'This book takes a new approach to the battle between pro-dam and anti-dam movements, emphasizing storylines and what lies underneath their discourses. It uncovers the motivations of each, and questions the way each uses sustainability arguments to their own purposes.'

Emilio F. Moran, *John A. Hannah, Distinguished Professor,*
Michigan State University

'Hydroelectric dams are not made only of concrete. As this engaging book shows, they are also built out of storylines that construct justifications for them that call them sustainable. Atkins uses a deeply researched study of two Brazilian dam projects to show how heterogenous opposition movements can also wield storylines to repoliticise and resist such projects, and even to challenge the broader claim that hydropower is a sustainable energy choice.'

Kathryn Hochstetler, *Professor of International Development, LSE*

Contesting Hydropower in the Brazilian Amazon

In *Contesting Hydropower in the Brazilian Amazon*, Ed Atkins focuses on how local, national, and international civil society groups have resisted the Belo Monte and São Luiz do Tapajós hydroelectric projects in Brazil. In doing so, Atkins explores how contemporary opposition to hydropower projects demonstrate a form of 'contested sustainability' that highlights the need for sustainable energy transitions to take more into account than merely greenhouse gas emissions.

The assertion that society must look to successfully transition away from fossil fuels and towards sustainable energy sources often appears assured in contemporary environmental governance. However, what is less certain is who decides which forms of energy are deemed 'sustainable.' *Contesting Hydropower in the Brazilian Amazon* explores one process in which the sustainability of a 'green' energy source is contested. It focuses on how civil society actors have both challenged and reconfigured dominant pro-dam assertions that present the hydropower schemes studied as renewable energy projects that contribute to sustainable development agendas. The volume also examines in detail how anti-dam actors act to render visible the political interests behind a project, whilst at the same time linking the resistance movement to wider questions of contemporary environmental politics.

This interdisciplinary work will be of great interest to students and scholars of sustainable development, sustainable energy transitions, environmental justice, environmental governance, and development studies.

Ed Atkins is a Lecturer at the School of Geographical Sciences, University of Bristol, UK, where he conducts interdisciplinary research on the ways in which environmental and energy policy are negotiated and contested. This is with a particular focus on working to ensure a just energy transition.

Routledge Studies in Sustainability

Urban Social Sustainability
Theory, Practice and Policy
Edited by Ramin Keivani and M. Reza Shirazi

Holistic Sustainability through Craft-design Collaboration
Rebecca Reubens

Sustainable Development Teaching
Ethical and Political Challenges
Katrien Van Poeck, Leif Östman and Johan Öhman

Utopia in the Anthropocene
A Change Plan for a Sustainable and Equitable World
Michael Harvey

Sustainability Governance and Hierarchy
Philippe Hamman

Energy, Environmental and Economic Sustainability in East Asia
Policies and Institutional Reforms
Edited by Soocheol Lee, Hector Pollitt and Kiyoshi Fujikawa

Green Skills Research in South Africa
Models, Cases and Methods
Eureta Rosenberg, Presha Ramsarup and Heila Lotz-Sisitka

Sustainability and the Automobile Industry in Asia
Policy and Governance
Edited by Aki Suwa and Masahiko Iguchi

Smart Green World?
Making Digitalization Work for Sustainability
Steffen Lange and Tilman Santarius

Contesting Hydropower in the Brazilian Amazon
Ed Atkins

For more information on this series, please visit www.routledge.com/Routledge-Studies-in-Sustainability/book-series/RSSTY

Contesting Hydropower in the Brazilian Amazon

Ed Atkins

LONDON AND NEW YORK

First published 2021
by Routledge
2 Park Square, Milton Park, Abingdon, Oxon OX14 4RN

and by Routledge
52 Vanderbilt Avenue, New York, NY 10017

Routledge is an imprint of the Taylor & Francis Group, an informa business

© 2021 Ed Atkins

The right of Ed Atkins to be identified as author of this work has been asserted by him in accordance with sections 77 and 78 of the Copyright, Designs and Patents Act 1988.

All rights reserved. No part of this book may be reprinted or reproduced or utilised in any form or by any electronic, mechanical, or other means, now known or hereafter invented, including photocopying and recording, or in any information storage or retrieval system, without permission in writing from the publishers.

Trademark notice: Product or corporate names may be trademarks or registered trademarks, and are used only for identification and explanation without intent to infringe.

British Library Cataloguing-in-Publication Data
A catalogue record for this book is available from the British Library

Library of Congress Cataloging-in-Publication Data
A catalog record has been requested for this book

ISBN: 978-0-367-33340-9 (hbk)
ISBN: 978-0-429-31928-0 (ebk)

Typeset in Goudy
by Deanta Global Publishing Services, Chennai, India

For Jo

Contents

List of Illustrations		x
Acknowledgements		xi
1	Introduction	1
2	Redesigning hydrology	23
3	Damming the Amazon	44
4	'By hook or by crook'	71
5	Belo Monstro	94
6	'A country that cannot live with difference'	120
7	Refusing to celebrate victory	146
8	Final remarks	167
Appendix		180
Bibliography		184
Index		218

Illustrations

Table

3.1 Characteristics of the Belo Monte and São Luiz do Tapajós projects 46

Figures

6.1 O Tapajós Precisa 123
6.2 Alter do Chão mural 134

Acknowledgements

This project began as my doctoral research at the School of Sociology, Politics and International Studies, University of Bristol. I am forever grateful to my supervisors, Adrian Flint and Karen Tucker for their unwavering support, kindness, and guidance in taking this research from an unformed idea to how it is presented today. A doctorate is a long – and often lonely – process and I am grateful to colleagues for journeying with me. Ben Hudson, Cameron Hunter, Jack Nicholls, Lydia Medland, James Mitchell, Solene Mosley, and Alice Venn – I owe you all a pint.

In 2018, I made the short move to the School of Geographical Sciences, University of Bristol. It has been a privilege to translate this work from a doctorate to a monograph in such a collegial, supportive department. My thanks to my colleagues for their insights, humour, and aid in these early stages of my career. Special thanks go to Oliver Andrews, Eddie Cole, Gemma Coxon, Alix Dietzel, Rachel Flecker, Sean Fox, Joe Gerlach, Franklin Ginn, Jessica Hope, Jo House, Eleni Michalopoulou, Susan Parnell, Margherita Pieraccini, and Chris Preist.

Beyond Bristol, I am grateful to the discussants, fellow panellists, and attendees at the numerous workshops, conferences, and events where the ideas and analysis that form this text were presented. My thanks to Christopher Rootes and Marieke Riethof, who examined the thesis on which this text is based. For the opportunity to discuss the work presented here – and out of continued admiration of their own work – I am grateful to Barbara Arisi, Eve Bratman, Phillipe Hanna, Filippo Menga and Jeroen Warner. Segments of this book stem from work that has been published in *Area*, *Political Geography*, *Singapore Journal of Tropical Geography*, and *Water*. I am grateful to the Editors of these respective journals and the various reviewers for their guidance. My utmost thanks also go to Rebecca Brennan, Oindrila Bose, and Trudy Varcianna at Routledge for their hard work in shepherding this book through the publication process.

This work was generously supported by the Economic & Social Research Council. I extend my thanks to those staff who have managed this support, as well as providing numerous other opportunities. My thanks to Molly Conisbee, Sonja Foster, Rob Keegan, and Joanna Williams. My gratitude also goes to all of those in Brazil who opened their doors to me, providing me with a home away from home and sharing their thoughts, advice, and ideas. Particular thanks go to Rafael Tauil and Paula and Tereza Ramos.

To my family – Carmel and Mark Dunmall, Kelvin Atkins, Jim Atkins, and Margaret and John Withers – thank you for giving me roots. To my friends – for your irreverence and love. Finally, I struggle to express my gratitude to the one person whose care and companionship has both sustained me as a person and driven this work forward. My partner in everything, Jo Wright has stood with me throughout. Your presence (and patience) makes everything worthwhile.

Bristol, July 2020

1 Introduction

The planning and construction of dams is not a new phenomenon. Understood broadly, a dam is a barrier that is built to hold back water and raise its level, either to provide water resources (for agriculture or cities) or to generate energy. However, both historically and in the contemporary context, the dams of the world are linked to broad questions of how we use and manage water resources. Dams are understood to have been built over 8,000 years ago in Mesopotamia, channelling waters from the Tigris and Euphrates in modern-day Iraq to irrigation networks. The Roman Empire consisted of more than just aqueducts, bridges and roads to Rome – dams were also constructed in North Africa and modern-day Spain to ensure a continuous supply of water to the baths, latrines, and fountains of urban centres. The Roman-built Cornalvo Dam, located in the Badajoz province of western Spain, now a UNESCO heritage site, is still in use – its earth and stone cladding is understood to date back to the first or second century AD.

The 20th century saw unprecedented levels of development of water infrastructure, both in scale and scope. From the canalisation of the Isthmus of Panama to the iconic concrete structures of the Hoover, Grand Coulee, and Glen Canyon Dams of the American West, states turned to massive infrastructure projects to redirect water to meet agricultural and urban demand or to generate hydroelectricity by manipulating a river's flow. The commitment to dam construction continued into the late 20th century, with the Itaipu (joint project by Brazil and Paraguay), Sayano–Shushenskaya (modern-day Russia), and Atatürk (Turkey) Dams all representing the 'Promethean impulse' that characterised water engineering as a route of societal progress (Gandy, 2014, p. 10).

At the turn of the new millennium, the World Commission on Dams (WCD), a multi-stakeholder consultative body formed by the World Conservation Union and World Bank, published a set of wide-ranging guidelines for planning and building hydroelectric dams in the 21st century in response to growing resistance to – and popular disapproval of – large hydroelectric projects. The WCD was formed in May 1998 to review the effectiveness of dams in achieving economic and development goals. The Commission, chaired by Kader Asmal and including members of industry, civil society, and government among its number, examined over 1,000 dams in 79 countries, interviewing 1,400 stakeholders and commissioning 130 technical papers. The publication of the World Commission on Dams report in 2000 represented a low point for the global dam-construction industry. After several years of research, the Commission concluded that:

> Dams have made an important and significant contribution to human development … [but in] too many cases an unacceptable and often unnecessary price has been paid to secure those benefits, especially in social and environmental terms, by people displaced, by communities downstream, by taxpayers and by the natural environment.
> (World Commission on Dams, 2000, p. xxviii)

The Commission put forward a framework consisting of seven strategic priorities and 26 'guidelines for good practice' – that aimed to improve the development outcomes of future hydroelectric dam projects. These ranged from the need for increased transparency and participation in the planning process and the payment of compensation to those impacted to the requirement for a basin-wide assessment of the potential impact on ecosystem health and biodiversity in the region (World Commission on Dams, 2000).

Yet, despite vocal criticism of these projects by the WCD and others (McCully, 1996; Scudder, 2005), the construction of hydroelectric dams has continued. From the Three Gorges Dam on the Yangtze River in Hubei Province, China, to the Grand Ethiopian Renaissance Dam that spans the Blue Nile in Ethiopia, these projects continue to have a traumatic impact on both those who are displaced or see their livelihoods and the morphology, biodiversity, and ecosystem health of the river basin itself disrupted. More than half of the 292 large river basins globally have been dislocated by hydroelectric infrastructure, including 45,000 large dams (Nilsson et al., 2005; Baghel and Nüsser, 2010). Although hydroelectric dams may have appeared to be under fire in 2000, they have enjoyed a global resurgence in the decades since. As of 2019, the total global installed capacity of hydroelectricity-generation stood at 1,307 gigawatts (GW) (International Energy Agency, 2019a).

This book explores this resurgence of dam construction in the 21st century by focusing on two projects in the Legal Amazon Region of Brazil[1] – namely, the Belo Monte and São Luiz do Tapajós Dams. Both projects are located on tributaries of the Amazon River (the Xingu and Tapajós Rivers, respectively), both have large energy generation capacities (11,233 and 8,040 megawatts [MW], respectively), and both have been subject to periods of contestation by multi-actor resistance coalitions. However, while Belo Monte has entered into operation, the São Luiz do Tapajós project was 'archived' (a term used to describe a project's removal from national energy plans) in August 2016, following the demarcation of the Sawré Muybu indigenous territory of the Munduruku community. Both projects represented constituent parts of the dam-building programme of the government led by the Partido dos Trabalhadores (Workers' Party, PT) that held power in Brazil from 2003 to 2016. During this period, Presidents Lula Inácio da Silva (2003–2011) and Dilma Rousseff (2011–2016) enacted a series of policy packages centred on stimulating economic growth through the construction of infrastructure, progressive social policies, and the championing of domestic companies within international markets (Casanova and Kassum, 2013; Hochstetler and Montero, 2013). A centrepiece of these policies was the 2007 *Programa de Aceleração do Crescimento* (Growth Acceleration Programme, PAC) and its successor plan, the 2010 *Programa de Aceleração do Crescimento* (PAC-2). The Belo Monte project secured investment in the 2007 PAC, while the São Luiz do Tapajós project was present in the 2010 PAC-2. At the time when they were planned, these projects were two parts of an extensive programme of dam building in the Legal Amazon Region that has taken place in Brazil over a number of decades. As of 2016, the Belo Monte and São Luiz do Tapajós projects were 2 of 79 dam projects planned for the lower and middle parts of the Amazon Basin (Lees et al., 2016).

Dam construction in Brazil is not a new process. The (now-decommissioned) Marmelos Zero Dam on the Paraibuna River, Minas Gerais, was built in 1896. The majority of Brazil's dams are earth-filled embankment dams, built to provide freshwater storage as a means of minimising the effects of droughts linked to the El Niño phenomenon (Brazilian Committee on Dams, 2009). Until the 1950s, most hydropower plants were small, privately owned facilities that provided limited output. During the military dictatorship (1965–1984), the exploitation of hydropower accelerated in a context in which extensive economic growth (itself underpinned by cheap energy) was an important legitimising strategy for the military regime. The 1960s witnessed the commissioning of the Furnas Dam (completed in 1963) and Peixotos Dam (1968) on the Rio Grande, and the Três Marias Dam on the São Francisco River (1961), all in Minas Gerais. The following decade saw the construction of a number of large dams, such as the Jupiá Dam (now the Engineer Souza Dias Dam) that blocked the Paraná River in Mato Grosso do Sul, creating a reservoir with a surface area of 330 km². Ninety-one dams were built in the 1970s, with this number including the Marimbondo (Minas Gerais), the Capivara (Paraná), and the Paulo Afonso Hydroelectric Complex in Bahia. Sixty such structures were built in the 1980s (including the iconic Itaipu on the Paraná River, completed in 1984), and fewer than 30 in the 1990s (Khagram, 2004). The 21st century witnessed numerous projects built to provide hydroelectricity, including the Barra Grande (in Santa Catarina/Rio Grande do Sul state, completed in 2005), the Irapé (Minas Gerais, 2006), Campos Novos (Santa Catarina, 2006), Mauá (Paraná, 2012), and the Simplício (Rio de Janeiro/Minas Gerais, 2013) Dams. Dams built in the Amazon region include the Santo Antônio and Jirau Dams (Rondônia, 2012 and 2016, respectively), Teles Pires (Mato Grosso/Pará, 2016), and Belo Monte (Pará, 2016) complexes. Contemporary dam-construction efforts may be less monumental now than they were in the age of Itaipu and Tucuruí, but they are just as large (Belo Monte will have an energy generation capacity of 10,233 MW) and expensive as before, with respective budgets calculated in the billions of Brazilian *reais* (R$).

Pro-dam actors increase the legitimacy of a dam project by presenting it as a solution to various issues, previously seen as distinct from the building of this infrastructure project (Warner, Hoogesteger, and Hidalgo, 2017). To gain this support, storylines that accompany hydropower projects co-opt pre-existing demands (such as for employment, energy security or secure water supply) as justifications for a dam project. For example, assertions related to energy security in contemporary pro-dam storylines represent the absorption of popular demands for secure and affordable energy supply to generate consent to – and to legitimise – the project in question. It is by absorbing these additional popular demands that the pro-dam actors position the hydropower projects they support as indispensable to ensuring future energy security, maximising the number of supposed beneficiaries of the project (with the promise of energy security extended to various constituents) and appealing to fears of a loss of power (Atkins, 2017). In doing so, the infrastructure project is presented as a key part of national economic and energy policy agendas.

In subsequent chapters, I focus on an emerging storyline of legitimacy, one which presents hydropower projects using the language of sustainability (Ahlers et al., 2015; Bratman, 2015; Atkins, 2018b). While the promise of economic development has in the past provided a legitimising storyline for historic dam projects, climate change mitigation now provides a key driver for the contemporary development of hydropower (Moore, Dore, and Gyawali, 2010; Huber and Joshi, 2015; Warner, Hoogesteger, and Hidalgo, 2017). I understand this as demonstrative of a *storyline of sustainability*, defined as the assertion of the perceived sustainability of the scheme and its location within contemporary sustainable energy transitions and sustainable development agendas. In the cases of the Belo Monte and São Luiz do Tapajós Dams, pro-dam actors have argued that contemporary hydropower projects in the Legal Amazon Region represent 'clean' energy that contributes to Brazil's sustainable development agenda. For example, at a 2010 rally in Altamira, President Lula Inácio da Silva (2003–2011) asserted the need to 'use clean energy and preserve the environment. This is my commitment' (da Silva, 2010). The Brazilian government sponsored a set of billboards in Rio de Janeiro, timed to coincide with the 2012 United Nations Conference on Sustainable Development, that portrayed the Belo Monte as 'clean energy' (Bratman, 2015). With a majority of the Brazilian population reporting a concern with environmental protection and health (Ministério do Meio Ambiente, 2012), these statements appeal to a 'moral legitimacy' in which the project is located within the dominant value system of the time (Bezerra et al., 2014). I argue that this represents the absorption of new elements into pro-dam storylines, with the infrastructure project taking on a new meaning as a constituent part of sustainable development and climate change mitigation agendas.

The energy landscape of the 21st century is rapidly changing, with renewable energy sources – such as wind power, solar power, and hydropower – representing significant proportions of energy matrices across the globe. While policies related to energy efficiency are often present, the dominant mode of contemporary discussions of sustainable energy transitions is the decarbonisation of energy supply – or the reduction of the carbon dioxide emissions associated with energy production. A key factor in the characterisation of hydropower as *sustainable* is its assumed role in schemes of climate change mitigation, with proponents of dams arguing that large dams emit relatively low levels of greenhouse gases (GHGs) when compared with fossil fuel energy sources (Biswas and Tortajada, 2001; Altinbîlek, 2002; Berga, 2016). For example, Berga (2016, p. 313) describes hydropower as a 'clean, renewable and environmentally friendly source of energy.' After characterising hydropower as both 'clean' and 'environmentally friendly,' Berga goes on to argue for the importance of this energy source in climate change mitigation and sustainable development (Berga, 2016). This is despite research linking hydroelectric dams – and their reservoirs in particular – to emissions of methane gas into the atmosphere (Giles, 2006; Delsontro et al., 2010; Marcelino et al., 2015). While carbon dioxide is released by vegetation protruding above the water level, the decomposition of plants and trees below the surface creates methane. This gas is subsequently released when it is processed by the turbines. Worryingly, methane can have 20 times the warming potential of carbon dioxide – a key GHG in climate change mitigation agendas – over a 100-year period (Giles, 2006). Despite this, the mitigative potential of hydropower remains a key part of national and international policies, and it continues to be characterised as a 'green' source of energy.

A key factor in the characterisation of hydropower as a sustainable energy source is the Clean Development Mechanism (CDM), created by Article 12 of the 1997 Kyoto Protocol. The CDM was created as a mechanism for Annex I states (wealthier states, primarily in the Global North, who have accepted a maximum limit on their emissions) to provide funding for sustainable development and climate change mitigation projects in Annex II states (emergent states, primarily in the Global South, without a national cap on emissions). Hydropower projects are categorised as a source of energy with low GHG emissions within the CDM and are eligible for Certified Emission Reduction certificates (CERS, carbon credits) (CDM Executive Board, 2009).[2] As of July 2020, 2,182 hydropower projects are provided with carbon credits under the CDM (CDM Pipeline, 2020). As we move forward towards a sustainable future, this energy source is expected to play a major role in decarbonising national energy systems (United Nations Symposium on Hydropower and Sustainable Development, 2004). The IEA (2019b) has affirmed the role of hydropower in its Sustainable Energy Scenario, which outlines its vision of a decarbonised energy system and the fulfilment of the comprehensive vision and targets set out by the SDGs. Within this scenario, global hydroelectric generation must increase by 2.5% every year until 2030. With global capacity standing at 1,307 GW, this represents a growth of 32.6 GW per year. In 2018, 21.8 GW of hydroelectric capacity was put into operation globally (International Hydropower Association, 2019). As the website for the United Nations Framework Convention on Climate Change (UNFCCC) (2018) stated in the run-up to the 2018 Conference of Parties (COP) in Katowice, Poland:

> The rapid and responsible deployment of clean, renewable energy is crucial to meet the goals of the Paris Climate Change Agreement, which is to limit the global average temperature so that the worst impact of climate change can be avoided, including ever more severe storms and droughts ...

The evolution of solar and wind energy has been the driving force of the transition to a low-carbon world in the past years, but despite the rise of new energy sources, one technology remains a cornerstone of the renewable energy mix in some regions of the Earth: hydropower.

In policy documents, the sustainability credentials of hydropower are often predicated on its characterisation as a renewable energy source. Both the 2004 Bonn International Conference on Renewable Energies and the United Nations Beijing Declaration on Hydropower and Sustainable Development have recognised hydropower as a renewable energy source with a synergistic role in sustainable development agendas. The characterisation of hydropower as renewable energy is based on the belief that water resources represent a non-finite source of energy, in comparison with the conventional fossil fuels of coal, oil and natural gas.

Sustainable development is a policy-based term that came of age at the 1992 Earth Summit in Rio de Janeiro, which is based on finding synergies between goals of economic development, social sustainability, and environmental protection. It can be broadly defined using the oft-cited Brundtland definition, as representing 'Development that meets the needs of the present without compromising the ability of future generations to meet their own needs' (World Commission on Environment and Development, 1987). The Brundtland definition represents the paradigmatic understanding of environmental issues and possible solutions in contemporary environmental governance. This is evident in its adoption at international events, including the 1992 United Nations Conference on Environment and Development (UNCED 1992, also known as the Earth Summit) and the 2015 Sustainable Development Goals, with the asserted compatibility between economic development and environmental protection providing a dominant paradigm in contemporary environmental policy and international development. Hydropower is often discussed in relation to the policy of Sustainable Development due to its role in simultaneously addressing issues of energy security, water (and, with it, food) security, and climate change mitigation (World Bank, 2009; Berga, 2016; United Nations Framework Convention on Climate Change, 2018). Hydropower projects provide job opportunities, reduce seasonal flooding, and provide energy and water security to populations. As a result of these multifaceted benefits, hydropower has become positioned as having a part to play in the fulfilment of the 2015 Sustainable Goals (SDGs), part of the United Nations' 2030 Agenda for Sustainable Development (Lane, 2015; Berga, 2016). This is with particular reference to Sustainable Development Goal 7, which aims to 'ensure access to affordable, reliable, sustainable, and modern energy for all,' with hydropower providing a route to simultaneously provide energy to more and more people and reduce GHG emissions. As Tracy Lane (2015), writing for the International Hydropower Association has argued:

> There is broad consensus that, when properly planned and implemented, hydropower is an affordable, reliable, sustainable and modern technology. It can help communities, nations and regions to acquire a reliable supply

of electricity, supporting economic and social development throughout the world.

What could perhaps be seen as a trade-off between climate change mitigation and energy security and social development, due to the role of dams in stimulating population displacement and loss of livelihoods, has instead become understood as synergistic. The World Bank (2009) has labelled hydropower as a key facet in ensuring both poverty alleviation and sustainable development, stating that it is the 'multi-dimensional role' and flexibility of hydropower that assists in addressing these challenges. In 2013, Rachel Kyte, the World Bank's vice president for sustainable development, argued that hydropower offered the most promising way to balance the institution's twin goals of continuing to lift people out of poverty and mitigate greenhouse gas (GHG) emissions globally:

> Large hydro is a very big part of the solution for Africa and South Asia and Southeast Asia. I fundamentally believe we have to be involved. [A previous move away from hydropower] was the wrong message. That was then. This is now. We are back.
>
> (Schneider, 2013)

The location of hydropower in these twinned policy agendas of climate change mitigation and sustainable development has accompanied – and legitimised – a resurgence of dam construction in the 21st century. The World Bank started to provide investment to large hydroelectric dams across the globe, including projects in Nepal, Congo, and Zambia, as well as technical assistance to governments building such facilities. Between 2002 and 2004, World Bank investment in hydropower projects was less than US$250 million per year. In 2008, the figure exceeded US$1 billion (World Bank, 2009). Numerous states have turned to hydropower expansion to increase their generation capacity and energy supply and have been able to secure international financial support. State interests are no longer only investing money in dam projects within their own countries but have regularly become involved in projects overseas. For example, as part of its 'going out' strategy, Chinese state institutions, state-owned enterprises, and private companies have provided funding and support and tendered contracts for dam projects across the globe (McDonald, Bosshard, and Brewer, 2009; Murton, Lord, and Beazley, 2016; Siciliano et al., 2019). The global environmental organisation (EO), International Rivers has argued that just one Chinese company, PowerChina controls nearly 50% of the international market in hydropower-construction (Jensen-Cormier, 2019). In the context of these investments, global dam building has become a key site of economic cooperation among states across the Global South, with China, Brazil, and India providing finance, technical assistance, and tendering contracts associated with the new dams of the 21st century.

Furthermore, new private actors, drawn from circuits of both regional and global finance, provide increasing amounts of financial support to dam projects

(Merme, Ahlers, and Gupta, 2014). For example, the Nam Theun 2 project in Laos is owned by three parties – the French energy company, EDF, the Thai Electricity Generating Public Company and the Laotian state – but is financed by a total of 27 parties from across the globe. With the emergence of these new streams of investment, many of the more traditional funders of hydroelectric dams (such as the World Bank) have taken a back seat, acting as facilitators of funding relationships (Merme, Ahlers, and Gupta, 2014). This increased investment is somewhat surprising. Hydroelectric schemes have been found to often go overbudget, with 20% of all dams built costing twice as much as first envisaged and one in three costing three times as much (Ansar et al., 2014). The Three Gorges Dam in China cost an estimated 254.2 billion yuan (US$37.23 billion), close to five times the estimated cost of 57 billion yuan (US$8.35 billion) first envisaged in 1992 (Reuters, 2009). However, the logic behind these new investments can be found in how private actors, in particular, are attracted to invest in hydroelectric schemes by additional incentives, such as state-promised tax exemptions and the potential to assert control over a river basin and local or regional energy grids (Merme, Ahlers, and Gupta, 2014). Much of the interest in the Nam Theun 2 project in Laos was enticed to the project following a series of policy reforms by the Laotian government, including the relaxing of labour standards and provision of extensive tax exemptions (Merme, Ahlers, and Gupta, 2014). The emergence of these new private or state–private hybrid actors into the dam-building business in the 21st century represents an important change, complicating understandings of accountability, costs and benefits, and financial risk.

Twenty years on, the World Commission on Dams has influenced contemporary patterns of large dam construction, with researchers employing innovative methods to ensure that the WCD report's recommendations and guidelines are followed (Schulz and Adams, 2019). In response to the World Commission on Dams report, the global hydropower sector (broadly defined) has made efforts to address previous criticism of hydroelectric dams, issuing a set of Sustainability Guidelines in 2004 and subsequently convening a multi-stakeholder forum to collate, discuss, and disseminate best practices. Between 2007 and 2010, a multistakeholder forum was formed of representatives from government, industry, financial donors, and civil society actors working to create a new global framework to increase the sustainability credentials of hydropower in the 21st century. The resulting Hydropower Sustainability Assessment Protocol (HSAP) defines both good and bad practices in dam building at all stages of the lifecycle of a project (from early stages to operations) and across 24 elements, including environmental, social, economic, and technical aspects. The HSAP calls for an independent review of sustainability factors, sustained and productive communication with impacted communities and reduction of the financial risks associated with overspending.

As hydroelectric dams continue to be built across the globe, their social and environmental impacts continue to proliferate. Claims of hydropower's role in sustainability are not necessarily supported. Previous studies have linked large hydroelectric dams to numerous ecological, economic, and social impacts, ranging from the disruption of fisheries, the transformation of river geomorphology, and population displacement (von Sperling, 2012). Hydroelectric projects are designed to flood land, leading to a loss of biodiversity and fragmentation of habitats. They disrupt the communities living on the riverbanks, as they are linked not only to population displacement but also to increases in criminality and disease transmission. This results in a disconnect between the infrastructure's classification as 'renewable' energy and the consequences of its construction. I follow the argument of Ahlers et al. (2015, p. 198), who stated that 'repackaging hydropower infrastructure as clean energy is confusing the resource with the instrument: water is renewable, yet dams are not.' While the benefits of hydropower may be multifaceted and positive in the eyes of their proponents, their impacts can be traumatic, irreversibly changing the region in which it is built.

Why how we talk about 'sustainability' matters

The construction of a hydroelectric dam is not a straightforward process. It represents more than the mere (re-)engineering of hydrology. For a dam to be built, pro-dam actors must secure acceptance of the project from those who may otherwise oppose it. Following the work of others, I argue that to understand these moments of contestation, researchers must engage with the ways in which different actors describe a dam and endow it with meaning (Molle, Mollinga, and Wester, 2009; Ahlers et al., 2014; Crow-Miller, 2015; Warner, Hoogesteger, and Hidalgo, 2017). Pro-dam actors have previously legitimised dam construction in a number of ways, including notions of the 'conquering' of nature, hydropower as a technical solution to socio-political problems, the role of infrastructure in economic development, dams as symbolic of a nationalist project, and assertions of the economic development to be stimulated by the project's construction (Bakker, 1999a; Kaika, 2003; Akhter, 2015a). The putting forward of these legitimising discourses by pro-dam actors positions the respective dam project within a wider social, political, or economic context, be it one centred around economic growth, nationalism, or the consolidation of a certain political order. As a result, the dam project in question becomes inscribed with a wider political significance, endowing it with a wider legitimacy.

The ways in which policymakers describe infrastructure, policies, or problems (and solutions) position these referents within a wider context, which is linked to the previous knowledge, political affiliation, emotion, embodiment and environment of the audience (Goffman, 1974; Lakoff, 2010). To explore the importance of how both proponents and opponents of hydropower projects describe particular schemes, I draw on the concept of *storylines* (Hajer, 1993, 1995). A storyline is understood as an overarching narrative in which various discourses are combined into a coherent whole, with their respective complexity simplified and concealed (Hajer, 1993). The imposition and entrenchment of a storyline, which provides a means of understanding a project and its wider consequences, has a central role in the contentious interaction that surrounds the construction of a dam, presenting it as a solution to a prescribed problem or asserting a necessity of action. These storylines are provided by both pro-dam and resistance actors, with each group locating a given dam project within a wider narrative of problems, solutions, and impacts. For example, historic pro-dam storylines have incorporated a variety of discourses, including those related to industrialisation, energy supply, utilitarian notions of the greatest good for the greatest number, and the importance of infrastructure, into a coherent storyline that is put forward to legitimise a dam project. Although a storyline may contain a range of demands, it can become fused by a homogenising logic that presents the demands as sharing the same goal(s), coming to have what Hajer (1993) terms *discursive affinity*. Storylines that draw together assertions of economic development, statehood, and nationalism or the need for an urgent solution to water scarcity appeal to these devices to simplify the debate surrounding the project by presenting it within a wider policy context based on what the country needs. Equipped with these storylines, pro-dam actors seek to impose a prescribed meaning on a dam project, overcome contestation and achieve *discursive closure*.

I understand the current storylines that locate dam projects within sustainable development and climate change mitigation agendas as a *storyline of sustainability* – that frame projects within wider concerns related to climate change mitigation and sustainable development. Rather than representing the construction of a new link, pro-dam actors present a dam as a solution to a particular problem (the need for 'sustainability'), tapping into a moral or ideological understanding of the issue and its significance (linked to either GHG-mitigation or sustainable development). In successfully positioning an issue in such a way, the speaker delimits the routes of action available, sanctioning the dam project as a particular solution to a defined set of problems, while denying the legitimacy of others (Benford and Snow, 2002). A dam project is inscribed with a particular meaning, linked to wider demands, simultaneously legitimising a project and reducing the grounds for critique by those opposed to it.

In conceptualising the term *sustainability*, I draw on the definition provided by Arias-Maldonado (2013, p. 438) in understanding sustainability as a term that describes 'any kind of socio-natural relationship which is balanced enough to be maintained in the indefinite future.' The term is used across a variety of disciplines and in numerous contexts. As a result, the definition of the term is context-dependent, ranging from the need for sustainable yields in fishery or forestry policy to the ability of certain economic practices to persist unaided. We all have different definitions of what sustainability is and what it looks like. Such visions of sustainability are rooted in different epistemologies and worldviews, everyday experience and personal history. While these may complement one another at times, they often find themselves in conflict.

Any claim of sustainability involves a value judgement – defining a problem, a solution, which resources should be sustained and by which means (Sikor and Norgaard, 1999). As a result, the utterance of a storyline of sustainability not only functions to assert a particular vision and definition of what sustainability is, and how hydropower is located within it, but also excludes other, alternative definitions that are dismissed as undesirable, culturally specific, or unscientific

(Redclift, 2005; Scoones, 2007, 2016; Leach, Scoones, and Stirling, 2010). Within this process of exclusion, storylines of sustainability represent the differentiation between legitimate and illegitimate actors and demands. I understand this as depoliticisation. Processes of depoliticisation are defined as 'discursive strategies in which legitimate and responsible actors' demands are distinguished from illegitimate, irresponsible actors and unrealistic and impossible demands' (Pepermans and Maeseele, 2014, p. 223). In exploring this concept of depoliticisation, I draw from the distinction between the political and politics proposed by Chantal Mouffe (1993, p. 262–263). Within this reading, 'politics' refers to the numerous practices, institutions, and acts of discourse that establish a certain order and organise society and 'the political' refers to the occurrence of antagonism that is present in all society, with no actor able to truly attain a fixed identity and no discourse able to fully achieve a hegemonic position (Mouffe, 1993). In putting forward a storyline of sustainability, pro-dam actors not only highlight the links between a respective project and policy goals related to sustainable energy transitions and sustainable development but also exclude other grievances and demands (related to impacts or costs and benefits, for example) to present the respective projects as the result of technical, rather than political, decisions. Pro-dam actors conceal alternative interpretations and visions of a project's sustainability, as well as the interests and identities that underpin pro-dam assertions of its sustainability credentials (Swyngedouw, 2010, 2011, 2015; Kenis and Lievens, 2014; Raco, 2014). Following the work of Mouffe (1993, 2000, 2005), I understand this concealing of alternatives as representing the denial of political conflicts, social demands and ideological contests about what society should be. As Mouffe (2013, p. 3) argues, 'political questions are not merely technical issues to be solved by experts. Proper political questions always involve decisions that require making a choice between conflicting alternatives.' Within this reading, the planning and construction of a hydroelectric project do not merely represent a technical decision regarding GHG-mitigation and sustainable development. It represents the collision of the vision of what sustainability is and how large hydroelectric dams fit into such visions. It is this character of the political that depoliticisation limits, denying the legitimacy of alternative positions and storylines and the political character of dam projects, raising it above the terrain of the political and delegitimising resistance actors (Chhotray, 2007; Huber and Joshi, 2015). A language of sustainability becomes a route of anti-politics, in which dissenting views and divergent definitions of what should be sustained are excluded.

Depoliticisation is not just a discursive process. With its role in sustainable energy transitions widely subscribed to, dam construction has gathered pace across the globe. In response, anti-dam movements against such projects across the globe are increasing in frequency also – from the resistance to the Tokwe-Mukorsi Dam in Zimbabwe to the continued opposition to hydroelectric projects to the Condor Cliff (formerly the Néstor Kirchner) Dam in Argentina. Research has found evidence of 220 dam-related conflicts across the globe (del Bene, Scheidel, and Temper, 2018). These conflicts can often be violent – with opponents of hydropower projects criminalised, ostracised, and at times threatened, assaulted, and murdered. From the 2016 murder of Berta Caceres, who was resisting the Agua Zarco Dam in Honduras, to Margarito J. Cabal, murdered in 2012 while opposing the Pulangi V project in the Philippines, anti-dam activists have faced extensive violence. These processes of criminalisation, demonisation, and violence function to depoliticise projects further both by intimidating those opposing projects and by presenting their grievances as unworthy of discussion. The presence of such violence highlights how the planning and construction of hydroelectric projects across the globe risk repeating the violence, marginalisation, and human rights abuses associated with other extractivist activities – leading Del Bene et al. (2018) to adopt the term 'extractivism of renewables' to describe the use of repression as a tool to delegitimise alternative definitions of sustainability.

The paradigmatic character of policies and rhetoric of sustainable development is evident in its wide application across and beyond contemporary environmental policy to describe supply chains, consumer goods and industrial practices. Yet, as different actors link principles of sustainable development to additional policy realms (such as supply chains or infrastructure), the originally asserted compatibility between environmental protection and economic growth has become emptied of its initial attachment to principles of environmentalism (Brown, 2016). The term sustainability remains contested, malleable, and open to other actors providing alternative definitions to challenge dominant understandings. There are diverse understandings of 'sustainability,' including environmental justice, climate justice, and the 'environmentalism of the poor,' that contest dominant assertions of sustainability as rooted in the reduction of GHG emissions (Martinez-Alier et al., 2016). Local communities often hold different definitions of the sustainability of a particular project or policy to those who devised, planned or built it. Following Cavanagh and Benjaminsen (2017), I understand these as 'alternative sustainabilities' that resist the dominant apolitical and technical conceptualisation of sustainable development, reasserting its political character and providing an alternative vision of environmental politics and climate change (del Bene, Scheidel, and Temper, 2018).

Environmental challenges, and their solutions, are perceived in different ways. For example, the material consequences of building a dam (rising water levels, population movement) are presented in the storylines put forward by competing groups in different ways. The population displacement caused by a dam will be articulated differently by those for and those against the respective project. While opponents may present this experience as damaging and rupturing to society, a proponent of a project may argue that those being displaced are well-compensated and are moving to safer, modern dwellings. Anti-dam storylines challenge pro-dam storylines of sustainability by illuminating grievances, demands, and impacts – and asserting alternatives. In doing so, they illuminate the incompatibility of large-scale hydroelectric dam projects (and their social and environmental impacts) and the wider goals of sustainable development policies and plans for climate change mitigation. The storylines put forward by anti-dam actors interact with and challenge dominant assumptions of a dam project's sustainability credentials and legitimacy. From movements that called for the end of World Bank funding for hydropower in the 1990s to those fighting for 'energy sovereignty' across the globe, anti-dam movements put forward alternative visions of not only particular dam projects but also their definition as sustainable pursuits.

In this book, I explore how anti-dam actors in Brazil have not only contested the planning and construction of the Belo Monte and São Luiz do Tapajós Dams but have also put forward an alternative vision that reconfigures the pro-dam storyline of sustainability. In subsequent chapters, I detail how anti-dam actors in Brazil, drawn from a wider coalition, illuminate overlooked impacts (labelled as 'rendering visible'), highlight the political interests, impunity, and motivations behind construction ('repoliticisation'), and foreground their resistance within the wider context of demands and grievances in contemporary Brazil ('scaling up'). Taken together, advancing these storylines simultaneously challenges and reconfigures the pro-dam storyline of sustainability by exposing its narrow focus on GHGs and highlighting the social and ecological impacts of hydropower in the 21st century. Although the provision of storylines can be found in the words and actions of both pro-dam and resistance actors, the dominant trend in scholarship has been to focus on the pro-dam storylines that legitimise the construction of dam projects. In exploring the ways in which anti-dam actors contest and reconfigure pro-dam storylines, this text shines a light on how pro-dam storylines remain contestable and contested.

While scholarship has explored how anti-dam actors contest the planning and construction of dams by forwarding storylines that illuminate the social and environmental impacts of respective projects (Ahlers et al., 2015; Huber and Joshi, 2015; Warner et al., 2017), it is important to also explore how these resistance storylines simultaneously challenge and reconfigure dominant pro-dam narratives. Groups and individuals opposed to a dam project put forward their own storylines of resistance to not only critique the dam project itself (illuminating impacts, etc.) but also challenge the pro-dam storylines of legitimacy. I argue that it is important for contemporary research to explore this process of interplay and contestation further – analysing the numerous ways in which resistance actors contest dominant pro-dam storylines. In light of Sustainable Development Goal 7, which calls for 'access to affordable, reliable, sustainable and modern energy for all,' this book explores how the 'greener' technologies included within this call continue to be contested, with their sustainability credentials subject to both disagreement and opposition. In doing so, the conclusions provided call for greater attention to the contested sustainability of contemporary green technologies, policies and projects.

Research strategy

Anti-dam movements are not homogenous. Their members do not necessarily share backgrounds, ways of seeing the world, or definitions of sustainability. Instead, they represent broad, multi-scalar coalitions of different actors with a

14 *Introduction*

shared goal: the cancellation of the hydropower project that they oppose. The subsequent analysis focuses its attention on the ways in which members of the resistance coalition for national and international non-governmental organisations (NGOs), environmental organisations, and journalists interact with, critique, and reconfigure the pro-dam storyline of sustainability. These organisations are important to anti-dam movements, collaborating with local networks of opposition to present their resistance to a wider audience, link it to broader concerns, and change the terms of debate (Keck and Sikkink, 1998; Hochstetler and Keck, 2007). This research focused on this segment opposition to gauge the ways in which they understand *sustainability*, how they locate hydropower within such a definition, and the arguments that make against hydroelectric dams in the 21st century.

This book draws on 37 interviews conducted (both in-person and virtually) between 2016 and 2019 with actors in the resistance coalition. These actors are drawn from local, national, and international organisations, as well as academics and journalists who have discussed and critiqued the Belo Monte and São Luiz do Tapajós projects. In addition, interviews were also conducted with high-profile representatives of the Brazilian environment agency, Instituto Brasileiro do Meio Ambiente e dos Recursos Naturais Renováveis (Brazilian Institute of the Environment and Renewable Natural Resources, IBAMA), Fundação Nacional do Índio (the National Indian Foundation, FUNAI), the government Ministério de Minas e Energia (Ministry of Mines and Energy, MME), and the Ministério Público Federal (Federal Public Ministry, MPF). These government organisations represent key actors in the planning, construction, and operation of dams in Brazil. Furthermore, an interview was conducted with a construction manager of Norte Energia in December 2016. Interviews were conducted, both in-person and over Skype, in the cities of Rio de Janeiro, São Paulo, Brasília, Santarém, Belém, and Manaus. Interviews were designed to encourage personal reflections on a number of key events in the construction of the Belo Monte and São Luiz do Tapajós projects (such as the 2016 cancellation of the latter) and to respond to a number of arguments provided by the dams' proponents seeking to legitimise the schemes (such as those related to sustainability).[3]

Data taken from interviews is supplemented by the analysis of over 400 primary documents. These documents have been taken from numerous sources disseminated by various organisations and groups. Primary sources were selected through targeted online searches, using a series of key search terms. The sources discussed include documents created by government bodies, international civil society groups, domestic arms of international non-governmental organisations, national civil society, and local campaigning groups. I understand these primary materials as 'communicative devices,' which are written and distributed to a specific, targeted audience for a particular purpose (Flick, 2009). They represent a partial and specific account of the projects researched. For example, a published report by WWF Brasil will be likely to report on the environmental impacts of the project, due to the organisation's focus on environmental protection, while a news article by Movimento dos Atingidos por Barragens (Movement of Dam-Affected

People, MAB) would, instead, focus on the social impacts. This contrast does not represent a denial of certain impacts but, instead, represents the parameters of the respective respondent's views, definition of sustainability and understanding of the Belo Monte and São Luiz do Tapajós projects.

I have clear ethical responsibilities to the participants in this work. This was particularly the case working with environmental organisations in Brazil, who have faced a number of increasing threats in recent years, as detailed in subsequent chapters. With accusations of corporate espionage against environmental organisations and the deaths of environmental and human rights activists often discussed in interviews, I need to ensure that I have fulfilled my ethical responsibilities. Although many research participants indicated that they would consent to being named in this research, I have made the decision to anonymise everyone who appears in this work. While some are identified via their affiliation with particular organisations, others, at their request, are not.

Chapter outline

This book is organised into eight chapters. Setting the next chapter aside, the subsequent chapters explore the ways in which anti-dam actors contest, critique, and reconfigure the pro-dam storyline of sustainability put forward to legitimise the Belo Monte and São Luiz do Tapajós Dam projects in the Brazilian Amazon.

In Chapter 2, I outline the importance of analysing how hydropower projects become inscribed with wider significance due to their linkages and entanglements with wider political discussions, projects, problems and solutions. I assert the central role of storylines within this before introducing the *storyline of sustainability*. In doing so, I argue that pro-dam actors demonstrate an adaptive capacity, coopting new demands and grievances into their legitimising storylines. However, this storyline remains contestable and, as I argue, research needs to explore the ways in which anti-dam actors contest and reconfigure pro-dam storylines.

In Chapter 3, I contextualise the Belo Monte and São Luiz do Tapajós projects. I explore the importance of hydropower in contemporary Brazilian politics, foregrounding the planning and construction of these two projects within a wider history of energy insecurity, developmentalism, and core–periphery relations. Furthermore, I highlight how dam-building policies in Brazil remain open to contestation, with resistance networks providing powerful acts of dissent against the projects studied. I also profile the pro- and anti-dam actors involved in the contests surrounding hydropower in Brazil.

The text now turns to the empirical analysis of the materials collected. In Chapter 4, I focus on how national and international anti-dam actors work to reground the Belo Monte and São Luiz do Tapajós projects within a political context that serves to illuminate how both projects were constituent parts of policy agendas with particular motivations and goals. While pro-dam actors asserted the dual role of this infrastructure project as contributing to Brazilian climate change mitigation goals, anti-dam actors argued that the projects represented a wider process of exclusion from decision-making. This represents a process of *repoliticisation*, with anti-dam actors detailing how political interests, corruption, and impunity forced the project forward, regardless of its impacts. In doing so, resistance actors highlight the political interests behind the construction of Belo Monte and São Luiz do Tapajós to illuminate how a language of sustainability has been captured and harnessed by political actors with what are deemed limited environmentalist credentials.

In Chapter 5, I turn my attention to how, in response to the dissemination of official environmental impact assessments (EIAs) for the Belo Monte and São Luiz do Tapajós Dams, opposition actors have engaged in the provision and dissemination of alternative assessments of the social and environmental impacts associated with these projects. Within the storylines analysed, anti-dam actors emphasised the links of the projects studied to a number of impacts, including socio-economic impacts on the local area and indirect, cumulative impacts. While official EIAs (and the storyline of sustainability) adopted a narrow understanding of the projects' impacts, rendering them 'technical' and excluding the grievances and demands of others, anti-dam actors illuminate such impacts. I understand this as a process of *rendering visible* – with anti-dam actors shining a light on the forgotten, overlooked, and unmitigated consequences of hydropower in the Brazilian Amazon.

In Chapter 6, I explore the multifaceted and central role of indigenous communities in the opposition to the Belo Monte and São Luiz do Tapajós dams. This chapter explores the process through which civil society actors disseminated materials across the globe to assert the different ways in which the projects would (both directly and indirectly) impact indigenous communities living in the respective regions. Indigenous groups – in particular, the Kayapó and Munduruku communities – have been key actors in anti-dam action against the projects studied and the images of these actors dominated anti-dam materials disseminated across the globe. As a result, these communities – and their relationship with the projects studied – provided a focal point for the resistance against hydropower projects in the Brazilian Amazon. In opposition materials, national and international civil society actors highlighted how the projects studied represented a direct threat to the cultural identity and human rights of the traditional communities impacted. It is by illuminating these links that anti-dam actors assert the ties between the projects studied and a wider context of violence against indigenous groups, anti-indigenous rhetoric, and the systemic neglect of traditional communities in contemporary Brazil. As a result, the opposition to the Belo Monte and São Luiz do Tapajós projects is 'scaled up' and the respective dams are characterised as single sites in a far wider struggle.

In Chapter 7, I turn to the 2016 decision to 'archive' the São Luiz do Tapajós project, removing it from the environmental licensing process. The chapter comes in two parts. First, I profile the reasons – official and otherwise – behind the 2016 removal of the São Luiz do Tapajós project from national energy plans, detailing their context and validity. The official reasoning for this decision – asserted by the Brazilian environmental regulator – is the uncertainty surrounding the social and environmental impacts of the project. Despite this, anti-dam actors discussing the decision highlighted a number of additional reasons – including the exposure of corruption, a prolonged economic recession and the 2016 impeachment of President Dilma Rousseff. Second, I will turn to how, although the suspension of the São Luiz do Tapajós Dam project could be considered to represent a victory for the resistance coalition, opposition actors quickly looked to the future. In this chapter, I explore the reasoning for this. For many, the projects studied were intricately linked to an emergent political antagonism, related to the growing tension between environmental protection and the expansion of agribusiness into the Legal Amazon Region. This is with particular reference to the policies of the government of President Michel Temer (2016–2019) and the *ruralista* political faction. As a result, civil society actors presented the São Luiz do Tapajós project as only one stage in a wider contest between resistance actors and political interests threatening environmental protection and the rights of indigenous communities. As I discuss in this chapter, such assertions became prophetic, as is evident in the 2018 election of Jair Bolsonaro as president. In making this argument, resistance actors assert that the contest over hydropower is far from over, with the construction of hydroelectric dams in the Brazilian Amazon a constituent part of a wider threat of extractivism in the region. Resistance actors look to the future and argue that the São Luiz do Tapajós project represents just one site in the continued antagonism between, on the one side, Brazil's indigenous communities and contemporary environmentalism, and, on the other, successive governments' economic policies.

In the concluding chapter, I explore the arguments and related implications developed throughout the previous chapters and reflect on how the resistance coalition, opposed to the Belo Monte and São Luiz do Tapajós Dam projects, advanced storylines that reconfigure the dominant storylines of sustainability adopted by the pro-dam coalition. I detail the transformative potential of the new storylines of sustainability detected and look to the future, tracing the trajectories of an emergent 'just sustainability.' Finally, I reflect on political events in Brazil since 2018, discussing the environmental policies of President Jair Bolsonaro, looking to the future and discussing the continued presence of – and need for – environmental resistance in the Brazilian Amazon.

Notes

1 Defined as the nine federal states that overlap with the Amazon River basin (Acre, Amapá, Amazonas, Pará, Rondônia, Roraima, and Tocantins, and parts of Mato Grosso and Maranhão).
2 Under the 2011 Marrakech Accords, a project's eligibility for CDM funding is approved by the host country, with the government issuing a Letter of Approval certifying the sustainable development credentials of the project. In Brazil, this decision is made based on the submission of an additional document, detailing the project's integration into local and regional sustainable development policies (Fernández et al., 2014).
3 A number of interviews were translated by a third party and are not analysed for the discourse present within them. Rather than analyse these materials for the lexical choices made in them, I analyse how these materials frame the Belo Monte and São

Luiz do Tapajós projects and provide data and case studies that challenge the pro-dam storyline of sustainability.

Bibliography

Ahlers, R, Brandimarte, L, Kleemans, I, and Said, HS (2014). Ambitious development on fragile foundations: criticalities of current large dam construction in Afghanistan. *Geoforum*, 54: 49–58.

Ahlers, R, Budds, J, Joshi, D, Merme, V, and Zwarteveen, M (2015). Framing hydropower as green energy: assessing drivers, risks and tensions in the Eastern Himalayas. *Earth System Dynamics*, 6(1): 195–204.

Akhter, M (2015). Infrastructure nation: state space, hegemony, and hydraulic regionalism in Pakistan. *Antipode*, 47(4): 849–870.

Aledo Tur, A, García-Andreu, H, Ortiz, G, and Domínguez-Gomez, JA (2018). Discourse analysis of the debate on hydro-electric dam building in Brazil. *Water Alternatives*, 11(1): 125–141.

Altinbilek, D (2002). The role of dams in development. *International Journal of Water Resources Development*, 18(1): 9–24.

Ansar, A, Flyvbjerg, B, Budzier, A, and Lunn, D (2014). Should we build more large dams? The actual costs of hydropower megaproject development. *Energy Policy*, 69: 43–56.

Arias-Maldonado, M (2013). Rethinking sustainability in the Anthropocene. *Environmental Politics*, 22(3): 428–446.

Atkins, E (2017). Dammed and diversionary: the multi-dimensional framing of Brazil's Belo Monte dam. *Singapore Journal of Tropical Geography*, 38(3): 276–292.

Atkins, E (2018). Dams, political framing and sustainability as an empty signifier: the case of Belo Monte. *Area*, 50(2): 232–239.

Baghel, R, and Nüsser, M (2010). Discussing large dams in Asia after the World Commission on Dams: is a political ecology approach the way forward? *Water Alternatives*, 3(2): 231–248.

Bakker, K (1999). The politics of hydropower: developing the Mekong. *Political Geography*, 18(2): 209–232.

Benford, RD, and Snow, DA (2002). Framing processes and social movements: an overview and assessment. *Annual Review of Sociology*, 26: 611–639.

Berga, L (2016). The role of hydropower in climate change mitigation and adaptation: a review. *Engineering*, 2(3): 313–318.

Bezerra, RG, Prates, RC, EggertBoehs, CG, and Tripoli, ACK (2014). Discourse strategies to legitimize the Belo Monte project. *International Journal of Business and Social Science*, 5(12): 181–189.

Biswas, AK, and Tortajada, C (2001). Development and large dams: a global perspective. *International Journal of Water Resources Development*, 17(1): 9–21.

Bratman, E (2015). Passive revolution in the green economy: activism and the Belo Monte dam. *International Environmental Agreements: Politics, Law and Economics*, 15(1): 61–77.

Brown, T (2016). Sustainability as empty signifier: its rise, fall, and radical potential. *Antipode*, 48(1): 115–133.

Carvalho, G (2006). Environmental resistance and the politics of energy development. *Journal of Environment & Development*, 15(1): 245–268.

Casanova, L, and Kassum, J (2013). *The Political Economy of an Emerging Global Power: In Search of the Brazil Dream*. Basingstoke: Palgrave Macmillan.

Cavanagh, CJ, and Benjaminsen, TA (2017). Political ecology, variegated green economies, and the foreclosure of alternative sustainabilities. *Journal of Political Ecology*, 24(1): 200–216.

CDM Pipeline (2020). *CDM Pipeline, UNEP DTU Partnership*. Available at: http://www.cdmpipeline.org/cdm-projects-type.htm#3 (Accessed: July 21, 2020).

Chhotray, V (2007). The 'anti-politics machine' in India: depoliticisation through local institution building for participatory watershed development. *Journal of Development Studies*, 43(6): 1037–1056.

Crow-Miller, B (2015). Discourses of deflection: the politics of framing China's south-north water transfer project. *Water Alternatives*, 8(2): 173–192.

del Bene, D, Scheidel, A, and Temper, L (2018). More dams, more violence? A global analysis on resistances and repression around conflictive dams through co-produced knowledge. *Sustainability Science*, 13(3): 617–633.

Delsontro, T, McGinnis, DF, Sobek, S, Ostrovsky, I, and Wehrli, B (2010). Extreme methane emissions from a Swiss hydropower reservoir: contribution from bubbling sediments. *Environmental Science and Technology*, 44(7): 2419–2425.

Fernández, L, de la Sota, C, Andrade, JCS, Lumbreras, J, and Mazorra, J (2014). Social development benefits of hydroelectricity CDM projects in Brazil. *International Journal of Sustainable Development and World Ecology*, 21(3): 246–258.

Flick, U (2009). *An Introduction to Qualitative Research*. London: SAGE.

Gandy, M (2014). *Fabric of Space: Water, Modernity, and the Urban Imagination*. Cambridge, MA: MIT Press.

Giles, J (2006). Methane quashes green credentials of hydropower. *Nature*, 444(7119): 524–5.

Goffman, E (1974). *Frame Analysis: An Essay on the Organization of Experience*. Cambridge, MA: Harvard University Press.

Hajer, M (1995). *The Politics of Environmental Discourse: Ecological Modernization and the Policy Process*. Oxford: Clarendon Press.

Hajer, MA (1993). Discourse coalitions and the institutionalization of practice: the case of acid rain in Britain. In F. Fischer and J. Forester (eds) *The Argumentative Turn in Policy Analysis and Planning*. Durham, NC: Duke University Press.

Hochstetler, K, and Keck, ME (2007). *Greening Brazil: Environmental Activism in State and Society*. Durham, NC: Duke University Press.

Hochstetler, K, and Montero, AP (2013). The renewed developmental state: the national development bank and the Brazil model. *Journal of Development Studies*, 49(11): 1484–1499.

Huber, A, and Joshi, D (2015). Hydropower, anti-politics, and the opening of new political spaces in the Eastern Himalayas. *World Development*, 76: 13–25.

International Energy Agency (2019a). *Renewables 2019*. Available at: https://www.iea.org/reports/renewables-2019/power#hydropower (Accessed: March 30, 2020).

International Energy Agency (2019b). *Sustainable Development Scenario – World Energy Model*. Available at: https://www.iea.org/reports/world-energy-model/sustainable-development-scenario (Accessed: March 30, 2020).

International Hydropower Association (2019). *2019 Hydropower Status Report*. London: International Hydropower Association.

Jensen-Cormier, S (2019). *Watered Down: How Do Big Hydropower Companies Adhere to Social and Environmental Policies and Best Practices?* Oakland, CA: International Rivers.

Kaika, M (2003). Constructing scarcity and sensationalising water politics: 170 days that shook Athens. *Antipode*, 35(5): 919–954.

Keck, ME, and Sikkink, K (1998). *Activists beyond Borders: Advocacy Networks in International Politics*. Ithaca, NY: Cornell University Press.

Kenis, A, and Lievens, M (2014). Searching for 'the political' in environmental politics. *Environmental Politics*, 23(4): 531–548.

Khagram, S (2004). *Dams and Development: Transnational Struggles for Water and Power*. Ithaca, NY: Cornell University Press.

Kirchherr, J (2018). Strategies of successful anti-dam movements: evidence from Myanmar and Thailand. *Society and Natural Resources*, 31(2): 166–182.

Lakoff, G (2010). Why it matters how we frame the environment. *Environmental Communication*, 4(1): 70–81.

Lane, T (2015). Sustainable development goals: how does hydropower fit in? *International Hydropower Association*, October 1. Available at: https://www.hydropower.org/blog/sustainable-development-goals-how-does-hydropower-fit-in (Accessed: March 30, 2020).

Leach, M, Scoones, I, and Stirling, A (2010). *Dynamic Sustainabilities: Technology, Environment, Social Justice*. London: Earthscan.

Marcelino, A, Santos, MA, Xavier, VL, Bezerra, CS, Silva, CRO, Amorim, MA, Rodrigues, RP, and Rogerio, JP (2015). Emissões difusivas de metano e de dióxido de carbono oriundas de dois reservatórios hidrelétricos. *Brazilian Journal of Biology*, 75(2): 331–338.

Martinez-Alier, J, Temper, L, del Bene, D, and Scheidel, A (2016). Is there a global environmental justice movement? *The Journal of Peasant Studies*, 43(3): 731–755.

McCormick, S (2010). Damming the Amazon: local movements and transnational struggles over water. *Society and Natural Resources*, 24(1): 34–48.

McDonald, K, Bosshard, P, and Brewer, N (2009). Exporting dams: China's hydropower industry goes global. *Journal of Environmental Management*, 90(3) Supplement 3: 294–302.

McCully, P (1996). *Silenced Rivers: The Ecology and Politics of Large Dams*. London: Zed Books.

Merme, V, Ahlers, R, and Gupta, J (2014). Private equity, public affair: hydropower financing in the Mekong Basin. *Global Environmental Change*, 24(1): 20–29.

Ministério do Meio Ambiente (2012). Meio ambiente: Brasileiro está mais consciente. *Ministério do Meio Ambiente*, 6 June. Available at: https://www.mma.gov.br/informma/item/8386-o-que-o-brasileiro-pensa-do-meio-ambiente-e-do-consumo-sustent%C3%A1vel (Accessed: March 30, 2020).

Molle, F, Mollinga, P, and Wester, P (2009). Hydraulic bureaucracies and the hydraulic mission: flows of water, flows of power. *Water Alternatives*, 2(3): 328–349.

Moore, D, Dore, J, and Gyawali, D (2010). The World Commission on Dams + 10: revisiting the large dam controversy. *Water Alternatives*, 3(2): 3–13.

Mouffe, C (1993). *The Return of the Political*. London: Verso.

Mouffe, C (2000). *The Democratic Paradox*. London: Verso.

Mouffe, C (2005). *On the Political*. London: Verso.

Mouffe, C (2013). *Agonistics: Thinking the World Politically*. London: Verso.

Murton, G, Lord, A, and Beazley, R (2016). A handshake across the Himalayas: Chinese investment, hydropower development, and state formation in Nepal. *Eurasian Geography and Economics*, 57(3): 403–432.

Nilsson, C, Reidy, CA, Dynesius, M, and Revenga, C (2005). Fragmentation and flow regulation of the world's large river systems. *Science*, 308(5720): 405.

Pepermans, Y, and Maeseele, P (2014). Democratic debate and mediated discourses on climate change: from consensus to de/politicization. *Environmental Communication*, 8(2): 216–232.

Raco, M (2014). The post-politics of sustainability planning: privatisation and the demise of democratic government. In: Wilson, J, and Swyngedouw, E (eds) *The Post-political and Its Discontents: Spaces of Depoliticisation, Spectres of Radical Politics*. Cambridge: Cambridge University Press.

Redclift, M (2005). Sustainable development (1987–2005): an oxymoron comes of age. *Sustainable Development*, 13(4): 212–227.

Reuters (2009). China says Three Gorges Dam cost $37 billion. *Reuters*, September 14. Available at: https://www.reuters.com/article/idUSPEK84588 (Accessed: March 30, 2020).

Riethof, M (2017). The international human rights discourse as a strategic focus in socio-environmental conflicts: the case of hydro-electric dams in Brazil. *International Journal of Human Rights*, 21(4): 482–499.

Rothman, FD (2001). A comparative study of dam-resistance campaigns and environmental policy in Brazil. *Journal of Environment and Development*, 10(4): 317–344.

Schneider, H (2013). World Bank turns to hydropower to square development with climate change. *The Washington Post*, 8 May. Available at: https://www.washingtonpost.com/business/economy/world-bank-turns-to-hydropower-to-square-development-with-climate-change/2013/05/08/b9d60332-b1bd-11e2-9a98-4be1688d7d84_story.html (Accessed: 30 March 2020).

Scoones, I (2007). Sustainability. *Development in Practice*, 17(4/5): 589–596.

Scoones, I (2016). The politics of sustainability and development. *Annual Review of Environment and Resources*, 41(1): 293–319.

Scudder, T (2005). *The Future of Large Dams: Dealing with Social, Environmental, Institutional and Political Costs*. London: Routledge.

Siciliano, G, del Bene, D, Scheidel, A, Liu, J, and Urban, F (2019). Environmental justice and Chinese dam-building in the global South. *Current Opinion in Environmental Sustainability*, 37: 20–27.

Sikor, T, and Norgaard, R (1999). Principles for sustainability: protection, investment, cooperation and innovation. In: Kohn, J, Gowdy, JM, Hinterberger, D, and Van der Straaten, J (eds) *Sustainability in Question: The Search for a Conceptual Framework*. Cheltenham: Edward Elgar.

Swyngedouw, E (2010). Impossible sustainability and the post-political condition. In: Cerreta, M, Concilio, G, and Monno, V (eds) *Making Strategies in Spatial Planning*. Dordrecht: Springer Netherlands.

Swyngedouw, E (2011). Depoliticized environments: the end of nature, climate change and the post-political condition. *Royal Institute of Philosophy Supplements*, 69: 253–274.

Swyngedouw, E (2015). The non-political politics of climate change. *ACME: An International Journal for Critical Geographies*, 12(1): 1–8.

United Nations Framework Convention on Climate Change (2018). How hydropower can help climate action. *United Nations Framework Convention on Climate Change*, November 21. Available at: https://unfccc.int/news/how-hydropower-can-help-climate-action (Accessed: March 30, 2020).

United Nations Symposium on Hydropower and Sustainable Development (2004). *Beijing Declaration on Hydropower and Sustainable Development*. Beijing, China: United Nations.

von Sperling, E (2012). Hydropower in Brazil: overview of positive and negative environmental aspects. *Energy Procedia*, 18: 110–118.

Warner, JF, Hoogesteger, J, and Hidalgo, JP (2017). Old wine in new bottles: the adaptive capacity of the hydraulic mission in Ecuador. *Water Alternatives*, 10(2): 322–340.

Whitehead, M, Jones, R, and Jones, M (2007). *The Nature of the State: Excavating the Political Ecologies of the Modern State*. Cambridge: Cambridge University Press.

World Bank (2009). *Directions in Hydropower*. Washington, DC: World Bank.
World Commission on Dams (2000). *Dams and Development: A New Framework for Decision-Making*. London: World Commission on Dams.
World Commission on Environment and Development (1987). *Our Common Future*. Oxford: WCED.

2 Redesigning hydrology

For over a century, geographers, historians, and political scientists have explored the intersection of water, politics and power asymmetries to interrogate how these three phenomena become linked within processes of water resource management and the construction of hydraulic infrastructure (Menga and Swyngedouw, 2018; Radkau, 2008; Wittfogel, 1957; Worster, 1985). From Wittfogel's (1957) assertion that the construction of irrigation networks made the monopolisation of water resources possible and led to the acquisition and consolidation of political power in ancient civilisations in Mesopotamia and Sri Lanka (among others) to Crow-Miller's (2015) work on the role of the South–North Water Transfer Project (SNWTP) in China's economic growth strategies, researchers have drawn attention to the ways in which hydraulic infrastructure projects, such as dams, become inscribed with a wider political significance.

In this chapter, I explore the forms that this political significance can take, as well as the importance of 'storylines' in inscribing dam projects with meaning. In doing so, this book is indebted to scholarship that has explored the nexus between dams, politics, and the control of space, population, and territory to argue that the construction of infrastructure not only has an impact on the flow of water but also functions to produce (and reproduce) dominant social relations and contemporary power asymmetries (Bakker, 2013; Bakker and Bridge, 2006; Boelens et al., 2016; Budds, 2004; Díaz-Caravantes and Wilder, 2014; Linton and Budds, 2013; Menga, 2017; Menga and Swyngedouw, 2018; Swyngedouw, 1999, 2009).[1] Following Whitehead et al. (2007), I understand the links between political and social variables and the management of water resources as manifesting in a number of ways. First, there is a 'moment of consolidation' in which the construction of a dam becomes symbolic of a wider political or nationalist project and its related power asymmetries. Second, there is a 'moment of contestation' in which two opposing groupings present divergent visions of the symbolism of a project's construction and resulting impact (Whitehead et al., 2007).[2]

The advancement of pro- and anti-dam storylines is a key part of these moments of consolidation and contestation. The construction of a hydroelectric dam requires more than simply engineering and construction. It must also involve the acceptance of (or, at least, acquiescence to) the project both by the local community to be impacted and beyond. The need for legitimacy results in the physical process of dam building often being accompanied – and disrupted – by moments of contestation between pro- and anti-dam actors. This moment of contestation involves the interplay between pro- and anti-dam 'storylines,' which inscribes the project in question with its own significance, whether it be in positive or negative terms. While pro-dam actors may highlight the importance of a dam in terms of economic development or national cohesion (Molle et al., 2009; Warner et al., 2017), those opposed to a project also adopt their own storylines of resistance that critique pro-dam assertions, thus allowing for a moment of contestation to occur. This process of interplay demonstrates how the dominance of pro-dam storylines is not set in stone but instead remains open to critique and reconfiguration.

In this chapter, I explore and detail the ways that both pro- and anti-dam storylines inscribe a hydroelectric project with a wider significance – be it by linking it to nationalist visions of the future, economic development, or extensive cultural impacts. However, while the dams of the past were justified by promises of economic benefits, contemporary hydropower projects are often legitimised through the adoption of the language of sustainability, with the energy generated perceived as a 'green' energy source that contributes to sustainable development agendas. Within this chapter, I explore this trend, defining what I label a 'storyline of sustainability' that is put forward by those supporting contemporary hydropower projects. It is this storyline – and the prolonged and contentious interactions between pro- and anti-dam actors – that is the focus of this book, which explores the ways in which the storyline of sustainability, put forward to legitimise the Belo Monte and São Luiz do Tapajós projects in the Brazilian Amazon, is contested.

The structure of this chapter is as follows. First, it will detail the links between the planning and construction of hydraulic infrastructure and 'moments of consolidation,' in which a particular project can be inscribed with a significance that extends beyond its construction site or the provision of energy. Second, I explore the role of what I term 'storylines' within inscribing projects with such significance, highlighting their role in depoliticising such schemes before defining and delineating the focus of this book: the pro-dam storyline of sustainability. Finally, I detail the ways in which anti-dam actors contest hydroelectric projects by putting forward new, alternative storylines that interact with, critique and challenge pro-dam storylines before offering concluding remarks.

Moments of consolidation

A river – across which a dam may be planned or built – has numerous users, communities, and stakeholders living along its banks. It represents a common pool resource that supports a large number of people but that, if overused, will risk congestion or collapse, with each group's use of the river reducing the benefits that others might enjoy (Ostrom, 2008). For example, excessive withdrawal of water for agricultural use upstream may have a significant impact on those living downstream by reducing the river's flow (van Oel et al., 2009). Furthermore, these different groups and communities will likely have divergent interests in the river – as well as perspectives on its importance – both in terms of magnitude but also in what constitutes its importance in terms of economic benefits, cultural significance, or livelihoods. In response to this complexity, Hommes et al. (2016) coined the term 'hydro-social territory' to explain how a river cannot be characterised by hydrological factors alone but, instead, represents an amalgamation of river morphology and hydrology and socio-political, economic, and cultural elements in which different interests and worldviews coalesce and engage in a continuous process of negotiation and renegotiation to allocate resources.

Hydraulic infrastructure is a key site in such a process of negotiation, illuminating how social, political, or economic logics can come to dictate the flow of water to different stakeholders. The development of hydraulic infrastructure in a region can lead to the entrance of additional public or private projects. When a large dam is built, the biophysical transformation of a river by a hydroelectric dam is accompanied by a wider social, economic, political, and institutional reordering in which the rights to water, land, resources, and decision-making powers are transferred and rescaled (Ahlers et al., 2017). Local common property resources, livelihood strategies of local communities and socio-cultural relationships can also be fragmented by the diversion and/or restriction of the river's flow. Its presence leads to road building and population movements, connecting previously disparate locations and communities and leading to the entrance of new interests, motives, and stakes in the region while redistributing those already present. It is within this process of social, political, and economic reordering that the river comes to possess a new purpose, with the redistribution of hydrological resources representing the restructuring of social meanings and the rearrangement of powers and responsibilities in both the region of construction and beyond (Ahlers et al., 2017; Middleton et al., 2013). For example, in Turkey, government investment in hydroelectricity has been accompanied by a redefinition of use-rights to water, with rivers not only physically diverted from local communities but also legally privatised, with new laws prioritising 'productive' use by private actors (Islar, 2012). Similarly, in Laos PDR, powerful actors – both in Laos PDR and neighbouring Thailand – have controlled the benefits of hydropower expansion in the country, exporting energy for profit, while neglecting the social and environmental impacts of the infrastructure (Matthews, 2012).

I understand such a process as representing the occurrence of territorialisation, or the act of 'excluding or including people within particular geographic boundaries, and about controlling what people do and their access to natural resources within those boundaries' (Vandergeest and Peluso, 1995, p. 388). The social impact of hydroelectric projects often represents a structural intervention in the landscape, based on core–periphery relations, that seeks to appropriate the rural landscape for development or extractive activities (Blake and Barney, 2018). As Mohamud and Verhoeven (2016, p. 187) have highlighted, this may also involve the subjugation of the communities living on the river's banks – the construction of a number of dams in Sudan, justified by the nation's 'Green Revolution,' involved the subjugation of populations via displacement, restriction of access, and ecological marginalisation, while consolidating the political position of the ruling group. In Laos PDR, the construction of hydropower projects is often coupled with wider governmental programmes of agricultural intensification and irrigation infrastructure within the region, with local populations resettled to make way for both the dam and additional projects (Blake and Barney, 2018). This process represents the territorialisation of the region, which revolves around the enrolment of regions, previously on the economic periphery, into state-led policies of accumulation (Nathan Green and Baird, 2016).

These episodes illustrate how the planning and construction of hydroelectric dams can come to represent 'moments of consolidation' in which these infrastructure projects come to be symbolic of a 'national nature' whereby the respective river is subject to a process of territorialisation and is incorporated into political visions of statehood or nationalism (Dinmore, 2014; Swyngedouw, 2015b; Worster, 1985). Historical dam projects have often been built within a context of what has been labelled the hydraulic mission – a worldview that asserts that every drop of water that makes it from the river to the sea is wasted – which has provided an impetus for the development of water infrastructure in the 20th century (Molle et al., 2009).[3] For example, in Spain, Joaquín Costa, the founder of the Spanish regeneracionismo ('regenerationism') movement declared 'Let's tame the rivers with the brakes of dams and the chains of canals' as part of a wider political effort to modernise the Spanish state (Ibor et al., 2011, p. 259). This worldview has parallels with James Scott's (1999) high modernism, assuming that societal progress can be found in schemes that re-engineer and enlist space, nature, and populations into a quest for economic development. Scholarship has highlighted how numerous projects have been justified in such a way, with the projects presented as being key to national economic growth and a symbol of 20th-century modernity, defined as the anthropocentric 'conquering' and 'harnessing' of nature (Crow-Miller, Webber, and Rogers, 2017; Dinmore, 2014; Isaacman and Isaacman, 2013; Klingensmith, 2007; Swyngedouw, 2015b). Such claims function to not only legitimise a project but also justify the social and environmental impacts associated with its construction. For example, the construction of the Volta River Project in Ghana in the 1960s was justified by pro-dam actors as a gateway to renewed national economic development and progress, with local communities regarded as sacrificing their homes and livelihoods for the good of the wider population (Johnson et al., 2015).

In studying 'moments of consolidation,' a number of researchers have argued that the persistence of the hydraulic mission represents the consolidation of the worldview of a group of pro-dam actors labelled the 'hydraulic bureaucracy' which calls for the continued use of infrastructure to control water resources (Evers and Benedikter, 2009; Molle et al., 2009; Wester et al., 2009). Both the Rogun Dam in Tajikistan and Tarbela Dam in Pakistan came to be key sites of an emergent nationalism in the respective states, consolidating a new form of national identity and governance in previously fragmented states (Akhter, 2015a; Menga, 2015). Within this context, the concrete, turbines, and electricity grids that make up a hydroelectric project reflect – but also preserve – the structures of political and economic power, as well as the dominant visions of what the world should be at the time of their construction. For example, the Kariba dam in Zambia represented the elevation of a particular vision of statehood, nation-building, and economic development over others, in which preference was given to a vision of a centralised, urban, industrialised nation, while rural populations, particularly the rural poor, were neglected (Tischler, 2014). In a post-colonial political context, the building of a large dam not only demonstrates national technical progress but also represents a process of emancipation from the former colonial powers and a new dawn for infant nations (Akhter, 2015a, 2015b; Miescher, 2014; Mossallam, 2014). A dam develops a nationalist significance that extends well beyond its technological character. For example, the Akosombo Dam in Ghana became a symbol of President Kwame Nkrumah's personal power, with the project dubbed 'Nkrumah's baby' by the Ghanaian media (Miescher, 2014). The Aswan High Dam became a similar symbol of the bright future of President Gamal Abdel Nasser's Egypt, with the project presented as representative of an Egyptian future of economic development and technological prowess (Mossallam, 2014). The embrace of hydraulic works as a symbol of progress is well illustrated in the oft-cited words of Jawaharlal Nehru who, when inaugurating the Bhakra Nangal Dam in 1963, labelled dams the 'temples of modern India' (Everard, 2013, p. 28). In making this statement, Nehru presented the construction of dams in a spiritual sense, highlighting the perception that the projects represented a landmark of national progress and modernity. The planning and construction project becomes what has been described as a 'set-piece' of nationhood, comparable to the hosting of a global sports event or having a space programme or nuclear bomb in defining a particular type of national identity (Bromber et al., 2014, p. 290). It is in this context of regime-consolidation and nationalism that the construction of a dam develops a symbolic character, representing a political project and the consolidation of a worldview related to national progress.

The 'hydraulic bureaucracy,' described in this book as the 'pro-dam coalition,' is resilient, maintaining its legitimacy into the 21st century – as is evident in the resurgence of large-scale dam building, desalination projects and inter-basin transfers in contemporary water policy (Crow-Miller, Webber, and Molle, 2017; Molle et al., 2009; Warner et al., 2017). Across the globe, hydroelectric dams continue to maintain a wider significance in policy; however, they find legitimacy in different ways, with pro-dam actors adopting different narratives and tropes to justify them, which I term 'storylines.' It is to the importance of these storylines that I turn below.

The role of storylines

For a large-scale hydropower project to be built, numerous audiences need to be convinced to support (or, at least, acquiesce to) the project. The work of numerous researchers has explored the ways in which such legitimacy is found and secured in the narratives and tropes that are put forward by pro-dam actors committed to the project's development (Abbink, 2012; Crow-Miller, 2015;

Cunningham, 2007; Kaika, 2003; le Mentec, 2014; Warner, 2004; Yong and Grundy-Warr, 2012). These narratives have previously been labelled 'nirvana concepts' (Molle, 2008) and 'discourses of deflection' (Crow-Miller, 2015) and are deemed to obscure the political and economic interests behind a project and, instead, justify its planning and construction as representative of a unifying goal. In this book, I draw on the work of Hajer (1995, p. 56) and label these legitimising tropes and narratives 'storylines,' defined as 'a generative sort of narrative that allows actors to draw upon various discursive categories to give meaning to specific physical or social phenomena.'

Storylines provide an important medium through which pro-dam actors can impose their worldview on others by simplifying problems, rationalising their solutions, and increasing the legitimacy of the planning and construction of a dam by creating a 'catchy one-liner' that accommodates multiple demands (Hajer, 1995, p. 59). An example of this can be seen in modern storylines that present infrastructure projects as a solution to problems of water insecurity (Alatout, 2008; Bakker, 1999b; Buchs, 2010; Mehta, 2001; Urquijo, de Stefano, and La Calle, 2015). Storylines of naturalised scarcity – with shortages presented as a result of climate change – have been put forward by pro-dam actors to dispute opposition assertions of potential alternatives, such as the management of demand (Crow-Miller, 2015). The use of a storyline of scarcity has two consequences: first, the creation of a necessity of action (van Wijk and Fischhendler, 2017; Warner, 2004; Yong and Grundy-Warr, 2012) and, second, the restriction of alternatives (Alatout, 2008; Mehta, 2001; Urquijo, de Stefano, and La Calle, 2015).

Pro-dam storylines both simplify and rationalise certain definitions of problems or solutions, rallying actors into supporting projects and following courses of action. They are instrumental in legitimising a dam project (Molle, 2008). The failure of such storylines to gain support can, in turn, heighten potential opposition to the respective project (Akhter, 2015a). While historical patterns of dam construction have been legitimised by storylines of economic development or national progress, more contemporary storylines have linked hydropower projects to emergent grievances and demands (such as for employment, energy security, or secure water supply), transforming these calls into legitimising devices. For example, international storylines about the War on Terror have been absorbed into storylines legitimising the Ilisu Dam in Turkey (Warner, 2010). Similarly, the use of a language of Sumak Kawsay and Buen Vivir in contemporary pro-dam storylines in Ecuador has also been adopted by pro-dam actors (Warner et al., 2017), despite its foundation in a movement calling for respect for Mother Earth. The absorption of these additional demands demonstrates that pro-dam storylines do not have a fixed character but are reconfigured by pro-dam actors over time, with new concepts and tropes providing dams with renewed legitimacy (Warner et al., 2017).

Following Warner et al. (2017), I understand the persistence of the hydraulic mission in the 21st century as rooted in the ability of pro-dam actors to link the planning and construction of hydraulic infrastructure to wider storylines, endowing projects with a renewed degree of legitimacy. The hydraulic mission is reinvented, moving from a storyline of nationalism or economic development to emergent demands, problems, and solutions. This represents an 'adaptive capacity' (Warner et al., 2017). The storylines put forward to legitimise a dam project hold an adaptive capacity to adopt new storylines to address and absorb the grievances and demands of additional groups. These storylines are continually changing and adjusting to enlist new demands and narratives (Bellette Lee, 2013; Edwards, 2013). For example, dominant storylines in Spanish water policy have transformed over time – from narratives of rural modernisation by irrigation in the 1970s to contemporary storylines adopted to justify the reallocation of water towards more profitable uses (Lopez-Gunn, 2009; Lopez-Gunn et al., 2012). Similarly, pro-dam actors in India, having faced extensive pressure from anti-dam movements in the 1990s, have switched from previous storylines of economic development to a more technocratic and managerial storyline of the need to preserve and maintain the health of rivers (Baviskar, 2019). This illustrates the dynamism of the storylines put forward to support a dam project, with these storylines absorbing new demands (for example, related to water insecurity) to legitimise a dam project.

The storylines put forward by pro-dam actors have an additional function. They also result in the exclusion of anti-dam voices, alternative worldviews, and criticism of the project in question, as those who express such views become demonised, ostracised, or criminalised (Crow-Miller, 2015; Huber and Joshi, 2015; Yong and Grundy-Warr, 2012). The assertion that a dam represents a particular form of statehood, nationalism, and community invariably results in the exclusion of others (Nixon, 2011). An assertion of ownership and control over a resource often involves framing others as outsiders with no legitimate claim to the resource (Neville and Weinthal, 2016). For example, within the evoking of a nationalist symbolism of a dam project, pro-dam actors constitute their own identity (and the meaning of the dam) by linking it to an area's water resources and infrastructure, while dismissing the demands and identities of others as illegitimate. The result is often a division between 'our' or 'my' water and those who stand in the way of a particular project (Allouche, 2005). Storylines of nationalism locate those opposing a respective project as both existing outside of the status quo and blocking the path of societal progress (Abbink, 2012; Cunningham, 2007; Ozen, 2014). This is seen in the construction of dams on the Omo River: the Ethiopian pro-dam coalition put forward storylines to cast international opposition networks as a roadblock to national progress (Abbink, 2012). As Prime Minister Meles Zenawi argued in 2011, 'they don't want to see [a] developed Africa; they want us to remain undeveloped and backward to serve their tourists as a museum' (Abbink, 2012).

These storylines are deployed by pro-dam actors to configure the normative divide between legitimate and illegitimate thinking, national progress, and regressive activity and isolate the opposition network from the wider community. For example, the Turkish government has previously attacked groups opposing dam construction by labelling them criminals and terrorists who are intent on blocking the economic progress of the nation (Ozen, 2014). These actors draw a normative divide between legitimate and illegitimate grievances, discrediting opposition networks and deflecting their criticism. This results in a transformation of the moment of contestation surrounding a project, with opposition groups cast as existing on the other side of a simple binary of 'for/anti-project' and 'patriotic/treasonous' (Pepermans and Maeseele, 2014). I understand this as a process of depoliticisation, or the elevation of the 'moment of contestation' surrounding hydroelectric dams above the terrain of the collision of competing storylines. I understand this process as rendering a project or policy process as technical and apolitical, deflecting opposition criticism, restricting the field upon which anti-dam movements can mobilise and contest contemporary hydroelectric projects, and defining their concerns and activism as illegitimate and subversive (Chhotray, 2007; Crow-Miller, 2015; Ferguson, 1994; Pepermans and Maeseele, 2014). It represents a form of anti-politics in which certain knowledges, worldviews, and perceptions of sustainability are excluded. This depoliticising tendency, evident in pro-dam storylines, provides a route to control the policy agenda, diverting attention from opposition movements that have been deemed illegitimate, restricting alternatives, and consolidating the hydraulic mission.

While historically storylines legitimised dam construction by articulating an equivalence between the infrastructure and notions of economic development, nationalism, and the 'conquering' of nature (Molle et al., 2009), this book explores contemporary storylines that illuminate the perceived links between dams and notions of sustainability and environmental health. I define this as a storyline of sustainability, or the deployment of assertions related to the perceived sustainability of the scheme and its role in contemporary sustainable development agendas (Ahlers et al., 2015; Bratman, 2015; Warner et al., 2017). A storyline of sustainability has been put forward by numerous actors to legitimise the return of large hydropower projects in recent years. For example, in Costa Rica, pro-dam actors have enrolled the expansion of hydroelectricity in the Pacuare basin into wider policy agendas to achieve carbon neutrality (Fletcher, 2010). Similarly, in the Eastern Himalayas of Nepal, the framing of hydropower as 'green' energy has allowed for the positioning of the energy source as synergistically positive, providing a route forward to policy agendas of economic growth and GHG-mitigation (Huber and Joshi, 2015). I understand this storyline of sustainability as representative of an 'adaptive capacity,' with pro-dam actors absorbing additional demands related to environmental protection into the storylines that legitimise hydropower projects (Warner et al., 2017). In putting forward this storyline, the proponents of contemporary hydropower projects present an equivalence between the respective projects and concerns of climate change and processes of mitigation and adaptation, presenting the infrastructure as a renewable source of energy (Bellette Lee, 2013; Yong and Grundy-Warr, 2012). The dam project is bestowed with new meaning, becoming positioned within a wider agenda of climate change mitigation and adaptation and characterised as a source of clean, sustainable, and renewable energy.

These claims of sustainability neglect and contradict the extensive episodes of contestation and conflict (both historically and in contemporary patterns) that have characterised dam construction. I understand this as concealing the struggle over the project and the alternative definitions of sustainability and criticism that argues that hydroelectric projects are environmentally and socially damaging (WCD, 2000) and accompanied by financial risk (Ansar et al., 2014). Putting forward a storyline of sustainability allows pro-dam actors to not only affirm the apparent sustainability of a project but also exclude alternative understandings of the social and environmental impact of the projects studied. This act of exclusion constitutes the depoliticisation of the projects that the storyline of sustainability describes, raising them above everyday politics and dissent (Kenis and Lievens, 2014; Kenis and Mathijs, 2014; Wilson and Swyngedouw, 2014). Local communities hold definitions, perceptions, and ways of understanding the sustainability of a particular scheme or policy that does not correspond with official, top-level understandings (Harris, 2009). Dominant definitions, which are often overly technical, can dismiss these localised views as culturally specific and unscientific, failing to fit the dominant rationale and narrative of sustainability (Leach et al., 2010). Similarly, in adopting a language of sustainability, decision-making actors may conceal the social and political character of environmental problems and solutions – which are linked to questions of power, conflict, and exclusion – by presenting them as technical pursuits, as well as asserting sustainability credentials that may not be accurate or present (Leach et al., 2010; Redclift, 2005). Similar to Ferguson's (1994) 'anti-politics machine,' the storyline of sustainability can undermine potential challenges to the political system and, with it, the supremacy of the hydraulic bureaucracy. Any assertion of 'sustainability' by powerful actors is not a benign act – it evokes a set of value judgements – defining which resources are to be sustained, why, how, and for whom (Sikor and Norgaard, 1999). Through this process, interests, grievances, and demands become excluded from dominant storylines. For example, the dominant understanding of sustainable development has been critiqued for being grounded in a technocratic worldview that excludes alternative articulations of sustainability. This functions to close down political space and the potential for organisation. Within a storyline of sustainability, the decision to build a dam is 'rendered technical,' fitting a narrow, depoliticised definition (Li, 2007) and limiting the terrain upon which people can critique and challenge a project of powerful actors, thus allowing it to continue.

It is within this context that the task of an opposition movement against these projects comes to not only contest the dams themselves but resist the storyline of sustainability adopted to endow them with legitimacy. While research has described the emergence of this storyline of sustainability both internationally (Ahlers et al., 2015; Huber and Joshi, 2015; Warner et al., 2017) and in Brazil (Bratman, 2015), the processes through which anti-dam actors challenge this storyline are less understood. With the concept of sustainability characterised by ambiguity and open to contestation, the resistance struggles against hydropower provide an example of how environmentalist movements put forward emergent and alternative storylines of sustainability that challenge the location of hydropower schemes in contemporary sustainable development agendas. As Huber and

Joshi (2015) have demonstrated in exploring the case of hydropower in Nepal, opposition movements against dam projects are able to repoliticise these schemes, opening up new political spaces. In this case, the construction of hydroelectric schemes catalysed an anti-dam movement which politicised environmental decision-making and exposing a historic democratic deficit (Huber and Joshi, 2015). In doing so, the movement not only critiqued the storyline of sustainability but also broadened it, exposing it to different demands and grievances. It is this process of critique, challenge, broadening, and reconfiguring the dominant storyline of sustainability that I explore in the subsequent chapters.

With the contest over dams hinging on the imposition of a storyline, which provides a lens for understanding the project and its wider consequences, it is important for researchers to analyse the different ways in which anti-dam actors contest, critique, and reconfigure dominant storylines. The term 'sustainability' is appealed to by multiple actors, albeit with different meanings and logics of use. There are diverse understandings of 'sustainability,' including environmental justice, climate justice, and the 'environmentalism of the poor,' that contest dominant assertions of sustainability. These contested sustainabilities are put forward to resist the dominant apolitical and technical conceptualisation of sustainable development, reasserting its political character and providing an alternative vision of environmental politics movements across the globe have called for the 'energy sovereignty' of local communities, highlighting the maldistribution of costs and benefits in the planning and construction of renewable infrastructure, with the benefits enjoyed by those in urban centres and the costs borne by already-marginalised communities in rural areas. From the Movimento Rios Vivos in Colombia to Energy Vikalp Sangam in India, popular movements have rejected hydropower projects and the energy models that they represent (del Bene et al., 2018). In doing so, these movements interact with the dominant storyline of sustainability by challenging the assumptions of pro-dam actors about what sustainability means, who it is for and how it is achieved.

It is important to explore how this emergent storyline can be contested. The analysis of dominant pro-dam storylines involves not only the investigation of why the respective project is so easily represented in such a way; it must also study the avenues of resistance against this representation. It is by exploring the contested character of contemporary pro-dam storylines that this book engages in the analysis of the different ways in which pro-dam storylines are contested by anti-dam actors and how these resistance storylines of critique interact with dominant storylines about environmental politics. In doing so, the subsequent chapters move beyond the analysis of the malleability of pro-dam storylines, and towards an understanding of how anti-dam actors not only oppose the planning and construction of a dam project but advance storylines that critique and reconfigure the storylines put forward to legitimise the project. Pro-dam storylines are not set in stone and, instead, remain contestable. While these storylines are dynamic and able to absorb new concepts and demands, they remain open to contestation by anti-dam actors. However, these 'moments of contestation' remain understudied in scholarship. I will now turn to how pro-dam storylines are challenged below.

Moments of contestation

The storylines that accompany a dam's planning and construction are open to both contestation and restructuring. It is in these contests that the dynamism and adaptability of pro-dam storylines are tested, with anti-dam actors not only opposing the project itself but critiquing its location within wider storylines, such as those related to development or nationalism. Neither pro- nor anti-dam storylines exist in isolation from one another. Instead, they are engaged in the process of contestation, critique, and reconfiguration – deflecting each other's criticism, critiquing rival claims, and highlighting inaccuracies. While opposition to dam projects is often predicated on local concerns related to social and environmental impacts and participation in decision-making (Sneddon and Fox, 2008), anti-dam actors also link these localised demands to wider storylines, putting forward an idea of the respective projects as a site with a far wider significance in social, political, or cultural terms. For example, anti-dam activists in Myanmar have previously opposed hydropower on cultural grounds, arguing that construction would disrupt spiritual and cultural activities in the region, and, in doing so, linking it to wider discussions of cultural diversity and protection in the country (Kirchherr et al., 2017) In doing so, these actors who resisted the project were able to not only oppose it but contest its definition as a project with limited impact.

Drawing from the work of Neville and Weinthal (2016), I understand the putting forward of a storyline that locates opposition within a wider context and importance as a 'scaling up' of local protests and activism. It is within this process that a moment of contestation that originated at the local level is presented within a storyline of regional, national, or global importance. This 'scaling up' involves the adoption of a universalising storyline to generate wider support for local grievances and demands and contest dominant storylines (Garavan, 2007; Rootes, 1999). Scholarship in the field of environmental politics has argued that it is by putting forward these wider storylines that localised environmental protests can come to represent wider political questions, becoming detached from their immediate environmentalist or ecological origins and taking on a greater political significance. In doing so, opposition networks against dams engage in the provision of alternative meanings, problems, and solutions to rearticulate the project within a context divergent from the storylines of the proponent. The provision of these storylines by environmental movements performs a strategic function. Although moments of contestation in environmental politics – including the construction of a dam project – often occur at the local level, local resistance movements contesting policies or infrastructure locate their opposition within wider (be they national or global) storylines, appealing to a broader constituency and linking their opposition to environmental problems or solutions of greater importance. To provide examples from environmental policy, Neville and Weinthal (2016) have explored such a process in the Yukon of Canada, where a movement against the siting of a liquid natural gas facility (LNG) in the area articulated the struggle in local (regarding safety and costs), regional (risks to landscape and water security), and global (climate change) terms. These activists gained regional and national support by linking local concerns regarding the siting of infrastructure to broader issues of water and air pollution and climate impacts (Neville and Weinthal, 2016).

This process of 'scaling up' is constituted by actors advancing storylines that demonstrate the wider resonance of their opposition, casting an infrastructure project as not only socially and environmentally damaging at the local level but as having a wider political symbolism. For example, the opposition to the Tryweryn dam project in Wales in the 1950s foregrounded its opposition to this relatively small project within a wider discussion of the protection of Welsh culture and language (Atkins, 2018a; Griffiths, 2014). In putting forward such storylines, anti-dam actors illuminated a number of cultural impacts of the project that remained unaddressed in the assertions of pro-dam actors, challenging pro-dam storylines of the 'national interest' (Atkins, 2018a). This, in turn, inscribed the Tryweryn project – as well as the village of Capel Celyn that was lost to its reservoir – with a significance that extended far wider than the site of its construction. The project, which displaced only 48 people, became a key site of a resurgence of Welsh nationalism, due to its symbolism of a loss of Welsh culture and an asymmetrical relationship between the Welsh nation and the British government (Atkins, 2018a; Griffiths, 2014). This symbolism and significance persist to this day – over 50 years after the project was completed.

Anti-dam actors, in particular, appeal to and challenge storylines put forward by pro-dam actors to both raise awareness of a project's impact and critique official assertions (Abbink, 2012; Yasuda, 2015). For example, activists opposed to the Kamchay dam in Cambodia have directly challenged pro-dam arguments that hydropower has a central role in national economic development, while drawing attention to the project's impact (Hensengerth, 2015). This anti-dam storyline illuminated a series of impacts that were unaddressed in pro-dam storylines, that were instead focused on legitimising the project as a route of economic growth, while directly challenging such a storyline. The importance of anti-dam storylines illuminating social impacts was a key part of the widespread opposition to hydropower that led to the formation of the World Commission on Dams. In 1994, numerous anti-dam groups released the Manibeli Declaration, which called for the World Bank to withdraw funding from large dams. This declaration directly critiqued the high modernist storylines that had previously justified dam projects, arguing that not only did the projects have extensive environmental impacts but their social costs went against the policies of the World Bank itself:

> The environmental and social costs of [the] World Bank-funded large dams, in terms of people forced from their homes, destruction of forests and fisheries, and spread of waterborne diseases, have fallen disproportionately on women, indigenous communities, tribal peoples and the poorest and most marginalised sectors of the population. This is in direct contradiction to the World Bank's often–stated 'overarching objective of alleviating poverty.'
> (Manibeli Declaration, 1994)

The 1994 Manibeli Declaration challenged dominant pro-dam arguments that hydropower projects assisted with the fulfilment of goals of economic development by illuminating the links between the energy source and wider patterns of spatial injustice (Schulz and Adams, 2019). It argued that World Bank funding, far from assisting the lifting of people out of poverty, had actually led to the further spatial differentiation of costs and benefits, with much of the electricity generated transmitted a great distance from those exposed to a project's impacts. The Manibeli Declaration called for the World Bank to withdraw funding from dam schemes, to organise reparations for communities impacted by previously funded projects and to develop new forms of project appraisal, monitoring, and evaluation. It is this highlighting of social impacts that resulted in the escalating discrediting of large dams towards the end of the 20th century, as is evident in the 2000 report by the World Commission on Dams, which highlighted the numerous social issues faced by communities impacted by dam construction (World Commission on Dams, 2000).

An example of a moment of contestation in which anti-dam actors contested dominant pro-dam storylines that is well-studied in scholarship is that of resistance against the construction of a series of dams in the Narmada Valley in India in the 1980s (Baviskar, 1995; Marino, 2012; Routledge, 2003). Scholarship exploring this opposition has demonstrated how the resistance against the Narmada projects not only directly opposed the dams but also engaged in a critique of the pro-dam storylines that associated the projects with notions of economic development (Baviskar, 1995; Chapman, 2007; Marino, 2012). The opposition network, the Narmada Bachao Andolan (NBA) presented an alternative to this pro-dam storyline of development, highlighting additional issues and impacts that were absent in pro-dam storylines. Within anti-dam storylines, the project was presented as a form of cultural erasure of the traditional Adivasi population of the area, with the way of life of these communities celebrated by opposition actors as 'an ecologically respectful, democratically communitarian, alternate route to development' (Baviskar, 1995, p. 272). In putting forward this storyline, anti-dam actors not only opposed the project but contested the high modernist storyline of development and highlighted the asymmetry in the sharing of the costs and benefits of the project (Palit, 2003; Routledge, 2003). Although the Sardar Sarovar Dam was later built, the opposition of the NBA to the project illustrates how pro-dam storylines, while seemingly dominant, can be contested and reconfigured. The anti-dam storyline highlighted alternative visions of economic development, incorporating the protection of Adivasi populations and ensuring an equal distribution of costs and benefits that allowed for the further expansion of the anti-dam network, with both national and international actors joining its ranks (Haynes, 1999). The opposition network became multi-scalar, incorporating numerous grievances, and priorities into an overarching, simplified storyline of opposition to the project (Haynes, 1999).

Anti-dam movements across the globe do not just highlight the environmental and social impacts of a hydroelectric project. The storylines that they put forward move towards questioning the ways in which pro-dam actors understand, perceive, and measure the sustainability of this energy (del Bene et al., 2018). Movements have disputed the links between hydropower and what is broadly understood as sustainability by highlighting numerous impacts that challenge pro-dam storylines of sustainability (Scheidel et al., 2018; Temper et al., 2018). The 2010 Declaration of Temaca, stemming from a meeting of anti-dam activists in Mexico, is a case in point. The declaration affirmed a new form of sustainability, one including traditional knowledge, equity, and community-owned energy, while challenging the dominant pro-dam storyline of sustainability:

> Big dams reduce the ability of societies and ecosystems to adapt to global warming. The changing climate is causing grave harm to people and ecosystems and making dams even less safe, less economically viable, and shorter-lived. Large reservoirs are a significant source of greenhouse gases ... We oppose the misnamed 'Clean Development Mechanism,' promoted by powerful governments and private capital to enable them to offset their GHG emissions, including by building dams.
>
> (Declaration of Temaca, 2010)

From the Barro Blanco project in Panama, which was criticised for its failure to consult local indigenous communities (Giraldo, 2017) to the Poçem Dam in Albania, opposed for its violation of the human rights of local communities (EcoAlbania, 2016), anti-dam actors are not only opposed to the sustainability credentials of respective projects; they are also providing new vocabularies to understand and describe the 'sustainability' of hydropower projects in the 21st century. In doing so, these movements illuminate alternative pathways towards a sustainable energy transition (del Bene et al., 2018). This can be understood as a form of 'alternative sustainabilities,' a term coined by Cavanagh and Benjaminsen (2017) to describe ground-level definitions of sustainability that challenge dominant conceptualisations of 'green energy.' As is evident with the opposition to the Narmada river dams in India in the 1990s, anti-dam movements illuminate overlooked impacts, highlight political motivations and injustices, and render forgotten communities visible. They continue to do so, stretching and challenging the asserted sustainability credentials of hydropower in the 21st century. As I will explore in subsequent chapters, these movements open up new spaces in which to rethink the role of hydropower in contemporary sustainability politics.

Conclusion

In this chapter, I have explored the ways in which the planning and construction of a dam can come to hold a wider significance, as well as the vital role of storylines in inscribing the projects with such importance. I have detailed how the construction of a dam can represent the consolidation of a political project – often related to notions of economic development or nationalism – and its related power asymmetries. These 'moments of consolidation' hinge upon the imposition of a pro-dam storyline, which defines a set of problems and legitimises prescribed solutions.

However, the planning and construction of a dam project may also result in a 'moment of contestation,' in which anti-dam actors challenge and reconfigure pro-dam storylines. As the example of opposition to the Narmada dams in India illustrates, the storylines provided by anti-dam actors not only oppose a project but also critique and reconfigure dominant storylines put forward by pro-dam actors. However, the role of anti-dam storylines remains understudied in the scholarship surveyed. Research must explore how the contestation of a hydropower project also represents the provision of anti-dam storylines that discredit pro-dam assertions and provides an alternative view and understanding of the project in question. In focusing on this process of contestation, I explore how these dominant storylines are challenged by anti-dam actors in different ways that act to reconfigure pro-dam storylines of sustainability. In doing so, resistance storylines contest not only the Belo Monte and São Luiz do Tapajós projects in Brazil but also their definition as sustainable projects. It is this point that subsequent chapters take as their starting point.

Notes

1 This book is positioned within a field of scholarship that explores the intersection between hydraulic infrastructure (such as dams) and political power (Isaacman and Isaacman, 2013; Menga and Swyngedouw, 2018; Swyngedouw, 2015b; Wittfogel, 1957; Worster, 1985). Following Menga (2017), I label this field of scholarship 'Critical Hydropolitics,' defined as exploring how the management of water and construction of its associated infrastructure represents a political process in which cultural, social, political, and economic norms interact with the laws of hydrology.
2 Whitehead et al. (2007) also draw attention to a third 'moment,' one of 'simulacrum' – in which, following Baudrillard, representations of the past become understood as more viable than the past itself. This moment is unexplored in this text.
3 This 'mission' is rooted in the state-led development of irrigation that occurred in the colonies of Great Britain, the Netherlands, and France in the 1800s, as well as similar processes in the United States (Molle et al., 2009).

Bibliography

Abbink, J (2012). Dam controversies: contested governance and developmental discourse on the Ethiopian Omo River dam. *Social Anthropology*, 20(2): 125–144.

Ahlers, R, Budds, J, Joshi, D, Merme, V, and Zwarteveen, M (2015). Framing hydropower as green energy: assessing drivers, risks and tensions in the Eastern Himalayas. *Earth System Dynamics*, 6(1): 195–204.

Ahlers, R, Zwarteveen, M, and Bakker, K (2017). Large dam development: from Trojan Horse to Pandora's Box. In: B Flyvbjerg (ed.) *The Oxford Handbook of Megaproject Management*. Oxford: Oxford University Press.

Akhter, M (2015a). Infrastructure nation: state space, hegemony, and hydraulic regionalism in Pakistan. *Antipode*, 47(4): 849–870.

Akhter, M (2015b). The hydropolitical cold war: the Indus Waters Treaty and state formation in Pakistan. *Political Geography*, 46: 65–75.

Alatout, S (2008). 'States' of scarcity: water, space, and identity politics in Israel, 1948–59. *Environment and Planning D: Society and Space*, 26(6): 959–982.

Allouche, J (2005). *Water Nationalism: An Explanation of the Past and Present Conflicts in Central Asia, the Middle East and the Indian Subcontinent?* Thèse N ° 699, submitted to University of Geneva.

Ansar, A, Flyvbjerg, B, Budzier, A, and Lunn, D (2014). Should we build more large dams? The actual costs of hydropower megaproject development. *Energy Policy*, 69: 43–56.

Atkins, E (2017). Dammed and diversionary: the multi-dimensional framing of Brazil's Belo Monte dam. *Singapore Journal of Tropical Geography*, 38(3): 276–292.

Atkins, E (2018a). Building a dam, constructing a nation: the 'drowning' of Capel Celyn. *Journal of Historical Sociology*, 31(4): 455–468.

Atkins, E (2018b). Dams, political framing and sustainability as an empty signifier: the case of Belo Monte. *Area*, 50(2): 232–239.

Bakker, K (1999). Deconstructing discourses of drought. *Transactions of the Institute of British Geographers*, 24(3): 367–372.

Bakker, K (2013). Neoliberal versus postneoliberal water: geographies of privatization and resistance. *Annals of the Association of American Geographers*, 103(2): 253–260.

Bakker, K, and Bridge, G (2006). Material worlds? Resource geographies and the 'matter of nature.' *Progress in Human Geography*, 30: 5–27.

Baviskar, A (1995). *In the Belly of the River*. Oxford: Oxford University Press.

Baviskar, A (2019). Nation's body, river's pulse: narratives of anti-dam politics in India. *Thesis Eleven*, 150(1): 26–41.

Bellette Lee, YC (2013). Global capital, national development and transnational environmental activism: conflict and the Three Gorges Dam. *Journal of Contemporary Asia*, 43(1): 102–126.

Blake, DJH, and Barney, K (2018). Structural injustice, slow violence? The political ecology of a 'best practice' hydropower dam in Lao PDR. *Journal of Contemporary Asia*, 48(5): 808–834.

Boelens, R, Hoogesteger, J, Swyngedouw, E, Vos, J, and Wester, P (2016). Hydrosocial territories: a political ecology perspective. *Water International*, 41(1): 1–14.

Bratman, E (2015). Passive revolution in the green economy: activism and the Belo Monte dam. *International Environmental Agreements: Politics, Law and Economics*, 15(1): 61–77.

Bromber, K, Féaux de la Croix, J, and Lange, K (2014). The temporal politics of big dams in Africa, the Middle East, and Asia: by way of an introduction. *Water History*, 6(4): 289–296.

Brown, T (2016). Sustainability as empty signifier: its rise, fall, and radical potential. *Antipode*, 48(1): 115–133.

Buchs, A (2010). Water crisis and water scarcity as social constructions: the case of water use in Almería (Andalusia, Spain). *Options Méditerranéennes*, A(95): 207–211.

Budds, J (2004). Power, nature and neoliberalism: the political ecology of water in Chile. *Singapore Journal of Tropical Geography*, 25(3): 322–342.

Cavanagh, CJ, and Benjaminsen, TA (2017). Political ecology, variegated green economies, and the foreclosure of alternative sustainabilities. *Journal of Political Ecology*, 24(1): 200–216.

Chapman, J (2007). India's Narmada dams controversy. *Journal of International Communication*, 13(1): 71–85.

Chhotray, V (2007). The 'anti-politics machine' in India: depoliticisation through local institution building for participatory watershed development. *Journal of Development Studies*, 43(6): 1037–1056.

Crow-Miller, B (2015). Discourses of deflection: the politics of framing China's south-north water transfer project. *Water Alternatives*, 8(2): 173–192.
Crow-Miller, B, Webber, M, and Molle, F (2017). The (re)turn to infrastructure for water management? *Water Alternatives*, 10(2): 195–207.
Crow-Miller, B, Webber, M, and Rogers, S (2017). The techno-politics of big infrastructure and the Chinese water machine. *Water Alternatives*, 10(2): 233–249.
Cunningham, M (2007). Public policy and normative language: utility, community and nation in the debate over the construction of Tryweryn reservoir. *Parliamentary Affairs*, 60(4): 625–536.
Declaration of Temaca (2010). Endorsed at Rivers for Life. *The 3rd International Meeting of Dam Affected People and their Allies, un Temacapulín, Mexico, 1–7 October 2010*. Available at: https://www.internationalrivers.org/resources/declaration-of-temaca-4290
del Bene, D, Scheidel, A, and Temper, L (2018). More dams, more violence? A global analysis on resistances and repression around conflictive dams through co-produced knowledge. *Sustainability Science*, 13(3): 617–633.
della Porta, D, and Piazza, G (2007). Local contention, global framing: the protest campaigns against the TAV in Val di Susa and the bridge on the Messina Straits. *Environmental Politics*, 16(5): 864–882.
Delsontro, T, McGinnis, DF, Sobek, S, Ostrovsky, I, and Wehrli, B (2010). Extreme methane emissions from a Swiss hydropower reservoir: contribution from bubbling sediments. *Environmental Science and Technology*, 44(7): 2419–2425.
Díaz-Caravantes, RE, and Wilder, M (2014). Water, cities and peri-urban communities: geographies of power in the context of drought in northwest Mexico. *Water Alternatives*, 7(3): 499–517.
Dinmore, EG (2014). 'Mountain dream' or the 'submergence of fine scenery'? Japanese contestations over the Kurobe Number Four Dam, 1920–1970. *Water History*, 6(4): 315–340.
EcoAlbania (2016). NO dams in Vjosa, 'NO' to Poçem dam. *EcoAlbania*. http://www.ecoalbania.org/no-dams-in-vjosa-no-to-pocem-dam/
Edwards, G (2013). Shifting constructions of scarcity and the neoliberalization of Australian water governance. *Environment and Planning. Part A*, 45(8): 1873–1890.
Everard, M (2013). *The Hydropolitics of Dams*. London: Zed Books.
Evers, HD, and Benedikter, S (2009). Hydraulic bureaucracy in a modern hydraulic society: strategic group formation in the Mekong delta, Vietnam. *Water Alternatives*, 2(3): 416–439.
Ferguson, J (1994). *The Anti-politics Machine*. Minneapolis, MN: University of Minnesota Press.
Fletcher, R (2010). When environmental issues collide: climate change and the shifting political ecology of hydroelectric power. *Peace & Conflict Review*, 5(1): 1–17.
Garavan, M (2007). Resisting the costs of 'development': local environmental activism in Ireland. *Environmental Politics*, 16(5): 844–863.
Giraldo, CM (2017). Panama's Barro Blanco dam to begin operation, indigenous pleas refused. *Mongabay*. 24 March. Available at: https://news.mongabay.com/2017/03/panamas-barro-blanco-dam-to-begin-operation-indigenous-pleas-refused/ (Accessed: 30 March 2020).
Griffiths, H (2014). Water under the bridge? Nature, memory and hydropolitics. *Cultural Geographies*, 21(3): 449–474.
Hajer, M (1995). *The Politics of Environmental Discourse: Ecological Modernization and the Policy Process*. Oxford: Clarendon Press.

Harris, LM (2009). Contested sustainabilities: assessing narratives of environmental change in southeastern Turkey. *Local Environment*, 14(8): 699–720.

Haynes, J (1999). Power, politics and environmental movements in the Third World. *Environmental Politics*, 8(1): 222–242.

Hensengerth, O (2015). Where is the power? Transnational networks, authority and the dispute over the Xayaburi Dam on the Lower Mekong Mainstream. *Water International*, 40(5–6): 911–928.

Hommes, L, Boelens, R, and Maat, H (2016). Contested hydrosocial territories and disputed water governance: struggles and competing claims over the Ilisu Dam development in southeastern Turkey. *Geoforum*, 71: 9–20.

Huber, A, and Joshi, D (2015). Hydropower, anti-politics, and the opening of new political spaces in the Eastern Himalayas. *World Development*, 76: 13–25.

Ibor, CS, Mollá, MG, Reus, LA, and Genovés, JC (2011). Reaching the limits of water resources mobilization: irrigation development in the Segura river basin, Spain. *Water Alternatives*, 4(3): 259–278.

Isaacman, AF, and Isaacman, BS (2013). *Dams, Displacement and the Delusion of Development: Cahora Bassa and Its Legacies in Mozambique, 1965–2007*. Athens, OH: Ohio University Press.

Islar, M (2012). Privatised hydropower development in Turkey: a case of water grabbing? *Water Alternatives*, 5(2): 376–391.

Johnson, LB, Howell, JP, and Evered, KT (2015). 'Where nothing was before': (re)producing population and place in Ghana's Volta River Project. *Journal of Cultural Geography*, 32(2): 195–213.

Kaika, M (2003). Constructing scarcity and sensationalising water politics: 170 days that shook Athens. *Antipode*, 35(5): 919–954.

Keck, ME, and Sikkink, K (1998). *Activists beyond Borders: Advocacy Networks in International Politics*. Ithaca, NY: Cornell University Press.

Kenis, A, and Lievens, M (2014). Searching for 'the political' in environmental politics. *Environmental Politics*, 23(4): 531–548.

Kenis, A, and Mathijs, E (2014). Climate change and post-politics: repoliticizing the present by imagining the future? *Geoforum*, 52: 148–156.

Klingensmith, D (2007). *'One Valley and a Thousand': Dams, Nationalism and Development*. Oxford: Oxford University Press.

le Mentec, K (2014). The Three Gorges Dam and the demiurges: the story of a failed contemporary myth elaboration in China. *Water History*, 6(4): 385–403.

Leach, M, Scoones, I, and Stirling, A (2010). *Dynamic Sustainabilities: Technology, Environment, Social Justice*. London: Earthscan.

Li, TM (2007). *The Will to Improve: Governmentality, Development and the Practice of Politics*. Durham, NC: Duke University Press.

Linton, J, and Budds, J (2013). The hydrosocial cycle: defining and mobilizing a relational-dialectical approach to water. *Geoforum*, 57: 170–180.

Lopez-Gunn, E (2009). Agua para todos: a new regionalist hydraulic paradigm in Spain. *Water Alternatives*, 2(3): 370–394.

Lopez-Gunn, E, Zorrilla, P, Prieto, F, and Llamas, MR (2012). Lost in translation? Water efficiency in Spanish agriculture. *Agricultural Water Management*, 108: 83–95.

Manibeli Declaration (1994). Manibeli declaration calling for a moratorium on World Bank funding of large dams. https://www.internationalrivers.org/resources/manibeli-declaration-4334 (Accessed: 30 March 2020).

Marino, A (2012). 'The cost of dams': acts of writing as resistance in post-colonial India. *Citizenship Studies*, 16(5–6): 705–719.
Martinez-Alier, J, Temper, L, del Bene, D, and Scheidel, A (2016). Is there a global environmental justice movement? *The Journal of Peasant Studies*, 43(3): 731–755.
Matthews, N (2012). Water grabbing in the Mekong basin – An analysis of the winners and losers of Thailand's hydropower development in Lao PDR. *Water Alternatives*, 5(2): 392–411.
Mehta, L (2001). The manufacture of popular perceptions of scarcity: dams and water-related narratives in Gujarat, India. *World Development*, 29(12): 2025–2041.
Menga, F (2015). Building a nation through a dam: the case of Rogun in Tajikistan. *Nationalities Papers*, 43(3): 479–494.
Menga, F (2017). Hydropolis: reinterpreting the polis in water politics. *Political Geography*, 60: 100–109.
Menga, F, and Swyngedouw, F (2018). *Water, Technology and the Nation-State*. Abingdon: Routledge.
Middleton, C, Grundy-Warr, C, and Yong, ML (2013). Neoliberalizing hydropower in the Mekong basin: the political economy of partial enclosure. *Social Science Journal*, 43(2): 299–334.
Miescher, SF (2014). 'Nkrumah's Baby': the Akosombo Dam and the dream of development in Ghana, 1952–1966. *Water History*, 6(4): 341–366.
Mohamud, M, and Verhoeven, H (2016). Re-engineering the state, awakening the nation: dams, Islamist modernity and nationalist politics in Sudan. *Water Alternatives*, 8(2): 182–202.
Molle, F (2008). Nirvana concepts, narratives and policy models: insight from the water sector. *Water Alternatives*, 1(1): 131–156.
Molle, F, Mollinga, P, and Wester, P (2009). Hydraulic bureaucracies and the hydraulic mission: flows of water, flows of power. *Water Alternatives*, 2(3): 328–349.
Mossallam, A (2014). 'We are the ones who made this dam "High"!' A builders' history of the Aswan High Dam. *Water History*, 6(4): 297–314.
Nathan Green, W, and Baird, IG (2016). Capitalizing on compensation: hydropower resettlement and the commodification and decommodification of nature-society relations in Southern Laos. *Annals of the American Association of Geographers*, 106(4): 853–873.
Neville, KJ, and Weinthal, E (2016). Scaling up site disputes: strategies to redefine 'local' in the fight against fracking. *Environmental Politics*, 25(4): 569–592.
Nixon, R (2011). *Slow Violence and the Environmentalism of the Poor*. Cambridge, MA: Harvard University Press.
Ostrom, E (2008). The challenge of common-pool resources. *Environment: Science and Policy for Sustainable Development*, 50(4): 8–21.
Ozen, H (2014). Overcoming environmental challenges by antagonizing environmental protesters: the Turkish Government discourse against anti-hydroelectric power plants movements. *Environmental Communication*, 8(4): 433–451.
Palit, C (2003). Monsoon risings. *New Left Review*, 21: 80–100.
Pepermans, Y, and Maeseele, P (2014). Democratic debate and mediated discourses on climate change: from consensus to de/politicization. *Environmental Communication*, 8(2): 216–232.
Radkau, J (2008). *Nature and Power: A Global History of the Environment*. Cambridge: Cambridge University Press.

Redclift, M (2005). Sustainable development (1987–2005): an oxymoron comes of age. *Sustainable Development*, 13(4): 212–227.

Rootes, C (1999). Environmental movements: from the local to the global. *Environmental Politics*, 8(1): 1–12.

Routledge, P (2003). Voices of the dammed: discursive resistance amidst erasure in the Narmada Valley, India. *Political Geography*, 22(3): 243–270.

Scheidel, A, Temper, L, Demaria, F, and Martínez-Alier, J (2018). Ecological distribution conflicts as forces for sustainability: an overview and conceptual framework. *Sustainability Science*, 13(3): 585–598.

Schulz, C, and Adams, WM (2019). Debating dams: the World Commission on Dams 20 years on. *Wiley Interdisciplinary Reviews: Water*, 6(5): e1396.

Scott, JC (1999). *Seeing Like a State: How Certain Schemes to Improve the Human Condition Have Failed*. New Haven, CT: Yale University Press.

Sikor, T, and Norgaard, R (1999). Principles for sustainability: protection, investment, cooperation and innovation. In: Kohn, J, Gowdy, JM, Hinterberger, D, and Van der Straaten, J (eds) *Sustainability in Question: The Search for a Conceptual Framework*. Cheltenham: Edward Elgar.

Sneddon, C, and Fox, C (2008). Struggles over dams as struggles for justice: the World Commission on Dams (WCD) and anti-dam campaigns in Thailand and Mozambique. *Society and Natural Resources*, 21(7): 625–640.

Swyngedouw, E (1999). Modernity and hybridity: nature, regeneracionismo, and the production of the Spanish waterscape, 1891–1930. *Annals of the Association of American Geographers*, 89(3): 37–41.

Swyngedouw, E (2009). The political economy and political ecology of the hydro-social cycle. *Journal of Contemporary Water Research & Education*, 142(1): 56–60.

Swyngedouw, E (2015). *Liquid Power: Contested Hydro-modernities in Twentieth-Century Spain*. Cambridge, MA: MIT Press.

Temper, L, Walter, M, Rodriguez, I, Kothari, A, and Turhan, E (2018). A perspective on radical transformations to sustainability: resistances, movements and alternatives. *Sustainability Science*, 13(3): 747–764.

Tischler, J (2014). Cementing uneven development: the Central African Federation and the Kariba Dam scheme. *Journal of Southern African Studies*, 40(5): 1047–1064.

Urquijo, J, de Stefano, L, and La Calle, A (2015). Drought and exceptional laws in Spain: the official water discourse. *International Environmental Agreements: Politics, Law and Economics*, 15: 273–292.

van Oel, PR, Krol, MS, and Hoekstra, AY (2009). A river basin as a common-pool resource: a case study for the Jaguaribe basin in the semi-arid Northeast of Brazil. *International Journal of River Basin Management*, 7(4): 345–353.

van Wijk, J, and Fischhendler, I (2017). The construction of urgency discourse around mega-projects: the Israeli case. *Policy Sciences*, 50(3): 469–494.

Vandergeest, P, and Peluso, NL (1995). Territorialization and state power in Thailand. *Theory and Society*, 24(3): 385–426.

Warner, JF (2004). Plugging the GAP working with Buzan: the Ilisu Dam as a security issue. SOAS Water Issues Study Group, School of Oriental and African Studies/King's College London, Occasional Paper No 67, 1–24.

Warner, J (2010). Hydro-hegemonic politics: a crossroads on the Euphrates-Tigris. In: Wegerich, K, and Warner, J (eds) *The Politics of Water: A Survey*. London: Routledge.

Warner, JF, Hoogesteger, J, and Hidalgo, JP (2017). Old wine in new bottles: the adaptive capacity of the hydraulic mission in Ecuador. *Water Alternatives*, 10(2): 322–340.

Wester, P, Rap, E, and Vargas-Velázquez, S (2009). The hydraulic mission and the Mexican hydrocracy: regulating and reforming the flows of water and power. *Water Alternatives*, 2(3): 395–415.

Whitehead, M, Jones, R, and Jones, M (2007). *The Nature of the State: Excavating the Political Ecologies of the Modern State*. Cambridge: Cambridge University Press.

Wilson, J, and Swyngedouw, E (eds) (2014). *The Post-political and Its Discontents: Spaces of Depoliticisation, Spectres of Radical Politics*. Cambridge: Cambridge University Press.

Wittfogel, K (1957). *Oriental Despotism: A Comparative Study of Total Power*. London: Random House.

World Commission on Dams (2000). *Dams and Development: A New Framework for Decision-Making*. London: World Commission on Dams.

Worster, D (1985). *Rivers of Empire: Water, Aridity, and the Growth of the American West*. Oxford: Oxford University Press.

Yasuda, Y (2015). *Rules, Norms and NGO Advocacy Strategies: Hydropower Development on the Mekong River*. London: Routledge Earthscan.

Yong, ML, and Grundy-Warr, C (2012). Tangled nets of discourse and turbines of development: lower Mekong mainstream dam debates. *Third World Quarterly*, 33(6): 1037–1058. doi: 10.1080/01436597.2012.681501

3 Damming the Amazon

Brazil has the greatest reserves of surface water in the world – totalling approximately 19.4% of the planet's total surface water resources (Soito and Freitas, 2011) and is home to monumental river basins, including the Araguaia-Tocantins (with a drainage basin covering 967,059 km^2) and large parts of the Amazon (7,500,000 km^2) and Paraguai (1,095,000 km^2) Rivers. Since the 1930s, the state-led exploitation of waterscapes – lakes, groundwater, rivers, and marine space – has formed an important part of Brazilian national and regional development plans. This wealth in water resources has allowed Brazil to develop an energy matrix heavily dependent on hydropower generation. Despite recent expansions in both wind and solar power, hydropower remains a dominant part of the national energy matrix, providing for 64% of the total national installed energy capacity (International Hydropower Association, 2019).

Hydropower appeals to energy planners as a predictable and price-effective source of power that can convert up to 90% of water's energy into transmittable energy (Kumar et al., 2011). The method of energy generation is widely adopted across the South American continent and is particularly prevalent in the states of Paraguay, Colombia, and Uruguay. Although energy strategies have indicated a potential decrease in hydropower capacity in comparison to other sources, hydropower continues to play an important strategic role. Although current installed capacity is spread geographically across the nation, the focus has been on the Legal Amazon Region of Brazil, a basin home to a predicted hydroelectric potential of 106 GW (Agência Nacional de Energia Elétrica, 2009; Tolmasquim, 2007). Recent analysis has found that Brazil has nearly exhausted its hydroelectric potential in many regions of the country, resulting in the Amazon region becoming transformed into a 'new hydroelectric frontier' (Soito and Freitas, 2011, p. 3165); 90% of Brazil's surface water reserves are found in the Amazon and Tocantins Rivers, with 63% of its hydroelectric potential calculated to be in the basin (Soito and Freitas, 2011). While more than 100 hydroelectric dams have already been built in the Amazon region (Latrubesse et al., 2017), a further 79 dams have been planned for the lower and middle parts of the Amazon Basin in Brazil, with 16 of these having a planned installed capacity of over 30 MW (Lees et al., 2016).[1]

In this chapter, I contextualise subsequent analysis by introducing the Belo Monte and São Luiz do Tapajós hydropower projects, locating them within the wider terrain of contemporary Brazilian energy politics and detailing the role of contestation within the planning and construction of these projects. Both the Belo Monte and São Luiz do Tapajós projects are located on tributaries of the Amazon River, with the former currently under construction on the Volta Grande ('Great Bend') of the Xingu River and the latter project planned for the Tapajós River. These basins are understood as key centres of the hydroelectric potential of the Amazon Basin (Ministério de Mines e Energia and Empresa de Pesquisa Energética, 2007). Following the line of argument introduced in the previous chapter, I characterise these projects as representative of a contest between two distinct, heterogeneous groups that I term the 'pro-dam' and the 'resistance' coalitions. These groupings are understood as temporary alliances that involve numerous actors and groups from various backgrounds with different strategies and expertise. In this chapter, I profile the diverse actors that support the construction of a dam or contest it before moving to explore the interplay between these coalitions. In the final section, I detail the pro-dam storyline of sustainability put forward to legitimise the construction of hydroelectric dams in Brazil and delegitimise resistance networks.

The projects studied

The planning and construction of the Belo Monte Dam have a long history of contestation. The original plans for the project were made in 1975, during the years of Brazil's military dictatorship (1964–1985). These plans, commissioned by the regional company responsible for energy supply in the north of Brazil, Centrais Elétricas do Norte do Brasil SA (Eletronorte), were completed in 1979. The project outlined in these plans included five dams on the Xingu River and one on the nearby Iriri River, which were expected to generate 19 GW and flood over 18,000 km^2 of the Xingu River Basin (de Moya Figueira Netto et al., 2007). These dams form part of the modern-day Belo Monte project (formed of two large dams, named Kararaô and Babaquara). The project was formally presented in the 1987 Plano Nacional de Expansão Energética and, as will be discussed in subsequent sections, became an important site of contestation in Brazilian energy politics, as evident in the extensive opposition from local communities and national and international environmental organisations. The project was subsequently removed from national energy plans.

The project – now renamed Belo Monte – re-emerged in 1998, when redeveloped versions of the Kararaô and Babaquara Dams (now renamed Belo Monte and Altamira, respectively) were included in that year's Plano Decenal de Expansão de Energia 1998–2008. The surface area of the dam's reservoir had been reduced to 440 km^2 by moving the project upstream (de Moya Figueira Netto et al., 2007). In the current incarnation of the project, Belo Monte is a 'run-of-the-river' (ROR) project, designed to generate hydroelectricity without relying on a large reservoir.[2] The turbines are powered by water diverted from the Volta Grande ('Big Bend') of the Xingu River, resulting in the 100 kilometre stretch of water losing 80% of its total flow and a reservoir of 516 km^2. Although competing projections differ, it was estimated that the plant would displace 25,000 people in the city of Altamira, as well as 18,000 members of indigenous and riverside populations (Villas-Bôas et al., 2015). The project is advertised as having a total generation capacity of 11,233 MW and is able to serve up to 60 million people in all 26 federal states (Norte Energia, 2020). The electricity generated will be transmitted over 2,000 km to the well-populated southeast of the country by two transmission lines – built by, among others, China's State Grid company – to south-eastern Rio de Janeiro and Minas Gerais (L. Costa, 2017; Teixeira and Costa, 2015).

The São Luiz do Tapajós Dam is part of a proposed complex of hydroelectric dams located on the Tapajós and Jamanxim Rivers. The proposed complex, including the Jatobá, Cachoeira dos Patos, Jamanxim and Cachoeira do Cai Dams, was planned to generate 12,000 megawatts (MW) of energy. The São Luiz do Tapajós complex was planned for the Tapajós River, near the village of Pimental. It was expected to flood 722 km² of forest to create its reservoir and have a total installed capacity of 8,040 MW. If built, it would have been the second-largest dam in Brazil (after Belo Monte).[3] It was 1 of 43 large dam complexes planned or under construction in the Tapajós River Basin, including the Teles Pires project (involving the São Manoel, Teles Pires, Sinop and Colíder Dams). The project was removed from national energy plans in August 2016, when IBAMA refused to provide the necessary environmental licence. Contextual details for both the Belo Monte and São Luiz do Tapajós projects can be found in Table 3.1.

As discussed in Chapter 2, the planning and construction of dams across the globe are often characterised by a moment of contestation, with both pro- and anti-dam actors seeking to inscribe the project with a particular significance. Brazil is no different. The development and implementation of energy policy in Brazil have historically been dominated by the long-term contestation between

Table 3.1 Characteristics of the Belo Monte and São Luiz do Tapajós projects

	Belo Monte	São Luiz do Tapajós
Total Number of Dams in Complex	3	5
State	Pará, North-Eastern Brazil	Pará, North-Eastern Brazil
Basin	Xingu	Tapajós
River[s]	Xingu	Tapajós, Jamanxim
Total Capacity	11,233 MW	8,040 MW
Area Flooded	668 km²	729 km²
Affected People (Official Estimates)	20,000	977
Predicted Cost, R$ (US$)[4]	30 billion (US$14 billion)	18 billion (US$4–8 million)
Operational Status	Operational	Suspended
Owner	Norte Energia, SA	Eletrobras

the pro-dam interests that lobby for large-scale energy projects and an opposition movement that highlights a project's environmental and social impact (Carvalho, 2006; Hochstetler, 2011). Previous anti-dam struggles include those against the Murta and Eliézer Batista Dams in Minas Gerais, the Barra Grande project on the border of Rio Grande do Sul and the Santa Catarina and the Dardanelos and Manso projects in Mato Grosso. Local groups, indigenous communities, and international organisations had previously mobilised against the Jirau and Santo Antônio Dams on the Madeira River, Rondônia, between 2006 and 2016, when the project was completed. These groups argued that the large dam projects had extensive social and environmental impacts, that local communities had not been adequately consulted in the planning process and, as a result, that the projects should not go ahead. An opposition activist against these projects, Nilce de Souza Magalhães, known as Nicinha, was found murdered in January 2016. Nicinha's body, missing for five months, was discovered in the project's reservoir, with her hands and feet bound by rope and her body kept weighed down underwater by a rock (Morais, 2016).

It is within this context that, as Hochstetler and Keck (2007, pp. 45–46) have stated, 'individual licensing decisions often become crucibles for the airing of giant social conflicts that really should be settled in other ways.' Moments of contestation inscribe a hydroelectric project with a significance within wider political struggles. While pro-dam actors put forward storylines that legitimise the project as a solution to a defined problem, those opposed to the project may 'scale up' such opposition by positioning the dam as one site in a wider set of grievances or demands. As Jacob Blanc (2019) has shown, the mobilisation of rural communities against the Itaipu Dam in the 1970s and 1980s highlighted how the project was entwined with the isolation and mistreatment of local farmers, disputing the military junta's pro-dam storyline that cast the project as a symbol of Brazilian economic development and national progress. While anti-dam actions such as the occupation of offices and the construction site did lead to notable concessions, this resistance movement provided a space in which the military junta itself – and its authoritarian character – became contested (Blanc, 2019). As a result, the project became located within wider contexts that provide it with a symbolism linked to either notion of economic development or environmental impact.

Both the pro- and anti-dam groupings in Brazil are formed of numerous actors, operating across scales and levels (i.e. local, national, and international) and holding numerous (at times, divergent) experiences and views, and putting forward different storylines. As a result, these groups should not be understood as homogenous or as holding a sole ideological position (Baviskar, 1995). In response to this heterogeneity of backgrounds and interests, I follow Hochstetler (2011) in labelling these groups 'coalitions' to illustrate the diverse and shifting linkages between the state, commercial actors, and non-governmental organisations in the debate over the Belo Monte and São Luiz do Tapajós projects. A focus on coalitions allows for an exploration of the variance among these groups, with the groups representing a dynamic network, rather than a sole ideological position. I adopt this definition to allow for a continued focus on respective actors as individual groups engaged in temporary coalitions with others (Saunders, 2013). These groupings involve numerous actors and groups from various backgrounds with different strategies and expertise. While Hochstetler (2011, p. 350) characterises these groups as the 'enabling coalition' and the 'blocking coalition,' I provide an alternative label. I define these groups as the 'pro-dam coalition' (formed of the project's proponents) and the 'resistance coalition' (consisting of opponents to the scheme). I adopt the term 'resistance' to describe the coalition opposing the Belo Monte and São Luiz do Tapajós projects to refer to how opposition to these projects is not merely focused on the 'blocking' of a particular hydropower project but, instead, locate their opposition to the project as part of a wider effort, linked to notions of environmental protection, human rights, and equity. I will now detail these coalitions below.

Pro-dam coalition

The planning and construction of Belo Monte were managed by a specially formed company, Norte Energia. The consortium was formed by numerous actors, including the national energy utility, Eletrobras, regional energy companies (Companhia Hidro-Elétrica do São Francisco (CHESF), Centrais Elétricas do Norte do Brasil SA (Eletronorte) and Neoenergia SA), national financial institutions (both Banco do Brasil and, its subsidiary, BB Banco de Investimento SA), private companies (such as the mining conglomerate, Vale SA) and pension funds run by both the Brazilian oil utility Petrobras and the Caixa Econômica Federal, respectively (Tribunal de Contas da União, 2015).

The São Luiz do Tapajós project was managed by the Grupo de Estudos Tapajós consortium, which included Eletrobras and Eletronorte, the electricity companies Cemig, Copel, and Neoenergia, the international energy companies Électricité de France SA (EDF), Engie (previously GDF Suez), and Endesa, and the construction company Camargo Corrêa. However, the projects studied were supported by a broad pro-dam coalition, including government actors, national banks, and construction companies. I will now turn to this below.

Both Belo Monte and the São Luiz do Tapajós represent central projects within the development policy agenda pursued by the Partido dos Trabalhadores (Workers' Party, PT) governments of Presidents Luiz Inácio Lula da Silva (hereafter Lula) (2003–2011) and Dilma Rousseff (hereafter Dilma) (2011–2016). The years of the PT government were characterised by the roll-out of redistributive economic policies and the expansion of domestic production and industry, funded by centralised funding mechanisms (such as via the BNDES) (Casanova and Kassum, 2013; Gómez Bruera, 2015; Hochstetler and Montero, 2013; Schwarcz and Starling, 2018). Within this development model, the policies of Lula and Dilma emphasised the expansion of the transportation, agribusiness, and energy sectors to both create jobs and stimulate economic growth. At the core of these plans were a number of wide-reaching infrastructure plans. The Programas de Aceleração do Crescimento (Growth Acceleration Program) I and

II, launched in 2007 and 2010, respectively, proposed extensive government investments in construction, transport systems, and energy projects (Ribeiro and Zimmermann, 2007). Under PAC-1, 6,377 km of highway and 909 km of railways were constructed or improved, over 5,000 housing and sanitation projects were built, 12 new gas platforms entered operation, and 3,776 km of gas pipelines were constructed in this period (Burrier, 2014). These works were intricately tied to national development agendas, allowing for the movements of raw materials, goods, and people across the region and towards global markets (Bratman, 2020). The Iniciativa de Integração da Infraestrutura Regional da América do Sul (Initiative for the Integration of the Regional Infrastructure of South America, IIRSA) supplemented these plans, providing a regional development plan across the economies of South America to integrate transportation networks, energy grids, and stimulate cross-national trade across numerous regions. These IIRSA plans included numerous bi-national hydroelectric dam projects, including a plan to build a hydroelectric dam and waterway complex on the Madeira River, near the Bolivian border (Switkes, 2008). This plan included the now-completed Santo Antônio and Jirau Dams. Belo Monte was listed within the 2007 Programa de Aceleração do Crescimento (Growth Acceleration Plan, PAC). Similarly, a number of hydropower projects on the Tapajós River were present in the PAC's successor plan, the 2010 Programa de Aceleração do Crescimento II (PAC-2).

With an estimated 55% of the budget of the PAC allocated to energy infrastructure, particularly large dams (Zhouri, 2010), the two projects studied were inscribed with a wider significance based on the asserted need for increased energy security in Brazil. At the turn of the millennium, Brazil experienced an energy shortage that resulted in nine months of electricity rationing (between June 2001 and March 2002) and saw a reduction of 16.3% in average energy use (Carvalho, 2006). The years succeeding 2002 were characterised by a renewed impetus for the transformation of Brazilian energy policy, a renewed search for additional energy resources, and a significantly increased interest in large-scale energy generation projects (Carvalho, 2006). When Lula came into office in 2003, the PT administration grew concerned that 35 hydroelectric plants had stalled during the licensing process, often due to opposition from local communities. Decision-making surrounding hydropower projects in Brazil became more coordinated and centralised than had previously been the case (da Costa, 2014). To allow this coordination, Lula set up what became known as the Sala de Situação (Situation Room), in which members of different governmental departments could meet with technical staff to develop strategies to allow the construction of these projects (Hochstetler, 2011). Subsequent reforms to the energy sector provided incentives for expanding energy capacity, particularly involving hydropower, and assurances were made that Brazilian society would not face future energy shortages. In 2004, the Empresa de Pesquisa Energética (Energy Research Company, EPE) was founded to provide specialised technical knowledge in conducting research and planning for the energy sector and support future project planning and construction (da Costa, 2014). It is within this context that the Belo Monte project, in particular, became inscribed with a wider

50 *Damming the Amazon*

significance. In 2011, Dilma defined the Belo Monte project as a 'fundamental undertaking for the development of the region and the country' (Brasil Portal do Planalto, 2011). In the same year, Francisco Dornelles, the then-senator for Rio de Janeiro, argued that 'the construction of Belo Monte Dam is of [the] greatest importance for the development of the country … to sustain economic growth, [and] job creation' (Senado Federal, 2011). José Carlos Aleluia, a former president (1987–1989) of CHESF and federal deputy for Bahia (Partido da Frente Liberal, PFL), declared that the project was 'not a government project, [but] a project of the nation' (Aleluia, 2005).

As discussed in Chapter 1, the re-emergence of hydropower as a 21st-century energy source has been accompanied by the entrance of new funding interests and instruments. This is also evident in Brazil, where both Chinese interests and funding via the Clean Development Mechanism have secured the planning, construction, and management of hydroelectric plants. For example, in 2016, the Three Gorges Corporation acquired the Ilha Solteira and Jupiá Dams (São Paulo) (China Daily, 2016). China's State Power Investment Corp had previously acquired the São Simão Dam (Goiás/Minas Gerais) and has been linked to the purchasing of other dams, such as the Três Irmãos Dam (São Paulo) and Santo Antônio Dam (Rondônia) (Bautzer, 2018; Costa, 2018). The Santo Antônio Dam itself – along with the Jirau and Teles Pire projects – was funded in part through the Clean Development Mechanism.

While hydroelectric dams in Brazil have attracted financial interest and investment from new funding actors, the projects studied highlight the importance of the Banco Nacional de Desenvolvimento e Social (National Bank for Economic and Social Development, BNDES) had a key role in the financing of the projects of the PT's PACs. Described by Casanova and Kassum (2013, p. 35) as the 'visible hand of the state,' the size of BNDES' investment portfolio doubled during the Lula administration, with the institution assuming a central position in the PT's ambitious economic policy. Through its investment arm, BNDESPar, BNDES has invested in a number of economic activities (Casanova and Kassum, 2013). Between 2002 and 2011, the institution issued 2,115 short loans, ranging from less than R$1 million to over R$1 billion (Montero, 2014). Energy-related spending was a particularly large area of BNDES' loan portfolio in the years between 2002 and 2011, with six of the institute's eight largest loans in this period made to energy generation or distribution projects (Hochstetler and Montero, 2013). Total BNDES investment in the Belo Monte project amounted to R$22.5 billion (US$11 billion) in 2012 (BNDES, 2012). The organisation was a key funder of the Madeira River dams (completed in 2011 and 2013), providing a reported R$42.9 billion (US$11.4 billion) to these projects. With São Luiz do Tapajós having never emerged from its planning stage, the extent of BNDES' (real or potential) financial support for the scheme remains unknown. BNDES financing is supplemented by investment from public pension funds. In what Datz (2013) has labelled 'pension fund developmentalism,' national pension funds have invested heavily in infrastructure projects, becoming key levers in the provision of long-term investment for such schemes. The pension funds of both the Petrobras oil company and the Caixa Econômica Federal (National Savings Bank), both state-owned enterprises, have invested in the Belo Monte project.

Despite being primarily state-led and state-funded, the pro-dam coalition includes national Brazilian construction companies, including Andrade Gutierrez, Camargo Corrêa, Odebrecht, Queiroz Galvão, and OAS. These companies are understood to hold a degree of political power in contemporary Brazil, due to their close relationship with numerous political parties and a central role in both PAC and PAC-2. Notably, these companies are increasingly involved in planning and building hydroelectric dams outside of Brazil (Dye, 2020). The role of the construction companies is evident in the consortiums responsible for the construction of both Belo Monte and São Luiz do Tapajós. The Belo Monte project is being built by the Consórcio Construtor Belo Monte (Construction Consortium [of] Belo Monte, CCBM). Eleven companies are involved in the consortium's contracts for Belo Monte, including Andrade Gutierrez, Odebrecht, OAS, and Queiroz Galvão, as well as the smaller construction companies Contern, Galvão Engenharia, Serveng-Civilsan, Cetenco, and J. Malucelli (Vieira, 2016). The initial planning of the São Luiz do Tapajós project was conducted by a consortium named Diálogo Tapajós, consisting of Eletrobras, Eletronorte, Neoenergia, Camargo Corrêa, Endesa Brasil, Cemig, and Copel, as well as the multinational companies Engie and EDF. However, due to the project's cancellation, the involvement of the Brazilian construction sector remained limited.

In the case of Belo Monte, these national actors were joined by a number of local groups that have voiced support for the project. O Fórum Regional de Desenvolvimento Econômico e Socioambiental da Transamazônica e Xingu (The Regional Forum for Economic and Socio-Environmental Development of the Transamazônica and Xingu, FORT Xingu) represents an umbrella group of 178 entities that have aligned themselves in support of the Belo Monte project (Fleury and Almeida, 2013). Similarly, other local groups, such as Fundação Viver, Produzir e Preservar (Live, Produce, and Preserve Foundation, FVPP), have given their backing for the project. However, support for the development is not assured, as demonstrated by the criticism of Belo Monte by FORT Xingu in 2011 and 2012, with the organisation condemning the chaotic construction of Belo Monte and its effect on the local area and calling for more intervention in the scheme, with the organisation paying for a number of billboards in Altamira, the nearest urban centre to the project's construction site, to publicise such criticism (Fleury and Almeida, 2013). Nevertheless, although the group criticised the schemes and their consequences, it has maintained a commitment to the importance of its construction for the local economy and the further development of the region around Altamira (Fleury and Almeida, 2013).

The resistance coalition

Anti-dam movements across the globe involve diverse groups of opposition, including local communities, indigenous groups, local organisations and political parties, recreational users, and religious groups. Lining up against the pro-dam lobby in Brazil is a broad coalition, representing a number of interests (Bratman, 2014; Fleury and Almeida, 2013) Anti-dam movements in Brazil are multi-scalar, existing at multiple levels, with local, regional, national, and transnational organisations and activists all engaged in challenging the project in different ways (McCormick, 2010; Rothman, 2001; Thorkildsen, 2018). There is a diverse group of opponents to the Belo Monte and São Luiz do Tapajós projects, including members of indigenous communities to be impacted by the respective projects,[5] small-scale farmers, urban dwellers, ribeirinhos (riverine populations), and garimpeiros (artisanal miners). One of the key actors in the contemporary resistance coalition against Belo Monte is the Movimento Xingu Vivo para Sempre (Xingu Alive Forever Movement, MXVS). Created in 2008, Xingu Vivo – as it is commonly referred to – emerged from the splintering of the activist group, the Movimento pelo Desenvolvimento da Transamazônica e Xingu (Movement for the Development of Transamazon and Xingu, MDTX). MDTX was historically opposed to the Kararaô Dam, organising the local *ribeirinho* population against the project. Ademir 'Dema' Alfeu Federicci, a leader of MDTX, was killed in 2001 in an attack thought to have been motivated by his stance against hydropower in the region (Bratman, 2014). However, in 2008, members of MDTX publicly declared that they would not oppose Belo Monte in exchange for government commitments to pave stretches of the Trans-Amazonian Highway in the region (Bratman, 2014). This resulted in the fragmentation of the local opposition network, with members divided into groups opposed to and supporting the project.

Following the withdrawal of MDTX from the opposition, Xingu Vivo, founded in 2008, became the main local movement against Belo Monte, providing a focal point for various campaigning groups to gather and articulate a shared message. The organisation employs both direct and indirect action to oppose the dam. For example, in 2012, Xingu Vivo, working with Amazon Watch, organised a three-day occupation and protest at Belo Monte's construction site, welcoming members of both local indigenous communities and other groups (Bratman, 2014). Members of the community, joined by indigenous communities, also occupied government offices (Anderson, 2017; Movimentos dos Atingidos por Barragens, 2012, 2015, 2016). These efforts have delayed the Belo Monte project, with a representative of Norte Energia explaining that 400 days of construction had been delayed by direct opposition action by local actors between the start of its construction and late 2016 (Interview, 6 December 2016). The organisation's website (www.xinguvivo.org.br) provides a number of documents, disseminated among the local community, describing the project's impact, as well as reporting on opposition activity. A similar organisation, Movimento Tapajós Vivo (Tapajós Alive Movement, MTV), was established in opposition to the São Luiz do Tapajós Dam project in 2010. Like Xingu Vivo, MTV provides a formal point of resistance for the numerous actors and groups opposing the Tapajós project, organising events and disseminating news of the project's planning and contestation.

Within these local networks, numerous interests and identities (such as women's movements, student movements, Afro-Brazilian activists, and urban and

Damming the Amazon 53

rural campaigners) are represented within a shared avenue of resistance against the scheme, often demonstrated by public protests, open letters, and the dissemination of information to the local community and national and international observers. In providing these resistance materials, both organisations provide a forum for members of the local community to disseminate detailed information on the local impact of construction to allied groups at the national and international level. These communities have engaged in opposition to these schemes in a number of ways, including the occupation of construction sites and the blockading of roads, open protests, and national and international lobbying for support. There is some crossover between the two movements, with members of both networks engaging in the process of dialogue and support for one another, as well as projects being built elsewhere. For example, in 2015, a Caravana de Resistência saw the Munduruku, Apiaká, Kayabi, and Rikbaktsa communities unite and travel to protest the São Manoel Dam on the Teles Pires River, a tributary of the Tapajós.

The resistance coalition includes a number of national organisations, such as the Coordenação das Organizações Indígenas da Amazônia Brasileira (Coordination of Indigenous Organisations of the Brazilian Amazon, COIAB), the Instituto Socioambiental (Socio-Environmental Institute, ISA), and the Movimento dos Atingidos por Barragens (Movement of People Affected by Dams, MAB). These organisations provide specialist support, based on their own mission, background and expertise. For example, COIAB provides critiques based on the impact of dam projects on indigenous communities, while organisations such as SDDH, Justica Global (Global Justice), and Terra de Direitos (Land Rights) file legal appeals against the Brazilian government at the Inter-American Commission on Human Rights, in an effort to suspend the licensing and construction of the Belo Monte project. The Movimento dos Atingidos por Barragens is a key actor within the resistance coalition. The movement, formed in opposition to the construction of dams in the south of Brazil in the late 1970s, has supported localised resistance to hydroelectric projects across Brazil in the decades since, while illuminating the social impacts on displaced communities and protesting against the failure of pro-dam actors to mitigate these effects. The organisation collates news on the impact of hydroelectric projects across Brazil, disseminates research and lobbies the government for improved protection of dam-affected communities. As dos Santos (2014) has argued, in doing so, the MAB provides the fulcrum for the counter-hegemonic struggle against the construction of dams in Brazil, widening the understanding of who is impacted by such projects (and how) and 'scaling up' localised struggles against hydropower into wider forms of resistance at the regional and national levels.

National religious organisations and figures have voiced opposition to the planning and construction of dam projects in the Brazilian Amazon, often presenting the projects as having a negative impact on the region's indigenous communities. For example, Conselho Indigenista Missionário (Missionary Indigenous Council, CIMI), an organ of Brazil's National Council of Bishops, regularly provides support to indigenous communities in the region while advocating for their protection at the national level. A leading member of CIMI, Dom Erwin Kräutler, the Prelate of Xingu, has campaigned against the Belo Monte project. This opposition resulted in a number of threats against Kräutler, who started to wear a bulletproof vest under his clerical vestments (Bratman, 2014). In 2010, Kräutler was awarded the Right Livelihood Award (commonly known as the Alternative Nobel Prize) for his work in defending the rights of indigenous groups.

In this text, I focus on the role of these national and international environmental organisations (EO) and non-governmental organisations (NGOs) in the resistance coalitions studied.[6] Such organisations are key actors in contemporary environmental and energy politics, linking localised environmental issues to wider national and global political discussions (Keck and Sikkink, 1998). Anti-dam movements elsewhere have benefited from the advocacy provided by NGOs and EOs operating at different levels, which allow for the translation of localised struggles into wider storylines in environmental and energy politics (Bellette Lee, 2013; Yasuda, 2015). For example, the progressive church in Brazil has previously 'scaled up' anti-dam movements in southern Brazil to correspond to wider grievances related to land-ownership and demands for land reform (Rothman and Oliver, 1999). These organisations are able to reconfigure the scale of the resistance movement, rescaling localised issues and impacts into national storylines and global networks, thus redefining the struggle (Arts, 2004). NGOs and EOs have an important relationship with local populations in contemporary environmental networks in Brazil (Barbosa, 2015; Hochstetler and Keck, 2007; McCormick, 2010). The collaboration between local networks and national and transnational organisations represents an important tactic of contemporary environmental networks, with different groups working together to achieve shared aims (Eden et al., 2006; Hochstetler and Keck, 2007; Keck and Sikkink, 1998; McCormick, 2006, 2010; Saunders, 2013). This networked character can allow for the movement to develop wider resonance and clout, changing the terms of the debate and leading to further opposition (Bratman, 2020; Keck and Sikkink, 1998; Rothman, 2001). For example, localised anti-dam movements in Minas Gerais in the 1980s were supported and enabled by support from both religious and educational institutions, as well as environmental activists (Rothman, 2001).

Brazilian national arms of international environmental organisations, such as WWF Brasil and Greenpeace Brasil and international organisations, such as Amazon Watch and International Rivers, are also present within the resistance coalition.[7] A large number of these EOs and NGOs are active within the resistance coalition. For example, in a series of summits organised against the Belo Monte project between 2002 and 2010, 113 social, environmental, and human rights organisations voiced dissent against the scheme (Bratman, 2014). These national and international organisations provide logistical or technical assistance to local resistance movements. For example, members of Greenpeace Brasil have supported the Munduruku community opposed to São Luiz do Tapajós by providing technological equipment to assist the community's effort to self-demarcate the Sawré Muybu territory (discussed in Chapter 7). In addition to this logistical support, organisations have funded international trips for local resistance figures, produced, and distributed films that detail the impact of the respective projects and disseminated resistance materials that critique the projects.

All anti-dam movements adopt particular 'repertoires of contention,'or tactics of protest and dissent (Tilly, 1986, 2008). Opposition activity has taken a number of forms at different levels, from celebrity activism to the dumping of 3 tonnes of manure outside the offices of the Agência Nacional de Energia Elétrica (National Electric Energy Agency, ANEEL). At the local level, the occupation of facilities remains an important tactic, with indigenous groups and the MAB occupying construction sites and blocking access roads as a form of both sabotage and symbolic dissent (Bratman, 2014). Numerous telephone and email campaigns have been launched at the national level, with physical petitions submitted to Dilma in February 2011 and December 2011, signed by 500,000 and 1.3 million people, respectively (Amazon Watch and Xingu Vivo para Sempre, 2011). Celebrity activism has also provided a particularly visible form of national and international opposition. Opposition networks in Brazil developed the Goto d'Agua ('Drop of Water') alliance, bringing together activists and high-profile actors in Brazil to oppose the project. International figures who have publicly voiced opposition to hydropower projects in the Brazilian Amazon include Arnold Schwarzenegger, Sigourney Weaver, and James Cameron. Similar international support for the struggle against the São Luiz do Tapajós project can be found, with figures voicing opposition to the project including Sir Ranulph Fiennes, Joanna Lumley, and Sir Paul McCartney (*The Guardian*, 2016).

Following della Porta and Diani (1999), I understand the resistance coalitions studied as more than their actions and protests. They have a greater significance than the blocking of roads, the circulation of information, and the occupation of buildings – an anti-dam movement also represents an articulation of a collective vision, a shared identity, and, often, an overarching storyline of resistance, all of which provide a degree of common purpose for its members (della Porta and Diani, 1999). Resistance coalitions put forward storylines in which more individualised or localised grievances become structured into broader claims and demands. The relationship between local movements and national and international organisations functions to 'scale up' the struggle against dam projects, locating them within wider arguments as a means of generating national and international support. These storylines draw on different identities, networks and forms of organisation, both within the movement and beyond (Tilly and Tarrow, 2007). In doing, so they locate the resistance to the Belo Monte and São Luiz do Tapajós projects within a wider terrain of struggle or, to use the terminology used in Chapter 2, they 'scale up' the anti-dam movement. Doing so allows for the movement to draw more people into its numbers, assuring potential members that they are not alone and giving a wider meaning to their grievances and demands (Tarrow, 2011; Tilly and Tarrow, 2007).

In addition, subsequent chapters include evidence drawn from interviews with representatives from a number of Brazilian state institutions, including the State Prosecutor's office, Ministério Público Federal (Public Prosecutor's Office, MPF), the national agency for indigenous communities, Fundação Nacional do

Índio (the National Indian Foundation, FUNAI), and the Brazilian environmental regulator, Instituto Brasileiro do Meio Ambiente e dos Recursos Naturais Renováveis (Brazilian Institute of the Environment and Renewable Natural Resources, IBAMA). While these agencies are governmental actors, they interact with anti-dam movements in Brazil in a number of ways. Local movements are provided legal assistance by the advocates at the MPF both locally and nationally. Prosecutors in the MPF act similarly to how we understand public interest lawyers to act in other countries, pursuing cases against individuals deemed to have a negative impact on society (McAllister, 2008). Second, anti-dam movements have supported, enabled, and created space for these regulators to introduce new measures, such as environmental restrictions, social safeguards, and demarcation of indigenous territories (Rothman, 2001). Environmental agencies in Brazil tend to have limited resources and thus fewer bureaucratic resources and less political capital than other ministries, such as the Ministry of Mines and Energy (Burrier, 2016). As a result, these agencies often encounter difficulties in ensuring environmental protections when such policies conflict with other government priorities (McAllister, 2008). This can result in some surprising alliances between civil society and state actors that can lead to policy change. For example, in the case of Belo Monte, fishing communities formed an alliance of convenience with the Ministério da Pesca e Aquicultura (Ministry of Fisheries and Aquaculture, MPA) to make demands of Norte Energia for increased participation (Klein, 2015). This relationship is driven by the creation of political leverage, with government agencies supporting resistance coalitions widening the scope of dissent and successful movements enabling regulatory policy change.

These networks and alliances that are present in the resistance coalition are not necessarily new, as this broad, multi-scalar grouping was involved in resistance to previous hydroelectric dams in Brazil, such as Belo Monte's predecessor project, Kararaô, in the late-1980s. It is this moment of contestation – and the storylines forwarded by anti-dam actors that functioned to 'scale up' the struggle – that I turn to below.

A history of resistance

A landmark event of the resistance to the Kararaô project can be found in the 1989 Altamira Gathering. This meeting, organised by the Coordenação das Organizações Indígenas da Amazônia Brasileira (Coordination of the Indigenous Organisations of the Brazilian Amazon, COIAB), provided a forum in which local resistance actors, most notably from the indigenous Kayapó community, engaged with numerous national and international organisations, 200 members of the global press and over 100 additional observers (Park, 2002), including the musician, Sting, and, the entrepreneur, Anita Roddick (Indigenous People's Cultural Support Trust, n.d.). These efforts by the organisers of the meeting and those present resulted in the resistance coalition receiving extensive international coverage. In stimulating this international audience, the 1989 Altamira Gathering provided a space for the grievances and demands of indigenous communities to be heard at the international level (Turner, 1993; Zanotti, 2015, 2016). A central moment of the 1989 Altamira Gathering was an act of hostility made by a member of the Kayapó community against José Antônio Muniz Lopes, the head of the government electrical company, Eletronorte, who had been sent to argue for the necessity of the project. In a now-famous act, Tuíra, a Kayapó warrior, approached Lopes and placed her machete to his cheek, making a statement that has since been translated as:

> You are a liar – we do not need electricity. Electricity is not going to give us food. We need our rivers to flow freely: our future depends on it. We need our jungles for hunting and gathering. We do not need your dam.
> (International Rivers, 2008)

The 1989 Altamira Gathering attracted hundreds of foreign journalists, all of whom returned to their home countries with news of Tuíra's act of defiance (Conklin and Graham, 1995). In making this statement, Tuíra presents an antagonism – a division between 'us' and 'them' – separating the Kayapó community from the economic benefits of the Kararaô project. The community, instead, presented the project as a direct threat to its rights to both territory (to be flooded by Kararaô's reservoir) and culture (deemed to be under threat by the encroachment on territory). It is at the Altamira Gathering that these demands were presented within a wider storyline. The Kayapó drew upon an international logic of opposition, directly appealing to storylines of biodiversity and environmental protection and enrolling them into their demands for recognition and land demarcation (Fleury and Almeida, 2013; Turner, 1993; Zanotti, 2015, 2016). In doing so, the 1989 resistance to Kararaô represents an important process of 'scaling up,' in which the Kayapó leadership framed the struggle against hydropower as part of a wider movement to protect the Amazon rainforest from encroachment and extraction (Zanotti, 2016). For many of those present, the resistance of the Kayapó became positioned as a defence of the natural environment and biodiversity of the Brazilian Amazon region against the impact of the construction of a hydroelectric dam (Turner, 1993; Zanotti, 2015, 2016). This presents a local–global storyline of opposition that drew on an emergent environmentalist worldview that asserted the potential of traditional knowledge systems and sustainable management practices of indigenous communities to contribute to global carbon sequestration (Fisher, 1994; Zanotti, 2016).[8] In doing so, the resistance storyline provided a bridge between the social and the environmental repercussions of dam construction and voiced them at the international level, allowing for the development of a strong coalition compelled by both local demands and more international storylines of environmental protection. For civil society groups, the 'scaling up' of the Kayapó opposition to Kararaô served two purposes. First, it provided an emergent route to mobilise supporters. With indigenous communities holding local ecological knowledge, they provided an important human face for the abstract notion of biodiversity and the spatially distant occurrence of deforestation. For example, civil society actors and journalists adopted the imagery of key Kayapó figures, such as Paulinho Paiakan, a community leader, to both inform others of the battle against Kararaô and to 'represent' the forest itself (Conklin and Graham, 1995) The presentation of Paiakan and other figures to the international community allowed civil society actors a degree of authenticity, with the images of indigeneity foregrounding the need to protect the Brazilian Amazon within one community's struggle. Second, this 'scaling up' provided a further political legitimacy to international campaigns against deforestation in Brazil – with the connection of localised struggles allowing civil society groups to involve themselves in Brazil's internal affairs due to their concern for communities as well as forests (Conklin and Graham, 1995). This fusion of demands proved successful, with Kararaô later being removed from national energy plans. The Altamira Gathering was successful in deterring international lenders from providing funding to the Kararaô project (Hochstetler, 2011). Keck and Sikkink (1998) describe this as a 'boomerang strategy,' in which a local community is able to change national government policy by influencing institutions on the international stage. At the time, the World Bank was the most prominent funder of hydropower projects internationally (Goldman, 2004) and was expected to provide funding to Kararaô (Chernela, 1988). In response to the 1989 opposition, the World Bank withdrew its potential support.

However, the opposition to the contemporary Belo Monte and São Luiz do Tapajós Dams has not shared the success of the 1989 Altamira Gathering (Barbosa, 2015; Bratman, 2014; Carvalho, 2006; Hochstetler, 2011). Within the cases studied, the contest of pro-dam and resistance coalitions has largely favoured the lobby supporting the projects (E. Bratman, 2015; Hochstetler, 2011). There are a number of reasons for the ineffectiveness of opposition networks. First, pro-dam actors are able to conduct an extended effort to secure construction of the schemes. The perceived gains of the successful completion of the scheme far outweigh any potential costs for the pro-dam coalition (Carvalho, 2006). With the apagão (power shortages) of 2001 and 2002 presented as providing an impetus for the planning and construction of the Belo Monte project (Atkins, 2017; Carvalho, 2006; Vieira and Dalgaard, 2013), the pro-dam coalition has remained committed to the project's completion.

Second, while previous infrastructure projects in Brazil have relied on international funding and support, contemporary schemes are not dependent upon this support (Barbosa, 2015; Carvalho, 2006). With BNDES having an important role in financing the Belo Monte project, scholars have highlighted how this domestic source of funding has weakened the opposition by insulating the project from the 'boomerang strategy' that had seen local opposition to Kararaô change national policy by influencing the multilateral World Bank to withdraw funding (Barbosa, 2015; Carvalho, 2006; Hochstetler, 2011; Keck and Sikkink, 1998). With many of the tactics adopted by the resistance coalition, such as protests and petitions, having a short-term nature and anti-dam actors lacking the necessary resources to sustain public attention via campaigns or to enter protracted legal proceedings, the pro-dam coalition has been able to 'ride out' the opposition to successive projects.

Furthermore, pro-dam actors have taken advantage of the plurality of demands and grievances present in the resistance coalition to divide opposition to the Belo Monte project. For example, at the local level, pro-dam actors have put forward a number of policies and storylines that act as a 'wedge' to divide the resistance coalition. As discussed above, the local resistance networks opposing Belo Monte were divided by government promises of supplementary infrastructure, with MDTX publicly declaring that they would not oppose the project in exchange for government promises to improve road infrastructure in the region (Bratman, 2014). In doing so, pro-dam actors provided concessions to groups to both highlight the plurality of interests, motivations, and demands in the local resistance network and to divide this opposition (Bratman, 2014).

However, in the next section, I illuminate an additional factor that explains how recent anti-dam movements have struggled to find the success enjoyed in Altamira in 1989. This concerns the emergence of a new storyline of legitimacy – one that affirms hydropower's sustainability credentials. It is this that I turn to below.

The pro-dam storyline of sustainability

In this research, I focus on an emergent storyline in the presentation of hydropower projects by pro-dam actors in Brazil: the storyline of sustainability, or the location of hydropower within overarching policy agendas of sustainable energy transitions and sustainable development. This pro-dam storyline, asserting the sustainability credentials of hydropower projects, can be seen in the words of prominent proponents of the Belo Monte project. For example, at a 2010 rally in Altamira, Lula presented the Belo Monte Dam as representative of contemporary notions of sustainability, asserting its role as clean energy with minimal impact on the environment (da Silva, 2010). Chico Lopes, a federal deputy, would later argue that Belo Monte represents 'a clean and renewable energy source that will prevent future non-green energy' (Lopes, 2011). Furthermore, the Empresa de Pesquisa Energética (Energy Research Company, EPE) has argued that Belo Monte should be understood as representative of Brazil's commitment to sustainable development (Empresa de Pesquisa Energética, 2010).

Hydroelectric projects have been widely presented as being key to economic development for both local and national populations. This storyline of economic development has persisted: in 2011, Dilma presented Belo Monte as a 'fundamental undertaking for the development of the region and the country' (Rousseff, 2011). Similarly, Francisco Dornelles, the senator for Rio de Janeiro (2007–2014), argued in the same year that 'the construction of Belo Monte Dam is of [the] greatest importance to the development of the country ... to sustain economic growth, [and] job creation' (Senado Federal, 2011). In justifying Belo Monte using a storyline of sustainability, proponents of the dam have adapted these storylines of dams as a route to economic development and prosperity to include an environmental component (Vieira and Dalgaard, 2013). A fluidity of storylines can be detected, which allows for the provision of a rebuttal to opposition networks' criticism of the Belo Monte and São Luiz do Tapajós projects.

The storyline of sustainability in Brazil has two advantages. First, it draws on an increasing environmentalist consciousness in the Brazilian state itself. Pro-dam storylines often appeal to a 'moral legitimacy,' with the project presented as a part of the value system that is dominant at the time (Bezerra et al., 2014). Pro-dam storylines of sustainability position hydropower projects within a growing environmental consciousness in the Brazilian population to ensure the legitimacy of and widen the perceived benefits of the project. A 2012 poll by the Ministério do Meio Ambiente (Ministry of the Environment, MMA) showed that 82% of respondents were unwilling to have more economic development at the expense of the environment (Ministério do Meio Ambiente, 2012). In the same survey, 51% of respondents stated that they would be willing to provide financial assistance to protect the Amazon region, an increase of 38% from 2006. It is by positioning the Belo Monte and São Luiz do Tapajós projects within this political context that pro-dam actors are able to present the projects as complementary to the environmentalist values of the populace, locating the dams within wider sustainable development agendas and securing the legitimacy necessary for planning and construction.

The second advantage of a pro-dam storyline of sustainability is its potential to depoliticise the project discussed. With the storyline put forward to appeal to popular moral legitimacy, it is also able to position those opposed to the projects as existing outside of and beyond such legitimacy. For example, in 2012, Edison Lobão, the then Minister of Mines and Energy (2008–2011; 2012–2015) argued that:

> There is a lot of misinformation about the Belo Monte project. We will make the project a global example of respect for the environment and the people in the project's area of influence ... We are not going to stop ... We will not be intimidated by these objections ... We preserve the environment as never before, but we will be obstinate in defending the country's economic expansion.
>
> (Oswald and Tavares, 2012)

This paints anti-dam actors as holding Brazil back from the sustainable development promised by the planning and construction of hydroelectric projects. In asserting that the arguments used by opponents of the dams are 'misinformation,' Lobão draws a dividing line between 'legitimate' and 'illegitimate' grievances and demands, casting the latter as, at best, misleading and, at worst, fabricated. Opposition actors are cast as existing beyond the order of legitimate debate, meaning that it is not necessary to listen to their demands and grievances. This is particularly evident in the language adopted by President Lula in a 2010 speech made in Altamira that was subject to protests. In this public address, Lula compared the resistance to Belo Monte to his own previous opposition to the Itaipu Dam built on the Paraná River at the Brazil–Paraguay border:

> If they [those protesting] had the patience to listen to what I have learned all along. When I was their age, I went to Paraná to demonstrate against the

construction of Itaipu. We said that Itaipu would be used to flood Argentina ... [addressing protestors] Spend half the day screaming and then spend half putting your positive energy towards something important.

(Savarese, 2010)

Lula provides an image of resistance being grounded in naivety and mistaken assumptions, with anti-dam grievances showing both a limited knowledge of the project and its role as a solution to wider problems. He draws on his own experience – highlighting his belief that, with time, the contemporary anti-dam movements will understand the project's importance – just as he did (Atkins, 2017; Eletrobras, 2012). This assumption of the naivety of anti-dam actors is evident in an argument made in 2011 by Francisco Dornelles (Partido Progressista, PP), the senator for Rio de Janeiro (2007–2014). Dornelles, stressing the importance of Belo Monte, stated that the PT government – and Brazilian society more broadly – could not 'allow partial views of reality to prevail in the face of general interest' (Senado Federal, 2011). Within these statements, pro-dam actors raise the Belo Monte project above the terrain of everyday politics, debate, and dissent. The project thus becomes apolitical and technical; those against it hinder the benefits of the project, based on unfounded and illegitimate demands. While pro-dam actors are fulfilling promises of sustainable development and the mitigation of fossil fuel emissions, anti-dam activists are cast as ignorant and restricting such benefits of the project.

However, the storyline of sustainability put forward by pro-dam actors in Brazil is narrow, with the environmentalist credentials of Belo Monte predicated on its role in reducing greenhouse gas (GHG) emissions. Pro-dam actors often discuss the 'sustainability' of the hydroelectricity generated by Belo Monte's turbines, in contrast with the emissions of fossil fuel energy sources (Atkins, 2018b). The federal deputy, Fernando Ferro argued that:

If we do not build hydroelectric plants, we shall have to follow other paths: using nuclear energy, using thermal energy and generating energy from fossil fuels, thus increasing greenhouse gas emissions, which will cause significant losses to our differential of generating clean energy.

(Ferro, 2010)

In making this statement, Ferro affirms the assumed role of hydropower in sustainable energy transitions, highlighting how if Brazil were not to build hydroelectric dams, it would be likely to have to turn to fossil fuels. A similar sentiment is evident in the words of Chico Lopes, federal deputy for Ceará, in 2011:

The Brazilian government must ... continue with the construction of the Belo Monte hydroelectric plant ... for it is a clean and renewable energy source that will prevent future non-green energy sources from being used.

(Lopes, 2011)

Lopes, Ferro, and Lobão assert a dichotomy between hydropower and greenhouse gas emissions, casting the project as 'clean' and arguing that the GHGs emitted from dams are far less than the alternatives (defined as coal, oil, and natural gas) (Atkins, 2017, 2018). The result is that the pro-dam storyline of sustainability is exclusive, focusing on certain elements of sustainability in a world where climate change awareness and concern is increasing. This leads to the further depoliticisation of the Belo Monte project by limiting the ground upon which the project's sustainability credentials can be debated. It denies the complexity of a dam's social and environmental impact beyond the potential reduction of GHG emissions. However, this a particularly narrow vision of sustainability which neglects the wider impact of hydropower on river morphology, biodiversity, and local communities, all of which were discussed by the World Commission on Dams in 2000. This provides room for anti-dam actors to contest and reconfigure the pro-dam storyline of sustainability. With the definition of the term 'sustainability' and the policy concept of sustainable development characterised by ambiguity and malleability (Leach et al., 2010; Redclift, 2005), the contests over dam construction represent an example of alternative sustainabilities, in which the sustainability credentials of a project are challenged, critiqued, and reconfigured by anti-dam actors (Cavanagh and Benjaminsen, 2017).

Brazilian environmental movements have historically provided alternative understandings of sustainability, reconciling the disconnect between the social and the natural realms by adopting a narrative of environmental justice that asserts the connection between social and ecological marginalisation (Hochstetler and Keck, 2007; Wolford, 2010; Zhouri, 2010; Zhouri and Laschefski, 2010). Labelled as 'socio-environmentalism,' this storyline reconciles the disconnect between the social and the natural realms by adopting a narrative of environmental justice that asserts the connection between social and ecological marginalisation (Hochstetler and Keck, 2007). In doing so, socio-environmental movements in Brazil have often moved beyond the illumination of the environmental impact and calls for environmental conservation and, instead, put forward demands for social justice, political autonomy, and cultural recognition in the management of land, water, and energy resources (Hecht, 2011). Such movements provided a new form of environmentalism that broadens the definition of 'sustainability' to include social as well as environmental factors and puts forward calls for equitable and participatory environmentalism (Zhouri and Laschefski, 2010). This alternative definition of sustainability, which broadens the focus beyond GHG-emission mitigation alone, has gained ground in recent years. For example, a growing environmental consciousness can be seen in the political rise of the former government minister, Marina Silva in the 2010 and 2014 Presidential elections (Nunes and Peña, 2015). Marina Silva is one of the most widely known and popular environmentalists in contemporary Brazil and has a significant pedigree in Amazonian environmental politics, having worked closely with historic figures, such as Chico Mendes (Hochstetler and Keck, 2007). Previously serving as a Minister for the Environment in Lula's cabinet (2003–2011), she is credited with implementing policies that resulted in an unprecedented decrease in deforestation in the Brazilian Amazon after 2005 (Hochstetler, 2011). The 'Marina Phenomenon' represented the elevation of socio-environmental issues into the political landscape, with environmental issues presented within a wider mosaic of social injustice, political corruption, and reform. Silva and the Partido Verde (Green Party, PV) were able to position and mobilise sustainability as a key election demand in the 2014 election, gaining 21.3% of the popular vote in the first round (Hochstetler and Viola, 2012; Nunes and Peña, 2015).

In presenting issues of social injustice within an environmental setting, these movements also increased the visibility – both in Brazil and beyond – of communities living in the Amazon region, allowing for their positioning as actors within the global sustainable development policy. This represents an environmental storyline that scales up localised issues into national and global storylines, establishing a bridge between issues of environmental conservation, territorial rights, and social justice (Fleury and Almeida, 2013). Like the 1989 Altamira Gathering, environmentalist movements highlight the links between the social, cultural, and environmental to broaden contemporary definitions of sustainability.

Conclusion

In this chapter, I have explored how the Belo Monte and São Luiz do Tapajós projects became inscribed with a wide-reaching significance within the development strategies of the Partido dos Trabalhadores. It is within this policy context of state investment in and infrastructure building of hydroelectric projects in the Brazilian Amazon that the moment of contestation surrounding such projects takes place. This interplay between the storylines of the pro-dam and resistance coalitions is not a new occurrence but can instead be traced to the cancellation of Belo Monte's predecessor project, Kararaô, in 1989. In presenting storylines of territorial and cultural rights at the 1989 Altamira Gathering, the opposition to this scheme engaged in the process of 'scaling up,' demonstrating the links between their local demands and a universal storyline of environmental protection. However, while this storyline proved successful in 1989, the resistance coalition has encountered difficulties in its opposition to the Belo Monte project. I have profiled the storyline of sustainability and its underpinnings within both Brazilian society and international policy.

This storyline of sustainability remains contested and contestable. It is within this context that the resistance coalition is able to contest, critique, and reconfigure the pro-dam storyline of sustainability that is put forward to legitimise hydropower projects in the Brazilian Amazon. To do so, anti-dam actors broaden the focus and definition of sustainability used by pro-dam actors to incorporate additional and emergent demands and grievances. In doing so, they challenge both the location of the Belo Monte and São Luiz do Tapajós projects in sustainable energy transitions (in terms of their being 'green' and renewable) and in sustainable development agendas (in terms of their synergistic environmental and social benefits). It is to this that I turn in subsequent chapters.

Notes

1 Between 1975 and 2013, 13 large dams were built by successive governments on tributaries of the Amazon River, including Tucuruí and Balbina (built under the Brazilian military junta), Manso and Samuel (completed in the late 1980s), and Santo Antônio and Jirau (completed in 2011 and 2013, respectively).
2 The Belo Monte project is a complex of three dams, with two additional dams named Pimental and Bela Vista. These supplementary projects supply water to the Dos Canais Reservoir and the complex's main power station at Belo Monte.
3 The Itaipu project (completed in 1984 and located on the Paraná River at the border between Brazil and Paraguay) is not included in this statement, due to it being a joint venture between the Brazilian and Paraguayan governments.
4 Finding costs for the two projects is a difficult task. The costs listed above are taken from estimates published in the Brazilian media (Pereira, 2013 in the case of Belo Monte; Goy and Rochas, 2014; Calixto, 2016 in the case of São Luiz do Tapajós). The conversion of these costs into US$ is calculated based on the currency exchange rates for the dates when the above sources were published) using oanda.com.
5 The Belo Monte project impacted the territories of the Kayapó, Arara, Juruna, Araweté, Xikrin, Asurini and Parakanã communities. Before being removed from national energy plans, the São Luiz do Tapajós project was projected to impact the Apiaká de Pimental, Akaybãe, Boca do Igarapé Pacu, Remédio, Sai Cinza, Munduruku, and São Martinho communities.
6 The aims and remits of civil society organisations present in the resistance coalition are diverse and, as a result, I differentiate between 'environmental organisations' (organisations focused exclusively on environmental protection, conservation or policy) and non-governmental organisations (more varied but, in the cases studied, primarily focused on human rights protection).
7 A number of international EOs, such as Greenpeace, World Wildlife Fund, and the Nature Conservancy, have subsidiary offices in Brazil. These Brazilian arms of international organisations can be understood as semi-autonomous organisations, staffed by Brazilians and rooted in the Brazilian environmental movement (Hochstetler and Keck, 2007). I treat these groups as distinct from other environmental organisations that are international in nature but located outside of the Brazilian state (such as Survival International).
8 The link between indigenous groups and notions of sustainable development can be seen in subsequent international environmental governance. Principle 22 of the 1992 Rio Declaration emphasises that indigenous communities have 'a vital role in environmental management and development because of their knowledge and traditional practices.' The document later argues that all states must 'support their [indigenous communities'] identity, culture and interests and enable their effective participation in the achievement of sustainable development.' Furthermore, both the 1992 Biodiversity Convention and Agenda 21 emphasised the role of traditional knowledge and resource management processes in sustainable development agendas.

Bibliography

Agência Nacional de Energia Elétrica (2009). *Atlas de Energia Elétrica do Brasil*. Brasilia: Agência Nacional de Energia Elétrica.
Aleluia, JC (2005). *Diário da Câmara dos Deputados, ANO LX N° 110 (07/07/2005)*. Brasilia: Câmara dos Deputados.
Amazon Watch and Xingu Vivo para Sempre (2011). Millions Join Belo Monte Protest in Brazil. *Amazon Watch*, 20 December. Available at: https://amazonwatch.org/news/2 011/1220-millions-join-belo-monte-protest-in-brazil (Accessed: 30 March 2020).

Anderson, M (2017). Displaced by Brazil's giant Belo Monte hydroelectric dam, 'river people' reoccupy reservoir. *Mongabay*, 13 March. Available at: https://news.mongabay.com/2017/03/displaced-by-brazils-giant-belo-monte-hydroelectric-dam-river-people-reoccupy-reservoir/ (Accessed: 30 March 2020).

Arts, B (2004). The global-local nexus: NGOs and the articulation of scale. *Tijdschrift Voor Economische En Sociale Geografie*, 95(5): 498–510.

Atkins, E (2017). Dammed and diversionary: the multi-dimensional framing of Brazil's Belo Monte dam. *Singapore Journal of Tropical Geography*, 38(3): 276–292.

Atkins, E (2018). Dams, political framing and sustainability as an empty signifier: the case of Belo Monte. *Area*, 50(2): 232–239.

Barbosa, LC (2015). *Guardians of the Brazilian Amazon Rainforest: Environmental Organizations and Development*. London: Routledge Earthscan.

Bautzer, T (2018). China's state power considering bids for Brazilian hydro and thermal plants. *Reuters*, 19 September. Available at: https://www.reuters.com/article/brazil-power-china/chinas-state-power-considering-bids-for-brazilian-hydro-and-thermal-plants-idUSL2N1WY25M (Accessed: 30 March 2020).

Baviskar, A (1995). *In the Belly of the River*. Oxford: Oxford University Press.

Bellette Lee, YC (2013). Global capital, national development and transnational environmental activism: conflict and the Three Gorges Dam. *Journal of Contemporary Asia*, 43(1): 102–126.

Bezerra, RG, Prates, RC, EggertBoehs, CG, and Tripoli, ACK (2014). Discourse strategies to legitimize the Belo Monte project. *International Journal of Business and Social Science*, 5(12): 181–189.

Blanc, J (2019). *Before the Flood: The Itaipu Dam and the Visibility of Rural Brazil*. Durham, NC: Duke University Press.

BNDES (2012). BNDES approves R$ 22.5 billion in financing for Belo Monte. *BNDES*, 26 November. Available at: https://www.bndes.gov.br/SiteBNDES/bndes/bndes_en/Institucional/Press/Noticias/2012/20121126_belomonte.html (Accessed: 30 March 2020).

Brasil, Portal do Planalto (2011). Conversa com a Presidenta - Presidenta Dilma Rousseff conversa em sua coluna semanal sobre internet banda larga de baixo custo, política habitacional e Lei da Aprendizagem. *Portal Do Planalto*, 9 August. Available at: http://www.biblioteca.presidencia.gov.br/presidencia/ex-presidentes/dilma-rousseff/conversa-presidenta/conversa-com-a-presidenta-09-08-2011 (Accessed: 30 March 2020).

Bratman, E (2014). Contradictions of green development: human rights and environmental norms in light of Belo Monte Dam activism. *Journal of Latin American Studies*, 46: 261–289.

Bratman, E (2015). Passive revolution in the green economy: activism and the Belo Monte dam. *International Environmental Agreements: Politics, Law and Economics*, 15(1): 61–77. doi: 10.1007/s10784-014-9268-z.

Bratman, EZ (2020). *Governing the Rainforest: Sustainable Development Politics in the Brazilian Amazon*. Oxford: Oxford University Press.

Burrier, G (2014). *Ordem e Progresso: The Programa de Aceleração do Crescimento, Developmentalism, and Democracy in Brazil*. Thesis submitted to Department of Political Science, University of New Mexico.

Burrier, G (2016). The developmental state, civil society, and hydroelectric politics in Brazil. *The Journal of Environment & Development*, 25(3): 332–358.

Carvalho, G (2006). Environmental resistance and the politics of energy development. *Journal of Environment & Development*, 15(1): 245–268.

Casanova, L, and Kassum, J (2013). *The Political Economy of an Emerging Global Power: In Search of the Brazil Dream.* Basingstoke: Palgrave Macmillan.

Cavanagh, CJ, and Benjaminsen, TA (2017). Political ecology, variegated green economies, and the foreclosure of alternative sustainabilities. *Journal of Political Ecology*, 24(1): 200–216.

Chernela, J (1988). Potential impacts of the proposed Altamira-Xingu hydroelectric complex in Brazil. *Cultural Survival Quarterly*, 12-(2): 20–24.

China Daily (2016). Chinese dam builders powering the Amazon nation. *Daily*, 9 May. Available at: https://www.chinadaily.com.cn/business/2016-05/09/content_25146582.htm (Accessed: 30 March 2020).

Conklin, BA, and Graham, LR (1995). The shifting middle ground: Amazonian Indians and ecopolitics. *American Anthropologist*, 97(4): 695–710.

Corrêa dos Santos, M (2014). O conceito de 'atingido' por barragens: Direitos humanos e cidadania. *Direito e Praxis*, 6(1): 113–140.

Costa, L (2017). UPDATE 1-State Grid, Eletrobras to deliver line for Brazil dam early – Reuters. *Reuters*, 16 October. Available at: https://www.reuters.com/article/brazil-utilities/update-1-state-grid-eletrobras-to-deliver-line-for-brazil-dam-early-idUSL2N1MR1H3 (Accessed: 30 March 2020).

Costa, L (2018). China's power investment group seeks new Brazil targets after $2 billion deal. *Reuters*, 16 May. Available at: https://www.reuters.com/article/us-spic-brazil/chinas-power-investment-group-seeks-new-brazil-targets-after-2-billion-deal-idUSKCN1IH08M (Accessed: 30 March 2020).

da Costa, A (2014). Sustainable dam development in Brazil: the roles of environmentalism, participation and planning. In: Scheumann, W, and Hensengerth, O (eds) *Evolution of Dam Policies: Evidence from the Big Hydropower States.* Berlin: Springer Berlin Heidelberg.

da Silva, LIL (2010). Discurso do Presidente da República, Luiz Inácio Lula da Silva, no ato por Belo Monte e pelo desenvolvimento da região do Xingu – Altamira-PA. *Presidencia Da Republica, Biblioteca*, 22 June. Available at: http://www.biblioteca.presidencia.gov.br/presidencia/ex-presidentes/luiz-inacio-lula-da-silva/audios/2010-audios-lula/22-06-2010-discurso-do-presidente-da-republica-luiz-inacio-lula-da-silva-no-ato-por-belo-monte-e-pelo-desenvolvimento-da-regiao-do-xingu-altamira-pa-08min36s/view (Accessed: 30 March 2020).

Datz, G (2013). Brazil's pension fund developmentalism. *Competition & Change*, 17(2): 111–128.

de Moya Figueira Netto, CA, de Barros Franco, HC, and Souto Rezende, PFV (2007). *AHE Belo Monte: Evolução Dos Estudos.* Paper presented at XXVII Seminário Nacional De Grandes Barragens, Belém, PA, 3–7 June. Available at: http://symbiont.ansp.org/ixingu/library/timeline_sources/Moya_et_al_2007.pdf (Accessed: 30 March 2020).

della Porta, D, and Diani, M (1999). *Social Movements: An Introduction.* London: Blackwell.

Dye, B (2020). What holds back dam building? The role of Brazil in the stagnation of dams in Tanzania. Available at SSRN: https://doi.org/10.2139/ssrn.3538214

Eden, S, Donaldson, A, and Walker, G (2006). Green groups and grey areas: scientific boundary-work, nongovernmental organisations, and environmental knowledge. *Environment and Planning. Part A*, 38(6): 1061–1076.

Eletrobras (2012). Assessoria de Comunicação da Eletrobras: Pela energia limpa. *Eletrobras*, 26 April. Available at: http://eletrobras.com/pt/Lists/noticias/ExibeNoticias.aspx?ID=590&ContentTypeId=0x0100C80727F9FEABA9499C54B2148B8BE07E (Accessed: 30 March 2020).

Empresa de Pesquisa Energética (2010). *Belo Monte Fatos e Dados*. Brasilia: Empresa de Pesquisa Energética. Available at: http://antigo.epe.gov.br//leiloes/Documents/Leilão Belo Monte/Belo Monte – Fatos e Dados – POR.pdf (Accessed: 30 March 2020).

Ferro, F (2010). *Diário da Câmara dos Deputados, ANO LXV No 51 (15/04/2010)*. Brasilia: Câmara dos Deputados.

Fisher, WH (1994). Megadevelopment, environmentalism, and resistance: the institutional context of Kayapó indigenous politics in Central Brazil. *Human Organization*, 53(3): 220–232.

Fleury, LC, and Almeida, J (2013). A construção da Usina Hidrelétrica de Belo Monte: Conflito ambiental e o dilema do desenvolvimento. *Ambiente e Sociedade*, 16(4): 141–156.

Goldman, M (2004). Imperial science, imperial nature: environmental knowledge for the World (Bank). In: Jasanoff, S, and Martello, ML (eds) *Earthly Politics: Local and Global in Environmental Governance*. Cambridge, MA: MIT Press.

Gómez Bruera, HF (2015). *Lula, the Workers' Party and the Governability Dilemma in Brazil*. Abingdon: Routledge.

Hecht, SB (2011). The new Amazon geographies: insurgent citizenship, 'Amazon Nation' and the politics of environmentalisms. *Journal of Cultural Geography*, 28(1): 203–223.

Hochstetler, K (2011). The politics of environmental licensing: energy projects of the past and future in Brazil. *Studies in Comparative International Development*, 46(4): 349–371.

Hochstetler, K, and Keck, ME (2007). *Greening Brazil: Environmental Activism in State and Society*. Durham, NC: Duke University Press.

Hochstetler, K, and Montero, AP (2013). The renewed developmental state: the national development bank and the Brazil model. *Journal of Development Studies*, 49(11): 1484–1499.

Hochstetler, K, and Viola, E (2012). Brazil and the politics of climate change: beyond the global commons. *Environmental Politics*, 21(5): 753–771.

Indigenous People's Cultural Support Trust (n.d.). Press release: Indians rally to fight dam proposal in the Amazon. *Indigenous People's Cultural Support Trust*. Available at: http://www.ipcst.org/Pdfs/AltamiraPR.pdf (Accessed: 2 April 2020).

International Hydropower Association (2019). *2018 Hydropower Status Report*. London: International Hydropower Association.

International Rivers (2008). A knife in the water. *International Rivers*, 3 July. Available at: https://www.internationalrivers.org/blogs/232/a-knife-in-the-water (Accessed: 30 March 2020).

Keck, ME, and Sikkink, K (1998). *Activists beyond Borders: Advocacy Networks in International Politics*. Ithaca, NY: Cornell University Press.

Klein, PT (2015). Engaging the Brazilian state: the Belo Monte dam and the struggle for political voice. *Journal of Peasant Studies*, 42(6): 1137–1156.

Kumar, A, Schei, T, Ahenkorah, A, Rodriguez, RC, Devernay, J-M, Freitas, M, Hall, D, Killingtveit, Å, and Liu, Z (2011). Hydropower. In: O Edenhofer, R Pichs-Madruga, Y Sokona, K Seyboth, P Matschoss, S Kadner, T Zwickel, P Eickemeier, G Hansen, S Schlömer, and C von Stechow (eds) *IPCC Special Report on Renewable Energy Sources and Climate Change Mitigation*. Cambridge: Cambridge University Press.

Latrubesse, EM, Arima, EY, Dunne, T, Park, E, Baker, VR, d'Horta, FM, Wight, C, Wittmann, F, Zuanon, J, Baker, PA, Ribas, CC, Norgaard, RB, Filizola, N, Ansar, A, Flyvbjerg, B, and Stevaux, JC (2017). Damming the rivers of the Amazon basin. *Nature*, 546(7658): 363–369.

Leach, M, Scoones, I, and Stirling, A (2010). *Dynamic Sustainabilities: Technology, Environment, Social Justice*. London: Earthscan.

Lees, AC, Peres, CA, Fearnside, PM, Schneider, M, and Zuanon, JAS (2016). Hydropower and the future of Amazonian biodiversity. *Biodiversity and Conservation*, 25(3): 451–466.

Lopes, C (2011). *Diário da Câmara dos Deputados, ANO LXVI No 060 (13/04/2011)*. Brasilia: Câmara dos Deputados.

McAllister, LK (2008). *Making Law Matter: Environmental Protection and Legal Institutions in Brazil*. Redwood City, CA: Stanford University Press.

McCormick, S (2006). The Brazilian anti-dam movement: knowledge contestation as communicative action. *Organization and Environment*, 19(3): 321–346.

McCormick, S (2010). Damming the Amazon: local movements and transnational struggles over water. *Society and Natural Resources*, 24(1): 34–48.

Ministério de Minas e Energia and Empresa de Pesquisa Energética (2007). *Plano Nacional de Energia 2030*. Brasil: Ministério de Mines e Energia.

Ministério do Meio Ambiente (2012). Meio ambiente: Brasileiro está mais consciente. *Ministério do Meio Ambiente*, 6 June. Available at: https://www.mma.gov.br/informma/item/8386-o-que-o-brasileiro-pensa-do-meio-ambiente-e-do-consumo-sustent%C3%A1vel (Accessed: March 30, 2020).

Montero, AP (2014). *Brazil: Reversal of Fortune*. Cambridge: Polity Press.

Morais, H (2016). Militante social desaparecida foi assassinada a tiros em Rondônia. *G1*, 15 January. Available at: http://g1.globo.com/ro/rondonia/noticia/2016/01/militante-social-desaparecida-foi-assassinada-tiros-em-rondonia.html (Accessed: 30 March 2020).

Movimentos dos Atingidos por Barragens (2012). Índios e pescadores ocupam Belo Monte. *Movimentos Dos Atingidos Por Barragens*, 9 October. Available at: http://www.mabnacional.org.br/noticia/ndios-e-pescadores-ocupam-belo-monte (Accessed: 30 March 2020).

Movimentos dos Atingidos por Barragens (2015). Indígenas bloqueiam acesso à canteiro de Belo Monte. *Movimentos Dos Atingidos Por Barragens*, 11 January. Available at: http://www.mabnacional.org.br/noticia/ind-genas-bloqueiam-acesso-canteiro-belo-monte (Accessed: 30 March 2020).

Movimentos dos Atingidos por Barragens (2016). Agricultores ocupam Incra para exigir reassentamento. *Movimentos Dos Atingidos Por Barragens*, 22 April. Available at: http://mabnacional.org.br/noticia/agricultores-ocupam-incra-para-exigir-reassentamento (Accessed: 30 March 2020).

Norte Energia (2020). Belo Monte. *Norte Energia*. https://www.norteenergiasa.com.br/pt-br/ (Accessed: 30 March 2020).

Nunes, J, and Peña, AM (2015). Marina Silva and the rise of sustainability in Brazil. *Environmental Politics*, 24(3): 506–511.

Oswald, V, and Tavares, M (2012). País não se intimida com pressão contra Belo Monte, diz Lobão. *Jornal O Globo*, 2 January. Available at: https://oglobo.globo.com/economia/pais-nao-se-intimida-com-pressao-contra-belo-monte-diz-lobao-3555541 (Accessed: 30 March 2020).

Park, CC (2002). *Tropical Rainforests*. Abingdon: Routledge.

Redclift, M (2005). Sustainable development (1987–2005): an oxymoron comes of age. *Sustainable Development*, 13(4): 212–227.

Ribeiro, AP, and Zimmermann, P (2007). Com PAC, governo espera investimento de R$ 504 bi até 2010. *Folha de S.Paulo*, 22 January. Available at: https://www1.folha.uol.com.br/folha/dinheiro/ult91u113888.shtml (Accessed: 30 March 2020).

Rothman, FD (2001). A comparative study of dam-resistance campaigns and environmental policy in Brazil. *Journal of Environment and Development*, 10(4): 317–344.

Rothman, FD, and Oliver, P (1999). From local to global: the anti-dam movement in Southern Brazil, 1979–1992. *Mobilization: An International Quarterly*, 4(1): 41–57.

Saunders, C (2013). *Environmental Networks and Social Movement Theory*. London: Bloomsbury.

Savarese, M (2010). Lula visita local de obras da usina de Belo Monte e se irrita com manifestantes. *UOL Notícias*, 22 June. Available at: https://noticias.uol.com.br/politica/ultimas-noticias/2010/06/22/lula-vai-local-de-obras-de-belo-monte-e-se-irrita-com-manifestantes.htm (Accessed: 30 March 2020).

Schwarcz, LM, and Starling, HM (2018). *Brazil: A Biography*. London: Allen Lane.

Senado Federal (2011). Pronunciamento de Francisco Dornelles em 25/04/2011. *Senado Federal*, 25 April. Available at: https://www25.senado.leg.br/web/atividade/pronunciamentos/-/p/texto/387756 (Accessed: 30 March 2020).

Soito, JLDS, and Freitas, MAV (2011). Amazon and the expansion of hydropower in Brazil: vulnerability, impacts and possibilities for adaptation to global climate change. *Renewable and Sustainable Energy Reviews*, 15(6): 3165–3177.

Switkes, G (2008). The Madeira hydroelectric and hidrovia project – cornerstone of IIRSA. *International Rivers*, 25 June. Available at: https://www.internationalrivers.org/resources/introduction-and-article-the-madeira-hydroelectric-and-hidrovia-project-%E2%80%93-cornerstone-of (Accessed: 30 March 2020).

Tarrow, SG (ed) (2011). *Power in Movement: Social Movements and Contentious Politics*. Cambridge: Cambridge University Press.

Teixeira, M, and Costa, L (2015). UPDATE 1-China's State Grid to build Brazil's longest power line. *Reuters*, 17 July. Available at: https://www.reuters.com/article/brazil-power-auction/update-1-chinas-state-grid-to-build-brazils-longest-power-line-idUSL2N0ZX0P420150717 (Accessed: 30 March 2020).

The Guardian (2016). Brazil must recognise Munduruku lands. *The Guardian*, 10 August. Available at: https://www.theguardian.com/environment/2016/aug/10/brazil-must-recognise-munduruku-lands (Accessed: 30 March 2020).

Thorkildsen, K (2018). 'Land yes, dam no!' Justice-seeking strategies by the anti-dam movement in the Ribeira Valley, Brazil. *The Journal of Peasant Studies*, 45(2): 347–367.

Tilly, C, and Tarrow, SG (2007). *Contentious Politics*. Oxford: Oxford University Press.

Tolmasquim, MT (2007). *Presentation at Public Audience, Organised by Comissões de Minas e Energia e de Meio Ambiente*. Rio de Janeiro: Câmara dos Deputados, 12 April. Available at: http://www2.camara.leg.br/atividade-legislativa/comissoes/comissoes-permanentes/cme/audiencias-publicas/anos-anteriores/2007/12-04-2007-leiloes-de-energia-a-5-2007-e-a-3-2007-e-mercado-de-energia-eletrica-para-o-proximo-decenio/EPE-Mauricio Tolmasquim.pdf (Accessed: 30 March 2020).

Tribunal de Contas da União (2015). Acórdão TCU 1569/2015. *Tribunal de Contas da União*, 24 June. Available at: https://pesquisa.apps.tcu.gov.br/#/documento/acordao-completo/*/KEY%253AACORDAO-COMPLETO-1456217/DTRELEVANCIA%2520desc/0/sinonimos%253Dfalse (Accessed: 30 March 2020).

Turner, T (1993). The role of indigenous peoples in the environmental crisis: the example of the Kayapo of the Brazilian amazon. *Perspectives in Biology and Medicine*, 36(3): 526–545.

Vieira, M (2016). Fim de festa em Belo Monte. *Projecto Colabora*, 29 March. Available at: https://projetocolabora.com.br/florestas/fim-de-festa-em-belo-monte/ (Accessed 22 July 2020).

Vieira, MA, and Dalgaard, KG (2013). The energy-security–climate-change nexus in Brazil. *Environmental Politics*, 22(4): 610–626.

Villas-Bôas, A, Rojas Garzón, B, Reis, C, Amorim, L, and Leite, L (2015). *Dossiê Belo Monte: Não há condições para a Licença de Operação*. Brasilia: Instituto Socioambiental.

Wolford, Wendy (2010). *This Land Is Ours Now: Social Mobilization and the Meanings of Land in Brazil*. Durham, NC: Duke University Press.

Yasuda, Y (2015). *Rules, Norms and NGO Advocacy Strategies: Hydropower Development on the Mekong River*. London: Routledge Earthscan.

Zanotti, L (2015). Water and life: hydroelectric development and indigenous pathways to justice in the Brazilian Amazon. *Politics, Groups, and Identities*, 3(4): 666–672.

Zanotti, L (2016). *Radical Territories in the Brazilian Amazon*. Tucson, AZ: University of Arizona Press.

Zhouri, A (2010). 'Adverse forces' in the Brazilian Amazon: developmentalism versus environmentalism and indigenous rights. *The Journal of Environment & Development*, 19(3): 252–273.

Zhouri, A, and Laschefski, K (2010). Desenvolvimento e conflitos ambientais: um novo campo de investigação. In: Zhouri, A, and Laschefski, K (eds) *Desenvolvimento e Conflitos Ambientais*. Belo Horizonte: Editora UFMG.

4 'By hook or by crook'

On Tuesday 2 August 2014, a helicopter moved across the blue skies of Pará. Inside, the incumbent president, Dilma Rousseff, gazed down at the Belo Monte construction sites. Dilma was in campaign mode, staging visits in the region to drum up support for her re-election campaign. On landing in Vitória do Xingu, she visited the Belo Monte site, chatting to and posing for photographs with workers and the press, recording election broadcasts and, throughout, stressing the importance of the project (G1 PA, 2014).

On Thursday 5 May 2016, Dilma returned to Belo Monte. Having been re-elected to a second term as president in 2014, she arrived to inaugurate the project. Two of the plant's 24 turbines had been generating energy for close to a month. That morning, a group of Movimento dos Atingidos por Barragens (MAB) activists, indigenous communities, and ribeirinhos blocked the only road to the plant, setting barricades of wood and tyres ablaze (Pinto, 2016). During both visits, the social and environmental impacts of the project, the protests against it, and the numerous lawsuits and denunciations that characterised its construction went unmentioned. Nor did Dilma visit those impacted by the project. Despite these protests, Dilma arrived at the site, again by helicopter, and presented the Belo Monte project as one of the achievements of her presidency:

> I'm very proud of the choices that I've made. One of those that I want to emphasise, once again, is the construction of the Belo Monte hydroelectric plant. [It is] a legacy for the Brazilian population, a legacy for the people here in this region of Pará.
>
> (Bragança, 2016)

It is a strange twist that Belo Monte would – far from leaving a legacy of energy security and economic development – become a site in the decline of both Dilma's political career and the political legitimacy of the Partidos dos Trabalhadores (PT) that governed Brazil between 2003 and 2016. If the planning and construction of Belo Monte had become a 'set-piece' in the development policies of the PT, it also came to be a symbol for the impunity and corruption that came to be associated with this era. The construction of the project coincided with the recalibration of the political terrain in Brazil, including the uncovering of a network of bribery and corruption between politicians, construction companies, and state utilities and Brazilians across the country taking to the streets to protest an economic recession and continued inequality. In March 2015, millions of Brazilians across the country marched calling for Dilma's resignation or impeachment. By July 2015, Dilma had a presidential disapproval rating of 68%, the highest such rating since democratisation in 1985 (Matoso, 2015).

At the time of her 2016 visit to Belo Monte, the legitimacy of and support for Dilma's presidency was unravelling. Several weeks before, the president had been impeached by the Brazilian Congress. Accused of administrative misconduct for a process known as 'fiscal pedalling' – an accounting practice that gives the impression that more money was received than was spent, breaking Brazilian budgetary laws – Dilma saw her presidential powers suspended by the Senate on 12 May. On 31 August 2016, she was removed from office. The fact that, while facing the unravelling of her presidency, Dilma chose to visit Belo Monte was symbolic. Dilma had long before committed herself to this project and, for many, Belo Monte represented the pouring of Dilma's political ideology and aspirations into a concrete form and provided her with personal pride (Interview, 28 April 2017; Interview, 16 September 2017). As an interviewee based at the Department of Environmental Licensing of FUNAI noticed, during her re-election campaign, 'Belo Monte was the only place where she smiled' (Interview, 10 November 2016a).

In this chapter, I detail how, far from merely coinciding with the exposure of a network of corruption and an outpouring of public dissent, the planning and construction of the Belo Monte and São Luiz do Tapajós Dam projects provided a key site upon which the alliances between the PT and social movements were challenged and, for many, crumbled. As discussed in Chapter 3, the planning and construction of hydroelectric dams became a key part of the development policies of the PT. It is within this context that pro-dam actors sought to elevate the project above dissent, ensuring its construction regardless of the grievances or complaints of those opposed to the project. I understand this as a process of depoliticisation. In this chapter, I trace the contours of how, while proponents of the projects studied sought to depoliticise hydropower in Brazil – raising it above the terrain of everyday dissent – those opposing hydropower repoliticised the projects by illuminating the interests that underpin the projects' planning and construction. An alternative vision of the reasons for the projects' planning and construction was put forward, with anti-dam figures advancing a storyline that re-cast the dams as key symbols of government corruption and impunity, as well as critiquing the pro-dam storyline of sustainability as a mere 'tool' to secure legitimacy for planning and construction.

The 'head carnival float' and the circumvention of dissent

Many of those living in Altamira saw the election of Lula as a moment to celebrate, as it was assumed that the new president would take their side and shelve the project (Blasberg and Gluesing, 2016; Brum, 2019; Interview, 16 September 2017). The 2002 election of a PT government generated widespread optimism, with the party seen by many activists as 'one of them' (Baiocchi, 2004; Ottmann, 2005). The PT has historically been part of a strong alliance – and has had overlapping personnel – with social movements such as the Movimento dos Trabalhadores Sem Terra (Landless Workers' Movement MST), favelados (those living in informal urban settlements), environmentalists, feminists, trade unions, human rights activists, and cultural groups (Hochstetler and Keck, 2007; Hunter, 2010; Branford and Rocha, 2015). Lula was and, at the time of writing, remains the figurehead for this alliance, with his elevation to the presidency completing the rags to riches story of a child born into poverty in the north-eastern state of Pernambuco.

The election of Lula as president in 2002 completed a trajectory of the party and the alliance that it represented, from clandestine meetings during the years of military rule to a successful national political machine (Guidry, 2003; Hunter, 2010; Ribeiro, 2014). This coalition was relatively stable during Lula's first term, when the PT adopted many of the market-friendly macro-economic policies than its predecessor (French and Fortes, 2012). The party's historic role as a home to civil society, and as a social movement itself, as well as its continued position on the social-democratic left of the political spectrum, instilled loyalty in many activists that, for some, resulted in a reluctance to criticise the governments of Lula and Dilma. The presence of this coalition, and of social movements in the corridors of government, increased a concern that these movements and organisation must not 'destabilise' the government (Puzone and Miguel, 2019). As interviewees explained to me:

> You have this very sensitive arrangement of the relationship between the [PT] government, that was in power for 13 years and how they related to social movements and civil society – which made, somehow, the criticism more difficult. It was harder to criticise them.
> (Interview, 3 November 2016b)

> He [Lula] ... [makes] that [Belo Monte] project the biggest of his administration and, supported by charisma and relying on the importance of the Workers' Party and the influence it had and still has over the social movements, he managed to neutralise opposition.
> (Interview, 1 February 2017)

This coalition persisted during the PT's years in government, despite the party's incremental move from being a left-wing, transformist social movement[1] to becoming a more pragmatic, electorally focused, politically moderate and professional party between 1994 and 2012 (Samuels, 2004).[2] Although elected as a base for progressive change, the PT, once in government, embarked on a path that diverged from the party's main previous policy goals (Gómez Bruera, 2015). Structural redistribution of wealth gave way to forms of compensation; extensive land reform never occurred, and radical participatory democracy (a key part of the PT in opposition) was not transplanted to national governance (Gómez Bruera, 2015).

While the PT was able to temper the antagonism between its economic policy agenda and the expectations of its supporters in social movements, the expansion of energy, mining, and agri-business infrastructure projects that formed the PAC, PAC-2, and IIRSA, led to the emergence of a new series of antagonisms between social movements in Brazil and the state (Baletti, 2016). Hydroelectric dams in the Brazilian Amazon were a key site of these emergent antagonisms, highlighting how the PT's development policies were forcing displacement and environmental damage in the name of economic growth. For many opposed to dam projects in Brazil, the Belo Monte and São Luiz do Tapajós projects were landmarks in understanding the social and environmental repercussions of the PT's policy of economic development. Such projects had an important symbolism for Lula and Dilma, who were widely understood by anti-dam actors as subscribing to a *high modernist* view (discussed in Chapter 2) that prioritises the re-engineering of the natural world for economic development (Interview, 3 October 2016; Interview, 27 October 2016a; Interview, 27 October 2016b). As one interviewee explained, 'It's exactly like "progress is having big roads, big dams" A society's progress or capacity can be measured by its capacity to construct huge works of engineering … And they truly believe in that' (Interview, 27 October 2016b). It is within this mindset that the infrastructure projects of the PAC, PAC-2, and IIRSA came to be representative of the wider policies of the PT, with interviewees arguing that these projects fitted a 'logic of lifting the working class out of poverty, providing them with opportunities and spending public funds to do so' but caring little about the impacts of such infrastructure projects (Interview, 1 February 2017).

While pro-dam actors such as both Lula and Dilma framed hydroelectric projects as the fulfilment of goals of economic development, energy security, and sustainable development – and, as a result, in what is deemed the *national interest* (Atkins, 2019) – for many of those opposing them, the Belo Monte and São Luiz do Tapajós projects were inseparable from the particular development policies, politics, and principles held by the PT and their wider social and environmental impacts. The hydropower projects come to symbolise the PT's government, representing 'the head carnival float for the party. The showcase … to show that the party, the president, whatever, is … helping Brazil develop and so forth' (Interview, 1 December 2016a). As an interviewee at the Brazilian arm of the Nature Conservancy argued, the announcement of hydropower projects often coincided with election years:

> When Lula wanted to [be] re-elect[ed], he launched the Madeira dams … When Dilma came, she launched Belo Monte … When they wanted the second term of Dilma … [São Luiz do Tapajós was launched]. It was so weird … In 12 years, they had three big dams to launch exactly in the election year[s].
> (Interview, 27 October 2016a)

A common criticism made by anti-dam actors was that the projects were not only environmentally and socially damaging but planned and built with limited room for dissent or airing of grievances. When describing the projects, numerous opposition figures asserted that the projects studied represented the pursuit of a policy of 'development at all costs' by the PT, with the aim of economic development pursued with limited concern for the social or environmental impact or dissent from local populations (Interview, 3 October 2016; Interview, 27 October 2016b; Interview, 9 October 2017). A human rights activist explained to me that the projects were 'an ecologic[al] and human tragedy, where the absolute priority was given to "economic development," not to social well-being or nature conservation' (Interview, 1 December 2016a). The contestation over these incursions into the Amazon represent key sites of an emergent antagonism between the PT and political resistance against the deemed lost 'progressiveness' of the PT (Baletti, 2016).

As discussed in Chapter 1, a key part of repoliticisation is the revealing of the particular political interests that underpin and drive a project forward. Across my time in Brazil, anti-dam activists drew attention to the political interests that underpinned the planning and construction of hydroelectric projects. A key figure discussed by many was Dilma Rousseff. The daughter of Bulgarian immigrants, Dilma was a member of a left-wing guerrilla group that organised against the junta; she was arrested in São Paulo and imprisoned and tortured between 1970 and 1973. Later training as an economist, in the years after democratisation she served as a civil servant in Porto Alegre, including as Secretary of Energy of Rio Grande do Sul (1999–2002). She joined the PT in 2001, going on to serve as part of Lula's transition team in 2002, Minister of Mines and Energy (2003–2005) and Lula's Chief of Staff (2005–2010). Dilma's political career was rooted in finding solutions to energy problems, as was evident during her tenure as Secretary of Energy of Rio Grande do Sul and as Minister of Mines and Energy, and she played a major role in the planning and construction of hydroelectric projects during the years of PT rule. One interviewee went as far as to label Dilma 'the mother of Belo Monte' (Interview, 1 February 2017).

For many of those interviewed, the construction of hydroelectric dams became a 'pet issue' for Dilma, with her commitment to these projects rooted in her personal memory of the energy rationing of 2001/02, when she was Secretary of Energy for the state of Rio Grande do Sul (Interview, 30 September 2016). The result was what many described as a tunnel-vision, with Dilma focusing on hydropower as the *only* solution to problems of energy supply and dismissing all alternatives and circumventing those standing in a project's way. One interviewee explained that Dilma 'was always very dismissive of wind energy, for instance. She said: "You're kidding. This is kid's stuff. This will never provide energy, electricity for Brazil"' (Interview, 18 October 2016). Local activists interviewed described how a meeting with Antônia Melo of Xingu Vivo ended with Dilma punching the table and shouting that Belo Monte would most definitely be built, regardless of Melo's opposition (Interview, 16 September 2017). Numerous interviews also described the long-running tension between Dilma and Marina Silva, the Minister for the Environment between 2003 and 2011 (Interview, 30 September 2016; Interview, 18 October 2016). When Silva proposed an extractive reserve in the area to be flooded by Belo Monte's reservoir, to protect the lands and livelihoods of impacted populations, Dilma blocked it – arguing that such demarcation would hinder the building of other dams in the future (Angelo, 2010). This contest between the Minister of the Environment and Dilma Rousseff was widely presented by anti-dam actors as representing Dilma's steadfast commitment to the construction of hydroelectric dams in the Brazilian Amazon, as well as her inability to hear dissenting opinions. Silva left Lula's government in 2008, having become isolated within the Cabinet due to her outspoken views against hydroelectric dams and agricultural expansion and later being overlooked by Lula when devising a sustainable development plan for the Brazilian Amazon. She was subsequently replaced with ministers who were more amenable to the government's efforts to build infrastructure in the Amazon region, such as Carlos Minc (2008–2010) and Izabella Teixeira (2010–2016) (Hochstetler, 2011). As discussed in Chapter 3, Silva went on to run for president with the Partido Verde.

Both Lula and Dilma were accused by activists of ignoring the advice and information provided by scientists and researchers (Monteiro, 2016), of restricting the publication of reports that highlighted Belo Monte's impacts (Interview, 1 December 2016a), and of applying pressure to speed up the planning process. For many, this political pressure was evident in a string of resignations that accompanied the planning and construction of Belo Monte. In 2008, both the president of IBAMA, Bazileu Margarido and the head of Instituto Chico Mendes de Conservação da Biodiversidade (Chico Mendes Institute for Biodiversity Conservation, ICMBIO), João Paulo Capobianco, resigned citing pressure regarding legal barriers to new infrastructure projects and claiming a lack of support for performing their duties. In 2009, two senior officials at IBAMA – Sebastião Custódio Pires and Leozildo Tabajara da Silva Benjamin – resigned from their roles in the organisation, complaining of high levels of pressure to approve the Belo Monte project. One year later, IBAMA president Abelardo Bayma Azevedo also resigned, two weeks before a partial installation licence, with conditions, was permitted for the site. Anti-dam materials argued that extensive political pressure was applied to technical staff at IBAMA, resulting in the licensing of dams without meeting several conditions of the licence and addressing of consequences of construction (Hurwitz, 2011; Mongabay, 2011).

An oft-cited example of this refusal to hear dissenting opinions powering Belo Monte ahead can be seen in the response of the PT government to a 2011 decision made by the Inter-American Commission on Human Rights (IACHR) of the Organization of American States (OAS) that called for the suspension of Belo Monte's environmental licensing process due to its various impacts on the indigenous communities living in the Xingu basin. The IACHR supported complaints from civil society groups that the Brazilian government had failed in its obligation to uphold the rights of indigenous communities to free, prior, and informed consent (Inter-American Commission on Human Rights, 2011). This decision was swiftly dismissed in Brasília. Flexa Ribeiro, senator for Pará and president of the congressional subcommittee overseeing Belo Monte, labelled it 'absurd,' arguing the decision represented an encroachment into Brazilian sovereignty over the Amazon region (Oliveira, 2011). The response from Dilma was swift.

The Brazilian government recalled its delegate, Ruy Casaes, from the IACHR, withdrew its candidate for the OAS, Paulo Vanucchi, and withheld its payment of US$800,000 from the OAS, claiming that the organisation had overstepped its remit (Nery, 2011). The IACHR rescinded the decision soon after. However, it would later return to the case in 2016, ruling in 2018 that the Brazilian government still needs to address violations of the rights of the indigenous communities impacted by Belo Monte (AIDA, 2018).

This represents a process of depoliticisation in which the grievances and demands of those opposed to the project are pushed aside by a dominant pro-dam coalition intent on project construction. Perhaps due to its wider political symbolism, proponents of these projects attempted to render the dams a foregone conclusion, with the coercive, bureaucratic apparatuses of the state committed to ensuring project completion. As one interviewee explained, 'Belo Monte was a very important government decision ... The government said, "Belo Monte is decided on" and [this] never changed' (Interview, 3 November 2016b). With the project being a core component of the PT's development policy, dissenting opinions were treated with disdain, and contradictory evidence and findings were ignored. The political commitment of the governments of Lula and Dilma was presented by numerous anti-dam activists in Brazil as representative of a 'steamroller' that neglected the social and environmental impacts of the project, ignored local communities and continued its course towards construction (Aliança dos Rios da Amazônia et al., 2011; Brum, 2015; Vieira, 2016). A bias towards dam building was seen as part of a wider state economic project that neglected public debate and discussion surrounding the projects, with legally mandated consultations distilled into theatrical exercises (Millikan, 2014). As an international journalist, who writes extensively on the PT government, explained to me: 'They [the PT] basically rammed Belo Monte through, despite vast opposition within Brazil itself and from the international community' (Interview, 30 September 2016).

Suspensões de Segurança

The process of depoliticisation by pro-dam actors – raising the Belo Monte project above dissent – was particularly evident in the judicial arena. Between 2011 and 2016, the Ministério Público Federal (MPF) referred 25 lawsuits against the Belo Monte project to regional courts. The complaints put forward were diverse and reflected the grievances discussed in previous chapters, ranging from asserted inadequacies in consultation, methodological flaws in the Environmental Impact Assessments and the failure of Norte Energia to meet the conditions of its construction licence. These judicial actions found only limited success. Construction of the plant was halted in August 2012. However, this was overturned after six days. A stoppage in October 2013 lasted for only five days. In December 2013, a halt in construction was overturned in less than 72 hours.

These decisions were overturned using a Suspensões de Segurança ('Security Suspension'), a legal instrument that provides the judiciary with the power to reverse decisions in the name of the national interest. These instruments date back to the years of the military dictatorship (1964–1985) and Law 4,348/1964, which allowed for the suspension of judicial decisions based on the criteria that the act/decision could cause 'serious damage to the health, safety, order and public economy.' While this law was initially focused on the suspension of individual rights, as a means to guarantee national security or development, it was widened during Brazil's transition to democratic rule, when the injunction was extended to apply to collective rights (Law 8,437/1992). The law was further updated to include the suspension of community rights in 2001 under President Fernando Henrique Cardoso (1995–2003). These mechanisms were used widely by the PT government, including for decisions related to other hydroelectric projects (e.g. the Teles Pires Dam) and large-scale events (e.g. the 2014 World Cup and 2016 Olympics) (Justiça Global; et al., 2014; Santos and Gomes, 2015). Decisions are first made at the local courts and then reversed on the federal circuit or, ultimately, the Brazilian Supreme Court (Oliveira, n.d.). Once a proclamation is made, it cannot be challenged – with the right to appeal suspended by the decision.

The employment of a Suspensões de Segurança elevates the issue above the judicial terrain of dissent, access to justice and due process of Brazilian law. It provides a mechanism of both legal intervention and redefinition of the legal space itself (Fleury, 2014). Decisions are justified by the assumption – and commitment to the belief – that it is necessary to ensure the *public* interest over the interests of the individual or the community. In the case of the two projects studied, this public interest was linked to national energy security (Fleury, 2014). The importance of the Belo Monte and São Luiz do Tapajós projects becomes located at the national level, removing the significance of the local community and their grievances. The judiciary becomes a site of contestation between pro- and anti-dam actors and the (re)production of environmental knowledge, expertise, and the legitimacy of grievances that elevates certain demands and assertions above others (Eren, 2017). As a result, the use of Suspensões de Segurança represents a site of the depoliticisation of the projects studied – with the grievances of anti-dam actors, voiced in a legal setting, deemed illegitimate and as restricting the fulfilment of the national interest. Although construction was found to have numerous impacts on local communities, court judgements argued that the stoppage of works would represent a significant degree of damage to the nation, both in relation to the economy and energy security (Tribunal Regional Federal da Primeira Região, 2010). Dialogue was rejected, and the projects continued, with anti-dam actors, such as the MPF, having no real possibility of reversing such a decision. The project thus becomes exceptional in its importance, and above dissent.

The use of these legal mechanisms and neglect of the complaints of those opposed to the projects were presented by anti-dam actors as examples of the impunity held by pro-dam actors in Brazil. Suspensões de Segurança were presented by anti-dam activists as evidence of the circumvention of democratic practice by a corrupt pro-dam coalition intent on building hydroelectric dams in the Brazilian Amazon. An activist at the Instituto Socioambiental characterised the mechanisms as a 'way of eluding [the] rules … It's a way to enable you to do anything, in any way' and commented that the decisions were a wider symbol of 'the limits of the democratic institutions [of Brazil],' with democratic protest, state institutions (such as the MPF, IBAMA, and FUNAI) and appeals to human rights unable to adequately defend local populations from the impact of the schemes (Interview, 3 November 2016b).

With the security suspensions dating back to the rule of the military *junta* (1964–1985), their use in the 21st century to ensure the completion of infrastructure projects raised parallels to the authoritarianism of the dictatorship. Between 1964 and 1985, the military junta planned and completed numerous development projects that neglected both human rights and social and environmental impacts, including the Rodovia Transamazônica (Trans-Amazonian Highway) and the Projeto Grande Carajás, which included the Tucuruí Dam. With the initial plans for Belo Monte originating in the 1970s and the era of the military junta in Brazil, opposition materials present the project as a scheme that was 'designed by the military [dictatorship]' (Interview, 3 October 2016; Pontes Jr. 2011; Monteiro, 2016). Numerous anti-dam activists in Brazil characterised contemporary dam projects as representing the continuation of the authoritarian infrastructure projects of the junta. Similarly, an interviewee at a Brazilian environmental organisation explained to me that:

> Brazil today is just the same as [when] we were at the beginning of the dictatorship … 12 years of a government that was supposed to be more progressive, left-wing … In some senses, we are still the same country, and we haven't learnt from our previous mistakes.
> (Interview, 10 November 2016a)

For many, this adoption of authoritarian methods to secure construction was evident in the criminalisation of local resistance groups, stripping actors of their ability to protest the respective projects (Branford, 2013; MXVPS, 2013). One local activist characterised the period of Belo Monte's construction as an 'avalanche of attempts at intimidation, criminalisation and lawsuits against [resistance] leaders who resisted the project' (Interview, 16 September 2017). Examples of such criminalisation are plentiful. In 2012, members of Xingu Vivo, arrested for blockading the road leading to Belo Monte, were banned from protesting in public areas near the construction site (MXVPS, 2016). At other protests, Brazilian military units were reported to have fired rubber bullets at indigenous protesters and to have violently broken up workers' demonstrations (Adams, 2013; MPF/PA, 2014; Comitê Brasileiro de Defensoras e Defensores de Direitos Humanos, 2017). In the Tapajós basin, members of the Munduruku community reported the increased presence of police in the region, seen as an effort to intimidate opposition against hydroelectric dams in the region (Branford, 2013). High-profile members of the opposition against Belo Monte, such as Dom Erwin Kräutler and Melo (Nascimento, 2015; Vieira, 2016) faced threats of violence from unknown parties. Melo has, in response to such threats, installed metal bars on the windows of her home (Interview, 16 September 2017).[3]

Furthermore, these methods stifling dissent were not always explicit and obvious – they were also covert. In February 2013, a man who later admitted to having been hired by the Consórcio Construtor Belo Monte was found recording a meeting of Xingu Vivo (MXVPS, 2013; FIDH, 2014).[4] Similarly, the journalist Ruy Sposati (2013) accused the government of directing the Agência Brasileira de Inteligência (Brazilian Intelligence Agency, ABIN) to conduct surveillance on indigenous leaders and NGOs engaged in opposition to the Belo Monte and São Luiz do Tapajós projects. Resistance materials provided evidence to support Sposati's claim, with ISA reporting on how ABIN had identified a list of international NGOs working in Brazil for investigation (Amorim, 2011). These included Amazon Watch, International Rivers, Greenpeace, AIDA, Friends of the Earth, and WWF (Amorim, 2011).

For many, this criminalisation and exclusion harked back to the history of intimidation and violence of the military junta (Interview, 3 October 2016; Interview, 3 October 2016; Interview, 27 October 2016b). Both Xingu Vivo and the MAB presented the 2011 discovery of their meeting being recorded as an example of the increased criminalisation of the resistance movement, with the organisation making direct allusions to the experience of many activists during the military dictatorship (MAB, 2014; MXVPS, 2014; CDDH, 2017). An interviewee from a Brazilian EO explained that 'the way Belo Monte was implemented … is very similar to the way that the military dictatorship implemented the other infrastructure projects in the [19]70s in that same region' (Interview, 3 November 2016b). Despite her social-democratic politics and background, Dilma was often accused in opposition materials of reproducing the same circumvention of democracy as that associated with the military dictatorship (Aliança dos Rios da Amazônia et al., 2011; MAB, 2014; MXVPS, 2014). An open letter, written to Dilma by Xingu Vivo, argued that the president had demonstrated that she had got Belo Monte built by circumventing both Brazilian law and norms of justice, dislocating their lives and failing to hear their grievances (MXVPS, 2016).

The comparisons between the hydroelectric dams of the PT and the history of the military junta in Brazil function not only to repoliticise the projects studied by illuminating the political interests that underpinned and drove the Belo Monte and São Luiz do Tapajós Dams forward but also to shed light on the tactics of these actors. In a 2009 meeting in Altamira, Lula promised that 'Belo Monte will not be shoved down anyone's throat' (International Rivers, 2009); the president's failure to keep this promise provided a central narrative device for civil society opposition to the project, with numerous interviewees highlighting the different ways that Lula, Dilma, and other pro-dam actors had, instead, sought to circumvent dissent and force Belo Monte through regardless. A 2010 letter signed by numerous NGOs and EOs argued that:

> Regardless of the concerns from your fellow Brazilians and your earlier promises to them, we see that your government indeed intends to *shove Belo Monte*

down the throats of the directly affected Indigenous and riverine communities in the Amazon.

(Poirier, 2010, italics my own)

Within anti-dam storylines, pro-dam actors are presented as circumventing the judiciary, intimidating the opposition, and ignoring dissenting opinions. However, a key part of the repoliticisation of the projects comes in the exposure of what anti-dam actors present as the logic behind this behaviour and impunity. It is to this that I turn below.

Lava Jato

In 2008, Hermes Magnus, a businessman in the Itaim Bibi neighbourhood in the western area of São Paulo, reported suspicious financial activity, understood to be an attempt to launder money through his manufacturing company, Dunel Indústria e Comércio. The subsequent investigation provided those opposing the Belo Monte and São Luiz do Tapajós projects with a route to understanding why pro-dam actors had been so focused on pursuing these projects, as well as the dominant terrain upon which the projects became repoliticised, with hydroelectric projects in Brazil becoming linked to an extensive scheme of corruption. One of the first to be imprisoned by the Lava Jato investigation was Paulo Roberto Costa, the former director of supply at Petrobras (2004–2012), for irregularities linked to the purchase of an oil refinery in Pasadena, Texas in 2006. Costa later revealed that the irregularities surrounding the Pasadena purchase were linked to a wider, more complex scheme of corruption that provided kickbacks, funded by over-invoicing, from Brazilian state institutions to politicians. The resulting investigations led to the identification of a vast money-laundering ring that, over time, implicated national construction companies, public corporations, and politicians from numerous congressional parties, including Lula himself.[5]

The Lava Jato ('Car Wash') investigation, so named because it originated in an investigation into the Posto da Torre car wash in Brasília, uncovered a network of bribery, corruption, and money laundering spanning 12 countries that was estimated to have involved R$6.4–42.8 billion (US$2–13 billion) of public funds (Superintendência Regional De Polícia Federal no Paraná, 2015). The enquiry uncovered an extensive scheme of corruption centred on the semi-public oil company, Petróleo Brasileiro SA (Petrobras), where executives were allegedly paid bribes to award contracts to favoured construction companies. This money would be funnelled to politicians, funding election campaigns that kept the governing coalition in power. The resulting investigation ensnared the largest construction companies in Brazil (such as Camargo Corrêa, Odebrecht, Queiroz Galvão, and Andrade Gutierrez) and several political parties in government during the years of Lula and Dilma's presidencies, such as the PT, the Partido Progressista (Progressive Party, PP), and the Partido do Movimento Democrático Brasileiro (Brazilian Democratic Movement Party, PMDB). By 2019, after five years of investigations, the Lava Jato investigation, led by the then-Federal

Justice of Curitiba, Sergio Moro,[6] had resulted in 155 convictions totalling 2,242 years and 5 days (Schmitt, 2019). An additional 426 people were denounced by prosecutors (Schmitt, 2019). When Lava Jato began in 2014, there were fewer than 10,000 electronic tag anklets used to monitor home detentions in Brazil; by September 2017, that number had increased to over 24,000 (Whitefield, 2017). The judges and prosecutors presiding over the cases became national figures, with Newton Ishii, a police officer who regularly escorted suspects to and from courthouses, memorialised with a 6-m-high effigy at the 2017 Rio de Janeiro Carnival (Watts, 2017).

As the Lava Jato investigation became one of the premier issues in contemporary Brazilian politics, confessions and plea bargains provided by those implicated in the scandal signalled that Belo Monte was a key site of this corruption. Former Minister Antônio Palocci, João Vaccari Neto, and Edison Lobão (PMDB, then Minister of Mines and Energy) were all implicated in the payment of bribes related to the Belo Monte project (Carvalho and Dantas, 2016). In 2015, the CEO of Camargo Corrêa, Dalton Avancini, testified that the company paid over R$100 million in bribes to obtain the construction contracts for the Belo Monte plant (Freire, 2015). Avancini's testimony reveals that both the PT and PMDB received sums equal to 1% of the total value of the construction contracts awarded to Camargo Corrêa (totalling R$5.1 billion), only one of ten construction firms working at the site (Freire, 2015).

The exposure of this corruption constituted a key site in the resistance against Belo Monte, allowing it to develop a wider resonance in a Brazilian society already protesting corruption. The corruption scandal was not news to many of those opposing Belo Monte. The closeness of the relationships within the pro-dam coalition was criticised by anti-dam activists long before plea bargains provided evidence of corruption. As early as 2010, Zachary Hurwitz (2011), an activist for International Rivers, coined the term 'hydro-mafia' to describe the ways in which big construction companies in Brazil neglected regulations yet continued to receive extensive state subsidies. In a letter the same year, congratulating Dilma on her election as president, Xingu Vivo and numerous other anti-dam movements challenged the close relationship of those in government and construction companies, such as Odebrecht, Camargo Corrêa and Andrade Gutierrez, juxtaposing the impact of Belo Monte with what was described as 'relações promíscuas' ('promiscuous relationship') between these actors (Aliança dos Rios da Amazônia et al., 2011).

For anti-dam activists in Brazil, the uncovering of these relações promíscuas highlighted the reasons why the government had neglected grievances and demands related to social justice and environmental sustainability while ensuring the 'steamroller' behind dam projects continued moving forward at all costs (Aliança dos Rios da Amazônia et al., 2011). For many, the construction of large infrastructure projects such as Belo Monte and São Luiz do Tapajós represented a moment of alignment to sustain this political–institutional relationship, with these links creating the environment that allowed (and emboldened) the circumvention of dissent discussed in the previous section (Interview, 3 October

2016; Interview, 19 October 2016; Interview, 1 December 2016a; Interview, 28 April 2017). Evidence for such a claim can be found in the volume of political campaign contributions made by construction companies. Of the top ten donors to political parties during the 2014 presidential election, five were construction companies, including Andrade Gutierrez (which donated R$33 million), Queiroz Galvão (R$25 million), and Odebrecht (R$23 million) (De Toledo et al., 2014). These contributions were subsequently used in Dilma's 2014 electoral campaigns (Reuters, 2016). One interviewee said that this relationship explains 'the high priority for Belo Monte and the tremendous personal involvement of both of these presidents [Lula and Dilma] in forcing this through' (Interview, 1 December 2016a). For anti-dam actors, the construction of hydroelectric dams came to represent the corrupt relationship between construction companies and the PT government, which pushed projects forward with little concern for dissent, as a means of securing financial support from the construction companies subsequently contracted to build such projects.

The links between Belo Monte and Lava Jato received increasing coverage in both national and international media reporting on the project (Calixto, 2016; Chayes, 2017; O Globo, 2017). Although anti-dam activists had reported on potential corruption in the Belo Monte project, it was not until the exposure of the scandal by the Lava Jato investigation that public opinion turned against Belo Monte (Sakamoto, 2016). One interviewee, based at a domestic human rights NGO explained, 'We have been calling everybody's attention to that, but nobody heard that until the Lava Jato came and [everybody] started to find out [about the] crimes and corruption' (Interview, 3 October 2016). It was by drawing attention to this close relationship between political and commercial actors that the resistance coalition was able to put forward a storyline that repoliticised the Belo Monte and São Luiz do Tapajós projects by characterising their planning and construction as an 'opportunity for corruption' (Interview, 18 October 2016) within the pro-dam coalition. As an interviewee from Amazon Watch argued, the project was constructed as a corrupt enterprise designed to benefit the few: 'This project was perhaps not only a source of corruption, it was perhaps built because of corruption' (Interview, 28 April 2017). Within this anti-dam storyline, the projects became the sites of the corruption and impunity of a pro-dam coalition intent on construction regardless of the consequences.

Jornadas de Junho

The re-election of Dilma as president in 2014 occurred in the aftermath of a series of protests that took hold of Brazil in the summer months of 2013. On 1 June 2013, protests broke out in São Paulo to contest a series of rises in the cost of public transport in the city. Police repression of the initial mobilisation resulted in national attention, extensive media support, and a dramatic increase in the numbers of those protesting (Saad-Filho, 2013). These protests, known as the Jornadas de Junho (June Journeys), involved a diversity of actors expressing a variety of grievances and demands, voicing dissent about public services and the rising costs of transportation, the staging of the football World Cup and Olympics megaprojects in Rio de Janeiro (2014 and 2016, respectively), and the political status quo. Despite the massive expansion of social programmes of the PT and Lula enjoying approval ratings of over 70% when leaving office, the Jornadas de Junho (June Journeys) protests represented widespread popular dissatisfaction with the political program of the PT, which focused on addressing some economic problems while not fundamentally seeking to rebalance the inequity of power in Brazil (Baletti, 2016).

The Lava Jato scandal and the June Journeys led to a decline in Dilma's popularity ratings, placing the PT-led coalition government at risk. At the start of her second term as president, with Lula being arrested by Lava Jato and amid a growing economic crisis, Dilma sought to rebuild a political coalition with opposition parties (Doval and Actis, 2016). To do so, she elevated the vice president, Michel Temer (Partido da Social Democracia Brasileira, PSDB), to a more prominent position in designing, implementing, and presenting government policy – particularly economic policy. This led to a series of policy changes in Dilma's second term (2015–2016), with social policies giving way to public spending efficiency savings and the increased importance of the private sector (Doval and Actis, 2016). Numerous social programmes were affected, with the popular social housing programme, Minha Casa, Minha Vida being rolled back, with its budget cut by R$4.8 billion in September 2015 (Nascimento, 2015). With the PT government of Dilma Rousseff engaged in the process of austerity and budget-cutting, Brazilian civil society and social movements began to voice discontent. For example, Vagner Freitas, the president of the CUT, argued that 'Rousseff's economic agenda is the same as that of the candidate of the right we defeated at the ballot box in October' (Gosman, 2015).

While the coalition between the PT and social movements and civil society retained prominence in the face of the Lava Jato investigation, by the beginning of her second period in office Dilma Rousseff struggled to secure the support of the social movements which had previously thrown their weight behind Lula (Branford and Rocha, 2015). In the wake of the 2013 movements, social movement actors adopted new storylines and demands, resulting in the further polarisation of Brazilian politics and society (Bringel, 2016). Protests became linked to numerous urban and rural protests and struggles that had already been occurring throughout the decades of the PT government, including those driven by indigenous and traditional communities resisting the intensification of mining, agriculture, and dam-building activities in their territories (Baletti, 2016).

It is within this context that hydroelectric dams in Brazil ceased to be a 'set-piece' of the PT's development policies and became a symbol of the social and environmental impact of the infrastructure projects of the government – and of the relative impunity, circumvention, and neglect of dissent and corruption that accompanied such projects. If Belo Monte was to be a symbol of Dilma's presidency, it was re-cast as a representation of its demise. As Amazon Watch argued in March 2016:

> Time and again Brazil's courts halted its construction and operation only to be ignored or overruled as the Dilma administration pressed on in its relentless efforts to make the Belo Monte monstrosity a symbol of her administration. Ironically, it has now become a symbol of her administration's corruption.
>
> (Amazon Watch, 2016)

On the 2 December 2015, Eduardo Cunha, the president of the Chamber of Deputies of Brazil, opened the proceedings that ultimately led to the impeachment of President Dilma Rousseff. On 31 August 2016, senators took to the Senate floor to denounce or defend Dilma, ultimately voting 61–20 in favour of impeachment. The president was deemed to have broken federal laws surrounding budget processes, and she was removed from office, to be replaced by Temer. During this process of impeachment, some opposition figures were quick to support the PT government. Interviewees labelled the impeachment a 'coup,' describing the illegality of the subsequent government of Michel Temer (2016–2019) (Interview, 3 October 2016; Interview, 28 April 2017). However, many civil society activists interviewed found it difficult to support the government that had been linked to the construction of Belo Monte and the corruption uncovered by the Lava Jato investigation. As one activist in São Paulo interviewed in October 2016 explained to me:

> there was a window of opportunity [to support the PT], which we did not seize when we could, which is because of these clear linkages between corruption and big projects ... [This was] a choice.
>
> (Interview, 27 October 2016b)

Rather than springing to Dilma's defence (as the MAB did), many activists stayed away. The construction of hydropower in the Brazilian Amazon that they had resisted for years had provided an example of the persistent tensions between the development policies of the Partido dos Trabalhadores and social and environmental protection. The exposure of corruption and outpouring of dissent resulted in numerous social movements, previously allied to the PT, distancing themselves from government policies (Baletti, 2016; Loureiro and Saad-Filho, 2018).

Conclusion

I have argued in this chapter that, for many opposed to the Belo Monte and São Luiz do Tapajós projects, the planning and construction of dams in the Brazilian Amazon represented the narrow interests of political and commercial actors engaged in corrupt behaviour. At the core of the contestation over the Belo Monte and São Luiz do Tapajós Dam projects lays the continued tension between this view of development and progress and the demands and grievances of both indigenous communities and environmentalist groups. The use of security suspensions, the criminalisation of opposition and the circumvention of dissent are all presented as tactics adopted by pro-dam actors to ensure that the dam projects studied would be constructed, regardless of the costs.

This represents a process of repoliticisation – in which the resistance storyline illuminates the political actors, interests, and impunity surrounding the Belo Monte and São Luiz do Tapajós projects. The links between the corruption scandal and the projects studied were not merely highlighted but, instead, the projects were defined as the direct result of a corrupt political–commercial alliance. In foregrounding these projects within the economic policies of the PT government, the resistance coalition illuminated the political character of the Belo Monte and São Luiz do Tapajós projects and highlighted the political interests that underpinned their planning and construction. The pro-dam storyline of sustainability was presented as merely a legitimising device, forwarded by the pro-dam coalition to generate support for hydroelectric schemes in the Brazilian Amazon. For many interviewed, corruption not only led to Belo Monte's construction but also drove it forward, regardless of its social or environmental impact (Interview, 3 October 2016; Interview, 19 October 2016; Interview, 27 October 2016b).

In highlighting this political commitment to the Belo Monte and São Luiz do Tapajós projects, opposition figures challenge the storyline of sustainability put forward by pro-dam actors by repoliticising the respective projects and arguing that the political interests supporting the project had done so with little concern for the social and environmental impact of its construction (Interview, 3 October 2016; Interview, 19 October 2016; Interview, 27 October 2016b). As an interviewee at Amazon Watch argued: 'The environmental laws [and] human rights standards that are written into either legislation or [the Brazilian] Constitution were being bulldozed to expedite this project' (Interview, 28 April 2017). The pro-dam storyline of sustainability was critiqued and positioned by anti-dam actors as legitimising the construction of a dam and the corrupt practices that surrounded it. As one interviewee argued, the storyline of sustainability 'smacked of a pretence … to run the project forward for the benefit of the companies who are building it … and the politicians who were making sure that it [Belo Monte] moves forward by hook or by crook' (Interview, 1 February 2017). Rather than representing 'clean' and 'green' energy, the assertions of sustainability by pro-dam actors were characterised as:

> A political tool … a communications tool, a propaganda tool to try to convince not just [the] Brazilian public but foreign investors that this is a good idea … It's providing political cover to what is, in fact, an enormous fraud.
> (Interview, 28 April 2017)

As discussed in this chapter, the pro-dam steamroller that forced the projects forward, regardless of the impact, depoliticised the projects studied, raising them above dissent and challenge and neglecting the project's social and environmental impacts. The illumination of the impact of Belo Monte and São Luiz do Tapajós, respectively, provided a key route of opposition for the resistance coalition, who put forward storylines to not only highlight social issues and the environmental damage caused by hydroelectric dams but also challenge the environmental licensing process. It is to this that I turn in the next chapter.

Notes

1 Historically, the PT defined itself as ideologically 'socialist,' however, this was an open-ended commitment, allowing for the presence of various tendencies, demands and grievances within the party. Such a broad platform allowed it to develop an extensive opposition programme to the policies of President Fernando Henrique Cardoso (1995–2003) (Guidry, 2003).
2 The party experienced a change from the mid-1990s onwards, becoming professionalised and reorganised around electoral apparatuses and success, rather than organising and communication of social movement demands (Vieira, 2012). Voluntary political activists, who had previously enjoyed a central role, ceased to be a central part of the party apparatus, replaced by full-time professionals – lawyers, professors or public employees. Radical rhetoric was superseded by a more moderate, inclusive political message (Ribeiro, 2014). The election of Lula in 2002, secured with more than 52 million votes (62% of the total number of valid votes), was the culmination of such a process, blending the two 'souls' of the party into a coalition focused on social inclusion and improved living standards (Singer, 2010).
3 Violence has previously claimed the lives of activists in the region, with the 2001 assassination of Ademir Alfeu Federicci (Dema), a leader of the opposition to the Kararaô and Belo Monte project, and both Nicinha de Souza Magalhães, a prominent opponent to the Madeira River dams in Rondônia and Luis Alberto Araújo, the Altamira Municipal Secretary of Environment, both murdered in 2016.
4 The discovery of surveillance at the Xingu meeting resulted in a great deal of suspicion of outsiders within local resistance movements. This was evident in how one group, campaigning against the São Luiz do Tapajós project accused me of being a spy for the Grupo do Estudos Tapajós (personal communication). Although these concerns were eventually allayed, this episode represents the degree of suspicion held by local resistance groups towards those deemed 'outsiders' to the contemporary resistance movement. It provided a topic of humour for others. At the offices of a domestic NGO in Rio de Janeiro, an interview was interrupted by the repeated drilling into a wall in a nearby office. After the fourth occurrence of this noise, an interviewee joked 'I think that they are from Odebrecht,' a construction company implicated in the 2011 recording of a Xingu Vivo meeting (Interview, 3 October 2016).
5 In April 2015, the Federal Public Ministry of Brazil opened up an investigation into accusations of influence-peddling against Lula. He was accused of lobbying for government contracts in Ghana, Angola and the Dominican Republic, among others, for Odebrecht and of lobbying for BNDES funding for the resulting projects (Bronzatto and Coutinho, 2015). Lula's home in São Paulo was raided by authorities in March the following year. Prosecutors filed corruption charges against him on 14 September 2016. He was found guilty of accepting R$3.7 million in bribes (US$1.2 million), in the form of home improvements to his beachfront house, and was jailed. His appeal against the judgement was rejected in 2018. Lula left prison in November 2018. In June 2019, *The Intercept* published leaked messages between the judge in Lula's case, Sérgio Moro, and Deltan Dallagnol, the lead prosecutor in the *Lava Jato* investigation, in which they are alleged to have conspired to convict Lula to prevent his running as a presidential candidate in the 2018 election (won by Jair Bolsonaro) (Greenwald and Pougy, 2019).
6 Moro later served as the Minister of Justice and Public Security (2019-20) in the administration of President Jair Bolsonaro (2019–).

Bibliography

Adams, F. (2013). 'Trataram a gente igual bicho,' denúncia operário de Belo Monte. *Movimento dos Atingidos por Barragens*, 17 October. Available at: http://www.mabnacional.org.br/noticia/trataram-gente-igual-bicho-denuncia-oper-rio-belo-monte (Accessed: 8 January 2020).

Aliança dos Rios da Amazônia, Movimento Xingu Vivo para Sempre, Aliança Tapajós Vivo, Movimento Teles Pires Vivo, Campanha Popular Viva o Rio Madeira Vivo, Coordenação das Organizações Indígenas da Amazônia Brasileira and Movimento dos Atingidos por Barragens (2011). Carta a Aliança em Defesa dos Rios Amazônicos o Presidente Dilma. *International Rivers*, 8 February 2011. Available at: https://www.internationalrivers.org/pt-br/resources/carta-a-aliança-em-defesa-dos-rios-amazônicos-o-presidente-dilma-3076 (Accessed: 8 January 2020).

Amazon Watch (2016). Belo Monte a symbol of obscene destruction and corruption in Brazil. *Amazon Watch*, 17 March. Available at: https://amazonwatch.org/news/2016/0317-belo-monte-a-symbol-of-obscene-destruction-and-corruption-in-brazil (Accessed: 8 January 2020).

Amorim, PH (2011). ABIN identifica as ONGs estrangeiras que boicotam Belo Monte. *Conversa Afiada*, 5 July. Available at: https://www.conversaafiada.com.br/politica/2011/07/05/abin-identifica-as-ongs-estrangeiras-que-boicotam-belo-monte (Accessed: 8 January 2020).

Angelo, C (2010). PT tenta apagar fama 'antiverde' de Dilma. *Folha de S.Paulo*, 10 October. Available at: https://www1.folha.uol.com.br/poder/812470-pt-tenta-apagar-fama-antiverde-de-dilma.shtml (Accessed: 8 January 2020).

Associação Internacional de Direito de Seguros (2018). Inter-American Commission urges Brazil to address damages to indigenous peoples caused by Belo Monte Dam. *AIDA*, 13 November. Available at: https://aida-americas.org/en/press/inter-american-commission-urges-brazil-address-damages-to-indigenous-peoples-caused-by-belo-monte (Accessed: 16 July 2019).

Atkins, E (2019). Disputing the 'national interest': the depoliticization and repoliticization of the Belo Monte Dam, Brazil. *Water*, 11(1: 103).

Baiocchi, G (2004). The party and the multitude: Brazil s Workers Party (PT) and the challenges of building a just social order in a globalizing context. *Journal of World-Systems Research*, 10(1): 199–215.

Baletti, B (2016). Toward the worker state, or working for the state? Reorganization of political antagonisms in the Brazilian Amazon. *Latin American Perspectives*, 43(2): 22–47.

Blasberg, M, and Gluesing, J (2016). Brazil's Olympic-sized political headache. *Spiegel International*, 4 August. Available at: https://www.spiegel.de/international/world/a-visit-with-dilma-rousseff-on-eve-of-the-rio-olympics-in-brazil-a-1105811.html (Accessed: 8 January 2020).

Bornhausen, P (2010). *Diário da Câmara dos Deputados, ANO LXV N° 51 (15/04/2010)*. Brasilia: Câmara dos Deputados.

Bragança, D (2016). Dilma inaugura Belo Monte, maior obra do seu governo. OECO, 6 May. Available at: https://www.oeco.org.br/noticias/dilma-inaugura-belo-monte-maior-obra-do-seu-governo/ (Accessed: 8 January 2020).

Branford, S (2013). Prontos para resistir. In: Amaral, M (ed.) *Amazônia Pública*. São Paulo: Pública.

Branford, S, and Rocha, J (2015). *Brazil under the Workers Party: From Euphoria to Despair*. Rugby: Practical Action Publishing.

Bringel, B (2016). 2013-2016: polarization and protests in Brazil. *Open Democracy*, 18 February. Available at: https://www.opendemocracy.net/en/democraciaabierta/2013-2016-polarization-and-protests-in-brazil/ (Accessed: 8 January 2020).

Bronzatto, T, and Coutinho, F (2015). As suspeitas de tráfico de influência internacional sobre o ex-presidente Lula. *Epoca*, 30 April. Available at: https://epoca.globo.com/tempo/noticia/2015/04/suspeitas-de-trafico-de-influencia-internacional-sobre-o-ex-presidente-lula.html (Accessed: 8 January 2020).

Brum, E (2015). Belo Monte, empreiteiras e espelhinhos. *El Pais*, 7 July. Available at: https://brasil.elpais.com/brasil/2015/07/06/opinion/1436195768_857181.html (Accessed: 30 March 2020).

Brum, E (2019). *The Collector of Leftover Souls*. Translated from Portuguese by Diane Grosklaus Whitty. London: Granta.

Calixto, B (2016). A corrupção nas obras de Belo Monte – segundo a delação de Delcídio. *Epoca*, 15 March. Available at: https://epoca.globo.com/colunas-e-blogs/blog-do-planeta/noticia/2016/03/corrupcao-nas-obras-de-belo-monte-segundo-delacao-de-delcidio.html (Accessed: 8 January 2020).

Carvalho, C, and Dantas, D (2016). Palocci negociou propina de Belo Monte para PT e PMDB, diz delator. *O Globo*, 31 October. Available at: https://oglobo.globo.com/brasil/palocci-negociou-propina-de-belo-monte-para-pt-pmdb-diz-delator-20390567 (Accessed: 8 January 2020).

Chayes, S (2017). A hidden cost of corruption: environmental devastation. *The Washington Post*, 16 June. Available at: https://www.washingtonpost.com/outlook/a-hidden-cost-of-corruption-environmental-devastation/2017/06/16/03f93c1e-52b8-11e7-b064-828ba60fbb98_story.html?utm_term=.e3995169b07a (Accessed: 8 January 2020).

Comitê Brasileiro de Defensoras e Defensores de Direitos Humanos (CDDH) (2017). *Vidas em Luta Criminalização e Violência Contra Defensoras e Defensores de Direitos Humanos no Brasil*. Curitiba: CIDH. Available at: https://pdfs.semanticscholar.org/a26f/0c22df6d02d156c65af315e3dd3ee4055119.pdf.

de Oliveira, GJ (n.d.) 'A suspensão de segurança e as cláusulas pétreas da constituiçao.' Available at: https://ajufesc.org.br/wp-content/uploads/2017/02/Gelson-Jorge-de-Oliveira.pdf (Accessed: 30 March 2020).

de Toledo, JR, Burgarelli, R, and Bramatti, D (2014). Doações de campanha somam R$1bi, das quais metade vem de 19 empresas. *O Estado de S. Paulo*, 15 September. Available at: https://politica.estadao.com.br/noticias/geral,doacoes-de-campanha-somam-r-1-bi-das-quais-metade-vem-de-19-empresas-imp-,1560289 (Accessed: 8 January 2020).

Doval, GP, and Actis, E (2016). The political and economic instability of Dilma Rousseff's second government in Brazil: between impeachment and the pragmatic turn. *India Quarterly*, 72(2): 120–131.

Eren, A (2017). The political ecology of uncertainty: the production of truth by juridical practices in hydropower development. *Journal of Political Ecology*, 24: 386–405.

Fédération Internationale Pour Les Droits Humains (2014). Vale e Belo Monte sob suspeita de espionagem: a justiça tem que investigar. *Fédération Internationale Pour Les Droits Humains*, 17 February. Available at: https://www.fidh.org/pt/americas/brasil/14676-brasil-vale-e-belo-monte-sob-suspeita-de-espionagem-a-justica-tem-que (Accessed: 8 January 2020).

Fleury, LC (2014). Belo Monte e o 'interesse nacional': Entre ações civis públicas, suspensões de segurança e o estado de exceção. Presented at *29ª Reunião Brasileira de Antropologia*. Natal, RN. Available at: http://www.29rba.abant.org.br/resources/anais

/1/1402504521_ARQUIVO_2014_ABA_LorenaFleury_BeloMonteeoestadodeex cecao.pdf.
Freire, F (2015). Delator dirá que Camargo Corrêa pagou R$100 milhões em propina para PT e PMDB em Belo Monte. *O Globo*, 6 March. Available at: https://oglobo.globo.com/brasil/delator-dira-que-camargo-correa-pagou-100-milhoes-em-propina-para-pt-pmdb-em-belo-monte-15521906 (Accessed: 8 January 2020).
French, J, and Fortes, A (2012). Nurturing hope, deepening democracy, and combating inequalities in Brazil: Lula, the Workers' Party, and Dilma Rousseff's 2010 election as President. *Labor Studies in Working-Class History of the Americas*, 9(1): 7–28.
G1 PA (2014). Dilma visita obras de Belo Monte e faz campanha no Pará. *G1*, 5 August. Available at: http://g1.globo.com/pa/para/eleicoes/2014/noticia/2014/08/dilma-roussef-visita-obras-de-belo-monte-e-faz-campanha-no-para.html (Accessed: 8 January 2020).
Gómez Bruera, HF (2015). *Lula, the Workers' Party and the Governability Dilemma in Brazil*. Abingdon: Routledge.
Gosman, E (2015). Rechazo al rumbo económico de Dilma Rousseff. *Clarin Mundo*, 29 May. Available at: https://www.clarin.com/mundo/brasil-ajuste-dilma_rousseff-tercerizacion_0_H1geWsuFwml.html (Accessed: 8 January 2020).
Greenwald, G, and Pougy, V (2019). Hidden plot: Brazil's top prosecutors who indicted Lula schemed in secret messages to prevent his party from winning 2018 election. *The Intercept*, 9 June. Available at: https://theintercept.com/2019/06/09/brazil-car-wash-prosecutors-workers-party-lula/ (Accessed: 22 July 2020).
Guidry, JA (2003). Not just another labor party: the Workers' Party and democracy in Brazil. *Labor Studies Journal*, 28(1): 83–108.
Hochstetler, K (2011). The politics of environmental licensing: energy projects of the past and future in Brazil. *Studies in Comparative International Development*, 46(4): 349–371. doi: 10.1007/s12116-011-9092-1.
Hochstetler, K, and Keck, ME (2007). *Greening Brazil: Environmental Activism in State and Society*. Durham, NC: Duke University Press.
Hunter, W (2010). *The Transformation of the Workers' Party in Brazil, 1989–2009*. Cambridge: Cambridge University Press.
Hurwitz, Z (2011). IBAMA president resigns over Belo Monte licensing. *International Rivers*, 13 January. Available at: https://www.internationalrivers.org/blogs/258/ibama-president-resigns-over-belo-monte-licensing (Accessed: 8 January 2020).
Inter-American Commission on Human Rights (2011). *Comuidades indigenas da Bacia do Rio Xingu, Pará (MC-382-10)*. Washington, DC: Inter-American Commission on Human Rights. Available at: http://www.xinguvivo.org.br/wp-content/uploads/2010/10/Carta_otorgamiento_corregida_peticionario1.pdf.
International Rivers (2009). Lula promises not to shove Belo Monte down our throats. *International Rivers*, 27 July. Available at: www.internationalrivers.org/blogs/232/lula-promises-not-to-shove-belo-monte-down-our-throats (Accessed: 8 January 2020).
Justiça Global, Justiça nos Trilhos, Sociedade Paraense de Direitos Humanos, Terra de Direitos, Instituto Socioambiental, Asociación Interamericana para la Defensa Del Ambiente, International Rivers (2014). *Situação do Direito ao Acesso à Justiça e a Suspensão de Decisões Judiciais (Ação de Suspensão de Segurança) no Brasil*. Rio de Janeiro: Justiça Global. Available at: http://global.org.br/wp-content/uploads/2016/03/Acesso----Justica-no-Brasil-Suspens--o-de-Seguran--a-Final.pdf
Loureiro, PM, and Saad-Filho, A (2018). The limits of pragmatism: the rise and fall of the Brazilian Workers' Party (2002–2016). *Latin American Perspectives*, 46(1): 66–84.

Marsiglia, I (2013). O futuro que passou. *O Estado de S. Paulo*, 22 June. Available at: https ://www.estadao.com.br/noticias/geral,o-futuro-que-passou,1045705 (Accessed: 10 July 2018).

Matoso, F (2015). Governo Dilma tem aprovação de 9%, aponta pesquisa Ibope. *G1*, 1 July. Available at: https://web.archive.org/web/20170108192305/http://g1.globo.com /politica/noticia/2015/07/governo-dilma-tem-aprovacao-de-9-aponta-pesquisa-ibope .html (Accessed: 8 January 2020).

Millikan, B (2014). The Amazon: dirty dams, dirty politics and the myth of clean energy. *Tipití: Journal of the Society for the Anthropology of Lowland South America*, 12(2): 134–138.

Ministério Público Federal, Procuradoria da República no Pará (2014). Indígenas denunciam agressões no canteiro de Belo Monte. *Ministério Público Federal*, 26 May. Available at: http://www.mpf.mp.br/pa/sala-de-imprensa/noticias-pa/indigenas-de nunciam-agressoes-no-canteiro-de-belo-monte (Accessed: 8 January 2020).

Mongabay (2011). Brazil's environment chief resigns over controversial Amazon dam. *Mongabay*, 14 January. Available at: https://news.mongabay.com/2011/01/brazils-env ironment-chief-resigns-over-controversial-amazon-dam/ (Accessed: 9 January 2020).

Monteiro, T (2016). Lula, Belo Monte e a Lava Jato II. *Telma Monteiro Blog*, 19 September. Available at: https://www.telmadmonteiro.com/2016/09/lula-belo-monte-e-lava-jat o-ii.html (Accessed: 8 January 2020).

Movimentos dos Atingidos por Barragens (2014). Lula, Dilma e o Cavalo de pau. *Movimento dos Atingidos por Barragens*, 22 April. Available at: http://www.mabnacion al.org.br/noticia/lula-dilma-e-cavalo-pau (Accessed: 8 January 2020).

Movimento Xingu Vivo para Sempre (MXVPS) (2014). Xingu Vivo, No 50o aniversário do Golpe, ação pede condenação da Abin e de Belo Monte por espionagem. *Xingu Vivo para Sempre*, 1 April. Available at: http://www.xinguvivo.org.br/2014/04/01/no-50o -aniversario-do-golpe-acao-pede-condenacao-da-abin-e-de-belo-monte-por-espionage m/ (Accessed: 9 January 2020).

MXVPS (2013). Xingu Vivo é alvo de novo ato de repressão em Altamira. *Xingu Vivo para Sempre*, 14 March. Available at: http://www.xinguvivo.org.br/2013/03/14/xingu-vivo-e-alvo-de-novo-ato-de-repressao-em-altamira/ (Accessed: 9 January 2020).

MXVPS (2016). Fazem com você o que você fez conosco; mas nem assim, Dilma. *Xingu Vivo para Sempre*, 5 May. Available at: https://xinguvivo.org.br/2016/05/05/fazem-com -voce-o-que-voce-fez-conosco-mas-nem-assim-dilma/ (Accessed: 30 March 2020).

Nascimento, L (2015). Governo vai reduzir R$ 4,8 bilhões do Programa Minha Casa, Minha Vida. *Agencia Brasil*, 14 September. Available at: http://agenciabrasil.ebc.com.b r/economia/noticia/2015-09/governo-vai-reduzir-r-48-bilhoes-do-programa-minha-ca sa-minha-vida (Accessed: 9 January 2020).

Nascimento, S (2015). Antônia Melo, liderança do Movimento Xingu Vivo para Sempre. *DR*, Issue 2. Available at: http://www.revistadr.com.br/posts/antonia-melo-lideranc a-do-movimento-xingu-vivo-para-sempre (Accessed: 8 January 2020).

Nery, N (2011). Dilma retalia OEA por Belo Monte e suspende recursos. *Folha de S.Paulo*, 30 April. Available at: https://www1.folha.uol.com.br/fsp/mercado/me3004201117. htm (Accessed: 8 January 2020).

O Globo (2017). Odebrecht só fez Belo Monte e Itaquerão por pedido de Lula a Emílio. *O Globo*, 1 May. Available at: https://oglobo.globo.com/brasil/odebrecht-so-fez-belo-m onte-itaquerao-por-pedido-de-lula-emilio-21279782 (Accessed: 8 January 2020).

Oliveira, M (2011). Posição da OEA sobre Belo Monte é 'absurda,' diz subcomissão do Senado. *G1*, 5 April. Available at: http://g1.globo.com/politica/noticia/2011/04/posic

ao-da-oea-sobre-belo-monte-e-absurda-diz-subcomissao-do-senado.html (Accessed: 8 January 2020).
Ottmann, G (2005). What is the PT? Brazil's Workers Party (PT) between formal representative and participatory democracy. *Journal of Iberian and Latin American Research*, 11(2): 93–102.
Pinto, K (2016). Em dia de visita de Dilma, grupo fecha único acesso a Belo Monte. *Folha de S.Paulo*, 5 May. Available at: https://www1.folha.uol.com.br/paywall/login.shtml? https://www1.folha.uol.com.br/poder/2016/05/1768004-em-dia-de-visita-de-dilma-grupo-fecha-unico-acesso-a-belo-monte-no-para.shtml (Accessed: 8 January 2020).
Poirier, C (2010). Letter to President Luiz Inácio Lula da Silva. *Comité Pour Les Droits Humains En Amérique Latine*, 12 March. Available at: https://www.cdhal.org/open-letter-against-belo-monte-hydroelectric-dam-project-xingu-river-brazil/ (Accessed: 8 January 2020).
Pontes Jr, F (2011). Speaking at À margem do Xingu: Vozes não consideradas, 2011. *Rede Brasil Atual*, 15 September. Available at: https://www.redebrasilatual.com.br/ambiente/2011/09/projeto-da-ditadura-militar-belo-monte-significa-o-mesmo-retrocesso-de-30-anos-atras/ (Accessed: 8 January 2020).
Puzone, V, and Miguel, LS (eds) (2019). *The Brazilian Left in the 21st Century: Conflict and Conciliation in Peripheral Capitalism*. London: Palgrave Macmillan.
Reuters (2016). Rousseff benefited from Belo Monte dam graft: report. *Reuters*, 12 March. Available at: https://www.reuters.com/article/us-brazil-corruption-belomonte/brazils-rousseff-benefited-from-belo-monte-dam-graft-report-idUSKCN0WE04U (Accessed: 8 January 2020).
Ribeiro, PF (2014). An amphibian party? Organisational change and adaptation in the Brazilian Workers' Party, 1980–2012. *Journal of Latin American Studies*, 46(1): 87–119.
Saad-Filho, A (2013). Mass protests under 'left neoliberalism': Brazil, June–July 2013. *Critical Sociology*, 39(5): 657–669.
Sakamoto, L (2016). Belo Monte: Antes de denúncias de corrupção, um crime contra a humanidade. *Blog do Sakamoto*, 12 March. Available at: https://blogdosakamoto.blogosfera.uol.com.br/2016/03/12/belo-monte-antes-de-denuncias-de-corrupcao-um-crime-contra-a-humanidade/ (Accessed: 8 January 2020).
Samuels, D (2004). From socialism to social democracy party organization and the transformation of the Workers' Party in Brazil. *Comparative Political Studies*, 37(9): 999–1024.
Santos, LQ, and Gomes, EG (2015). *Suspensão de Segurança: Neodesenvolvimentismo e violações de direitos humanos no Brasil*. Curitiba: Terra de Direitos. Available at: https://terradedireitos.org.br/uploads/arquivos/suspensao-e-seguranca-min.pdf.
Schmitt, G (2019). Em quase cinco anos, Lava-Jato de Curitiba condenou 155 pessoas. *O Globo*, 7 March. Available at: https://oglobo.globo.com/brasil/em-quase-cinco-anos-lava-jato-de-curitiba-condenou-155-pessoas-23506151 (Accessed: 8 January 2020).
Singer, A (2010). A segunda alma do partido dos trabalhadores. *Novos estudos CEBRAP*, 88: 89–111.
Sposati, R (2013). Abin espionou indígenas e ONGs no governo Dilma. *Folha de S. Paulo*, 29 May. Available at: http://www1.folha.uol.com.br/poder/2017/05/1882257-abin-espionou-indigenas-e-ongs-no-governo-dilma.shtml (Accessed: 8 January 2020).
Tribunal Regional Federal da Primeira Região. (2010). *Suspensão de liminar ou antecipação de tutela 0022487-47.2010.4.01.0000/PA*. Belém: PAL Tribunal Regional Federal. Available at: https://aasp.jusbrasil.com.br/noticias/2160403/trf-1-suspensas-as-limi

nares-que-impediam-a-realizacao-do-leilao-de-usina?ref=amp (Accessed: 16 April 2020).

Vieira, M (2016). Belo Monte. 'Um monumento à insanidade.' Entrevista com D. Erwin Kräutler. *IHU-Online*, 5 April. Available at: http://www.ihu.unisinos.br/185-noticias/noticias-2016/553178-belo-monte-um-monumento-a-insanidade-entrevista-com-d-erwin-kraeutler (Accessed: 30 March 2020).

Vieira, R (2012). O transformismo petista: considerações acerca das transformações históricas do Partido dos Trabalhadores no Brasil. *Red de Revistas Científicas de América Latina, el Caribe, España y Portugal*, 17: 1–58. Available at: https://www.redalyc.org/articulo.oa?id=85524080003 (Accessed: 30 March 2020).

Watts, J (2017). Operation Car Wash: is this the biggest corruption scandal in history? *The Guardian*, 1 June. Available at: https://www.theguardian.com/world/2017/jun/01/brazil-operation-car-wash-is-this-the-biggest-corruption-scandal-in-history (Accessed: 8 January 2020).

Whitefield, M (2017). Brazil engulfed in a corruption scandal with plots as convoluted as a telenovela. *Miami Herald*, 5 September. Available at: https://www.miamiherald.com/news/nation-world/world/americas/article171222962.html (Accessed: 8 January 2020).

5 Belo Monstro

The opposition to Belo Monte, is, in many ways, a history of individuals, from the Kayapó warrior, Tuíra raising her machete to the cheek of José Antônio Muniz Lopes at the 1989 Altamira Gathering to the images of Chief Raoni being beamed across the globe; and from the political commitment of the project's proponents to the continued presence of natural scientists, lawyers from the Ministério Público Federal (MPF), and journalists in the resistance coalition. Many retained their prominence throughout the decades-long struggle over the project. Cacique Raoni dominates anti-dam materials from the late 1980s onwards, being photographed with international figures in solidarity, from Sting to Arnold Schwarzenegger.

The centrality of individuals is evident in the prominence of personal experiences and stories of the impact of Belo Monte – with materials distributed by anti-dam actors transmitting accounts and descriptions of people in Altamira leaving their homes to the rising floodwater and picking up the pieces of their former lives (Parracho, 2012; Freeman, 2013; Brum, 2016; Southgate, 2016). In these stories, new figures of the trauma, displacement, and destruction of Belo Monte come to light. The impact of the project is endowed with a human face. The message of many activists is clear: the project irreversibly, traumatically transformed the everyday experience of many Altamirenses (Freeman, 2013; Brum, 2015b; Instituto Socioambiental, 2015a). These experiences were presented to a wider, national, and international audience, whether through globally disseminated films, nationally distributed newspapers, or websites. They illuminated the impact of the project, presented the faces and voices of those left to face them and challenged the belief that hydroelectricity is a sustainable energy source.

Some of these stories are tragedies. When meeting with Norte Energia to discuss compensation, João Pereira da Silva became paralysed and collapsed when hearing the company's offer for the home that he and his wife Raimunda had built (Brum, 2019). João had had a stroke – from which he has not recovered (MPF/PA, 2015). João and Raimunda were displaced by the rising waters of the Xingu in 2015. On 31 August 2015, when visiting to collect the last of their possessions, Raimunda found the house had been burned down by agents working for Norte Energia (Brum, 2019). Other stories are full of strength. Antônia Melo moved to Altamira as a child in 1953. Active in the struggle against Kararaô, she was a founding member of the Movimento Xingu Vivo Para Sempre in 2008, which provides a fulcrum for both local opposition in Altamira and national and international activists visiting the region. Known by many as Dona Antônia, her activism centres around the impact of Belo Monte and securing recognition of how the project impacted the region's indigenous communities. Melo has spoken of her experience and activism at the United Nations and the 2015 Paris Climate Change summit, and in recognition of her activism, she received the Alexander Soros Foundation Award for Environmental and Human Rights Activism in 2017. On 11 September 2015, Dona Antônia was displaced from her home in Altamira, where she had lived since 1970 and raised her four children while working as a teacher. Her displacement was a traumatic experience – a representative of a domestic human rights organisation explained to me how Melo 'literally lost her heart. She had to undergo heart surgery during this whole process [of her displacement]' (Interview, 3 October 2016). Like João Pereira da Silva, Belo Monte took a physical and emotional toll on Antônia Melo's body, along with those of other figures of resistance who became what the prominent Brazilian journalist Eliane Brum (2015c) described as 'victims of an Amazon war.'

In this chapter, I turn my attention to how those opposed to both Belo Monte and São Luiz do Tapajós discuss the projects' social and environmental impacts. I argue that the narrow lens of analysis and definition of impacts evident in pro-dam materials represents a form of depoliticisation, in which the respective projects studied are 'rendered technical' (Li, 2007). Within this process, the validity and significance of impacts are restricted to a narrow band of impacts that were defined and mitigated by communities of experts – while others were excluded. However, this process is contested by the resistance coalition. In response to the dissemination of official environmental impact assessments (EIAs) for the projects studied, activists challenge the project by rendering *visible* impacts that remain undiscussed in official impact assessments. The illumination of these impacts functions to 'scale up' the resistance against the projects to include wider, cumulative, and indirect impacts that are overlooked, forgotten, or neglected in official assessments and illustrate the central role of knowledge in the moments of contestation surrounding the projects studied.

Official assessments

An EIA is a document that determines the impacts of the construction of a project, as well as outlining the necessary acts of mitigation. It plays a central role in the construction of infrastructure and energy projects across the globe – with proponents of schemes preparing the documents to identify potential impacts of construction and design pathways of mitigation. These documents are provided to an authority to determine the approval of the project, as well as any potential conditions and/or mitigation measures to be completed during construction. It is within these documents that potential issues are identified, mitigative measures provided, and the sustainability credentials of a project defined alongside existing environmental policy and regulations.

In Brazil, the development of an EIA contributes to the environmental licensing process, which provides regulatory approval for a project. The process consists of three stages: (1) the Licença Prévia (preliminary licence) approving the location and allowing for the beginning of planning; (2) the Licença de Instalação (construction/installation licence) authorising the start of construction; and (3) the Licença de Operação (operating licence) allowing for the beginning of operations. Both the EIA and the licensing process were instituted by Law 6938/1981 (establishing the National Environmental Policy) and have been subject to additional regulations in the 30 years since. Licences are provided by the Instituto Brasileiro do Meio Ambiente e dos Recursos Naturais Renováveis (IBAMA), with the process open to input from the MPF and the Fundação Nacional do Índio (FUNAI). The companies and interests involved in a respective project submit two documents: the primary Estudo de Impacto Ambiental (EIA) and a shorter, public-facing Relatório de Impacto Ambiental (RIMA) before the provision of the Licença Prévia.

Despite numerous issues – including their delayed use within the licensing process (Ritter et al., 2017) and an absence of discussions of socio-cultural impacts (Hanna et al., 2016) – these documents provide a central stage upon which the sustainability of a project is understood, asserted, and consolidated in the eyes of pro-dam actors. The official EIAs prepared for the respective projects studied are representations of the pro-dam storyline of sustainability, presenting key impacts and prescribing routes of mitigation. A project's approval depends on it securing IBAMA's consent and approval, with IBAMA interrogating projects for both social and environmental impacts. As a result, subsequent approval is understood by pro-dam actors as the consolidation of a project's sustainability credentials. In a 2016 interview, a Project Manager employed by Norte Energia explained that it was not the company that defined the project as *sustainable* but the licensing process itself, arguing that 'the evaluation of the environmental [impacts] … is IBAMA's work … If the government can provide a licence, we are a sustainable project' (Interview, 6 December 2016).

The environmental licensing process, due to its role in assessing social and environmental impacts and approving a particular project, is a key site in the development (and contestation) of the pro-dam storyline of sustainability due to the clarification that a project is being planned and built in accordance with contemporary legislation and norms (Atkins, 2018b). As a result, the granting of a Licença Prévia represents a key moment in the contentious politics that surrounds contemporary dam construction (Devlin and Yap, 2008; Hochstetler, 2011). It is within this process that the struggle between the pro- and resistance coalitions is distilled into a decision. If the pro-dam coalition is successful, the licence is approved, and the project is built. If the resistance coalition is successful, the project is redesigned, mitigative measures are improved, or the project is cancelled (Devlin and Yap, 2008).

'Rendering technical'

The Belo Monte EIA was completed by a technical group consisting of the Federal Government, Eletrobras, and the construction companies of Andrade Gutierrez,

Camargo Corrêa, and Odebrecht. The research for the documents was outsourced and completed by LEME Engenharia (a subsidiary of GDF Suez). The EIA for the São Luiz do Tapajós project was completed by CNEC Engenharia, a Brazilian engineering company owned by the Australian company, WorleyParsons. The documents themselves were exclusively the purview of scientists and technicians – frequently running to thousands of pages and numerous volumes, meaning that the documents were in practice inaccessible by those impacted (Zhouri, 2015). The scale of these documents was evident during my time in Brazil. On entering the Department of Environmental Licensing at FUNAI, I was shown the official documents related to FUNAI's contribution to the EIA for the Belo Monte project. 'This is Belo Monte,' said an employee, pointing to six piles of paper tied together with string – each at least 2 feet high, sitting across two full-size desks.

EIAs across the globe often adopt an overtly technical approach to understanding and mitigating the potential impacts of infrastructure projects (O'Faircheallaigh, 2007; Aguilar-Støen and Hirsch, 2017; Spiegel, 2017). The worldviews of the technicians completing and approving them – primarily drawn from techno-scientific backgrounds – are dramatically distinct from those of the local community near the site of construction (Harris, 2009; O'Faircheallaigh, 2010; Zhouri, 2018). As a result, the creation of an EIA and provision of a licence is bound up in a politics of expertise – in which impacts are defined as technical problems to be solved by expert-driven solutions (Li, 2007; Aguilar-Støen and Hirsch, 2017). The technical nature of the EIA not only functions to identify impacts and propose solutions but also – to borrow from Li (2007) – renders the project 'technical,' restricting room for dissent and separating 'legitimate' impacts and grievances from those deemed 'illegitimate' or outside the assessment's remit and area of impact. The process confirms expertise, constituting the boundaries between those deemed 'expert' and those who are not (Li, 2007). It represents a process of depoliticisation, with the prioritisation of certain forms of knowledge and exclusion of alternative perspectives from official EIAs and licensing procedures (Zhouri, 2018). For example, cultural impacts are often neglected in official EIAs in Brazil, as the relative intangibility of spiritual connections to land, traditional knowledge, and ancestral tenure makes them difficult to calculate, articulate, and mitigate within more technical understandings (Hanna et al., 2016; Nathan Green and Baird, 2016).

The 'rendering technical' of EIAs and the environmental licensing process forecloses the process from alternative claims regarding impacts, differentiating legitimate grievances that are worthy of discussion and solution within official documents from those deemed illegitimate and unworthy. This form of 'epistemological violence' means that the technical focus on EIAs leaves little space for alternative claims and marginalises the impacted communities in the planning process (Zhouri, 2018).[1] The technical focus of an EIA leaves little room for impacts linked to contextual and cultural factors, which do not fit into the technical lens adopted by many of those involved in the creation or interrogation of an EIA document but will carry great significance for local communities (Hanna et al., 2016; Zhouri, 2018). This is evident in the Lajeado hydroelectric dam in Tocantins, central Brazil – where social and environmental compensation policies disrupted the agricultural practices of the indigenous Xerente community, resulting in intra-community conflict (Hanna et al., 2016). In this case, the failure to take traditional cultural practices into account while developing mitigative measures intensified such impacts (Hanna et al., 2016). These communities did not necessarily lack knowledge of the hydroelectric project but, instead, were unable to articulate their grievances within the technical framework and language adopted within environmental impact assessments and, as a result, the measures approved by IBAMA in the official EIA. This exacerbated impacts, rather than mitigating them.

The 'rendering technical' of an EIA can be countered by public hearings, within which the project (and associated EIA) is presented to members of the local community who can question and critique plans. While not federally mandated, if a public hearing is requested by the local community, it should take place within 45 days of its notification. Public hearings, in theory, represent the opening up of the EIA – and, with it, the licensing process – to input from residents and interested parties. The alternative worldviews and knowledges present across a community are to be given time and space to be aired and contribute to any decision. Officials at CCBM, IBAMA, and FUNAI rigorously recorded and digitised 39 volumes (of approximately 600 pages each) of consultations, public hearings, and the environmental licensing process (Bratman, 2020). Norte Energia would go on to claim that, between 2007 and 2012, it held 12 public consultations, 10 community workshops, visits to over 4,000 households, 4 public hearings alongside IBAMA, and 2 technical forums, reaching over 6,000 people (G1 PA, 2017). In 2009, public hearings took place in Brasil Novo (9 September), Vitória do Xingu (12 September), Altamira (13 September), and Belém (15 September). However, these hearings were widely criticised. The location of these assemblies was often geographically distant from the villages of both indigenous and riverine communities to be impacted by the project (Barros and Ravena, 2011; Instituto Humanitas Unisinos, 2016) and the size of these venues was insufficient to accommodate those impacted, resulting in many attending being unable to either hear from Norte Energia or participate in subsequent discussions (Fearnside, 2018). Security forces were often present at the hearings, with hundreds of heavily armed members of the National Force, Federal Police, and Military Police at the hearing in Altamira (Salm, 2009; Fearnside, 2018). In Belém, security personnel built a barrier which prevented protesters from entering the venue (FASE, 2009). The presence of military personnel, as well as their weaponry, is deemed to have influenced proceedings, indicating the presence of a threat of violence against participants voicing grievances. The Federal Public Prosecutor, Rodrigo Costa, and Public Prosecutor of the State of Pará, Raimundo Moraes, labelled the hearings at Belém a scam and, in response to the presence of military personnel, called for those attending to leave (FASE, 2009). Within the room, the hearings were dominated by technical presentations from engineers and consultants employed by CCBM (Fearnside, 2018). These presentations were delivered using a language and tone that was overwhelmingly technical and inaccessible to those participating. Norte Energia failed to provide translators, resulting in many of those attending being unaware of what information was being communicated or of its magnitude (Interview, 1 December 2016a). While all attending were, in theory, entitled to ask a three-minute question, followed by a three-minute rejoinder, to make their own statements, the official presentations went on for hours, limiting the time left available for those attending to ask questions or raise concerns (Fearnside, 2018).

The performance of the EIAs – their creation and confirmation – can, at times, take precedence over what impacts are included within them (Li, 2015). These public hearings were understood to have been devised to communicate the findings and conclusions of the official environmental impact assessment, rather than allowing community contributions to its development (Fearnside, 2018). With the events taking place after the completion of the official EIA, the dialogue and discussions that took place in 2009 were widely understood to be merely a 'box-ticking exercise' in which the pro-dam coalition legitimised a decision that had already been made behind closed doors (Interview, 7 November 2016b; Interview, 1 December 2016a). The impacted communities were not heard, with the process merely a formality to be completed (Interview, 16 September 2017). One interviewee, laughing as they said so, argued that Norte Energia would declare routine social gatherings as representing processes of consultation, arguing that: 'people would ... invite friends to a barbecue and call that a "public hearing" and everyone [would] say "It [Belo Monte] is okay!"' (Interview, 28 October 2016). The image provided by the activist is striking, with the resulting approval and consent for the project following a limited whip-around at an exclusive social occasion held on an impulse. The result was the depoliticisation of the Belo Monte project, with alternative perspectives on the impacts that diverged from pro-dam viewpoints excluded from the decision-making process. However, this process was challenged by anti-dam actors. It is to this that I turn below.

'Rendering visible'

In light of the foreclosure of EIAs and the environmental licensing process, access to and the capacity to generate knowledge is a key factor for anti-dam groups seeking to influence government policy in Brazil (Rothman, 2001; McCormick, 2006). Both *Xingu Vivo para Sempre* and the MAB have whole sections on their respective websites dedicated to research papers that dispute hydroelectric projects. The MAB website carries a library in which not only photos and newspaper articles but also scientific studies and doctoral theses are collected. Xingu Vivo's website provides summaries of research related to environmental and socio-economic impacts. Belo Monte's construction stimulated scientific research – conducted by academic researchers across Brazil, and beyond – into the project's impacts. This includes studies on cumulative impacts (Latrubesse et al., 2017; Jiang et al., 2018), population displacement (Randell, 2016; Castro-Diaz, Lopez and Moran, 2018), greenhouse gas emissions (Lessa et al., 2015; Fearnside, 2017; De Araújo et al., 2019), and the project's impacts for health (Grisotti, 2016;

Marin and Da Costa Oliveira, 2016). Research was presented extensively to public audiences. For example, at a 2016 meeting to discuss the São Luiz do Tapajós project, the physician Erik Jennings explained to 500 members of the local opposition the impacts that previous hydropower projects have had on methylmercury levels in the river basin (MPF/PA, 2016). This dissemination of research represents the linking of localised opposition to the scheme – based on localised grievances and demands – to technical information and expertise (McCormick, 2006, 2010). Websites and archives make a wealth of scientific information available to activists, working closely alongside local communities, national and international organisations locate local demands within wider arguments – be they related to environmental protection, the territorial rights of indigenous communities or the protection of Amazonian forests and biodiversity (Barbosa, 2015).

For many of those interviewed, the provision of scientific evidence of a project's impacts was a key tactic of opposition and resistance, aimed at '[discrediting] the Environmental Impact Assessment, to make it either invalid or to cancel it – so that the government denies it [cancels the project]' (Interview, 19 October 2016). In the wake of the publication of the respective EIAs of the Belo Monte and São Luiz do Tapajós projects, environmental organisations opposed to their construction published alternative assessments. Following the publication of Belo Monte's EIA in 2009, a panel of experts – mainly drawn from the Brazilian scientific community – engaged in an extensive critique of the official assessment of Belo Monte's impacts (Magalhães and Hernandez, 2009). Similarly, in response to the publication of the São Luiz do Tapajós EIA in 2016, International Rivers, an international EO, organised and published *Ocekadi*, an extensive collection that highlighted numerous impacts of a project in the Tapajós basin (Alarcon, Millikan, and Torres, 2016). Both texts highlighted the methodological weaknesses of the respective EIAs, arguing that these limitations restricted their applicability and challenged pro-dam assertions of the assumed sustainability of the projects. Both reports highlighted numerous methodological and factual inaccuracies of official assessments – such as how such documents overlooked impacts on fisheries in the region, as well as an underestimation of the number of people to be directly affected by the project (Magalhães and Hernandez, 2009; Alarcon, Millikan, and Torres, 2016).

If the environmental licensing process represents the 'rendering technical' of a project and the exclusion of different social groups, visions and values, the use of scientific evidence to dispute official assessments and illuminate overlooked impacts can be understood as a process of 'rendering visible.' The provision and dissemination of scientific research into the impacts of Belo Monte have three benefits for those standing against it. First, it disputes the validity of the official EIAs, which endow the project with sustainability credentials. Second, it functions to 'scale up' the resistance against the project to include impacts that are excluded from the dominant storyline of sustainability that legitimises the projects studied. Third, it repoliticises the project studied – opening up the pro-dam storyline of sustainability to impacts, knowledges and worldviews that are otherwise excluded. Those opposed to the Belo Monte and São Luiz do Tapajós projects not only provided scientific, technical evidence to dispute the respective projects' sustainability but, instead, elevated the grievances of local populations – presenting them on a national and international stage. By shining a light on neglected issues, marginalised viewpoints and ignored uncertainties, activists rendered visible the overlooked, neglected impacts and forgotten populations affected by Belo Monte. It was by illuminating these impacts that anti-dam activists provided evidence of the unsustainability of Belo Monte that remained forgotten, unmentioned, and neglected within the pro-dam storyline of sustainability.

The rendering visible of impacts is primarily focused on social impacts and moves in two ways. First, the illumination of the transformation of the city of Altamira, the settlement nearest Belo Monte's construction site and, second, on the plight of those deemed to be unaffected by the project – namely those riverine communities living downstream from its turbines.

The tragedy of Altamira

Less than an hour's drive from the main construction site of Belo Monte, on the banks of Volte Grande of the Xingu River, lies the city of Altamira. There had been euphoria for many in Altamira at the announcement of Belo Monte. Drivers traversed the city's roads with bumper stickers praising the project (Fachin and Santos, 2015) and official billboards promised a bright future. Project proponents asserted the economic benefits of the project for the local population (Atkins, 2017) and the Belo Monte EIA promised development opportunities in terms of employment, workers achieving new qualifications, and prosperity for local and regional entrepreneurs (Eletrobras, 2009a). However, positivity soon gave way to grievance (Vieira, 2016), with the promises of economic benefits contrasting with the words of those opposed to the project, the majority of whom highlighted traumatic social and economic impacts that dislocated the lives and livelihoods of many in Altamira yet remained unaddressed in official EIAs (Interview, 19 October 2016; Interview, 9 January 2017; Interview, 28 April 2017).

The population of Altamira was 99,075 people at the start of Belo Monte's construction in 2010 (IBGE, n.d.). This population increased rapidly. Construction workers and those in subsidiary industries moved to the area to secure employment. Hydropower projects mobilise a wide labour force, triggering an influx of workers into the region and resulting in a population boom. The population of Tucuruí, the city near the dam which shares its name, increased from 10,901 in 1975 to 182,021 in 1985 (Calvi, 2019). Those who build dams in Brazil – known collectively as barrageiros – occupy a near-mythical place in Brazilian national consciousness, being responsible for great feats of engineering from Itaipu to Tucuruí. These individuals – predominantly men – move from dam to dam, either building their transient lives around new settlements or sending remittances to distant families. Many of those who arrived in Altamira to work on Belo Monte had worked on the Santo Antônio and Jirau Dams on the Madeira River near Porto Velho, Rondônia, which was completed in 2012, and moved to

Altamira without the promise of a job but under the assumption that one would be forthcoming.[2]

While Norte Energia made attempts to reduce the influx of barrageiros in Altamira by prioritising the hiring of local labour (Eletrobras, 2009b), tens of thousands of workers still migrated to the region. With the Belo Monte project's period of construction extending from 2011 to the time of writing, activists argue that the population influx into the city resulted in a process of upheaval and exclusion for the local Altamirense population (Amazon Watch, n.d.; Xingu Vivo para Sempre, 2010; Parracho, 2012). While official projections of peak-level employment stood at 18,700 direct employees and 23,000 indirect jobs (Eletrobras, 2009a), it was estimated by some that upwards of 30,000 workers arrived in Altamira (Interview, 3 November 2016b). *Xingu Vivo* argued that – when taking those employed in subsidiary industries and additional migrants (due to the promise of jobs or economic benefits) into account – the number would be closer to 100,000 (Xingu Vivo para Sempre, 2010).

The growing population increased demand for goods and accommodation across Altamira, leading to a rapid escalation in prices. One interviewee, who regularly travelled to Altamira from their home in São Paulo, reported struggling to find affordable accommodation, paying for a hammock in a shared area under a plastic roof at a price equivalent to a night's stay in an apartment in São Paulo (Interview, 28 October 2016). For the interviewee, a national print journalist who had written extensively on the Belo Monte project, the result was the financial exclusion of the local population, who had seen no change in their income. Many of them migrated away from Altamira to escape:

> So, they are now paying more, and a lot of people are leaving Altamira to live in other small cities around [the region] because they don't have enough money to pay or to sustain [their lives in] the new economy there [in Altamira].
>
> (Interview, 28 October 2016)

Although Belo Monte did bring economic development to the region, many feared that the local economy would collapse in the wake of the project's completion. Many of the benefits promised by Belo Monte's supporters were predicated on short-term gains, with the end of Belo Monte's construction leading to further economic change. Promises of jobs and employment are conditioned on the stage of construction – levels of investment and opportunity are at their greatest during construction. However, once construction is complete, the economic benefits promised will dissipate. A representative of Greenpeace Brasil argued, 'When you are building a dam, you employ a lot of people, but once it is over, these people lose their jobs' (Interview, 19 October 2016). Amazon Watch argued that, of the close to 40,000 jobs promised by the Belo Monte EIA, only 2,000 of them represent long-term employment, raising questions about the future of many of those employed by the construction consortium (Amazon Watch, 2014). As one interviewee who had recently returned to São Paulo from

Altamira explained, the employment brought by the project had a temporally limited character:

> The fact is that it's not going to generate jobs forever – jobs come and go ... the boom and the bust. [It is] the kind of project that hydropower dams are. They come, they generate a lot of activity and jobs on-site, and then they leave.
>
> (Interview, 18 October 2016)

With the demobilisation of the workforce taking place across a number of years, from 2015 onwards, *Norte Energia* implemented policies to encourage migrant workers to leave Altamira, including re-skilling employees and purchasing tickets to return home to workers (Estado de São Paulo, 2015). However, there was limited mitigation of the possible knock-on consequences of this managed departure for the local economy. In 2016, it was reported in the national media that the redundancy of 20,000 employees resulted in a 51% decline in the economy of Altamira, with thousands of workers staying in the city and applying for local jobs (G1 PA, 2016). In the first half of 2016, the local government alone received over a thousand resumes from prospective employees (G1 PA, 2016).

The job market was further crowded by those let go by local businesses who were struggling in the financial slump. The short-term nature of the economic development and employment promised was understudied within the official EIA provided by Norte Energia, which offered limited measures to mitigate the possible impact on the local economy of a rapidly stimulated reliance on Belo Monte. This widens the scope of the analysis of Belo Monte's impacts in Altamira, while highlighting the long-term consequences for those living there.

In the face of a population boom, Altamira experienced an upsurge in violence and criminality (Instituto Socioambiental, 2015a; MAB, 2017a). The Ministério da Saúde (Ministry of Health) reported that, in 2015, Altamira experienced 124 murders per 100,000 inhabitants in the city, making it the deadliest city in the world (Madeiro, 2017). This represented an increase of 147% from 2009, when Eletrobras requested the preliminary licence for the Belo Monte project (Madeiro, 2017). The globally distributed film, *Belo Monte: After the Flood*, which counted Amazon Watch and International Rivers among its producers, detailed how the city experienced eight murders in one night, with the local police force struggling to keep order (Southgate, 2016).

The violence and criminality stimulated by Belo Monte had a gendered dimension, disproportionately impacting women in the region. An interviewee at Instituto Socioambiental was clear – arguing that the population influx represented 'Men. That's 30,000 men [entering Altamira]' (Interview, 3 November 2016b). With the development of a hydropower project impacting upon women disproportionately (Hill et al., 2017), the illumination of sexual violence presents the social consequences of Belo Monte in a new light, illuminating the gendered impacts of the Belo Monte project. The MAB reported that the construction of Belo Monte led to an 18.5% increase in sexual violence and crime in the years after the project's entrance into Altamira (MAB, 2013).[3] In the years after 2010, sexual harassment on the streets of Altamira increased in frequency, leading to a grassroots campaign to both increase reporting and decrease incidents (Estronioli, 2016), and the number of cases of sexual violence against children and adolescents between 2010 and 2013 exceeded the number of such cases in Altamira for the previous decade (XVPS, 2011; Instituto Humanitas Unisinos, 2013a).

In February 2013, a police raid on a building named Boate Xingu found 15 women who had been held against their will and forced into sex work (Glass, 2013). The women – aged between 16 and 20 – had been trafficked from across Brazil. All had been told that they would earn up to R$14,000 per month yet when they arrived, they were confined to small, windowless rooms that were padlocked from the outside and forced into debt bondage to pay off the costs of transport, clothing, and food (Glass, 2013). This tragedy is not exceptional. Only days before, police raids had discovered 15 victims of sexual exploitation in nightclubs across Altamira (Instituto Humanitas Unisinos, 2013b). Boate Xingu, opened in 2012, was located on the edge of Belo Monte's construction site – a strategic decision to cater to the workers who were the primary clientele (Glass, 2013). Peak visiting times at these illicit operations coincided directly with the time when the construction workers employed by CCBM were paid (Pinho and Oliveira Costa, 2012). Other sources reported clients paying with food vouchers distributed to workers by their employer (Talento, 2014).

The increased population of Altamira also made it a lucrative destination and market for drug-traffickers; there were reports that criminal gangs from the favelas of Rio de Janeiro had moved to Altamira and 'killed the members of the local gang, to establish a new level of drug traffic.' (Interview, 28 October 2016). While this statement was made in 2016, there is evidence for this claim in a 2019 prison riot in Altamira. On 29 June 2019, tensions between the Comando Classe A (CCA, Class A Command) and Comando Vermelho (CV, Red Command) trafficking gangs led to staggering episodes of violence and the massacre of 58 prisoners in the prison at Altamira (Exame, 2019). Members of CCA broke into the wing where CV-affiliated prisoners were housed, killing indiscriminately, decapitating victims and setting mattresses on fire – leading to further deaths from asphyxiation. Four more were strangled while being transported from the prison (Barbon and Maissonnave, 2019). CV is a trafficking gang originating in Rio de Janeiro while CCA is affiliated with one of the biggest trafficking groups in north Brazil, lending credence to the interviewee's claims above. The violence of the morning of 29 June 2019 stemmed from the struggle to control key drug trafficking routes, as well as emerging markets in the region itself (Aroeira, 2019). The prison block where the 2019 prison riot took place was itself a site of overcrowding due to Norte Energia's failure to build a new prison building as per a condition in the licence. The delay in delivering this new space was criticised by activists in Altamira as leading, if only indirectly, to the deaths in June 2019. It was cited as further evidence of the failure of Norte Energia to mitigate the impacts of the alteration of the fabric of Altamira (Aroeira, 2019).

The Licença Prévia granted to build Belo Monte in 2010 contained 40 conditions for planning and construction, including the building of schools and health clinics, the expansion of sanitation systems, the conservation of both aquatic and terrestrial ecosystems, and the maintenance of the Xingu River's flow. These conditions were transferred to the installation licence, which was granted in 2011. Of the total budget of Belo Monte, 14% – or R$4 billion – was invested in mitigative measures and improvements to the area influenced by the project (Brasil MP, 2016). Norte Energia asserted that 27 basic health units had been built and equipped (with malaria cases in Altamira reduced by 90% between 2011 and 2014), 252 classrooms built and 102 expanded (benefiting more than 20,000 students) and that, as of 2014, a total of R$1.2 billion had been invested in social and environmental measures (PT, 2014). Despite these investments, Norte Energia was consistently accused of failing to fulfil these conditions and address the impacts of the project (Instituto Socioambiental, 2015a; Southgate, 2016). To mark the first anniversary of the project's operational licence, the Instituto Socioambiental (2015a) published a list of failings of the Belo Monte project, including the failure to complete sanitation works in Altamira, resulting in the discharge of raw sewage into the Xingu River. As an activist based at WWF Brasil explained, 'many things that were promised at the consultation of the dam … are not going on and not happening' (Interview, 7 November 2016a). Schools remained incomplete, hospitals unconnected to the electrical grid, and households faced electricity shortages, while others did not have running water or sewerage connections (Interview, 28 October 2016; Interview, 3 November 2016b; Interview, 28 April 2017).

While the project's supporters speak of the economic benefits that Belo Monte would bring to Altamira (see Chapter 1), those opposed to the project illuminate numerous impacts that remain undiscussed and unmitigated in official impact assessments. For many, the failure of Norte Energia to fulfil multiple conditions of its licence represented a lack of oversight and concern for the ways in which the construction of Belo Monte would impact Altamira, the surrounding area and its inhabitants. Interviewees argued that the increased violence was worsened by a stretched police force and that the precariousness of public services made it difficult to combat sexual violence (Instituto Humanitas Unisinos, 2013a). This transformation of Altamira was widely understood as the result of a lack of governance and mitigation of impacts when the construction started (Interview, 3 November 2016b; Interview, 16 September 2017; Interview, 28 April 2017). This governance and mitigation is found in the remit of both EIAs and the environmental licensing process – which, for many activists, had failed the people of Altamira.

This illumination of the impacts of Belo Monte on the social fabric of the city of Altamira represents a process of 'rendering visible,' with the official EIA's and Norte Energia's policies of mitigation widely presented as demonstrating the neglect of the long-term impacts felt by those living in Altamira – as was evident in the failure to complete the infrastructural improvements required to mitigate such consequences. While the official EIAs – and the storyline of sustainability that they represent – see the analysis and definition of impacts through a narrow, technical lens, the resistance coalition provides an alternative vision of the project's construction and consequences. For many, the city was irreversibly altered – subject to rapid population growth, extensive displacement of resident populations, increased pressure on public services, and spiralling incidents of crime and violence. It is here, on the banks of the Xingu, that Belo Monte was bestowed with its nickname: Belo Monstro, translated as 'Beautiful Monster' (XVPS, n.d.).

'Indirect' and cumulative downstream impacts

The Belo Monte project was built according to a run-of-the-river design. In contrast to the large reservoirs of other projects, the project diverts 80% of the Xingu River's flow via two man-made canals to its turbines. With the EIA focused on direct impacts (such as flooding), the storyline of sustainability put forward by pro-dam actors argued that the lack of flooding represented a limitation of the social and environmental impacts caused by the project. One interviewee at MME went so far as to label this design a 'victory' for the resistance coalition that had opposed the Kararaô project in 1989 (Interview, 3 November 2016a). While it did not cause extensive flooding, the design of the Belo Monte project transformed the hydrologic character of the region. In Altamira (upstream), water levels rose. Populations could no longer predict the behaviour of the river due to the presence of unforeseen floods that claimed lives (G1 PA, 2014b). Wells were contaminated in neighbourhoods of Altamira that had been considered to be unimpacted in official assessments (Gauthier et al., 2019) and floods caused by heavy rains inundated homes, many on stilts, in the Lagoa do Bairro Independente 1 neighbourhood, displacing many families (MAB, 2018). Residents of the Jardin Independente 1 neighbourhood claimed that flooding increased sanitation problems in the area – an impact overlooked in official assessments (Barros and Barcelos, 2017). One resident, Carlos Alves Moraes, spent 17 days living in a house inundated by the floodwaters caused by Belo Monte (Barros and Barcelos, 2017). In 2019, Norte Energia agreed to re-evaluate the siting of houses in the Jardim Independente 1 neighbourhood – an achievement for local activists who had been warning of the inadequacies of this settlement at the edge of a lagoon (MAB, 2019).

The construction of a dam does not only affect the population present in its immediate confines. Projects have a series of impacts downstream of their sites of construction. While Altamira experienced flooding and groundwater-contamination, downstream communities faced the dramatic alteration of the Xingu River that provided for their livelihoods. The construction of a dam transforms a river from a system of flowing waters into one that is still; flowing rapids were transformed into idle water. While the previous hydrological regime saw flows of between 20,000 and 25,000 m^3 of floodwater in the rainy season, the post-construction Xingu is, instead, in a state of permanent drought (MPF, 2019). Norte Energia's EIA for Belo Monte did make allowances for the release of water (arranged on an alternate basis of 4,000 m^3 one year and 8,000 m^3 the following year); the arrangements have not adequately mitigated the hydrological transformation caused by the diversion of 80% of the Xingu's flow. The result is sustained water stress downstream from Belo Monte – with a group of scientists labelling the new flow in the Xingu as making life 'impossible' (MPF, 2019). Fisheries have been disrupted and routes of transportation blocked. The reduction in water levels carried health risks, including an increased frequency of intestinal parasites, malaria and dengue fever (Pace, 2018).

At the start of construction, approximately 235 riverine households or around 1,175 people lived on the riverbanks that are now submerged by Belo Monte's reservoir (ISA, 2018b). Riverine communities – widely known as ribeirinhos[4] – were widely overlooked, neglected and unmentioned in the official EIA for Belo Monte. As the Xingu River was transformed into a lake and their homes were lost, this population was compulsorily removed and relocated. The construction of the hydroelectric project led to the simultaneous inundation of riverine communities, decline in river flow and fish stock – altering the way of life of these communities. Ribeirinhos saw their territory lost to the river, their access to natural resources stymied and their livelihoods, income, and connections to land dislocated. These communities, descended from the 'rubber soldiers' compulsorily drafted and sent into the region to harvest rubber during World War II (see Secreto, 2007), are considered traditional peoples under Brazilian law, holding a cultural specificity related to their river-based livelihoods and shared knowledge and history. Their rights – enshrined in law – recognise their need for traditional riverine territory. Yet, in building Belo Monte, Norte Energia removed these households and communities from their lands and relocated them in the city of Altamira, transforming their livelihoods, disconnecting them from their networks and dislocating their traditional identity (Magalhães and Carneiro da Cunha, 2017). Many households had entered discussions and negotiations with Norte Energia without the support of organisations such as the MPF, who concentrated their attention on urban displacement. The result was that many were underpaid for their land – gaining as little as R$20,000 (Álvares, 2019). The community became geographically dispersed, dislocated from the Xingu, and economically disrupted (ISA, 2018b). Hundreds of riverine families had their lives irreversibly disrupted by the construction of Belo Monte. These communities now find themselves housed in a Reassentamento Urbano Coletivo (RUC, Collective Urban Resettlement) built by Norte Energia – open to the hustle, insecurity, and crime that came to dominate Altamira in the Belo Monte years (Álvares, 2019). The new areas that many ribeirinhos now found themselves in were small, insecure, and distant from the new shoreline – making it impossible to follow the traditional riverine style of life that they had once lived (ISA, 2018b).

Further downstream, communities that remained living on the shoreline faced additional impacts. The previously flooded forests that many species called home were reduced in size, leading to a decrease in both the abundance and variety of fish species, including two of the most important species in the basin, the piraíba, and the tucunaré (Castro-Diaz et al., 2018). With fishing communities no longer catching the most valuable species, they were forced to travel further to catch less. Food-cultivation on land declined – both in terms of harvest and diversity of crops (Silva and Lucas, 2019). This decline of regional fisheries was accompanied by an increase in the price of other foodstuffs, with the price of farinha, or flour, increasing to R$13 (Castro-Diaz et al., 2018). In addition, gasoline to power the outboard engines of fishing boats also increased in price, rising to $R6 in 2016 (Castro-Diaz et al., 2018).[5,6]

These downstream impacts are widely neglected when understanding, discussing or asserting the 'sustainability' of hydroelectric projects – or mitigating their impacts. Hydroelectric projects have myriad impacts downstream from their turbines, transforming river morphologies and flow (Yang et al., 2014), disrupting ecosystems and biodiversity (McCartney, 2009), and impacting the migratory routes and stocks of fish (Power et al., 1996). These impacts have wide-ranging consequences for those communities living downstream – affecting health and livelihoods. This complexity is underrepresented in official EIAs in Brazil (Hanna et al., 2016). The official pro-dam environmental assessments divide the impacts of hydropower projects into two areas: defined as areas of 'direct' and 'indirect' influence (Eletrobras, 2009b; Grupo de Estudos Tapajós, 2014). This division distinguishes between the impacts occurring in the immediate vicinity of the construction site and those 'indirect' consequences occurring in areas considered beyond the responsibility of those planning and building the respective projects.

Traditional, riverine communities – while protected by Brazilian law – did not fit into the dominant understanding of the impacts of hydropower as being limited to 'direct' impacts near the site of construction. Many of those living downstream were understood as being merely 'indirectly' impacted and not requiring relocation, compensation, or support. Living downstream, many continued to live in their original homes. However, these homes were irreversibly transformed – the river's flow altered, fish stocks lost, and their livelihoods disrupted. These communities are, as Zhouri (2018) argues 'displaced in situ,' subject to the impacts of Belo Monte but unprotected. With the impacts of Belo Monte reduced to the areas immediately around its construction, the ribeirinhos were forgotten. While there were well-documented problems with the new housing built to accommodate those displaced by Belo Monte, many were not able to secure compensation by resettlement as they were deemed to be only 'indirectly' impacted by the project and able to withstand the changes brought by the changing hydrology of the basin. While primary displacement is easier to predict and quantify, secondary displacement is far less certain, existing in areas distant from the site and at times detached from a project's construction. This secondary displacement can be understood as a ripple effect, with communities and landscapes distant from the site of construction not experiencing the project's consequences until after the project's completion. The downstream impacts of Belo Monte and their disruption of the lives and livelihoods of ribeirinho communities were overlooked in official assessments. The official EIA was criticised for lacking key information related to the simulation and evaluation of changes in water levels downstream, had a lack of studies of sedimentation in the region and a lack of analysis of how Belo Monte may affect a rising water table (Magalhães and Hernandez, 2009). Norte Energia neglected the intrinsic culture and history of this community – most particularly, the need to take their connection to the river into account when managing displacement and resettlement. While indigenous communities strove to *protect* their territory, many riverine communities – deemed 'traditional' under Brazilian law – were attempting to *gain* and *secure* it (Interview, 7 November 2016b). Norte Energia had no adequate plan for their displacement or resettlement and was unable to guarantee any conditions related to the continuity of the riverine way of life.

While riverine communities joined indigenous groups in occupying the Belo Monte construction site (see Jornal de Brasília, 2013; Anderson, 2017), they also organised collectively to document the impacts of Belo Monte upon their livelihoods. In December 2016, the Conselho Ribeirinho ('Ribeirinho Council') was formed by gathering 26 representatives across the Xingu basin. Over the next two years, the Council met seven times to record the stories of those impacted and displaced by Belo Monte. The Council identified families – both in a relational context but also in the sense of an informal network of neighbours and friends – that had been displaced and called for their resettlement. A survey by the Council reported that more than 15 ribeirinhos had died due to diseases deemed linked to Belo Monte – including cancer, diabetes, and depression (MXVPS, 2019). They told the story of Lidia Fereira, who was displaced from her home on the island of Palhal in 2015 and moved to Altamira before spiralling into chronic illness and depression. She died on 19 May 2019. Riberinhos complained of hunger, disease, lack of finances, lack of shelter, and depression – highlighting the failure of Norte Energia to address their displacement and resettle them adequately (XVPS, 2019).

In 2018, the collective organisation of riverine households, the Conselho Ribeirinho do Xingu presented its plight to IBAMA and Norte Energia. Their former territory – now submerged – was mapped and put forward as a criticism of the official EIA's mapping of riverine communities (ISA, 2018a). This led to a redesign of the official map of impacts by Norte Energia in 2018 – with the riverine communities now rendered visible and the impacts on them understood, agreed upon, and discussed. It described their lives before this project before rendering visible the trauma of dislocation and displacement. Many had seen their homes lost to the rising water levels and were struggling to rebuild the life that they had lost. The council presented a list of residents who required recognition by Norte Energia as 'impacted' and as ribeirinho who, as a result, were entitled to cultural protection and adequate resettlement. In response to the efforts of the Conselho Ribeirinho, IBAMA recognised the problems of resettlement of riverine communities, the failings of Norte Energia and the need to mitigate both by following the guidelines put forward by the communities themselves (ISA, 2018a). It later decided that 307 riverine families would be relocated to nearby lands. However, in 2019, this was disputed by several landowners in the region, who protested the requisition of parts of their land to re-home these communities (Senado Federal, 2019). At the time of writing, this dispute continues.

Riverine communities do not easily figure in the technical view of direct impacts adopted by the technicians devising, presenting, and confirming official

EIAs (Zhouri, 2018). This resulted in their exclusion within a process that prioritised technical expertise over local experience in defining what impacts were mitigated and which were deemed 'indirect' and beyond the remit of Norte Energia. However, in response to this process, the Conselho Ribeirinho do Xingu rendered visible the multiple downstream impacts associated with Belo Monte – not only highlighting the plight of those displaced and resettled but also demanding support and compensation for those who had been neglected by those tasked with Belo Monte's construction. In doing so, anti-dam actors broadened the storyline of sustainability and highlighted the neglect of the wider impacts of the project, asserting the need to widen the spatial focus in official assessments and illuminate the equivalence between the projects and a number of impacts deemed 'indirect' in official assessments to broaden the horizons of the assessment of impacts of the Belo Monte and São Luiz do Tapajós Dam project and challenge the quality of official EIAs.

Conclusion

I have argued in this chapter that, with environmental impact assessments providing important tools in understanding, predicting, and mitigating the potential impacts of hydroelectric dam projects, they represent central sites of contestation between those who support a project and those who stand against it. The environmental licensing process provides a key moment in which the contest between these two groups is distilled into a decision (Hochstetler, 2011) and the sustainability credentials of a project are affirmed and consolidated, in accordance with existing environmental policy and regulation. With government decisions – such as those made within the environmental licensing process – predicated on expert evidence and technical information, anti-dam actors present their arguments on the technical stage, disputing the accuracy of scientific assessments (McCormick, 2006). With EIAs representing a technical worldview, language and perception of a project's impacts, the process excludes alternative voices and grievances. This is evident in the failure of the official EIA for the Belo Monte project in overlooking key indirect impacts (i.e. the plight of the ribeirinhos) and the long-term consequences of the project for the city of Altamira. In response to this 'rendering technical,' anti-dam activists opposed to Belo Monte produced and disseminated research that illuminated forgotten impacts and highlighted neglected areas and sectors. The putting forward of this storyline renders project impacts visible, and functions to broaden and reconfigure the pro-dam storyline of sustainability to demonstrate its narrowness and its neglect of those deemed unimpacted.

This contest offers two insights. First, while EIAs represent a process of 'rendering technical,' resulting in the foreclosure of the environmental licensing process from alternative perspectives, those opposed to the project 'render visible' extensive impacts that remain undiscussed, unmitigated and excluded within official assessments. Discussions of environmental licensing are controversial and discussed on newspaper front pages (Lima and Magrini, 2010). Scientific research was reported extensively in the Brazilian print and online media. For example, the 2017 publication of a study in *Nature* on the cumulative impacts of Belo Monte – and other hydroelectric projects – on the Amazon Basin (Latrubesse et al., 2017) was reported, commentated, and disseminated by both Folha de S.Paulo (Lopes, 2017), Mongabay (Salisbury, 2017) and El Pais Brasil (Criado, 2017). With many of the impacts discussed in this chapter underestimated or undiscussed in materials provided by Norte Energia and other pro-dam interests, anti-dam actors worked to demonstrate the neglect of localised impacts and communities by those behind the project. Yet, there is a risk that those opposing the process (and its EIAs) could repeat the same patterns of exclusion. The resistance storyline discussed in this chapter involved the work of scientists, journalists, lawyers and activists and EOs/NGOs but was driven by the residents themselves. The Conselho Ribeirinho monitored impacts, recorded stories of displacement and, at the time of writing, successfully lobbied for changes to policies of resettlement and compensation for communities that had been excluded from EIAs and the respective compensation mechanisms. The efforts by those opposing Belo Monte to both illuminate the neglect of local populations within official EIAs and render visible forgotten, overlooked and unmitigated social impacts highlight the rich potential that these actors have in disputing and altering the apparent sustainability of hydroelectric projects in the 21st century.

Second, the wider basin around hydroelectric dams became a site to illuminate the impacts of the project and widen the definition of the 'sustainability' of hydroelectric dams. This represents the 'scaling up' of the resistance against these projects – with the resistance coalition foregrounding their opposition within a wider terrain of impacts to dispute the pro-dam storyline of sustainability. An interviewee at *Instituto Socioambiental* explained that this process of highlighting impacts was motivated by the desire to discredit the economic benefits promised by pro-dam actors: 'we couldn't allow the government to sell that development and well-being rhetoric' (Interview, 3 November 2016b).

For many others, the monitoring of and reporting on the numerous impacts faced by Altamira in the wake of Belo Monte provided a key route to disputing pro-dam storylines surrounding its construction. This change was not a short-term alteration. The coming years will tell us more about Altamira's future – and the role of Belo Monte's construction – in dictating it. However, as the project's turbines enter operation, the localised legacy of this project is one of population displacement and influx, increased crime and violence, and an underestimation of social, cumulative, and indirect impacts, all of which directly challenging the assumed sustainability of the project. With the 'sustainability' of Belo Monte rooted in the international levels of greenhouse gas emissions and climate change mitigation, the illumination of localised impacts highlights the utter transformation of the lives, networks, and livelihoods of those living in the Xingu basin. As one interviewee from the World Rainforest Movement told me, there is 'nothing clean … nothing "renewable" about an energy type that causes so many impacts on the local populations and towns in the region and with a limited time span over the years. Just go to Altamira and look for yourself' (Interview, 2 November 2016).

Within the Brazilian environmental licensing system, individual projects are assessed on a case-by-case basis, resulting in a limited understanding of the cumulative impacts of development schemes that involve multiple projects in particular vicinities. However, the social impacts of hydroelectric dams discussed in this chapter do not exist in isolation. Instead, they were entwined within a wider context of overlapping, complex social and economic consequences that occur across projects and sectors (Baird and Barney, 2017; Athayde et al., 2019). Numerous anti-dam activists highlighted the idea that the Belo Monte and São Luiz do Tapajós projects are component parts of a wider scheme of encroachment and extraction in the regions. It is to this that I turn in the next chapter.

Notes

1. For Zhouri (2018), the use of a language of 'impacts' itself represents the supremacy of the technical lens – presupposing the environment as an objective reality that is (imp) acted on and that must be assessed using scientific knowledge and practices.
2. Those who migrated to the area were not immediately able to secure work, with reports of hundreds of workers sleeping on the streets, waiting to be offered employment (Pedruzzi, 2012).
3. Elsewhere, dam construction on the Madeira River in Rondônia led to a 208% increase in sexual assault cases in the surrounding area (MAB, 2013).
4. Although the term *ribeirinho* has been used a slur, it is now used as a form of self-definition and a signal of cultural difference (Bratman, 2020).
5. The impacts of this decline of fisheries on livelihoods are exacerbated within the history of the community, with there being limited experience of agricultural cultivation in the region. This is a consequence of the region's role in the rubber booms of both 1870–1912 and 1939–1945, when 'rubber barons' forbid rubber tappers in the region from planting crops in order to oblige them to buy supplies, creating long-term debt and service (see: Castro-Diaz, Lopez, and Moran, 2018).
6. In response to declining catches, many women who had previously divided their time between fishing and domestic work stayed at home due to the need to travel further for limited returns. This challenged their autonomy, with many women across this community becoming dependent on the men of the village for food and financial support (Castro-Diaz, Lopez, and Moran, 2018).

Bibliography

Aguilar-Støen, M, and Hirsch, C (2017). Bottom-up responses to environmental and social impact assessments: a case study from Guatemala. *Environmental Impact Assessment Review*, 62: 225–232.

Alarcon, DF, Millikan, B, and Torres, M (ed.) (2016). *Ocekadi: Hidrelétricas, Conflitos Socioambientais e Resistência na Bacia do Tapajós*. Brasília: International Rivers. Available at: https://www.internationalrivers.org/sites/default/files/attached-files/tapajos_digital.pdf.

Álvares, D (2019). Belo Monte, a violação de direitos humanos dos ribeirinhos e a ameaça ao Xingu. *The Huffington Post Brasil*, 4 September. Available at: https://www.huffpostbrasil.com/entry/belo-monte-altamira_br_5d6efef4e4b09bbc9ef644fd (Accessed: 8 January 2020).

Amazon Watch (n.d.). Belo Monte facts: 10 myths the Brazilian government wants you to believe about Belo Monte. *Amazon Watch*, no date. Available at: https://amazonwatch.org/work/belo-monte-facts (Accessed: 12 February 2020).

Amazon Watch (2014). Issue brief: Brazil's Belo Monte dam: a major threat to the Amazon and its people. *Amazon Watch*, no date. Available at: https://amazonwatch.org/assets/files/belo-monte-dam-issue-brief.pdf (Accessed: 12 February 2020).

Anderson, M (2017). Displaced by Brazil's giant Belo Monte hydroelectric dam, 'river people' reoccupy reservoir. *Mongabay*, 13 March. Available at: https://news.mongabay.com/2017/03/displaced-by-brazils-giant-belo-monte-hydroelectric-dam-river-people-reoccupy-reservoir/ (Accessed: 30 March 2020).

Aroeira, A (2019). Belo Monte forjou o massacre de altamira: novo presídio nunca entregue era obrigação da norte energia. *Intercept Brasil*, 7 August. Available at: https://theintercept.com/2019/08/06/belo-monte-forjou-massacre-altamira/ (Accessed: 8 January 2020).

Athayde, S, Matthews, M, Bohlman, S, Brasil, W, Doria, CRC, Dutka-Gianelli, J, Fearnside, PM, Loiselle, B, Marques, EE, Melis, TS, Millikan, B, Moretto, EM, Oliver-Smith, A, Rosette, A, Vacca, R, and Kaplan, D (2019). Mapping research on hydropower and sustainability in the Brazilian Amazon: advances, gaps in knowledge and future directions. *Current Opinion in Environmental Sustainability*, 37: 50–69.

Atkins, E (2017). Dammed and diversionary: the multi-dimensional framing of Brazil's Belo Monte dam. *Singapore Journal of Tropical Geography*, 38(3): 276–292.

Atkins, E (2018). Dams, political framing and sustainability as an empty signifier: the case of Belo Monte. *Area*, 50(2): 232–239.

Baird, IG, and Barney, K (2017). The political ecology of cross-sectoral cumulative impacts: modern landscapes, large hydropower dams and industrial tree plantations in Laos and Cambodia. *Journal of Peasant Studies*, 44(4): 884–910.

Barbon, J, and Maissonnave, F (2019). Maioria dos presos mortos no Pará era negra, tinha até 35 anos e cometeu crime violento. *Folha de S.Paulo*, 4 August. Available at: https://www1.folha.uol.com.br/cotidiano/2019/08/maioria-dos-presos-mortos-no-para-era-negra-tinha-ate-35-anos-e-cometeu-crime-violento.shtml (Accessed: 8 January 2020).

Barbosa, LC (2015). *Guardians of the Brazilian Amazon Rainforest: Environmental Organizations and Development*. London: Routledge Earthscan.

Barros, C, and Barcelos, L (2017). Conflitos, desmatamento e inundações marcam 6 anos das obras em Belo Monte. *UOL*, 7 November. Available at: https://noticias.uol.com.br/cotidiano/ultimas-noticias/2017/11/07/conflitos-inundacoes-e-desmatamento-marcam-6-anos-das-obras-em-belo-monte.htm (Accessed: 8 January 2020).

Barros, TA, and Ravena, N (2011). Representações sociais nas audiências públicas de Belo Monte: do palco ao recorte midiático. *Compolitica*, 13: 1–20.

Brasil, Ministério do Planejamento (2016). Dilma inaugura usina hidrelétrica de Belo Monte. *Brasil Ministério do Planejamento*, 6 May. Available at: http://pac.gov.br/noticia/7be96908 (Accessed: 8 January 2020).

Bratman, EZ (2020). *Governing the Rainforest: Sustainable Development Politics in the Brazilian Amazon*. Oxford: Oxford University Press.

Brum, E (2015a). O dia em que a casa foi expulsa de casa. *El Pais*, 14 September. Available at: https://brasil.elpais.com/brasil/2015/09/14/opinion/1442235958_647873.html (Accessed: 19 March 2019).

Brum, E (2015b). Vítimas de uma guerra amazônica. *El Pais*, 26 September. Available at: https://brasil.elpais.com/brasil/2015/09/22/politica/1442930391_549192.html (Accessed: 8 January 2020).

Brum, E (2016). Dilma compôs seu réquiem em Belo Monte. *El Pais*, 10 May. Available at: https://brasil.elpais.com/brasil/2016/05/09/opinion/1462804348_582272.html (Accessed: 25 April 2019).

Brum, E (2019). *The Collector of Leftover Souls*. Translated from Portuguese by Diane Grosklaus Whitty. London: Granta.

Calvi, MF (2019). *(Re)Organização Produtiva e Mudanças na Paisagem sob Influência da Hidrelétrica de Belo Monte*. Thesis submitted to Instituto de Filosofia e Ciências Humanas, Universidade Estadual de Campinas, Campinas.

Castro-Diaz, L, Lopez, MC, and Moran, E (2018). Gender-differentiated impacts of the Belo Monte hydroelectric dam on downstream fishers in the Brazilian Amazon. *Human Ecology*, 46(3): 411–422.

Criado, MA (2017). 500 presas amenazan con ahogar el Amazonas. *El País*, 14 June. Available at: https://elpais.com/elpais/2017/06/14/ciencia/1497430161_506854.html (Accessed: 19 March 2019).

de Araújo, KR, Sawakuchi, HO, Bertassoli Jr, DJ, Sawakuchi, AO, da Silva, KD, Vieira, TB, Ward, ND, and Pereira, TS (2019). Carbon dioxide (CO_2) concentrations and emission in the newly constructed Belo Monte hydroelectric complex in the Xingu River, Amazonia. *Biogeosciences*, 16(18): 3527–3542.

Devlin, JF, and Yap, NT (2008). Contentious politics in environmental assessment: blocked projects and winning coalitions. *Impact Assessment and Project Appraisal*, 26(1): 17–27.

Eletrobras (2009a). *Aproveitamento Hidrelétrico Belo Monte: Estudo de Impacto Ambiental*. Rio de Janeiro, RJ, Brazil: Eletrobras.

Eletrobras (2009b). *Relatório de Impacto Ambiental: Aproveitamento Hidrelétrico Belo Monte*. Brasilia, DF. Available at: http://restrito.norteenergiasa.com.br/site/wp-content/uploads/2011/04/NE.Rima_pdf (Accessed: 19 March 2019).

Estado de São Paulo (2015). O fim das obras dos 'barrageiros.' *Estado de São Paulo*, 27 June. Available at: https://economia.estadao.com.br/noticias/geral,-o-fim-das-obras-dos-barrageiros,1714868 (Accessed: 14 April 2020).

Estronioli, E (2016). Obras de belo monte aumentam casos de assédio e estupro. *Azmina*, 15 February. Available at: https://azmina.com.br/reportagens/obras-de-belo-monte-aumentam-casos-de-assedio-e-estupro/ (Accessed: 8 January 2020).

Exame (2019). Altamira é mais um capítulo da guerra de facções; relembre outros casos. *Exame*, 30 July. Available at: https://exame.abril.com.br/brasil/altamira-e-mais-um-capitulo-da-guerra-de-faccoes-relembre-outros-casos/ (Accessed: 8 January 2020).

Fachin, P, and Santos, JV (2015). A monstruosidade de Belo Monte e descalabro em Altamira que Dilma não teve coragem de ver. Entrevista especial com D. Erwin Kräutler. *IHU-Online*, 16 January. Available at: http://www.ihu.unisinos.br/entrevistas/539024-a-monstruosidade-de-belo-monte-dilma-nao-teve-coragem-de-ver-o-descalabro-provocado-pela-obra-entrevista-especial-com-d-erwin-kraeutler (Accessed: 30 March 2020).

FASE (2009). Belo Monte: Audiência discrimina e reprime população. *FASE*, 28 September. Available at: https://fase.org.br/pt/informe-se/noticias/belo-monte-audiencia-discrimina-e-reprime-populacao/ (Accessed: 8 January 2020).

Fearnside, PM (2017). Planned disinformation: the example of the Belo Monte Dam as a source of greenhouse gases. In: Issberner, LR, and Lena, P (eds) *Brazil in the Anthropocene: Conflicts between Predatory Development and Environmental Policies*. New York: Routledge.

Fearnside, PM (2018). Belo Monte: Lições da Luta 11 – A farsa da audiência pública. *Amazonia Real*, 5 March. Available at: https://amazoniareal.com.br/belo-monte-licoes-da-luta-11-farsa-da-audiencia-publica/ (Accessed: 30 March 2020).
Freeman, S (2013). Voices of the Xingu: interview with Maini Militão. *Amazon Watch*, 28 March. Available at: https://amazonwatch.org/news/2013/0328-voices-of-the-xingu-interview-with-maini-militao (Accessed: 25 April 2019).
G1 PA (2014). Cheia do rio Xingu deixa mais famílias desabrigadas em Altamira. *G1*, 12 March. Available at: http://g1.globo.com/pa/para/noticia/2014/03/cheia-do-rio-xingu-deixa-mais-familias-desabrigadas-em-altamira.html (Accessed: 8 January 2020).
G1 PA (2016). Fim das obras de Belo Monte ressalta desemprego no sudoeste do Pará. *G1*, 28 June. Available at: http://g1.globo.com/pa/para/noticia/2016/06/fim-das-obras-de-belo-monte-revela-cenario-de-desemprego-na-regiao.html (Accessed: 8 January 2020).
G1 PA (2017). MPF faz audiência pública em para debater impacto de Belo Monte no PA. *G1*, 20 March. Available at: http://g1.globo.com/pa/para/noticia/2017/03/mpf-faz-audiencia-publica-em-para-debater-impacto-de-belo-monte-no-pa.html (Accessed: 9 January 2020).
Gauthier, C, Lin, Z, Peter, BG, and Moran, EF (2019). Hydroelectric infrastructure and potential groundwater contamination in the Brazilian Amazon: Altamira and the Belo Monte dam. *The Professional Geographer*, Routledge, 71(2): 292–300.
Glass, V (2013). Adolescente é resgatada de prostíbulo em Belo Monte. *Reporter Brasil*, 14 February. Available at: https://reporterbrasil.org.br/2013/02/adolescente-e-resgatada-de-prostibulo-em-belo-monte/ (Accessed: 19 March 2019).
Grisotti, M (2016). The construction of health causal relations in the Belo Monte dam context. *Ambiente & Sociedade*, 19: 287–304.
Grupo de Estudos Tapajós (2014). *Avaliação Ambiental Integrada da Bacia do Tapajós: Sumário Executivo*. Available at: https://web.archive.org/web/20190217004707/http://www.http://grupodeestudostapajos.com.br/site/wp-content/uploads/2014/04/Sumario_AAI.pdf (Accessed: 30 March 2020).
Hanna, P, Vanclay, F, Langdon, EJ, and Arts, J (2016). The importance of cultural aspects in impact assessment and project development: reflections from a case study of a hydroelectric dam in Brazil. *Impact Assessment and Project Appraisal*, 34(4): 306–318.
Harris, LM (2009). Contested sustainabilities: assessing narratives of environmental change in southeastern Turkey. *Local Environment*, 14(8), 699–720.
Hill, C, Phan, TNT, Storey, J, and Vongphosey, S (2017). Lessons learnt from gender impact assessments of hydropower projects in Laos and Vietnam. *Gender & Development*, 25(3): 455–470.
Hochstetler, K (2011). The politics of environmental licensing: energy projects of the past and future in Brazil. *Studies in Comparative International Development*, 46(4), 349–371.
Instituto Brasileiro de Geografia e Estatistica (IBGE) (n.d.). *Altamira População*. Instituto Brasileiro de Geografia e Estatistica. Available at: https://cidades.ibge.gov.br/brasil/pa/altamira/panorama (Accessed: 8 January 2020).
Instituto Humanitas Unisinos (2013a). Violência sexual em Altamira: uma realidade crescente. Entrevista especial com Assis Oliveira. *IHU-Online*, 1 April. Available at: http://www.ihu.unisinos.br/entrevistas/518919-violencia-sexual-em-altamira-uma-realidade-crescente-entrevista-especial-com-assis-oliveira (Accessed: 8 January 2020).
Instituto Humanitas Unisinos (2013b). Boate Xingu: MPF/PA inicia investigação sobre exploração sexual em Belo Monte. *IHU-Online*, 19 February. Available at: http://www

.ihu.unisinos.br/noticias/517747-boate-xingu-mpfpa-inicia-investigacao-sobre-exp loracao-sexual-em-belo-monte (Accessed: 8 January 2020).
Instituto Humanitas Unisinos (2016). Belo Monte e a proposição formal de participação. Entrevista especial com Maíra Borges Fainguelernt. *IHU-Online*, 26 June. Available at: http://www.ihu.unisinos.br/entrevistas/521268-belo-monte-e-a-proposicao-for mal-de-participacao-entrevista-especial-com-maira-borges (Accessed: 8 January 2020).
Instituto Socioambiental (2015). *Dossiê Belo Monte: Não há condições para a Licença de Operação*. Brasilia, DF. Available at: https://documentacao.socioambiental.org/notic ias/anexo_noticia/31046_20150701_170921.pdf.
Instituto Socioambiental (2018a). Em articulação inédita, ribeirinhos atingidos pela usina Belo Monte determinam os caminhos para retornarem ao seu território. *Instituto Socioambiental*, 17 December. Available at: https://medium.com/@socioambiental/ em-articulação-inédita-ribeirinhos-atingidos-pela-usina-belo-monte-determinam- os-caminhos-para-3743b8440973 (Accessed: 8 January 2020).
Instituto Socioambiental (2018b). Ribeirinhos atingidos por Belo Monte exigem retomar seu território. *Instituto Socioambiental*, 9 February. Available at https://www.socioamb iental.org/pt-br/noticias-socioambientais/ribeirinhos-atingidos-por-belo-monte-e xigem-retomar-seu-territorio (Accessed: 8 January 2020).
Jiang, X, Lua, D, Moran, E, Freitas Calvi, M, Vieira Dutra, L, and Li, G (2018). Examining impacts of the Belo Monte hydroelectric dam construction on land-cover changes using multitemporal Landsat imagery. *Applied Geography*, 97: 35–47.
Jornal de Brasília (2013). Índios e ribeirinhos voltam a ocupar Belo Monte. *Jornal de Brasilia*, 21 March. Available at: https://jornaldebrasilia.com.br/economia/indios-e- ribeirinhos-voltam-a-ocupar-belo-monte/ (Accessed: 8 January 2020).
Latrubesse, EM, Arima, EY, Dunne, T, Park, E, Baker, VR, d'Horta, FM, Wight, C, Wittmann, F, Zuanon, J, Baker, PA, Ribas, CC, Norgaard, RB, Filizola, N, Ansar, A, Flyvbjerg, B, and Stevaux, JC (2017). Damming the rivers of the Amazon basin. *Nature*, 546(7658): 363–369.
Lessa, ACR, Santos, MA, Maddock, JEL, and dos Santos Bezerra, C (2015). Emissions of greenhouse gases in terrestrial areas pre-existing to hydroelectric plant reservoirs in the Amazon: the case of Belo Monte hydroelectric plant. *Renewable and Sustainable Energy Reviews*, 51(C): 1728–1736.
Li, F (2015). *Unearthing Conflict: Corporate Mining, Activism and Expertise in Peru*. Durham, NC: Duke University Press.
Li, TM (2007). *The Will to Improve: Governmentality, Development and the Practice of Politics*. Durham, NC: Duke University Press.
Lima, LH, and Magrini, A (2010). The Brazilian Audit Tribunal's role in improving the federal environmental licensing process. *Environmental Impact Assessment Review*, 30(2): 108–115.
Lopes, RJ (2017). Novas hidreletricas na Amazonia poden prejudicar clima e ecossistemas. *Folha de S.Paulo*, 14 June. Available at: http://www1.folha.uol.com.br/ambiente/20 17/06/1892979-novas-hidreletricas-na-amazonia-podem-prejudicar-clima-e-ecossiste mas.shtml (Accessed: 8 January 2020).
Madeiro, C (2017). Após Belo Monte, Altamira (PA) supera taxa de homicídios de país mais violento do mundo. *IHU-Unisinos*, 6th March. Available at: http://www.ihu.unisi nos.br/186-noticias/noticias-2017/565448-apos-belo-monte-altamira-pa-supera-taxa -de-homicidios-de-pais-mais-violento-do-mundo (Accessed: 19 March 2019).

Magalhães, SB, and Carneiro da Cunha, M (2017). *A Expulsão de Ribeirinhos em Belo Monte*. São Paulo. Sociedade Brasileira para o Progresso da Ciência: São Paulo. Available at: http://portal.sbpcnet.org.br/livro/belomonte.pdf.

Magalhães, SM, and Hernandez, FdM (eds) (2009). *Painel de Especialistas – Análise Crítica do Estudo de Impacto Ambiental do Aproveitamento Hidrelétrico de Belo Monte*. Belém, PA: Painel de Especialistas. Available at: https://www.socioambiental.org/banco_ima gens/pdfs/Belo_Monte_Painel_especialistas_EIA.pdf.

Marin, REA, and da Costa Oliveira, A (2016). Violence and public health in the Altamira region: the construction of the Belo Monte hydroelectric plant. *Regions and Cohesion*, 6(1): 116–134.

McCartney, M (2009). Living with dams: managing the environmental impacts. *Water Policy*, 11(1): 121–139.

McCormick, S (2006). The Brazilian anti-dam movement: knowledge contestation as communicative action. *Organization and Environment*, 19(3), 321–346.

McCormick, S (2010). Damming the Amazon: local movements and transnational struggles over water. *Society and Natural Resources*, 24(1): 34–48.

Ministério Público Federal (2019). MPF recomenda correção da licença de Belo Monte para preservar a vida na Volta Grande do Xingu (PA). *Ministério Público Federal*, 4 September. Available at: http://www.mpf.mp.br/pa/sala-de-imprensa/noticias-pa/mp f-recomenda-correcao-da-licenca-de-belo-monte-para-preservar-a-vida-na-volta-gra nde-do-xingu-pa (Accessed: 8 January 2020).

Ministério Público Federal, Procuradoria da República no Pará (2015). *Relatório de Inspeção Interinstitucional: Áreas ribeirinhas atingidas pelo processo de remoção compulsória da UHE Belo Monte*. MPF/PA: Altamira. Available at: http://pfdc.pgr.mpf.mp.br/tema s-de-atuacao/populacao-atingida-pelas-barragens/relatorios/relatorio-inspecao-interin stitucional-belo-monte (Accessed: 8 January 2020).

Ministério Público Federal, Procuradoria da República no Pará (2016). Em Santarém (PA), mais de 500 pessoas debatem usinas, mas governo não manda representante. MPF/PA, 29 January. Available at: http://www.mpf.mp.br/pa/sala-de-imprensa/noti cias-pa/em-santarem-mais-de-500-pessoas-debatem-usinas-mas-governo-nao-mand a-representante (Accessed: 8 January 2020).

Movimento dos Atingidos por Barragens (2013). MAB denuncia exploração sexual em áreas de barragens. *Movimento dos Atingidos por Barragens*, 20 March. Available at: http://www.mabnacional.org.br/noticia/mab-denuncia-explora-sexual-em-reas-barrag ens (Accessed: 8 January 2020).

Movimento dos Atingidos por Barragens (2017). Belo Monte faz de Altamira o município mais violento do Brasil. *Movimento dos Atingidos por Barragens*, 6 June. Available at: http://mabnacional.org.br/noticia/belo-monte-faz-altamira-munic-pio-mais-violent o-do-brasil (Accessed: 19 March 2019).

Movimento dos Atingidos por Barragens (2018). Inundação deixa atingidos por Belo Monte desabrigados. *Movimento dos Atingidos por Barragens*, 30 November. Available at: https://www.mabnacional.org.br/noticia/inunda-deixa-atingidos-por-belo-mont e-desabrigados (Accessed: 8 January 2020).

Movimento dos Atingidos por Barragens (2019). Conquista: Norte Energia vai refazer vistoria no entorno da Lagoa em Altamira. *Movimento dos Atingidos por Barragens*, 19 March. Available at: https://www.mabnacional.org.br/noticia/conquista-norte-energia-vai-refazer-vistoria-no-entorno-da-lagoa-em-altamira (Accessed: 8 January 2020).

Movimento Xingu Vivo para Sempre (MXVPS) (2010). *Letter to Secretary of Development, Science and Technology of the State of Pará*. Translated by Survival International. Available at: http://assets.survivalinternational.org/documents/406/SEDEC_letter_English.pdf (Accessed: 19 March 2019).

MXVPS (2011). Com Belo Monte, violência sexual contra criança e adolescente cresce 138%. *Xingu Vivo para Sempre*, 11 October. Available at: http://www.xinguvivo.org.br/2011/10/11/com-belo-monte-violencia-sexual-contra-crianca-e-adolescente-cresce-138/ (Accessed: 8 January 2020).

MXVPS (2019). Norte Energia descumpre acordos e provoca morte de ribeirinhos, denuncia Conselho. *Xingu Vivo para Sempre*, 21 May. Available at: http://www.xinguvivo.org.br/2019/05/21/norte-energia-descumpre-acordos-e-provoca-morte-de-ribeirinhos-denuncia-conselho/ (Accessed: 8 January 2020).

MXVPS (n.d.) *Belo 'Monstro' Não!* Altamira: MXVPS. Available at: http://assets.survivalinternational.org/documents/267/Xingu_Vivo_para_Sempre_panfle%0Ato.pdf.

Nathan Green, W, and Baird, IG (2016). Capitalizing on compensation: hydropower resettlement and the commodification and decommodification of nature-society relations in Southern Laos. *Annals of the American Association of Geographers*, 106(4), 853–873.

O'Faircheallaigh, C (2007). Environmental agreements, EIA follow-up and aboriginal participation in environmental management: the Canadian experience. *Environmental Impact Assessment Review*, 27(4): 319–342.

O'Faircheallaigh, C (2010). Public participation and environmental impact assessment: purposes, implications, and lessons for public policy making. *Environmental Impact Assessment Review*, 30(1): 19–27.

Pace, CA (2018). *Ripple Effects of the Belo Monte Dam: A Syndemic Approach to Addressing Health Impacts for the Downstream Community of Gurupá*. Thesis submitted to Department of Anthropology, University of South Florida.

Parracho, L (2012). Com obras de Belo Monte, Altamira enfrenta insegurança e alta de preços. *Terra*, 27 March. Available at: https://istoe.com.br/196393_COM+OBRAS+DE+BELO+MONTE+ALTAMIRA+ENFRENTA+INSEGURANCA+E+ALTA+DE+PRECOS/ (Accessed: 8 January 2020).

Partido dos Trabalhadores (PT) (2014). Norte Energia desmente Marina e investe R$ 1,2 bi em projetos de compensação. *Partido dos Trabalhadores*, 16 September. Available at: https://pt.org.br/norte-energia-desmente-marina-e-investe-r-12-bi-em-projetos-de-compensacao/ (Accessed: 14 March 2020).

Pedruzzi, P (2012). Centenas de desempregados dormem nas ruas de Altamira à espera de vagas em Belo Monte. *Agencia Brasil*, 18 April. Available at: http://memoria.ebc.com.br/agenciabrasil/noticia/2012-04-18/centenas-de-desempregados-dormem-nas-ruas-de-altamira-espera-de-vagas-em-belo-monte (Accessed: 8 January 2020).

Pinho, VA, and Oliveira Costa, A (2012). *Rodas de Direito: Diálogo, Empoderamento e Prevenção Não Enfrentamento da Humano Sexual Contra Crianças e Adolescentes*. Altamira, PA: Universidade Federal do Pará. Available at: http://pair.ledes.net/gestor/titan.php?target=openFile&fileId=1000.

Power, ME, Dietrich, WE, and Finlay, JC (1996). Dams and downstream aquatic biodiversity: potential food web consequences of hydrologic and geomorphic change. *Environmental Management*, 20(6): 887–895.

Randell, H (2016). The short-term impacts of development-induced displacement on wealth and subjective well-being in the Brazilian Amazon. *World Development*, 87: 385–400.

Ritter, CD, McCrate, R, Nilsson, RH, Fearnside, PM, Palme, U, and Antonelli, A (2017). Environmental impact assessment in Brazilian Amazonia: challenges and prospects to assess biodiversity. *Biological Conservation*, 206: 161–168.

Rothman, FD (2001). A comparative study of dam-resistance campaigns and environmental policy in Brazil. *Journal of Environment and Development*, 10(4): 317–344.

Salisbury, C (2017). International action a must to stop irreversible harm of Amazon dams, say experts. *Mongabay*, 19 June. Available at: https://news.mongabay.com/2017/06/international-action-a-must-to-stop-irreversible-harm-of-amazon-dams/ (Accessed: 8 January 2020).

Salm, R (2009). Belo Monte: a farsa das audiências públicas. *EcoDebate*, 8 October. Available at: https://www.ecodebate.com.br/2009/10/08/belo-monte-a-farsa-das-audiencias-publicas-artigo-de-rodolfo-salm/ (Accessed: 8 January 2020).

Secreto, MV (2007). A ocupação dos 'espaços vazios' no governo Vargas: do 'Discurso do rio Amazonas' à saga dos soldados da borracha,' *Estudos Históricos*, 2(40): 115–135.

Senado Federal (2019). Subcomissão de Belo Monte quer resolver disputa por terra com ribeirinhos no Pará. *Senado Federal*, 23 October. Available at: https://www12.senado.leg.br/noticias/materias/2019/10/23/subcomissao-de-belo-monte-quer-resolver-disputa-por-terra-com-ribeirinhos-no-para (Accessed: 8 January 2020).

Silva, GC, and Lucas, FCA (2019). Ribeirinhos e a hidrelétrica belo monte: a desterritorialização e influências no cultivo de plantas alimentícias. *Ambiente & Sociedade*, 22: e02961.

Southgate, T (2016). *Belo Monte: After the Flood*. Oakland, CA: International Rivers & Amazon Watch.

Spiegel, SJ (2017). EIAs, power and political ecology: situating resource struggles and the techno-politics of small-scale mining. *Geoforum*, 87: 95–107.

Talento, A (2014). Operarios de Belo Monte pagam sexo com vale alimentacao. *Folha de S.Paulo*, 14 June. Available at: https://www1.folha.uol.com.br/cotidiano/2014/06/1469550-operarios-de-belo-monte-pagam-sexo-com-vale-alimentacao.shtml (Accessed: 8 January 2020).

Vieira, M (2016). Belo Monte. 'Um monumento à insanidade.' Entrevista com D. Erwin Kräutler. *IHU-Online*, 5 April. Available at: http://www.ihu.unisinos.br/185-noticias/noticias-2016/553178-belo-monte-um-monumento-a-insanidade-entrevista-com-d-erwin-kraeutler (Accessed: 30 March 2020).

Yang, SL, Milliman, D, Xu, KH, Deng, B, Zhang, XY, and Luo, XX (2014). Downstream sedimentary and geomorphic impacts of the Three Gorges Dam on the Yangtze River. *Earth-Science Reviews*, 138: 469–486.

Zhouri, A (2015). From 'participation' to 'negotiation': suppressing dissent in environmental conflict resolution in Brazil. In: Bryant, RL (ed.) *The International Handbook of Political Ecology*. Cheltenham: Edward Elgar.

Zhouri, A (2018). Megaprojects, epistemological violence and environmental conflicts in Brazil. *Perfiles Económicos*, 5: 7–33.

6 'A country that cannot live with difference'

When seen from the air or in satellite imagery, the Legal Amazon Region of Brazil can appear to be an area characterised by vast swathes of forest that are only punctured by bodies of flowing water. For centuries, the region has been presented as pristine, as wilderness, or, more recently, as the 'lungs of the world.' However, Amazônia is a lived space – the product of millennia of historical settlement, day-to-day activities, population movement and displacement, and the economic agendas of successive political regimes (Bolaños, 2011; Heckenberger et al., 2007). The earliest evidence of human occupation in the region is dated to between 10,000 to 11,000 years ago (Roosevelt et al., 1996). Excavations in Mato Grosso have found evidence of 19 circular-shaped villages joined by roads that, between them, held public squares, bridges, dams and canals, land to cultivate cassava and other plants, and defensive palisades (Heckenberger et al., 2003). These villages, built between 1,200 and 1,600 AD, are estimated to have been home to up to 5,000 people (Heckenberger et al., 2008).

The history of the Amazon is one of encroachment. From the arrival of the Portuguese in 1500 to the modern-day government of Jair Bolsonaro, the Amazon has been transformed into a landscape of extractive riches, with its indigenous communities removed from their ancestral lands and decision-making (Ramos, 1998). The colonisation of the state by the Portuguese colonial regime is estimated to have resulted in the deaths of 90% of the 2.5 million indigenous peoples of Brazil in the region (Hemming, 1978). This experience continued into the 20th century, with the policies of the military junta resulting in extensive impacts on indigenous communities in Brazil. The construction of the Transamazônica occurred within a legacy of violence, with large numbers of indigenous people killed – by overwork, starvation, or murdered by those newly arrived in the region (Davis, 1977). Throughout this history, the fate of indigenous communities living in the Amazon became tied to the fate of the land at the hands of this form of development. As a result, the moments of contestation that surrounds the planning and construction of hydroelectric dams in the Brazilian Amazon must be understood as part of a wider, historical process of the defence of lands and livelihoods both within the development policies of the PT and a history of encroachment, assimilation, theft, and erasure (Zanotti, 2016).

A country that cannot live with difference 121

Opposition to hydropower projects from indigenous communities is not a new experience in Brazil, and these movements have linked their localised resistance to wider processes of encroachment on indigenous territory. As demonstrated by the 1989 Altamira Gathering, indigenous communities in the region have opposed dam projects by asserting their rights to territory and livelihoods. As described in Chapter 3, the community asserted that the construction of the Kararaô project represented the encroachment of external actors onto their territory and a direct threat to their culture and way of life. In 1989, the Kayapó community put forward a storyline of resistance that not only opposed the project but successfully 'scaled up' this struggle by asserting the links between their resistance and wider concerns for environmental protection.

In this chapter, I explore the ways in which the moments of contestation surrounding the Belo Monte and São Luiz do Tapajós projects continue to illuminate these links between hydropower projects in the Brazilian Amazon and processes of encroachment on their territories and cultures. While pro-dam actors argue that the impacts of the projects on indigenous communities will be limited, anti-dam actors illuminate the ways in which the dams will disrupt and dislocate the lives of many living in the region. This illumination occurs in two ways. First, anti-dam actors continue the process of 'rendering visible' discussed in Chapter 5 by highlighting the impacts of both projects on the lives and cultures of those communities impacted. Anti-dam actors draw attention to the traumatic disruption of the cultural lives of many of those living in the Xingu basin as a result of Norte Energia's mitigation plan. Second, anti-dam actors argue that the Belo Monte and São Luiz do Tapajós projects represent two sites in a wider process of encroachment and contestation between the development agendas of the Partido dos Trabalhadores administration and the indigenous communities of Brazil. In doing so, the resistance coalition illuminates how the construction of hydroelectric dams represents a 'spearhead' for further encroachment and extraction within the region by developmentalist interests.

Putting forward these storylines of opposition scales up the struggles against the Belo Monte and São Luiz do Tapajós projects by linking to them the wider neglect of and encroachment on the rights and territories of indigenous communities in Brazil. Taken together, this chapter argues that, within this resistance storyline, the planning and development of hydropower projects in the Brazilian Amazon become cast as more than a series of material, biophysical impacts (related to flooding or deforestation) but also as part of a wider struggle between indigenous communities and encroachment on their lands, lives, and cultures. In doing so, anti-dam actors reconfigure the pro-dam storyline of sustainability by demonstrating how the two projects studied embody similar logics of historical processes of encroachment.

The impacted communities

Within the official Environmental Impact Assessment, 12 indigenous lands were projected to be impacted by the Belo Monte project, with impacts including the alteration of the Xingu River's flow, the disruption of fisheries and a number of pressures associated with an increased population in the region (including increased competition for resources, biodiversity loss, and spread of disease) (Eletrobras, 2009a). These include the Paquiçamba and the Volta Grande do Xingu Macaw areas, both located within the territory of the indigenous Juruna territory located on the 'big bend' of the Xingu River. These lands are 'directly influenced' by the project, resulting in a number of communities being displaced from their traditional territories (Eletrobras, 2009a). Ten additional indigenous territories are listed as being located in areas of indirect influence, including the Xikrín, Xipaia, Kuruaya, and Kayapó communities (Fundação Nacional do Índio, 2011).

With the São Luiz do Tapajós Dam never moving forward in the planning process, its impacts on indigenous communities are less clear. Official assessments predicted that the project would affect seven indigenous communities, including the Apiaká de Pimental, Akaybãe, Remédio, Sai Cinza, São Martinho, and Boca do Igarapé Pacu communities, with segments of the territory of the Munduruku indigenous community to be flooded by the project's reservoir (Grupo de Estudos Tapajós, 2014). The predicted impacts included the flooding of land, loss of fisheries used for both subsistence and ornamental[1] fishing and an increase in waterborne diseases (Grupo de Estudos Tapajós, 2014).

Although additional groups – such as the ribeirinhos of the Xingu (discussed in Chapter 5) – are impacted by hydroelectric projects in Brazil and discussed in anti-dam materials (Movimento dos Atingidos por Barragens, 2014; MPF/PA, 2017), indigenous groups were widely presented as the figureheads of the resistance to the Belo Monte and São Luiz do Tapajós projects (Interview, 3 October 2016, Interview, 27 October 2016a, Interview, 27 October 2016b, Interview, 28 April 2017). Furthermore, despite other indigenous groups resisting the projects studied, the interviews and anti-dam materials collected focused extensively on the role of the Kayapó (resisting Belo Monte) and Munduruku (opposing São Luiz do Tapajós) communities, respectively (Interview, 3 October 2016, Interview, 27 October 2016a, 27 October 2016b, Interview, 6 December 2016, Interview, 28 April 2017; Alarcon et al., 2016; Amazon Watch, 2016). This omitted the actions of other communities such as the Juruna and Xikrín communities who have, themselves, participated in occupations of the Belo Monte project's construction site (Bratman, 2020).

An abundance of anti-dam materials – distributed nationally and internationally – incorporated images of indigenous communities in their presentation on the impacts of the Belo Monte and São Luiz do Tapajós projects (Alarcon et al., 2016; Marina. Amaral et al., 2013; de Aguiar et al., 2016; Greenpeace Brasil, 2016). Reports published and disseminated at the national and international level by Greenpeace featured prominent images of members of indigenous communities, presenting them as the core communities facing the social and environmental impacts of the Belo Monte project (de Aguiar et al., 2016; Greenpeace Brasil, 2016). Similarly, murals across Brazil present indigenous communities, particularly children, as key symbols of the respective projects. A

Figure 6.1 O Tapajós Precisa. Photograph taken by the author in Pinheiros, São Paulo (23/10/2016).

mural in Altamira presented an image of an indigenous child, their face circled by crosshairs (Hanna, 2016). Similar imagery was adopted in a series of posters found in Pinheiros, a suburb of São Paulo, in 2016 and distributed by unknown activists (see Figure 6.1). These posters provided images of indigenous children in their presentation of resistance to the São Luiz do Tapajós project. The poster engages in wordplay, changing the spelling of Amazônia to include 'Amar' (the verb for to love). The text below reads 'the Tapajós needs all,' creating an image of the indigenous communities needing support from across Brazil, and beyond, to oppose dams in the Tapajós basin.

This elevation of indigenous communities by NGOs and EOs opposed to hydropower projects as symbols of the resistance to the Belo Monte and São Luiz do Tapajós Dams follows previous opposition movements, such as that against the Kararaô Dam in 1989 (Turner, 1993; Zanotti, 2015). While many organisations have adopted an image of indigenous groups as marginalised traditional communities (Conklin and Graham, 1995; Zanotti, 2015) and indigenous groups in Brazil have, at times, adopted certain forms of imagery to fit this perception, this imagery can result in these communities being deprived of agency in the resistance to the projects studied (Ramos, 1998). Claims of the marginalisation of indigenous communities can give way to the creation of an image of indigenous communities as primitive, innocent, or helpless (Ramos, 1998). There are several cases of this occurring in the words of international actors in the resistance coalition studied. When describing the Munduruku opposition to the São Luiz do Tapajós Dam, Survival International, an international NGO based in the UK focused on securing the rights of indigenous communities, labelled the struggle as representative of 'industrialised society … trying to steal it [Munduruku territory] and plunder its resources in the name of "progress" and "civilisation"' (Survival International, 2016). Similarly, an actor in the UK who is a patron of Survival International argued that the projects represented how:

> the world that we live in now is forcing human beings, who are still in a different century, into the so-called 'Modern World.' We should not destroy or run roughshod over creatures who have not caught up with the world that we Westerners demand of them.
>
> (Interview, 5 September 2017)

Within these statements, a false dichotomy is created between the Munduruku community and 'industrialised society' or the 'modern world' which presents the Munduruku as distinct and detached from their livelihoods and patterns of interaction with other communities. It creates an image of the community as helpless and requiring international support and neglects the complexity of the community and its historical relationship with the Amazonian environment. While problematic, the logic behind this language can be found in the dissemination of these materials to international arenas. The use of imagery of indigenous figures and communities has been linked to the use of the community's rich cultural difference to represent the Amazon forest itself in the popular imagination of those living in the Global North (Conklin and Graham, 1995; Ramos, 1998). Nevertheless, this dichotomy demonstrates that, for some of those opposed to contemporary projects, this characterisation of indigenous communities in Brazil as distinct, passive, and requiring international support remains.[2]

However, many NGOs and EOs involved in the resistance coalition made great efforts to move beyond this dichotomy and, instead, focus attention and resources on the empowerment of the communities resisting the project. As one interviewee at a Brazilian human rights organisation that regularly worked with indigenous communities impacted by Belo Monte explained, many organisations saw their role as elevating members of indigenous communities as 'protagonists of their own stories' (Interview, 3 October 2016), with national and international organisations seeking to not only engage with these movements but facilitate their opposition at both the national and international levels (Interview, 3 October 2016, Interview, 19 October 2016, Interview, 28 April 2017). Other civil society actors interviewed consistently defined the struggle of indigenous communities against the respective projects studied as 'theirs,' with the agency of indigenous communities in opposing the projects studied reaffirmed (Interview, 3 October 2016; 27 October 2016b, 28 October 2016; 28 April 2017). In locating indigenous communities at the centre of the imagery, activities, and message of the resistance coalitions, the NGOs and EOs studied in this book sought to reassert the agency of these communities. Many of the organisations that I focus on in this book perceived themselves as a 'tool' to be used by the community, how and when they see fit (Interview, 19 October 2016). The funding and planning of international visits demonstrate this tactic of empowerment adopted by NGOs and EOs in the resistance coalition. For example, Greenpeace International supported Munduruku Caciques to travel internationally, allowing for the wider dissemination of resistance storylines and for the direct lobbying of international companies linked to the project, such as Siemens, which made hydroelectric turbines for hydroelectric projects in the Brazilian Amazon. Similarly, members of the Munduruku community spoke at the United Nations Framework Convention on Climate Change (UNFCCC) 21st Conference of Parties, held in Paris in 2015 (Amazon Watch et al., 2015). The visits – supported by national and international resistance actors – drew attention to the impacts of the projects studied at the international level.[3] An interviewee at Greenpeace Brasil explained to me that the opposition to São Luiz do Tapajós 'was a Munduruku struggle for a long time. We were a tool to help them increase awareness, [to] spread the word to the world' (Interview, 19 October 2016). In empowering the agency of indigenous groups, national and international actors in the resistance coalition elevate local communities and groups resisting the Belo Monte and São Luiz do Tapajós projects to become figureheads of a struggle defined as their own.

Many of those interviewed contrasted this facilitation of indigenous community's resistance with the failure of the pro-dam coalition to ensure the participation, consultation, and free, prior and informed consent (FPIC) of these communities in the development and construction of the projects studied (Interview, 30 September 2016; Interview, 27 October 2016a). Guaranteed in numerous international human rights mechanisms, the right to FPIC can be understood as representing the inherent rights of indigenous communities to their lands while respecting and protecting their authority over the use of such territory (Hanna and Vanclay, 2013). This authority is linked to the rights of such communities to self-determination, with both individuals and groups entitled to the control of their own destinies.[4] These processes provide a space in which accurate information is presented to local communities about a proposed project and, in turn, offer an opportunity for communities to ask questions, challenge apparent inaccuracies and contribute to the planning process.

As discussed in Chapter 5, members of the resistance coalition routinely criticised the participatory mechanisms around the Belo Monte project – arguing that the dialogue between the government and those impacted was instrumental, tokenistic, and suffered from numerous failings. It is particularly notable that a representative in the environmental licensing department of FUNAI argued that the organisation's claims of having hosted 50 meetings with indigenous communities were deceitful, with a substantial number of meetings not discussing either the project or its consequences:

> Free, prior and informed consent was not fulfilled properly ... After the [preliminary investigations] on the Xingu, they should have given specific briefings, saying that there was to be a hydroelectric plant. They weren't ... FUNAI held several meetings with the indigenous communities that were not for consultation [but they were] considered a consultation after the team returned from fieldwork ... We are perceived as liars by the indigenous

community, which is a valid criticism because the proper consultation was not done.

(Interview, 10 November 2016a)

Furthermore, numerous anti-dam actors questioned the validity of processes of FPIC surrounding the São Luiz do Tapajós project (Interview, 3 October 2016, Interview, 27 October 2016a, Interview, 03 November 2016b). Those interviewed argued that, throughout the planning process, there was little attempt to engage with the Munduruku community (Interview, 1 February 2017, Interview, 28 April 2017). In light of this absence of consultation, the community put together and published the 2014 Munduruku Protocol, stating that it was willing to hear the government's plans but required transparency and the provision of full and accurate information for such consultations to take place. This document, prepared in a series of meetings in September 2014 and approved by an Extraordinary Assembly of the Munduruku in December of that year, argued that the community wanted to hear the government's plans but required transparency and the provision of full and accurate information and for the consultation to represent dialogue, with the government hearing what the community has to say. For the Munduruku community, this process of consultation not only had to include discussion of the project but also had to involve respecting their wishes and rights to territory (Munduruku Consultation Protocol, 2014). The document never received an official reply from the government (Interview, 28 April 2017), which later published the official announcement of the auction of the São Luiz do Tapajós project without receiving the necessary consent from the Munduruku community (MXVPS, 2014).

This lack of consultation was linked by many anti-dam actors to the 'steamroller' (discussed in Chapter 4) that forced Belo Monte forward, regardless of the concerns of local communities. Interviewees from the resistance coalition argued that this represented the deliberate overruling of the rights of these communities by state actors in the name of economic development (Interview, 27 October 2016b; Interview, 9 November 2016; Interview, 10 November 2016a). As one Brazilian scientist argued, 'governments turned them [the projects] into a matter of "honour" to send the message to large corporations that ... [it] was willing to overrule indigenous rights, local traditional communities' rights' (Interview, 9 November 2016). The perceived failure of the pro-dam coalition to adequately consult the local indigenous communities was presented as illustrative of the pro-dam coalition not wanting to hear the voices of indigenous communities impacted by hydroelectric projects and, instead, concentrating on ensuring the passage of the projects from planning to construction (Interview, 27 October 2016b, Interview, 1 February 2017, Interview, 28 April 2017; Fachin and Santos, 2015; Poirier, 2010; Sakamoto, 2016).

While many of the organisations studied for this book argued that their role in the resistance coalition was one of supporting and empowering the opposition of the indigenous communities impacted by the Belo Monte and São Luiz do Tapajós projects, many of those interviewed did put forward storylines of resistance that discussed these communities and illuminated the ways in which they were impacted. It is to these storylines that I turn below.

Forgotten impacts

As I discussed in Chapter 5, anti-dam actors disputed the official Environmental Impact Assessments of the Belo Monte and São Luiz do Tapajós projects by 'rendering visible' a number of overlooked, neglected impacts. A similar process is evident in the ways in which those interviewed understood and defined the impacts faced by indigenous communities opposed to the respective projects. Despite a number of impacts of the Belo Monte and São Luiz do Tapajós projects on indigenous communities being discussed in the respective project's Environmental Impact Assessments (Eletrobras, 2009a; Grupo de Estudos Tapajós, 2014), pro-dam actors in Brazil argued that the magnitude of impacts on these groups was limited. In a regular public address in which she responded to questions from the public, President Dilma Rousseff assured Maria da Glória Souza, a 62-year-old retiree from Fortaleza, that:

> [Belo Monte's] reservoir will not reach any of the ten indigenous lands of the area. Indigenous peoples will not be removed from their villages ... The objective is to bring to the region [the] social and infrastructure investments that are fundamental to improving the quality of life of the local population.
> (Brasil Portal do Planalto, 2011)

By not creating a large reservoir, the run-of-the-river design of Belo Monte is in accordance with the obligations of the 1988 Brazilian Constitution, which made it illegal to flood parts of indigenous territories without authorisation from the Brazilian Congress. A similar assertion was evident in descriptions of the São Luiz do Tapajós project, with pro-dam actors denying that the planned project would have an impact on indigenous communities in the region. An interviewee at the Ministério de Minas e Energia (MME) described the indigenous groups living in the region as 'nomadic,' asserting that these communities were not fixed to the territory in any way and could easily move to escape the projected impacts of the dam (Interview, 3 November 2016a).

While a run-of-the-river design does result in less land inundation, its impacts move in different ways, with indirect and cumulative impacts just as important in gauging a project's 'sustainability.' With pro-dam actors asserting that the project would not flood any indigenous land, anti-dam materials argue that the impact was, in fact, the opposite. With 80% of the Xingu's flow being redirected, the resulting fluctuation in flow was described by many as the disappearance of the river that indigenous communities rely upon (Interview, 3 November 2016b, Interview, 7 November 2016b, Interview, 28 April 2017). The logic underpinning these assertions is that the reduced flow of the Xingu was to impact subsistence and ornamental fishing due to the loss of fisheries, disrupt river navigation, and increase waterborne diseases in the region. This distinction between 'directly impacted' and 'indirectly impacted,' discussed in Chapter 5, in official assessments neglects these impacts and was presented by a representative of the Ministério Publico Federal as representing a selection made by the designers of Belo Monte to limit the understanding of the numbers of those to be affected by the project. The interviewee argued:

> They know that they are going to affect [local populations] and I have been to Belo Monte … and indigenous people are begging to be recognised as dam-affected.
> (Interview, 7 November 2016b)

While anti-dam actors illuminated the absence of discussions of indirect impacts in these documents and the pro-dam storyline of sustainability, many went further and criticised the mitigative measures put in place by the owner of Belo Monte, Norte Energia. For these actors, the personal trauma for many impacted by the Belo Monte Dam can be found in the transformation of traditional livelihoods and their forced transition into a new form of economic organisation. The impacts of Belo Monte on indigenous communities should not be understood as being only related to direct, material impacts, such as flooding, as studied in official impact assessments. Instead, the indirect impacts – such as the disruption of livelihoods – represent an irreversible and dramatic transformation (Interview, 3 October 2016).

A central part of the storyline adopted by anti-dam actors to oppose the Belo Monte project concerned the impacts of the project on the cultural identity of the impacted communities of the Xingu, with a particular focus of criticism being on the ways in which the project's mitigation scheme resulted in numerous irreversible impacts for the indigenous way of life in the region. The Plano Emergencial (Emergency Plan), run by Norte Energia and linked to a condition present in the project's construction licence, allocated over funds to 11 indigenous areas impacted (both directly and indirectly) by the Belo Monte project to support the communities' adaptation to its impacts. Within this scheme, running from 2010 to 2012, R$30,000 (US$9,000) in financial support and goods were distributed to each village every month. The Caciques of each community submitted a list of goods required – including boats, fuel, televisions, sugar, and soft drinks – and the company would later deliver them. By 2012, the scheme, which had reached even the most remote community, had spent R$212 million. In 2014, Norte Energia reported that, under this policy, 699 houses were built and 1.2 million litres of fuel, 326 ships and sails, 564 outboard engines, 96 electricity generators, and 44 vehicles were delivered to the indigenous communities of the region (PT, 2014).

Anti-dam actors argued extensively that the Plano Emergencial resulted in the detachment of many members of the indigenous communities in the Xingu basin from their livelihoods and cultures. Within this argument, the transformation of the lives and livelihoods of indigenous communities comes to represent the traumatic transition from tradition to a particular view of modernity

(Interview, 27 October 2016b, 3 November 2016b). A journalist who had written extensively on issues of development in Amazônia argued that analysis of the Belo Monte Dam needed to explore 'how a project like that really changes [the] lives of people' (Interview, 21 November 2016). Under the Plano Emergencial, members of the indigenous community were able to visit the FUNAI office in Altamira and request goods and financial assistance. Many started buying goods in local marketplaces – saving labour grinding cassava flour by buying it, purchasing consumer goods (such as plasma televisions) and flatbed trucks (Arnold, 2018). As Carolina Reis, an activist at Instituto Socioambiental, notes, those devising the Plano Emergencial did not understand – or seek to mitigate – the ways in which this influx of new goods and ways of living might interact with communities who, up to recently, had had only limited interaction with consumer goods (Sullivan, 2016). Communities switched from a diet of cassava, fresh fruit and vegetables, and newly caught fish to one consisting of processed foods, and crops stopped being planted (Interview, 3 November 2016b; Sullivan, 2016). Resistance materials link the scheme to increased rates of alcohol abuse, diabetes, and hypertension due to the proliferation of junk food in their diet, increased infant mortality, increased household waste, and increased rates of drug use within the communities that experienced to the mitigative measures (Brum, 2014, 2015a, 2015c; Instituto Socioambiental, 2015b).

For many interviewees, while the conditions of Belo Monte's licence called for the provision of schools and health clinics, the Plano Emergencial had, instead, taken the form of series of giveaways, with material goods provided to placate potential resistance (Interview, 1 February 2017, Interview, 28 April 2017). As an interviewee explained, the scheme was designed to give

> [some] indigenous people ... a feeling of 'progress'... dividing the people, generating conflicts among the indigenous communities ... creating all the conditions for the construction to take place and at the same time for the destruction of a culture that had existed for millennia.
> (Interview, 1 February 2017)

The use of goods to gain the support of local communities was discussed by both pro-dam and resistance actors in interviews. An interviewee based at the Brazilian arm of an international EO explained that they had directly experienced this use of goods to co-opt indigenous peoples:

> I went to a dam, and there was a pile of poles ... Something like 50 [poles] ... And I say 'What's this for?' and [they say] 'for the indigenous chiefs.' They didn't know who [to give them to] but they had [them] already.
> (Interview, 27 October 2016a)

Maíra Irigaray, an activist for Amazon Watch, an NGO campaigning for the protection of the Amazon rainforest, argued that these policies represented a process of bribery, with Norte Energia using materials to provide incentives to indigenous communities to accept Belo Monte's construction (Irigaray, 2014). Irigaray translated the words of Sheyla Juruna, from the Juruna community affected by the Plano Emergencial, who argued that:

> Norte Energia came and because they couldn't 'buy me off,' they made promises to my cousin who took the leadership from me and got a truck instead, so he would stay quiet.
>
> (Irigaray, 2014)

A construction manager for Norte Energia at Belo Monte would later joke about the role of these goods in negotiations with indigenous communities. The interviewee argued that when indigenous communities occupied roads and construction sites: 'we have to negotiate with them and … we have to … give away more items [laughs] to open the roads and continue the construction' (Interview, 6 December 2016). With these words, this figure confirms the fear of many opposed to Belo Monte: that material goods were distributed to stifle opposition.

Many opponents of Belo Monte likened this use of material goods and items to encourage the support of Belo Monte from local indigenous populations to the historical experience of colonialism in Brazil (Interview, 3 October 2016, Interview, 27 October 2016b, Interview, 28 April 2017). The Plano Emergencial is presented as a repetition of the experience of indigenous communities in the colonial era, with the provision of funds and materials described as repeating the use of 'trinkets' to secure their trust and dependence of pre-1500 communities (Brum, 2014, 2015a; Santos, 2015). Resistance actors foreground the scheme's location in a long and violent history of incursion on indigenous and traditional lands in Brazil and the cultural loss experienced by many at the time (Interview, 19 October 2016; Interview, 27 October 2016b; Interview, 18 November 2016). The Plano Emergencial ceased to be a programme of impact-mitigation and compensation and became understood as a process of bribery that had disastrous consequences, disconnecting local communities from their culture and disrupting their livelihoods.

The links between the Plano Emergencial and the colonial era were further presented via the use of the language of ethnocide – understood as representing the systematic destruction of a group's culture – to describe the measures (Brum, 2014; Santos, 2015; Sullivan, 2016). In a 2014 interview in El Pais, Thais Santi, the public prosecutor in Altamira, described the village of Arara do Cachoeira Seca as a scene reminiscent of a holocaust (Brum, 2014):

> I saw their destroyed homes, with broken tiles, raining inside. And they were sleeping there … [it was] a holocaust. The Indians did not move. They just stood there motionless, stuck, asking for food, asking to have homes built for them … They have stopped talking and meeting each other. The only time they met was at night to watch a telenovela on a plasma screen. It was brutal … The Emergency Plan has created an absolute dependence on the company.
>
> (Brum, 2014)

In adopting the language of ethnocide, those civil and political society actors opposed to the project highlighted how the Plano Emergencial impacted upon, altered and fragmented the identity and culture of indigenous communities but also that the plan represented a conscious, deliberate effort by the pro-dam coalition to secure the acquiescence of indigenous communities, with little concern for the consequences. This argument is based on the assertion that Norte Energia had deliberately and consciously failed to comply with conditions present within the environmental licences for the protection of indigenous communities, instead relying on the use of the compensation and mitigative measures to gain support (Brum, 2014; Instituto Socioambiental, 2015b). In December 2015, the MPF presented this argument in a legal setting, filing a lawsuit that sought recognition of the Belo Monte scheme as representing an occurrence of ethnocide committed by both the Brazilian state and Norte Energia (Instituto Socioambiental, 2015b). Such assertions challenge the pro-dam storyline of sustainability by asserting the similarities between the experience of those in the Xingu and Tapajós basins and the fate of indigenous groups at the time of colonisation and extraction by the Portuguese Crown (Aleixos and Conde, 2016). In alluding to the experience of colonial violence, those opposed to the projects studied illuminated how the Brazilian state has not moved on from its historical subjugation of indigenous communities and remains a country that 'cannot live with difference' (Interview, 27 October 2016b).

While pro-dam actors have sought to deny the impacts of the Belo Monte and São Luiz do Tapajós projects based on a narrow understanding of the impacts linked to displacement caused by land inundation, such cultural impacts point to a wider process of dislocation and loss. Social relationships in these regions become frayed; obesity increased, drug and alcohol use skyrocketed – all due to the failure of the Plano Emergencial to adequately identify the social costs of Belo Monte in indigenous communities and mitigate them correctly. Such assertions challenge the pro-dam storyline of sustainability by illuminating the cultural impacts, absent in official storylines, faced by local indigenous communities and, in labelling the process an episode of 'ethnocide,' 'scaling up' resistance to the projects, which became representative of a wider defence of indigenous culture and difference (Interview, 19 October 2016; Interview, 27 October 2016b; Interview, 3 November 2016b; Aleixos and Conde, 2016).

Territorial visions

The election of Luiz Inácio Lula da Silva in 2002 and 2006 and Dilma Rousseff in 2010 represented a degree of hope for indigenous communities, with the Partido dos Trabalhadores offering numerous reforms to increase protection of traditional communities in Brazil. However, such hope was short-lived. The budget of the Brazilian indigenous agency, Fundação Nacional do Índio (FUNAI), was continually reduced (Interview, 10 November 2016a). Similarly, the demarcation and protection of indigenous territories decreased, reaching a low of 3.3 million hectares during Dilma's administration. As a journalist would explain to me:

For a long time, Brazil was really aggressive and doing a really interesting job of trying to create a mosaic of protected lands across the Amazon. That pretty much stopped under the PT governments and, obviously, who that impacts the most ... is the indigenous communities that have long called those areas home.

(Interview, 30 September 2016)

As discussed in Chapter 4, the years of PT government were also characterised by development policies, such as PAC and PAC 2, of which the Legal Amazon was a key arena. For example, within the first PAC, there were 82 highway and waterway works in the Legal Amazon Region, of which 43 projects affected one or more areas of land claimed by indigenous communities (Verdum, 2012). It is within this context that those opposed to the projects studied foreground the impacts faced by indigenous communities in the wider context of the PT government's dam-building agenda and a model of economic development that is described as encroaching upon indigenous territory, denying the rights, livelihoods and identities of these communities (Interview, 3 October 2016; Interview, 19 October 2016; Interview, 2 November 2016; Interview, 18 November 2016). For example, a letter disseminated by indigenous communities after the 2010 Terra Livre (Free Land) encampment foregrounded their resistance to Belo Monte in a wider context of encroachment, reporting that the Programa de Aceleração do Crescimento (Growth Acceleration Program, PAC) contained 426 projects that would affect indigenous lands (Various, 2010). Anti-dam actors argued that, within the context of PAC, PAC 2, and IIRSA, the respective projects represented a 'spearhead' for further state-driven encroachment and extraction in the region, with the construction of energy infrastructure providing a foundation for 'accessing some of the more remote regions of the Amazon for these developmentalist projects' (Interview, 1 February 2017). In doing so, the resistance coalition 'scaled up' the opposition to the projects studied, presenting them as one front in a wider moment of contestation between indigenous communities and the development policies of the PT.

A process of 'scaling up' is evident in how both projects were discussed within a context of the potential infrastructure, development and extractive projects that were expected to follow them, with the links between the Belo Monte and São Luiz do Tapajós projects and other infrastructure schemes highlighted by many. Many of those interviewed drew attention to the links between Belo Monte and the mining operations (Interview, 19 October 2016; Interview, 3 November 2016b; Interview, 1 December 2016a; Interview, 9 January 2017). The Brazilian mining giant Vale SA held a 9% stake in the Norte Energia consortium that owns Belo Monte. Despite selling 49% of this stake in April 2015, Vale SA maintained its right to 9% of the total energy to be produced by Belo Monte's turbines (Reuters, 2015). Between 2010 and 2013, numerous mining concerns were acquired by the Canadian company, Belo Sun. Redirecting 80% of the river's flow through its canals and spillways, the construction of Belo Monte exposed a 100 km stretch of the Xingu's resource-rich river bed, allowing for the acceleration of extractive operations in the region. The Belo Sun mining operation, located on the part of the Volta Grande left exposed by Belo Monte, is predicted to cover a 1,033 km area and become the largest open-pit gold mine in Brazil. This investment – understood to involve a US$380 million investment by the Canadian company and to be active over a period of 12 years, is expected to produce yields of over 200,000 ounces of gold per year – resulting in Belo Sun earning over US$7 billion in revenues (Bratman, 2020). While the Belo Sun operation is not legally or financially linked to the planning and construction of Belo Monte, its entrance into the Xingu River Basin provided a powerful example for many anti-dam actors of the overlapping geographies of hydropower and mining in the Brazilian Amazon.[5] The Belo Sun project was described by those opposed to it as being intimately linked to the construction of the dam (Hurwitz, 2011; Movimento dos Atingidos por Barragens [MAB], 2017; Poirier, 2017; Sullivan, 2017). One interviewee explained, 'it is very coincidental [laughs] that you have Belo Monte, [and then] you have this huge gold-mining proposal from a Canadian company in this dry stretch that is downstream from Belo Monte' (Interview, 1 December 2016a).

Similarly, the impacts of the São Luiz do Tapajós project were also widely presented as embodying the entrance of various other projects into the region. The São Luiz do Tapajós project was part of the Complex Tapajós (Tapajós Complex), consisting of five larger hydroelectric dams that were due to generate a total capacity of 12,589 MW for the Brazilian national grid. This complex itself will likely be a constituent part of a wider cascade of hydroelectric dams in the region. The project's official Environmental Impact Assessment reported the possibility of a total of 26 large dams in the region, with a total capacity of 26,408 MW (CNEC, 2014). In light of this potential for more projects to be built in the basin, the construction of the São Luiz do Tapajós project is widely understood as a constituent part of an objective that is far broader than the provision of hydroelectricity. The municipalities surrounding the planned São Luiz do Tapajós construction site already illustrate the role that this demand can play in stimulating infrastructure construction, particularly in terms of road construction. The city of Itaituba – one of the nearest population centres to the São Luiz do Tapajós site – is situated at the confluence of the Rodovia Transamazônica (Transamazon Highway) and the BR-163 highway, providing a fulcrum of the region's soy industry and global markets. The planning and construction of more dams in the Tapajós basin were widely asserted by those opposed to the project to be likely to enable the construction of ports in nearby cities, as well as the further development of the 4,476 km highway between Santarém and states in the south of Brazil and numerous mining operations. With expanding agribusiness activities in the region leading to increased demand for improved transport corridors to both national and international markets, the São Luiz do Tapajós project was understood to represent a part of a wider plan to convert the Juruena, Teles Pires and Tapajós Rivers into a 1,000-mile-long waterway, to transport soybeans from Mato Grosso in the south to the Atlantic ports at the mouth of the Amazon (Interview, 1 December 2016a; Interview, 1 February 2017; Interview, 28 April 2017).

The economic policy of the PT, described in Chapter 4, was presented by anti-dam activists as predatory and plundering the environment with limited concern for local communities. One domestic environmental campaigner argued that, in this context, the indigenous populations impacted by the Belo Monte and São Luiz do Tapajós projects are seen as 'undesirables and as something to be pushed out of the way of "development" and "progress"' (Interview, 18 November 2016). This statement highlights the view of resistance actors that, within the economic policy of 'development at all costs,' the indigenous communities impacted are considered dispensable and viewed by pro-dam actors as blocking the realisation of 'progress,' resulting in their being 'pushed out of the way' (Interview, 18 November 2016). Assertions of how the projects studied represent a process of further encroachment and exclusion are also provided by imagery in a mural found in the village of Alter do Chão, which was painted during a festival celebrating the Tapajós River (see Figure 6.2). The mural depicts a man in a suit (symbolising business), bloated in the face, sucking up the water of the Tapajós through a straw, leaving a boat carrying indigenous figures beached on an exposed riverbed. The individual or group responsible for the mural (unknown at the time of writing) presented a striking image of the São Luiz do Tapajós project.

Actors opposed to hydropower in the Brazilian Amazon characterised projects as symbolic of a wider disrespect of indigenous communities and their territories, with resistance actors arguing that these groups had become rendered surplus within the development policies underpinning the projects' planning and construction (Interview, 19 October 2016; Interview, 27 October 2016a; Interview, 27 October 2016b). As a representative of Greenpeace Brasil explained, 'They are seen as lazy, as people who do not have jobs, as people who do not contribute to their country' and, as a result, they are deemed disposable in development

Figure 6.2 Alter do Chão mural. Photograph taken by the author, Alter do Chão (14/11/2016)

A country that cannot live with difference 135

agendas (Interview, 19 October 2016).[6] For many, this disregard for indigenous communities resulted in the impunity on the part of pro-dam actors discussed in Chapter 4, who held little regard for the communities to be impacted by Belo Monte. As an interviewee at the Brazilian arm of the Nature Conservancy explained:

> They come, they don't care about their culture, they don't care about their livelihood ... [They say] 'They live like animals, they live inside the forest? They don't use full clothes' [laughs] 'They are stupid.' They go [unintelligible] ... 'Fuck them and let's build the dam.'
> (Interview, 27 October 2016a)

In highlighting these links, anti-dam actors widened the struggle against the projects, 'scaling up' their opposition to the project into a wider contestation surrounding a development strategy that was seemingly only one component in a wider series of threats to indigenous communities. With the construction of Belo Monte enabling the concessions required for Belo Sun and the São Luiz do Tapajós project linked to an expansion of hydroelectricity, waterways and commercial agriculture into the region, the projects were presented by many as representative of the shift to large-scale investments and infrastructure construction in the region that characterised the PAC, PAC-2, and IIRSA of the PT. In the eyes of the anti-dam actors interviewed, the project became illustrative of a wider policy towards the Legal Amazon Region, one which was focused on transforming the region, its lands, rivers, and communities, into a conduit for globalised resource extraction and trade (Interview, 3 October 2016; Interview, 10 November 2016a; Interview, 1 February 2017; Interview, 28 April 2017).

The Munduruku opposition

While the potential act of building the São Luiz do Tapajós Dam was widely presented as representative of a process of encroachment, extraction, and subjugation, national and international civil society figures also presented the Munduruku community, and their resistance to the project, in a particular light. Specifically, this community's opposition to the São Luiz do Tapajós Dam was often described in the context of the community's history of conflict with the Brazilian state. The Munduruku were presented as 'warlike' (Aranha and Mota, 2014a; Branford, 2013; Irigaray, 2015; Rosa, 2015) and described as engaged in a 'guerra moderna' ('modern war') against the Brazilian government (Pontes, 2016).

The antagonistic relationship between the Munduruku and the Brazilian government was evident in an episode in November 2012, when the Brazilian Federal Police raided an illegal gold-mining barge at the Munduruku village of Teles Pires (Branford and Torres, 2017b; Rocha and Millikan, 2013). During the raid, the barge was destroyed, and Adenilson Munduruku was shot dead. When describing this episode, a representative of a domestic human rights organisation compared the Munduruku community to 'guerrillas ... fight[ing] a giant' and described how the Munduruku community instilled fear in those working for Eletrobras and other companies engaged in dam construction: 'this guy from the government, he was telling me how afraid he was the Munduruku would take him hostage' (Interview, 3 October 2016). This bureaucrat's fear likely stemmed from an episode in 2013 when a group of Munduruku discovered three technicians conducting preliminary studies for the Tapajós hydroelectric project in indigenous territory. The three men, Djalma Nóbrega, Luiz Peixoto and José Guimarães, were kidnapped by Munduruku warriors in protest at the conducting of studies without their permission (Reuters, 2015). This abduction prompted a confrontation with the Brazilian Federal Police, sent by President Dilma Rousseff, with the police arriving in a helicopter, two large ships and 40 smaller vessels (Aranha and Mota, 2014a).

Rather than the application of a particular form of imagery and motivation by external actors, it is evident that the Munduruku community itself drew on its history of combat when expressing its opposition to the São Luiz do Tapajós project, which was presented as a government-sponsored invasion of their territory (Irigaray, 2015; Leite et al., 2013; Pontes, 2016; Rocha and Millikan, 2013; Rosa, 2015). In meetings and events, Munduruku attendees would display their bows and arrows throughout, providing a symbolism of resistance (Aranha and Mota, 2014a). This display links the historical reputation of the Munduruku with their contemporary resistance to the São Luiz do Tapajós project by providing a symbolic visual display of resistance.[7]

An antagonistic relationship can also be seen in an open letter released by the Munduruku community to an international audience:

> The great smoke of Djurupari (the evil spirit) is coming deeper into our lands. Ultimately, it will bring everything to an end – even the pariwat (white people) who brought it. But we indigenous people are strong. Despite all efforts to exterminate us, we have been preparing for many generations to defend our lands and our people and we will resist to the last Munduruku.
> (Members of the Pariri Indigenous Association and Ipereğ Ayũ Movement, 2017)

This statement 'scales up' the opposition to the São Luiz do Tapajós project – with the Munduruku community adopting a language of defence and resistance, transforming their opposition to the São Luiz do Tapajós project into a site of antagonism between their own cultural identity and an other (the pariwat) encroaching upon their lands. This warrior imagery is illustrative of a wider Munduruku ideology and movement against hydroelectric and mining activities on the community's lands. Ipereğ Ayũ is an indigenous movement based on the assertion of cultural identity and constitutional rights in the face of the encroachment of developmentalist activities. The term itself translates as 'We are strong – we know how to protect ourselves and all we believe in' and the concept simultaneously asserts the territorial rights and cultural identity of the

Munduruku community, foregrounding hydroelectric and extractive-driven encroachment within a wider contest over the community's way of life and cultural sites (Loures, 2018).

The São Luiz do Tapajós Dam threatened a number of Munduruku cultural sites, including Travessia dos Porcos ('Crossing of the Pigs'), a spiritual site linked to a revered ancestor, and Garganta do Diabo ('Devil's Throat'), a set of rapids having significance due to its vast wealth of fish (Nitta and Naka, 2015). It is at this site that the main complex of the São Luiz do Tapajós was to be built. The presence of these sites of spiritual symbolism meant that the projects represented a threat not only to indigenous territorial rights but also to their culture and intrinsic links to the land itself (Fearnside, 2015; Nitta and Naka, n.d.). The impact on these sites is presented as being of a similar magnitude to the destruction of the Munduruku sacred site of Sete Quedas by the neighbouring Teles Pires hydroelectric project, constructed on a tributary to the Tapajós (Nitta and Naka, 2015; Resk, 2017). The site was destroyed with dynamite in 2014, making way for the facility's reservoir. For the Munduruku, Sete Quedas is revered as the site of the spirits of deceased elders and has become a symbol of the effects of hydropower projects on sites of cultural and spiritual importance in Brazil (Branford and Torres, 2017a). The location of a hydroelectric complex at a site of spiritual significance for the Munduruku community is presented by many in the resistance coalition as a symbol of the government's disrespect for the community and their intrinsic relationship with the river, with these sacred sites absent in the project's official Environmental Impact Assessment (Fearnside, 2015; Nitta and Naka, 2015).

When discussing the Munduruku resistance to the São Luiz do Tapajós project, numerous anti-dam actors 'scaled up' the community's opposition, presenting it as part of a wider resistance to encroachment on Munduruku territory (Interview, 3 October 2016; Interview, 19 October 2016; Interview, 28 April 2017). Since the 1980s, pro-dam actors in Brazil have sought to introduce hydroelectric projects into the Tapajós basin, hindering decades-long efforts by the Munduruku community to secure demarcation of their territory. The Munduruku community had waited for 13 years for FUNAI to publish its report on the Sawré Muybu territory and announce its official demarcation. During those years, the community faced encroachment from logging and gold-mining operations and hydropower expansion, destroying their lands, sacred sites, and resources. In September 2014, Munduruku leaders met with the interim president of FUNAI, Maria Augusta Assirati, who declared to those gathered that the report recognising and creating the indigenous land had been approved months previously but was being blocked by government actors who were concerned about how the land demarcation might limit future activities in the region.

Due to the state's refusal to recognise their territorial rights to Sawré Muybu, the Munduruku community began to demarcate its territory in 2014, working alongside Greenpeace Brasil to traverse, geo-tag, map and claim the lands threatened by the São Luiz do Tapajós Dam. By mid-July 2016, the Munduruku community had finished this process of demarcation, mapping Sawré Muybu, which was formed of three villages (Sawré Muybu, Dace Watpu, and Karo Muybu) and a number of sites of spiritual importance, via 42 points. Munduruku villages raised informal demarcation signs designed to look similar to official FUNAI signs to demonstrate their territorial rights and delineate a dividing line between Sawré Muybu and the outside world (Pontes, 2016). The signs used block lettering on a white background, with green and yellow diagonal bands running diagonally from top-left to bottom-right; in bold red font are the words 'PROTECTED LAND.' This process extends beyond the mapping of territory and towards forms of monitoring that would usually be conducted by the state, such as safeguarding the integrity of such formalised claims.

An important element of this process of demarcation was the mapping and recording of the Munduruku territory, transforming it from an abstract landscape into a lived space. In mapping the Sawré Muybu territory, members of the Munduruku community were able to highlight their deep-seated relationship with the river, in terms of cultural and livelihoods. The map that came out of the Munduruku process of counter-mapping, labelled the 'Map of Life' and disseminated by Greenpeace Brasil, included key sites of spiritual significance, hunting and fishing grounds, and settlements. It highlights key species and their presence along the river, and it illustrates key points of encroachment, such as the BR 836 highway skirting around the edges of the territory. Official, technical processes of mapping – for Environmental Impact Assessments, for example – are narrow, simplifying space and neglecting its cultural and spiritual importance and patterns of use and settlement (Peluso, 1995; Zhouri, 2018). The Munduruku process of counter-mapping shifted the emphasis from the land to the people who live there and how they, as communities, interact with the Tapajós River Basin.

Conclusions

I have argued in this chapter that, when discussing the Belo Monte and São Luiz do Tapajós projects, many of those opposed to hydroelectric projects in the Brazilian Amazon foregrounded the contemporary resistance to the respective projects within a wider context of encroachment on indigenous territory, rights, and livelihoods. The projects are presented as one site in a wider struggle of indigenous communities against the encroachment of extractive and developmentalist practices into the Xingu and Tapajós basins, with the projects coming to represent a 'spearhead' that both allows for and stimulates the further expansion of extractive operations in the respective regions.

The storylines of anti-dam actors discussed in this chapter 'scale up' the opposition to the Belo Monte and São Luiz do Tapajós projects, widening the scope of resistance and presenting the links between these projects and wider patterns of encroachment. For many anti-dam activists interviewed for this book, the construction of both the Belo Monte and São Luiz do Tapajós projects represents a process of envelopment. The projects studied are deemed to be constituent parts of a wider encroachment into the area, with the river basins to be opened up for new mines and waterway projects. This represented a state-led process of extraction and displacement resulting in the displacement of indigenous communities from their territory and their dislocation from their culture. Evidence of this is found in both the tangible (the potential destruction of sites sacred to the Munduruku community of the Tapajós basin) and the cultural (the trauma and dislocation brought by the Plano Emergencial initiated by Norte Energia).

It is the latter that provides perhaps the most dramatic rebuke to the claims of sustainability and limited impacts made by pro-dam actors. In discussing Belo Monte, numerous proponents of the project argued that the project would not have impacts on indigenous communities, with many communities in the respective regions being either unaffected or mobile enough to avoid the impacts. However, similar to the discrediting of the division of 'direct' and 'indirect' influence and impacts present in official Environmental Impact Assessments, the illumination of the cultural losses of many in the Xingu River Basin functions to render visible the ways in which the impacts of hydropower may not always be what they seem at first. Activists against Belo Monte claimed that the Plano Emergencial represented the sudden and widespread disintegration of the way of life in the basin. Lifestyles and livelihoods were utterly transformed– all as a result of a scheme that is widely deemed to have been devised and implemented to divide communities and secure acquiescence.

This broadens the terrain on which the sustainability credentials of the two projects are set and understood. The projects became defined by those standing against them as a site upon which the cultural identity and territorial rights of the indigenous communities impacted collide with dominant commercial interests, anti-indigenous storylines, and global notions of indigeneity. The resistance storylines discussed in this chapter highlight how the indigenous communities impacted by the Belo Monte and São Luiz do Tapajós projects are seen as 'surplus' in the eyes of the pro-dam coalition, with their rights trampled upon and their cultures fragmented in the name of Brazilian development and energy security (Interview, 18 November 2016). The dominant storyline of sustainability advanced to legitimise the projects is reconfigured, with anti-dam actors foregrounding the resistance against the projects studied within a language of encroachment on territory and cultural loss.

In opposition to the São Luiz do Tapajós project, the Munduruku indigenous community adopted a process of counter-mapping to assert its cultural importance and mapped out customary land claims. This securing of land rights has provided (and continues to provide) a key route of community resistance to contemporary hydropower projects in Brazil – reasserting not only occupancy but also shared experience, history and cultural sites (Zanotti, 2016). In response to the Munduruku self-demarcation of Sawré Muybu, FUNAI formally published the identification and demarcation studies for Sawré Muybu in April 2016. The São Luiz do Tapajós project was later criticised for overlooking and simplifying impacts in official assessments and was removed from the environmental licensing process in August 2016. It is to this that I turn in the next chapter.

Notes

1 Catching live fish for sale to collectors is a key part of the livelihoods of the Juruna and Arara communities.
2 These quotes should not be taken as representative of Survival International's views or work. The organisation is committed to defending the rights of indigenous communities and has previously distanced itself from – and criticised – the dichotomy presented above. Stephen Corry, the organisation's director, argued in 2005: 'Tribal peoples are not backward: they are independent and vibrant societies which, like all of us always, are constantly adapting to a changing world. The main difference between tribal peoples and us is that we take their land and resources, and believe the dishonest, even racist, claim that it's for their own good. It's conquest, not development' (Ginzburg, 2006).
3 These international trips to generate support were foreshadowed by the activism of the rubber-tapper activist, Chico Mendes, who, in 1987, flew to Washington DC to convince the World Bank and International Monetary Fund to support the creation of extractive reserves (Ramos, 1998). Similarly, in 1988, two Kayapó leaders travelled to Washington, DC to meet with officials from the World Bank and to argue against the institution's potential funding of the Kararaô project (Revkin, 1990).
4 The foundations of the right to FPIC can be found in the 1989 Indigenous and Tribal Peoples Convention, Convention 169 of the International Labor Organization (ILO 169), which entered into force in 1991 and the 2007 United Nations Declaration on the Rights of Indigenous Peoples (UNDRIP). ILO 169 recognises the right of indigenous communities to exercise both autonomy and control over their lands and to freely participate in the decision-making processes that govern schemes within these territories. This right was also present in the World Commission on Dams' (World Commission on Dams, 2000) landmark report, which, among other recommendations, argued that the public acceptance of decisions, gained via broad participatory mechanisms, was essential for project development.
5 The ties between hydropower and the mining industry are as old as Brazilian hydropower itself. The first Brazilian hydroelectric plant was built in 1883 to provide energy to a diamond mining project in Minas Gerais. The Tucurui project, one of the biggest, was part of the wider Grande Carajas programme, providing energy for the mining and processing of iron ore (Barrow, 1988).
6 This imagery of a community being sacrificed for the generation of electricity and securing of economic development is a well-trodden trope in anti-dam movements in Brazil. For example, the logo of Movimento dos Atingidos por Barragens (Movement of Dam-Affected Peoples, MAB) features the silhouette of a figure, seemingly crucified on an electricity pylon. Two farming tools, symbolising a traditional livelihood, lie at the figure's feet. The logo articulates an equivalence between the building of a dam and loss of the figure's livelihood and the sacrifice of the figure to generate energy.
7 The name 'Munduruku' is rooted in a history of aggression, assigned by rival communities in the region, and is understood to mean 'red ant,' an allusion to the historical tactics of Munduruku attacks, which would take place at dawn and overwhelm the adult population of the defending communities (Rosa, 2015).

Bibliography

Alarcon, DF, Millikan, B, and Torres, M (ed.) (2016). *Ocekadi: Hidrelétricas, Conflitos Socioambientais e Resistência na Bacia do Tapajós*. Brasília: International Rivers. Available at: https://www.internationalrivers.org/sites/default/files/attached-files/tapajos_digital.pdf.

Aleixos, J, and Conde, N (2016). *Quem São os Proprietários das Hidrelétricas da Amazônia?* Rio de Janeiro: Mais Democracia. Available at: http://www.corecon-rj.org.br/corecon/ckfinder/userfiles/files/pdf/Quem%20sao%20os%20proprietarios%20das%20hidroeletricas.pdf (Accessed: 23 July 2020).

Amaral, M, Aranha, A, Barros, CJ, Branford, S, Mota, J, Castro, A, and Rabello, T (2013). *Amazônia Pública*. São Paulo: Agência Pública.

Amazon Watch (2016). Belo Monte a symbol of obscene destruction and corruption in Brazil. *Amazon Watch*, 17 March. Available at: https://amazonwatch.org/news/2016/0317-belo-monte-a-symbol-of-obscene-destruction-and-corruption-in-brazil (Accessed: 30 March 2020).

Amazon Watch, Greenpeace, and International Rivers (2015). Brazilian indigenous movement received prominent UN environmental price at COP21 in Paris. *Amazon Watch*, 7 December. Available at: https://amazonwatch.org/news/2015/1207-brazilian-indigenous-movement-receives-prominent-un-environmental-prize-at-cop-21-in-paris (Accessed: 30 March 2020).

Aranha, A, and Mota, J (2014). A batalha pela fronteira Munduruku. *Publica*, 11 December. Available at: http://apublica.org/2014/12/batalha-pela-fronteira-munduruku/ (Accessed: 30 March 2020).

Arnold, CF (2018). *The Third Bank of the River: Power and Survival in the Twenty-First Century*. London: Picador.

Barrow, C (1988). The impact of hydroelectric development on the Amazonian environment: with particular reference to the Tucurui project. *Journal of Biogeography*, 15(1): 67–78.

Bolaños, O (2011). Redefining identities, redefining landscapes: indigenous identity and land rights struggles in the Brazilian Amazon. *Journal of Cultural Geography*, 28(1): 45–72.

Branford, S (2013). Prontos para resistir. In: Amaral, M (ed.) *Amazônia Pública*. São Paulo: Pública.

Branford, S, and Torres, M (2017a). The end of a people: Amazon dam destroys sacred Munduruku 'Heaven.' *Mongabay*, 5 January. Available at: https://news.mongabay.com/2017/01/the-end-of-a-people-amazon-dam-destroys-sacred-munduruku-heaven/ (Accessed: 30 March 2020).

Branford, S, and Torres, M (2017b). Tapajós under attack 4: day of terror in Tapajós river basin. *Latin America Bureau*, 15 March. Available at: https://lab.org.uk/day-of-terror-in-tapajos-river-basin/ (Accessed: 30 March 2020).

Brasil, Portal do Planalto (2011). Conversa com a Presidenta – Presidenta Dilma Rousseff conversa em sua coluna semanal sobre internet banda larga de baixo custo, política habitacional e Lei da Aprendizagem. *Portal Do Planalto*, 9 August. Available at: http://www.biblioteca.presidencia.gov.br/presidencia/ex-presidentes/dilma-rousseff/conversa-presidenta/conversa-com-a-presidenta-09-08-2011 (Accessed: 30 March 2020).

Bratman, EZ (2020). *Governing the Rainforest: Sustainable Development Politics in the Brazilian Amazon*. Oxford: Oxford University Press.

Brum, E (2014). Belo Monte: a anatomia de um etnocídio. *El País*, 1 December. Available at: https://brasil.elpais.com/brasil/2014/12/01/opinion/1417437633_930086.html (Accessed: 30 March 2020).

Brum, E (2015a). Belo Monte, empreiteiras e espelhinhos. *El País*, 7 July. Available at: https://brasil.elpais.com/brasil/2015/07/06/opinion/1436195768_857181.html (Accessed: 30 March 2020).

Brum, E (2015b). Vítimas de uma guerra amazônica. *El Pais*, 26 September. Available at: https://brasil.elpais.com/brasil/2015/09/22/politica/1442930391_549192.html (Accessed: 8 January 2020).

CNEC Worley Parson Engenharia (2014). *Aproveitamento Hidrelétrico (AHE) São Luiz do Tapajós: Estudo de Impacto Ambiental*, 1–25. São Paulo: CNEC Worley Parsons Engenharia.

Conklin, BA, and Graham, LR (1995). The shifting middle ground: Amazonian Indians and ecopolitics. *American Anthropologist*, 97(4): 695–710.

Davis, S (1977). *Victims of the Miracle: Development and the Indians of Brazil*. Cambridge: Cambridge University Press.

de Aguiar, D, Rodrigues, L, Nakagawa, L, Lila, L, Minami, T, Leal, V, and Brasil, G (2016). *The battle for the river of life*. São Paulo: Greenpeace Brasil. Available at: https://www.greenpeace.de/sites/www.greenpeace.de/files/publications/greenpeace-report-the_battle_for_the_river_of_life-20160321.pdf (Accessed: 30 March 2020).

Eletrobras (2009). *Aproveitamento Hidrelétrico Belo Monte: Estudo de Impacto Ambiental*. Rio de Janeiro: Eletrobras.

Fachin, P, and Santos, JV (2015). A monstruosidade de Belo Monte e descalabro em Altamira que Dilma não teve coragem de ver. Entrevista especial com D. Erwin Kräutler. *IHU-Online*, 16 January. Available at: http://www.ihu.unisinos.br/entrevistas/539024-a-monstruosidade-de-belo-monte-dilma-nao-teve-coragem-de-ver-o-d escalabro-provocado-pela-obra-entrevista-especial-com-d-erwin-kraeutler (Accessed: 30 March 2020).

Fearnside, PM (2015). Brazil's São Luiz do Tapajós dam: the art of cosmetic environmental impact assessments. *Water Alternatives*, 8(3): 373–396.

Fundação Nacional do Índio (2011). Nota sobre as medidas cautelares da Comissão Interamericana de Direitos Humanos (CIDH) da OEA. *Fundação Nacional Do Índio*, 5 April. Available at: http://www.funai.gov.br/index.php/comunicacao/noticias/1885-nota-sobre-as-medidas-cautelares-da-comissao-interamericana-de-direitos-humanos-cidh-da-oea (Accessed: 30 March 2020).

Ginzburg, O (2006). *There you go!* London: Survival International.

Greenpeace Brasil (2016). *Damming the Amazon: the risky business of hydropower in the Amazon*. São Paulo: Greenpeace Brasil. Available at: https://www.greenpeace.org/usa/dam-amazon-hydropower/ (Accessed: 30 March 2020).

Grupo de Estudos Tapajós (2014). *Avaliação Ambiental Integrada da Bacia do Tapajós: Sumário Executivo*. Available at: https://web.archive.org/web/20190217004707/http://www.http://grupodeestudostapajos.com.br/site/wp-content/uploads/2014/04/Sumario_AAI.pdf (Accessed: 30 March 2020).

Hanna, P (2016). *The Social Impacts of Large Projects on Indigenous Peoples: Procedures, Processes and Protests*. Thesis submitted to Department of Cultural Geography, University of Groningen.

Hanna, P, and Vanclay, F (2013). Human rights, indigenous peoples and the concept of free, prior and informed consent. *Impact Assessment and Project Appraisal*, 31(2): 146–157.

Heckenberger, MJ, Kuikuro, A, Kuikuro, UT, Russell, JC, Schmidt, M, Fausto, C, and Franchetto, B (2003). Amazonia 1492: pristine forest or cultural parkland? *Science*, 301(5640): 1710–1714.

Heckenberger, MJ, Russell, JC, Fausto, C, Toney, JR, Schmidt, MJ, Pereira, E, Franchetto, B, and Kuikuro, A (2008). Pre-Columbian urbanism, anthropogenic landscapes, and the future of the Amazon. *Science*, 321(5893): 1214–1217.

Heckenberger, MJ, Russell, JC, Toney, JR, and Schmidt, MJ (2007). The legacy of cultural landscapes in the Brazilian Amazon: implications for biodiversity. *Philosophical Transactions of the Royal Society of London Series B Biological Sciences*, 362(1478): 197–208.

Hemming, J (1978). *Red Gold: The Conquest of the Brazilian Indians*. Cambridge, MA: Harvard University Press.

Hurwitz, Z (2011). Mining giant joins Belo Monte dam. *International Rivers*, 2 May. Available at: https://www.internationalrivers.org/blogs/258/mining-giant-joins-belo-monte-dam (Accessed: 30 March 2020).

Instituto Socioambiental (2015). MPF denuncia ação etnocida e pede intervenção judicial em Belo Monte. *Instituto Socioambiental*, 11 December. Available at: https://www.socioambiental.org/pt-br/noticias-socioambientais/mpf-denuncia-acao-etnocida-e-pede-intervencao-judicial-em-belo-monte (Accessed: 30 March 2020).

Irigaray, M (2014). Killing a people little by little: Belo Monte, human rights and the myth of clean energy. *Tipiti*, 12(2): 128–133.

Irigaray, M (2015). The Munduruku people: a living history of resistance. *Amazon Watch*, 30 April. Available at: https://amazonwatch.org/news/2015/0430-the-munduruku-people-a-living-history-of-resistance (Accessed: 30 March 2020).

Leite, M, Amora, D, Kachani, M, de Almeida, L, and Machado, R (2013). A batalha de Belo Monte. *Folha de. Sao Paulo*, 16 December. Available at: https://arte.folha.uol.com.br/especiais/2013/12/16/belo-monte/ (Accessed: 30 March 2020).

Loures, R (2018). The Karodaybi government and its invincible warriors: the Munduruku Ipereğ Ayũ Movement versus large construction projects in the Amazon. *Vibrant: Virtual Brazilian Anthropology*, 15(2): 1–23.

Members of the Pariri Indigenous Association and Ipereğ Ayũ Movement (2017). A government of death is plundering our ancient Munduruku lands. Help us stop it. *The Guardian*, 25 April. Available at: https://www.theguardian.com/global-development/2017/apr/25/a-government-of-death-is-plundering-our-ancient-munduruku-lands-help-us-stop-it-brazil-amazon (Accessed: 30 March 2020).

Ministério Público Federal, Procuradoria da República no Pará (2017). Ribeirinhos expulsos por Belo Monte apresentam lista de moradores que devem voltar ao Xingu. MPF/PA, 21 March. Available at: http://www.mpf.mp.br/pa/sala-de-imprensa/noticias-pa/ribeirinhos-expulsos-por-belo-monte-apresentam-lista-de-moradores-que-devem-voltar-ao-xingu (Accessed: 30 March 2020).

Movimento dos Atingidos por Barragens (2014). Ribeirinhos reafirmam não às barragens no Tapajós. *Movimento Dos Atinigos Por Barragens*, 7 May. Available at: http://www.mabnacional.org.br/noticia/ribeirinhos-reafirmam-n-s-barragens-no-tapaj-s (Accessed: 30 March 2020).

Movimento dos Atingidos por Barragens (2017). Por uma convivência sustentável com a Amazônia. *Movimento dos Atingidos por Barragens*, 2 August. Available at: http://www.mabnacional.org.br/noticia/por-uma-conviv-ncia-sustent-vel-com-amaz-nia (Accessed: 30 March 2020).

Movimento Xingu Vivo para Sempre (MXVPS) (2014). Leilão da usina de São Luiz do Tapajós: o governo mentiu para os Munduruku. *Xingu Vivo Para Sempre*, 14 September. Available at: https://xinguvivo.org.br/2014/09/14/leilao-da-usina-de-sao-luiz-do-tapajos-o-governo-mentiu-para-os-munduruku/ (Accessed: 30 March 2020).

Munduruku Community (2014). *Munduruku Consultation Protocol*. Available at: https://amazonwatch.org/assets/files/2014-12-14-munduruku-consultation-protocol.pdf (Accessed: 30 March 2020).

Nitta, R, and Naka, LN (2015). *Barragens do Rio Tapajós: Uma Avaliação Crítica do Estudo e Relatório de Impacto Ambiental (EIA/RIMA) do Aproveitamento Hidrelétrico São Luiz do Tapajós*. São Paulo: Greenpeace Brasil. Available at: http://greenpeace.org.br/tapajos/docs/analise-eia-rima.pdf (Accessed: 30 March 2020).

Partido dos Trabalhadores (PT) (2014). Norte Energia desmente Marina e investe R$ 1,2 bi em projetos de compensação. *Partido dos Trabalhadores*, 16 September. Available at: https://pt.org.br/norte-energia-desmente-marina-e-investe-r-12-bi-em-projetos-de-compensacao/ (Accessed: 14 March 2020).

Peluso, NL (1995). Whose forests are these? Territories in Kalimantan, counter-mapping forest Indonesia. *Antipode*, 274, 383–406.

Pinho, VA, and Oliveira Costa, A (2012). *Rodas de Direito: Diálogo, Empoderamento e Prevenção Não Enfrentamento da Humano Sexual Contra Crianças e Adolescentes*. Altamira, PA: Universidade Federal do Pará. Available at: http://pair.ledes.net/gestor/titan.php?target=openFile&fileId=1000.

Poirier, C (2010). Letter to President Luiz Inácio Lula da Silva. *Comité Pour Les Droits Humains En Amérique Latine*, 12 March. Available at: https://www.cdhal.org/open-letter-against-belo-monte-hydroelectric-dam-project-xingu-river-brazil/ (Accessed: 8 January 2020).

Poirier, C (2017). Toxic mega-mine looms over Belo Monte's affected communities. *Amazon Watch*, 4 April. Available at: https://amazonwatch.org/news/2017/0404-toxic-mega-mine-looms-over-belo-montes-affected-communities (Accessed: 30 March 2020).

Pontes, N (2016). Índios travam 'guerra moderna' contra hidrelétricas no Tapajós. *Deutsche Welle*, 12 July. Available at: https://www.dw.com/pt-br/%C3%ADndios-travam-guerra-moderna-contra-hidrel%C3%A9tricas-no-tapaj%C3%B3s/a-19394652 (Accessed: 30 March 2020).

Ramos, AR (1998). *Indigenism: Ethnic Politics in Brazil*. Madison, WI: University of Wisconsin Press.

Resk, SS (2017). Povo Munduruku defende patrimônio espiritual indígena. *Instituto Centro de Vida*, 30 August. Available at: https://www.icv.org.br/2017/08/povo-munduruku-defende-patrimonio-espiritual-indigena/ (Accessed: 30 March 2020).

Reuters (2015). Brazil's Vale concludes sale of 49 pct stake in Belo Monte dam. *Reuters*, 1 April. Available at: https://www.reuters.com/article/vale-cemig-belo-monte-idUSE6N0T70B120150401 (Accessed: 30 March 2020).

Revkin, Andrew (1990). *The Burning Season: The Murder of Chico Mendes and the Fight for the Amazon Rainforest*. New York: Collins.

Rocha, B, and Millikan, B (2013). Brazil: Operation Tapajós suspended. *International Rivers*, 18 April. Available at: https://www.internationalrivers.org/resources/brazil-operation-tapaj%C3%B3s-suspended-7932 (Accessed: 30 March 2020).

Roosevelt, AC, Lima da Costa, M, Lopes Machado, C, Michab, M, Mercier, N, Valladas, H, Feathers, J, Barnett, W, Imazio da Silveira, M, Henderson, A, Sliva, J, Chernoff, B, Reese, DS, Holman, JA, Toth, N, and Schick, K (1996). Paleoindian cave dwellers in the Amazon: the peopling of the Americas. *Science*, 272(5260): 373–384.

Rosa, G (2015). A política munduruku. *Reporter Brasil*, 21 December. Available at: https://reporterbrasil.org.br/2015/12/a-politica-munduruku/ (Accessed: 30 March 2020).

Sakamoto, L (2016). Belo Monte: Antes de denúncias de corrupção, um crime contra a humanidade. *Blog do Sakamoto*, 12 March. Available at: https://blogdosakamoto.blogosfera.uol.com.br/2016/03/12/belo-monte-antes-de-denuncias-de-corrupcao-um-crime-contra-a-humanidade/ (Accessed: 8 January 2020).

Santos, JV (2015). Belo Monte: Atualização do processo de destruição dos povos indígenas. *Instituto Humanitas Unisinos*, 30 November. Available at: http://www.ihuonline.unisinos.br/artigo/6284-thais-santi (Accessed: 30 March 2020).

Sullivan, Z (2016). Brazil's dispossessed: Belo Monte dam ruinous for indigenous cultures. *Mongabay*, 8 December. Available at: https://news.mongabay.com/2016/12/brazils-dispossessed-belo-monte-dam-ruinous-for-indigenous-cultures/ (Accessed: 30 March 2020).

Sullivan, Z (2017). Unexamined synergies: dam building and mining go together in the Amazon. *Mongabay*, 22 June. Available at: https://news.mongabay.com/2017/06/unexamined-synergies-dam-building-and-mining-go-together-in-the-amazon/ (Accessed: 30 March 2020).

Survival International (2016). 'Stop Brazil's genocide': Brazil blocks dangerous dam. *Survival International*, 5 August. Available at: https://www.survivalinternational.org/news/11378 (Accessed: 30 March 2020).

Turner, T (1993). The role of indigenous peoples in the environmental crisis: the example of the Kayapó of the Brazilian Amazon. *Perspectives in Biology and Medicine*, 36(3): 526–545.

Various (2010). Final declaration from the Terra Livre Encampment: 'In defense of the Xingu: against Belo Monte!' *Amazon Watch*, 12 August. Available at: https://amazonwatch.org/news/2010/0812-final-declaration-from-the-terra-livre-encampment (Accessed: 30 March 2020).

Verdum, R (2012). *As Obras de Infraestrutura do PAC e os Povos Indígenas na Amazônia Brasileira*. São Paulo: Instituto de Estudos Socio-Economicos. Available at: https://www.amazonia.org.br/wp-content/uploads/2012/10/Obras-de-Infraestrutura-do-PAC-e-Povos-Indigenas.pdf (Accessed: 30 March 2020).

World Commission on Dams (2000). *Dams and Development: A New Framework for Decision-Making*. London: World Commission on Dams.

Zanotti, L (2015). Water and life: hydroelectric development and indigenous pathways to justice in the Brazilian Amazon. *Politics, Groups, and Identities*, 3(4): 666–672.

Zanotti, L (2016). *Radical Territories in the Brazilian Amazon*. Tucson, AZ: University of Arizona Press.

Zhouri, A (2018). Megaprojects, epistemological violence and environmental conflicts in Brazil. *Perfiles Economicos*, 5: 7–33.

7 Refusing to celebrate victory

The office of the Instituto Brasileiro do Meio Ambiente e dos Recursos Naturais Renováveis (Brazilian Institute of the Environment and Renewable Natural Resources, IBAMA) is located near the eastern shore of the artificial Lake Paranoá. Housed in a low building of concrete walkways and surrounded by vegetation, it was here on its marbled floors that, in August 2016, the president of IBAMA, Suely Araújo (2016–2019) made the decision to 'archive' the licensing process of the São Luiz do Tapajós project. Rather than being related to the permanent suspension of the project, the term 'archival' instead concerns its temporary removal from the environmental licensing process. Nevertheless, the decision to 'archive' represents the assertion that the project, in its current formulation, was not of an adequate standard to move forward into the construction phase.

When I arrived in Brazil in September 2016, Araújo's decision had, in many ways, transformed the focus of this research. While a leading civil servant working on energy planning at the Ministerio de Minas e Energia had previously assured me in an interview that the São Luiz do Tapajós project was a key part of the government's energy matrix moving forward, the decision, formally based on FUNAI's approval of the Munduruku's autonomous demarcation of the Sawré Muybu territory, demonstrated that the steamroller driving hydropower expansion in the Brazilian Amazon forward could be disrupted and that it could be beaten. In previous chapters, I have detailed the different storylines put forward by anti-dam actors in Brazil and beyond – rendering visible impacts, highlighting political impunity, and illuminating the role of the projects studied in wider processes of encroachment on indigenous communities. With the archival of the project, seemingly representing the success of the opposition movement, it is important to explore how anti-dam actors made sense of IBAMA's decision and to trace the contours of their reactions.

As I explore in this final chapter, the 2016 decision was not celebrated as a victory by many in the resistance coalition. In response to this decision, anti-dam actors put forward new storylines that presented the cancellation of the São Luiz do Tapajós project as just one stage in a contest between resistance actors and political interests (first, the administration of President Michel Temer (2016–2019) and later that of President Jair Bolsonaro (2019 onwards)) threatening environmental protections and the rights of indigenous communities. The processes of repoliticisation and scaling up, discussed in previous chapters, continued within these new storylines. Resistance actors challenged the rationale present in official accounts that the 2016 decision was based on the uncertainties of environmental impacts, by locating it within a changing political context, which may change in the future. In foregrounding the 2016 decision in this shifting context, resistance actors continued the process of 'scaling up' discussed in Chapter 7 by putting forward a new storyline of vigilance that asserts that these political changes have resulted in emergent threats and, as this context changes further, will likely result in a return of the São Luiz do Tapajós project and their resistance to it.

The cancellation of the São Luiz do Tapajós project

On 19 April 2016, IBAMA suspended the environmental licensing process for the São Luiz do Tapajós project. This decision was made in response to the publication of a report by FUNAI that confirmed the demarcation of the 178,000 hectares of the Sawré Muybu territory of the Munduruku community. This area, now protected as traditional land, had been independently demarcated by the Munduruku community in 2014 in an effort to block the construction of the São Luiz do Tapajós Dam, which would have flooded 7% of the territory (Aranha and Mota, 2014; FUNAI, 2016). The suspension of the project was followed by an additional decision to deny the project its preliminary environmental licence (Licença Prévia), which certifies that a project is environmentally feasible, by IBAMA on 4 August 2016 (Instituto Brasileiro do Meio Ambiente e dos Recursos Naturais Renováveis, 2016).

With the environmental licensing process representing a key site in which a dam's sustainability credentials are asserted and accepted, IBAMA's 2016 decision to archive the São Luiz do Tapajós project based on the uncertainty of social and environmental impacts challenged the pro-dam storyline of sustainability, as well as the moral legitimacy to which it had previously appealed. When responding to the cancellation of the São Luiz do Tapajós project, few pro-dam actors continued to put forward a storyline of sustainability (Interview, 3 November 2016a; Interview, 4 November 2016; Interview, 10 November 2016a). Instead, supporters of the project returned to previous storylines to criticise the decision. Many sought to assert the importance of this project in ensuring national energy security, returning to previous storylines that located hydroelectric projects in the context of power cuts in the 2001 and 2002 energy crisis. Such assertions previously provided a storyline of legitimacy for the Belo Monte project (Atkins, 2017). Luiz Barroso, the president of EPE, told Folha de S. Paulo that the cancellation of the São Luiz do Tapajós project may result in increased energy costs for consumers (Amora, 2016). Similarly, a representative of the MME argued that, despite the cancellation of the São Luiz do Tapajós Dam, Brazil will need to continue to invest in hydroelectric dams to meet energy demand (Interview, 3 November 2016a). This represents a return to linking the construction of hydroelectric dams in the Brazilian Amazon with popular concerns regarding blackouts to both reiterate the legitimacy of dam projects and question the validity of IBAMA's decision. Other supporters of the São Luiz do Tapajós Dam returned to storylines that denied the impacts of the project on indigenous communities (Sales and Uhlig, 2016), demonstrating a focus on discrediting the arguments of resistance actors related to impacts on indigenous communities rather than asserting the sustainability of the project. In response to the cancellation of São Luiz do Tapajós, a representative of MME argued that those planning the dam had previously been unaware of the presence of an indigenous population in the region that was to be directly impacted by the project. In making this statement, this pro-dam actor was returning to a storyline, described in Chapter 6, that denies the impact of the project on indigenous populations in the region, despite anti-dam storylines arguing otherwise (Interview, 3 November 2016a).

With the project removed from national energy plans, many of the anti-dam actors interviewed looked to the future to present the cancellation of the São Luiz do Tapajós project as an opportunity to transform the energy sector. For several interviewees, primarily drawn from environmental organisations, the 2016 decision represented a turning point in the resistance against hydropower in Brazil (Interview, 18 October 2016; Interview, 19 October 2016; Interview, 27 October 2016a; Interview, 27 October 2016b), it was also seen as allowing a recalibration of the national energy matrix of Brazil. As an interviewee at WWF Brasil, who had been critical of the environmental impacts of hydropower, explained, the cancellation of the project was 'a good sign, a good indicator, that things should be done different[ly]' (Interview, 7 November 2016a). This interpretation was replicated in materials disseminated by Greenpeace Brasil, which presented the cancellation of the project as allowing for the transition to the construction of mega-dams in the Brazilian Amazon in the future (Interview, 19 October 2016; Interview, 27 October 2016a). Less than a month after IBAMA's decision, a prominent national journalist explained to me in an interview, 'Maybe, this is what is starting to happen now. I hope that the Brazilian government will go in that direction [of alternatives] ... maybe [the cancellation of] Tapajós is the beginning of it' (Interview, 18 October 2016).

While many anti-dam actors presented the archival of the São Luiz do Tapajós project as embodying a moment for the Brazilian government and energy planning authorities to recalibrate the national energy matrix, this optimism proved relatively short-lived. While both solar and wind energy are expanding at impressive rates, they still represent limited amounts of energy when compared to the mega-dams previously planned for the Brazilian Amazon. There was a belief, widely held among anti-dam activists in Brazil in 2016, that, despite IBAMA's decision, the São Luiz do Tapajós project is likely to return in the future. As a representative of an international EO explained 'I don't believe that this is a permanent archival in any way, I believe it's temporary ... We need to recognise this as a very important victory, but it can be reversed from one year to the next' (Interview, 28 April 2017).

The reasons behind this pessimism can be found in the logic behind IBAMA's 2016 decision. The official reasoning, based on consultation between IBAMA,

FUNAI and the Ministerio Publico Federal (MPF), was the incomplete nature of the Environmental Impact Assessments submitted to the regulator, which had failed to correct a number of inadequacies in previous submissions (Instituto Brasileiro do Meio Ambiente e dos Recursos Naturais Renováveis, 2016). In its decision, IBAMA had voiced concerns that the social and environmental impacts of the project were not clear – with this uncertainty rooted in the incomplete nature of the official EIAs. As a representative of IBAMA explained: 'The environmental assessment was ... very bad regarding [the absence of] technical information and we just said "No, with this, we won't give any licence with this kind of information."' (Interview, 4 November 2016). Interviewees from IBAMA, FUNAI and MPF highlighted the fact that the lack of information regarding the impacts of São Luiz do Tapajós was the result of the perceived complacency of the consortium submitting the documents, Grupo de Estudos Tapajós (Interview, 4 November 2016; Interview, 7 November 2016b; Interview, 10 November 2016a). The interviewee at IBAMA explained that the authority had requested information on at least a hundred issues or impacts but that the consortium behind the project had failed to address these concerns and provide updated information (Interview, 4 November 2016). Similarly, a representative from the environmental licensing division of FUNAI compared the EIA of the São Luiz do Tapajós project to that of Belo Monte, arguing that 'When [its EIA is] compared with São Luiz do Tapajós, Belo Monte was wonderful, São Luiz do Tapajós was rubbish' (Interview, 10 November 2016a). In making these statements, these bureaucratic actors argue that it was the weaknesses of the documents, which lacked the adequate technical information and failed to accurately detail impacts, that led to the removal of the São Luiz do Tapajós project from the environmental licensing process (Interview, 4 November 2016; Interview, 7 November 2016b; Interview, 10 November 2016a; Interview, 18 November 2016).

With the logic of the 2016 archival of the project based on the inadequacies of the official EIA, rather than the project's potential social and environmental impacts, anti-dam activists argued that the decision by Araújo and the team at IBAMA represented the mere repetition of the technical mindset that characterised the EIAs themselves, with the alternative claims of local communities excluded from the decision. With the project's archival based on a lack of information and certainty, rather than the impacts predicted by local communities and the resistance coalition, many anti-dam actors argued that, far from representing a sea-change in Brazilian energy policy, the decision represented a mere obstacle for the pro-dam coalition. As an interviewee at a domestic EO argued: 'it was a technical decision that said [that] there weren't enough studies. So that offers no assurance of any kind. It can come back at any moment.' (Interview, 28 April 2017) This assertion that a project, assumed to be cancelled and removed from energy plans, can return raises an important parallel between the São Luiz do Tapajós Dam and the Belo Monte Dam. After the 1989 Altamira Gathering, the Kararaô project was removed from government plans. However, the project (renamed Belo Monte) returned, albeit with a different design.

With the struggle over the Belo Monte project extending over 30 years, interviewees argued that the São Luiz do Tapajós project will return in a similar fashion (Interview, 2 November 2016; Interview, 1 December 2016a; Interview, 18 February 2017; Interview, 28 April 2017). A representative of Greenpeace Brasil argued, 'So, this dam can never happen the way it is but, if they change the project, it can. That's what happened with Belo Monte … So, this is still a threat' (Interview, 19 October 2016). For many, the project is likely to return in the future – just as Belo Monte did (Interview, 19 October 2016; Interview, 28 April 2017). Another interviewee argued, 'I think that it will come back. [I am] not sure if it will come back as São Luiz [do Tapajós], but I don't think that they will give up on hydropower in the Amazon' (Interview, 27 October 2016a). The logic underpinning these statements is that the decision made by IBAMA was not made to terminate the project, committing it to the history books, but to temporarily 'archive' the scheme. As a prominent scientist, opposed to the project, explained, 'It's being put out in the press as "It's cancelled! It's never going to happen!" but that's not … that's not a valid conclusion. It is just one step' (Interview, 1 December 2016a). IBAMA's 2016 decision was presented as momentary and not definitive, allowing for the government to return to the project again in the future – albeit under a new guise, name, or design (Interview, 18 February 2017; Interview, 16 September 2017). With the 2016 decision widely understood by opposition actors as motivated by a shifting political context, interviewees argued that a reversal in this context would allow for the project to be built in the future (Interview, 23 August 2017; Interview, 16 September 2017).

Many highlighted that it was not the social and environmental impacts that led to the project's cancellation, and the project could return at any time. This argument can be seen in a statement by the Movimento dos Atingidos por Barragens (2017c) which argued that it is likely that, as economic growth is restored, hydroelectric projects will return. As I discuss below, despite IBAMA's decision, those interviewed retained the widely held belief that the decision was of a political nature, rather than directly related to the disputed sustainability of the project, as asserted in the official logic of the decision (Interview, 19 October 2016; Interview, 28 April 2017; Interview, 23 August 2017). In presenting this storyline, resistance actors continued a process of repoliticisation – arguing that, if the project can be cancelled due to political motivations, a change in context would allow the project to return (Interview, 1 December 2016a).

In the next two sections, I explore the two logics behind the assertion, made by anti-dam actors, that the 2016 decision to remove the São Luiz do Tapajós project from the environmental licensing process did not necessarily equal the disappearance of the dam (or other hydroelectric projects) from future energy plans, nor did it represent the victory or end of contemporary movements of opposition to hydropower in Brazil. First, I explore how the anti-dam activists continued to repoliticise the project by foregrounding its archival in the political context of IBAMA's decision, asserting that when this context changes, the project may well return. Second, I discuss the ways in which anti-dam activists continued to 'scale up' their opposition to the São Luiz do Tapajós project, locating it within a wider contest between local communities and encroachment on their territory, and highlighting how such threats had not receded.

A 'good moment'

In Chapter 4, I explored the storylines advanced by anti-dam actors to illuminate the political character of the Belo Monte and São Luiz do Tapajós Dams and highlight the political interests committed to their construction. Taken together, the illumination of these contextual factors functioned to repoliticise the project, disputing claims made by pro-dam actors that the expansion of the Brazilian hydroelectric frontier into the Xingu and Tapajós was in the 'national interest' by re-grounding their planning and construction into a politicised context of ideology, the circumvention of dissent and corruption. The pro-dam storyline of sustainability became characterised as a 'tool' to justify and gain support for projects that were guided by political motivations (Interview, 19 October 2016; Interview, 28 April 2017; Interview, 23 August 2017).

While IBAMA's decision may have been predicated on technical factors, anti-dam actors continued to repoliticise the São Luiz do Tapajós project by shining a light on the ways in which the Brazilian political terrain in 2016 made such a decision possible. Many interviewees continued to focus on the importance of political agency and corruption in understanding the decision and its significance. As an interviewee from the Brazilian wing of an international EO argued, this was the first time that the Brazilian electrical sector had been rebuffed by the environmental regulator, and such a move required an accommodating political context (Interview, 27 October 2016a). With many having previously discussed the Belo Monte project as one characterised by extensive state support that allowed for it be steamrolled forward, regardless of its impacts; the cancellation of the São Luiz do Tapajós Dam was presented as the site upon which this steamroller dynamic came to an end.

For those who made the decision, it was taken at what was described as 'a good moment' (Interview, 4 November 2016), in which the cancellation of São Luiz do Tapajós represented a viable policy choice for the regulator. The exposure of corruption by the Lava Jato investigation, the public outpouring of dissent in 2013 that became known as the Jornadas de Junho (June Journeys), and the 2016 impeachment of Dilma Rousseff all led to the fragmentation of the political coalition that had, broadly, governed Brazil since 2003 and that had become synonymous with both the Belo Monte and the São Luiz do Tapajós projects. With the 'steamroller' of Belo Monte powered by the political influence and commitment of pro-dam actors, the exposure of corruption led to its deceleration and the fragmentation of the pro-dam coalition (Interview, 3 November 2016b; Interview, 23 August 2017; Interview, 16 September 2017). If Belo Monte represented an opportunity for corruption, the cancellation of São Luiz do Tapajós illuminated its demise. As an employee of the Instituto Socioambiental explained to me:

They [the pro-dam coalition] are unstructured, without money [and] in prison ... There's no one. There's no money. Everything is broken. I think that's what explains the cancellation of the São Luiz do Tapajós [dam]. [It] is much more a political and economic situation than the environmental focus that [IBAMA's decision] suggests.

(Interview, 3 November 2016b)

With the planning and construction of Belo Monte previously deemed to have been predicated on the impunity, corruption, and influence of the pro-dam actors, the fragmentation of the pro-dam coalition, caused by the Lava Jato investigation and the end of the PT government allowed the archival of the São Luiz do Tapajós Dam. Due to her asserted prominence in the planning and development of the dams studied, such a moment was discussed in interviews in relation to the political fall of President Dilma Rousseff (2011–2016). With the cancellation of São Luiz do Tapajós occurring in the same period as her removal from office in August 2016, many anti-dam actors argued that Dilma's removal from office had directly created the space for the cancellation of the São Luiz do Tapajós project (Interview, 19 October /10/2016). It is perhaps particularly significant that the claim that the impeachment of Dilma resulted in an opportunity for the pro-dam coalition to be broken and forced into retreat was also voiced by those at IBAMA who were involved in the decision to archive the project. A discussion of the reasons behind the cancellation was interrupted as follows:

Interviewee 1: I think that a lot of elements contribute to this. We have energy, [José] Sarney Filho, Lava Jato ...
Interviewee 2: The crisis.
I1: The crisis. The fiscal crisis. We don't have money and we must ...
I2: [whispers] Dilma
I1: We must use this ... [laughs] Dilma.
I2: [laughs] ...
I1: Dilma loved hydroelectric ... She loves hydroelectric dams!

(Interview, 4 November 2016)

The interviewees collapsed into laughter soon after. As discussed in Chapter 4, for many anti-dam actors, hydroelectricity generation in Brazil had become Dilma's pet project during her time in government, resulting in her commitment to Belo Monte, regardless of the criticism. With her removal from office, it became easier for IBAMA to deny the preliminary licence to the São Luiz do Tapajós scheme (Interview, 4 November 2016). As one interviewee, based at Greenpeace Brasil, argued, Dilma's decline diminished her ability to ensure the project went ahead, arguing that 'if Dilma had the same power that she [had previously] ... she would have just shoved it down our throats' (Interview, 19 October 2016). This statement returns to the imagery of hydropower projects being forced upon local populations, with the language adopted a direct allusion to the claims of Lula that the Belo Monte project would not be 'shoved down anybody's throats' (as discussed in Chapter 4). While, for many, the political connections and ideology of Lula and Dilma had propelled the Belo Monte project, by 2016, such political capital was spent, lost, and unable to secure the continuation of the São Luiz do Tapajós project. Both were out of government and a new administration – with new motivations – was making decisions. Dilma Rousseff was succeeded as president by her former vice president, Michel Temer (Partido do Movimento Democrático Brasileiro, PMDB), who governed Brazil from 2016 to 2019.

The exchange between IBAMA staff quoted above also provides a number of additional factors that must be taken into account. Several interviewees explained that the political influence held by José Sarney Filho, the Minister for the Environment (2016–2019) in Temer's administration that governed Brazil at the time, was a reason for the decision (Interview, 19 October 2016; Interview, 4 November 2016). An interviewee at IBAMA explained that the decision to archive the project was supported by Sarney Filho, who deferred to the expertise and judgement of Suely Araújo and her team of technicians and advisers. This contrasts with previous assertions of how Lula and Dilma would regularly apply pressure to the same figures, with numerous IBAMA employees – as well as Sarney Filho's successor, Marina Silva – having previously resigned citing government pressure to ensure the construction of Belo Monte. Sarney Filho, the son of the former president of Brazil, José Sarney (1985–1990), is from a political dynasty in Brazil, providing political capital that, in this case, gave strength to IBAMA to suspend the São Luiz do Tapajós project by affording a degree of political legitimacy and clout that protected those making the decision from similar pressures.

A deep economic recession experienced in Brazil between 2014 and 2017 was also presented as a primary factor in the decision to archive the São Luiz do Tapajós project. An economic slowdown in China led to a decline in the foreign demand for commodities that had driven the resurgence of the Brazilian economy under Lula, accompanied by a rapid fall in commodity prices. The political instability brought by the Lava Jato investigation exacerbated this economic uncertainty, driving away investment (Folha de S.Paulo, 2017). The investigation is estimated to have caused an economic downturn of between 1 and 1.5% of national GDP per year (Nogueira, 2017). In 2015, inflation hit 10.67%, the highest since 2002 (Boas, 2016). In July 2015, interest rates hit 14.25% (Martello, 2015). By the end of 2016, the unemployment rate stood at 12% (or 12.3 million Brazilians) (Cury, 2017). Anti-dam actors argued that it was within this context of an economic recession that the steamroller that had driven Belo Monte forward ran out of momentum. The Temer administration was focused on tackling this recession and, within this new context, the expansion of hydropower was no longer seen as a logical route for government spending. The focus of the government became managing government spending and implementing austerity measures across Brazil (Interview, 27 September 2016; Interview, 3 October 2016; Interview, 27 October 2016b). In addition, the contraction of the Brazilian economy, with a 3.8% drop in the gross domestic product (GDP) in 2015 (Cury and Caoli, 2016), led to a decrease in the energy demand that had made the expansion of hydropower a priority in the first place. This prompted a recalibration of government spending, particularly the amounts spent on energy infrastructure in Brazil. As an interviewee at the MPF explained, 'A [financial] crisis is always a good moment to rethink, to reflect on our past and to find better ways' (Interview, 7 November 2016b). Resistance actors argued that, with large dams representing substantial investments, the Temer administration would be less likely to pursue such projects in a precarious economic climate and would concentrate on alternatives (Interview, 19 October 2016; Interview, 10 November 2016b; Interview, 21 November 2016). It is within this new political context that the government led by President Michel Temer departed from the previous orthodoxy that saw the expansion of hydropower as a key to national economic development and energy security (Interview, 10 November 2016b), distancing itself from not just the São Luiz do Tapajós project but wider discussions of hydroelectric dams in the Brazilian Amazon in a January 2018 announcement (Branford, 2018).

In discussing the removal of the São Luiz do Tapajós project from the environmental licensing plans, those opposed to the project directed attention away from the official rationale related to uncertainty surrounding the project's social and environmental impacts. Instead, they further repoliticised the project, locating it within a terrain of political motivations and questions of economic growth and development. In repoliticising the project, many argued that a shifting political context resulted in a loss of the political capital committed to the scheme and the decreased power of the pro-dam coalition (Interview, 3 October 2016; Interview, 3 November 2016b; Interview, 1 December 2016b; Interview, 28 April 2017). Moreover, many felt that the impeachment of Dilma Rousseff from the Presidency created a moment in which IBAMA could act, and the economic recession that dominated Brazil at the time of the decision led to government actors no longer holding the same levels of interest in expanding hydropower as their predecessor. While the political commitment of Lula and Dilma was seen by many as a factor that explained the construction of Belo Monte despite vast opposition, the cancellation of the São Luiz do Tapajós project represented their no longer being in office.

Continued vigilance

In Chapter 6, I explored how numerous resistance actors foregrounded their discussions of the Belo Monte and São Luiz do Tapajós projects within a wider need to protect indigenous culture and territory in the Legal Amazon Region. Antidam actors 'scaled up' the resistance against the projects studied, presenting them as representative of a series of wider threats to indigenous communities in Brazil. Across the interviews and the documents explored, numerous anti-dam activists argued that, while the São Luiz do Tapajós project may have been removed from the licensing process, the root causes behind its planning and construction remain. Anti-dam actors reconfigured the pro-dam storyline of sustainability by illuminating both how the project studied impacted indigenous communities and by foregrounding them within a wider context of encroachment and the violation of the rights of indigenous communities.

The prominence of indigenous communities in the resistance coalition continued in the how anti-dam actors working in NGOs and EOs made sense of the archival of the São Luiz do Tapajós project. Many presented the actions of the Munduruku community in autonomously demarcating the Sawré Muybu territory as a central factor in the cancellation of the project (Interview, 19 October 2016; Interview, 10 November 2016a; Interview, 10 November 2016b; Interview, 21 November 2016). One interviewee described the Munduruku opposition as 'irreducible,' arguing that its resistance 'got really [widely] covered by the press and … television and … newspapers. In Brazil and outside of Brazil' (Interview, 21 November 2016). The community is presented in opposition materials as well-organised, visionary, and effective in their resistance and as themselves forcing the project's cancellation (Amazon Watch and International Rivers, 2016; Greenpeace Brasil, 2016). As a journalist explained to me, 'It was really ahead of its time … Tapajós was a national issue before it was built' (Interview, 10 November 2016b). This demonstrates the continued centring of indigenous communities in the resistance to the project by resistance actors, with the Munduruku community continuing to be cast as key actors in resisting the São Luiz do Tapajós project – and defeating it.

However, in describing the cancellation of the São Luiz do Tapajós project, resistance actors argued that, despite the Mundurukus' success, the encroachment on indigenous territory and culture continues, and the anti-dam movement in Brazil cannot rest (Interview, 3 October 2016; Interview, 18 November 2016; Interview, 9 December 2017; Interview, 28 April 2017). As with those discussed in Chapter 6, anti-dam storylines that addressed the archival of São Luiz do Tapajós 'scaled up' the resistance to the project – with it representing a single site in a far wider struggle. As a representative of an international NGO reminded me, São Luiz do Tapajós was 'only of many dams planned on the Tapajós,' alluding to the need for the resistance coalition to refocus its opposition to the construction of the Teles Pires and São Manoel projects also being built in the river basin (Interview, 9 December 2017). Similarly, an event to celebrate the project's archival in Itaituba quickly became a site for local resistance actors to reflect on anti-dam struggles elsewhere in the Brazilian Amazon that had not been successful, including those against Belo Monte. The report by the international EO Amazon Watch on the archival included a translated quote from Cacique Arnaldo Kabá Munduruku greeting the news, who said 'We, Munduruku people, are very happy with the news, this is very important for us. Now, we will continue to fight against other dams on our river' (Poirier, 2016).

While anti-dam actors asserted the persistence of contest between indigenous communities and external actors, their discussions became refocused, taking into account the new political context discussed above. While, as discussed in Chapter 4, many anti-dam actors struggled to reconcile their traditional support for the PT with the emerging knowledge of their corruption and graft, uncovered by the Lava Jato investigation, the political changes that surrounded Dilma's removal from power were criticised by a number of resistance actors. Resistance materials and actors opposed the impeachment of Dilma, describing the process as a 'coup' (Interview, 29 September 2016; Interview, 3 October 2016) and Temer as 'an illegitimate president' (Interview, 28 April 2017). It was this new administration – described as an illegitimate government – that was characterised as antagonists in the new, post-Tapajós political context (Interview, 3 October 2016).

The new storylines put forward by anti-dam actors discussing the removal of the São Luiz do Tapajós project focused on the need for continued vigilance against – and resistance to – the policies of the government of Dilma's successor, President Michel Temer. This was with a particular focus on Temer's relationship with the bancada ruralista faction in contemporary Brazilian politics. The bancada ruralista, a political alliance formed in 1985, is centred on opposition to measures directed at environmental protection or conservation, and lobbies for the expansion of the Brazilian agricultural sector. The ruralistas are understood as embodying the interests of the agricultural lobby, taking a firm stance against indigenous land demarcation and lobbying for the expansion of the agricultural frontier. Although this group supported the administration of Dilma Rousseff, numerous interviewees argued that the ruralistas had increased their political influence within the new government of Michel Temer (Interview, 3 October 2016; Interview, 10 November 2016b; Interview, 23 August 2017). The political and economic crisis provided the room for ruralistas to argue that environmental regulation was stifling the economic growth required to lift Brazil out of recession (Gerlak et al., 2019). Upon his taking office, the lobby submitted a list of demands to President Temer, arguing for the need for land reform and increased subsidies for agribusiness. It is reported that Temer committed to exploring these demands over lunch with members of the ruralist bloc (Benites, 2016).

For many of those interviewed, the political influence of the bancada ruralista at the time of the archival of the São Luiz do Tapajós necessitated a renewed vigilance. Those interviewed argued that, under Temer, the ruralistas had the power and autonomy to both influence government policy but also to block other decisions – resulting in a series of emergent threats against the protection of the environment and indigenous communities (Interview, 3 October 2016; Interview, 1 December 2016a; Interview, 28 April 2017). As a representative of Amazon Watch argued, 'they are pretty much calling the shots right now in Brazil' (Interview, 28 April 2017). A prominent member of the bloc, Senator Blairo Maggi, was subsequently appointed Minister for Agriculture between 2016 and 2019. The Temer government staged extensive budget cuts in the environmental sector and openly encouraged others to explore and lobby for the reduction of environmental protection and regulations, particularly involving the loosening of the environmental licensing process. This threatened environmental protection in Brazil in a number of ways, including a weakening of the environmental licensing process (allowing for the planning and construction of dams and other damaging schemes regardless of potential impacts), the opening up of protected areas for extractive industries and accelerated processes of deforestation as agricultural land expands into the Amazon region (Interview,

3 October 2016; Interview, 2 November 2016; Interview, 9 December 2017; Interview, 18 February 2017). As one interviewee at an international EO argued, 'one of the major targets of the ruralistas is to open up these territories to have access to them to build large agro-industrial projects but also large mines, roads, waterways, dams' (Interview, 28 April 2017). In discussing these threats to environmental, resistance actors argued that the Temer government, supported by the ruralistas, was likely to rollback current protections for traditional communities, as part of a campaign to 'open up' the Amazon region for further developmentalist activities (Interview, 3 October 2016; Interview, 19 October 2016). This linking of the protection of indigenous communities to the role of ruralistas centres on a number of policies. These include the Proposta de Emenda à Constituição 215/2000 (PEC 215), a bill that proposes to transfer legal responsibility for indigenous land demarcation from the executive to the legislature, ultimately allowing for the blocking of future territorial protection. In August 2017, Conselho Indigenista Missionario (CIMI) (2017) labelled the policies of the Temer government part of an 'institutional campaign' by the Brazilian government against indigenous communities. The year 2017 witnessed numerous protests against the policies of Michel Temer's government. A centrepiece of this resistance was the 14th Acampamento Terra Livre (Free Earth Camp, ATL), which gathered 1,600 indigenous people in Brasília for a four-day event of activities, discussions, and protests in April 2017. It was reported that this was the largest ATL ever held (Mobilização Nacional Indígena, 2017a, 2017b). At an indigenous demonstration held as part of this event, military police fired pepper gas canisters and rubber bullets at 2,000 indigenous people marching towards the Congresso Nacional (National Congress) (Mobilização Nacional Indígena, 2017c).

In putting forward this storyline, anti-dam actors continued to 'scale up' the resistance to the São Luiz do Tapajós project, even when it was removed from the environmental licensing process. The dam was portrayed as one front in the contemporary resistance to anti-indigenous policies – with the contest between indigeneity and development projects, such as hydropower, being far from over (Movimento dos Atingidos por Barragens, 2017c). While the previously discussed storyline of opposition sited this competition between indigeneity and developmentalism within the policies of the governments of Lula and Dilma, the reconfigured storyline discussed relocates this contest to focus on the politics of the ruralistas. As the programme director for Amazon Watch, Christian Poirier, has argued '[the] triumph must be weighed against the grim reality facing Brazil today, as the Amazon and its traditional communities confront a rising tide of existential threats' (Poirier, 2016). For many, the 2016 decision of IBAMA did not represent a moment of transformation of the Brazilian energy sector but instead signalled a pause in resistance, with the project likely to return in the future (Interview, 3 October 2016; Interview, 1 December 2016a). While a 'golden moment' allowed for this victory, it cannot be celebrated. The São Luiz do Tapajós Dam and projects like it are likely to return, bringing the same processes of displacement, deforestation, and emissions that were objected to by the anti-dam actors opposing Belo Monte.

The presidency of Jair Bolsonaro

At around 3 p.m. on Monday 20 August 2019, the city of São Paulo was plunged into darkness. This was not a blackout caused by a loss of energy supply, nor was it the end of days. Instead, the city of over 12 million bore witness to the smoke streams caused by fires in the Brazilian Amazon. The smoke trails stretched across the South American continent; they could be seen from space and blocked out the sun in the states of Mato Grosso and Paraná. São Paulo is 3,300 km from the city of Boa Vista, the state capital of Roraima. As I write this in Bristol, UK, I am closer to Athens, Greece than São Paulo is to the flames laying waste to the Amazon rainforest. Farmers across the region use slash-and-burn techniques to clear new land for farming and pasture. Illegal logging operations turn to fires to force indigenous communities from the lands, as well as to cover the destruction that they leave behind. On 10 August 2019, cattle ranchers in southern Amazonia staged a joint dia de fogo ('day of fire'), starting at least 134 forest fires around Novo Progresso, Pará alone (Maisonnave, 2019). The ranchers responsible were eager to show that they were 'ready to work' to expand the agricultural frontier further into the Brazilian Amazon.[1]

The calls for a renewed vigilance issued by anti-dam actors in 2016 came to seem particularly prescient from January 2019 onwards. For many environmentalists in Brazil, these fires – which seized the frontpages of media and minds of many across the globe in the August and September 2019 – were the direct result of Brazil's new president. Jair Bolsonaro was sworn in as president in January 2019, succeeding Temer, after winning an election in late 2018. Bolsonaro, a former military officer and leader of the Partido Social Liberal party, is a controversial figure. He has previously called for a military coup (Cuadros, 2017), labelled the crimes of the military junta, including rape, torture, and murder of civilians as 'little problems' of history, and has denied its characterisation as a dictatorship (Folha de S. Paulo, 2019). He has a persistent record of homophobic, misogynistic, and racist utterances (Ilg, n.d.; Folha de S. Paulo, 2020) and has promised to criminalise several social movements (Paiva, 2018). He has also employed racist rhetoric towards indigenous communities, characterising them as living 'prehistoric lifestyles' and insinuating that they are not yet 'human' (Exame, 2019b; UOL, 2020).

Before being elected as president, Bolsonaro had regularly spoken out against the demarcation of indigenous territory in Brazil and called for the opening up of such lands for mining operations. He has spoken out against what he labelled 'an indigenous land demarcation industry' that holds rural producers 'hostage' (Folhapress, 2018) and called for previous decisions of demarcation to be reversed to allow for farms and extractive activities to enter new frontiers (Gonzales, 2018). In a 2015 statement made when receiving a medal from the Brazilian Military Police, Bolsonaro argued that:

> The Indians do not speak our language, they do not have money, they do not have [a] culture. They are native peoples. How did they manage to get

13% of the national territory ... there is no indigenous land where there are no minerals. Gold, tin and magnesium are in these lands, especially in the Amazon, the richest area in the world. I am not part of this ploy to defend [the] land for the Indians.

(Marques and Rocha, 2015)

Although they have never been formally linked in a political alliance, the accession of Bolsonaro to the Presidency represents the continued political influence and power of the ruralista caucus and its vision of a stripped-back, deregulated environmental policy. Upon taking office, Bolsonaro appointed Rodrigo Salles, a ruralist and climate change denier to head the Ministry of the Environment (Bilenky and Fernandes, 2018). Salles and the government quickly went to work and, within a month of taking office, the government had revealed its plan for new large infrastructure megaprojects in the Brazilian Amazon, including numerous roads, dams, and mines (Rocha, 2019). Bolsonaro moved to dismantle FUNAI's authority on his first day in office, attempting to transfer the decision-making powers over the demarcation of indigenous reserves from FUNAI to the Ministry of Agriculture. However, this move, as well as creating a public outcry, was reversed by the Brazilian legislature, which affirmed FUNAI's powers, as well as its location within the Ministry of Justice (Mendes, 2019). Salles had previously called for reform of O Conselho Nacional do Meio Ambiente (National Environmental Council, CONAMA), merging it with up to 22 other councils and bodies linked to the Ministerio Meio Ambiente (Tuffani, 2019). On 1 January 2019 – Bolsonaro and Salles' first day in office – a document was leaked that called for a restructuring of environmental legislation and mechanisms in Brazil (Tuffani, 2019). Suely Araújo, the head of IBAMA who had previously removed the São Luiz do Tapajós project from the licensing process, resigned in January 2019, having found herself under intense criticism and attention from both Bolsonaro and Ricardo Salles, who questioned a truck rental contract signed by IBAMA in December 2018 (Peron, Zaia, and Brigatto, 2019). The contract, for an amount of R$28.7 million for 393 trucks to be used across the agency and including funds for fuel, maintenance, and insurance, was presented by Salles and Bolsonaro as irregular and as evidence of the 'financial violation' of Brazilians by civil servants (Mazui, 2019; Peron, Zaia, and Brigatto, 2019). Araújo, a civil servant working on Brazilian environmental policy since 1991, resigned from office with a parting shot, labelling the president and his Minister of the Environment as 'ignorant' (Mazui, 2019).

These attacks on regulation occurred during a period when the Brazilian population was forced to confront an example of the intense failure of environmental regulation in the country. On 25 January 2019, in Brumadinho, Minas Gerais, a tailings dam at the Córrego do Feijão iron ore mine owned by Vale failed, collapsing and releasing a mudflow that inundated the mine's facilities, including a cafeteria packed with workers on their lunch break, before flooding countless nearby homes. Two hundred and seventy are understood to have perished in the disaster (Freitas and Almeida, 2020). Twelve million m^3 of tailings flooded the nearby area, polluting the Paraopeba River (G1 Minas, 2019). For many in Brazil, the disaster provided a tragic example of the ineffectiveness of environmental regulations in the country and the intransigence of mining companies (Cruz, 2019; FGV DAPP, 2019). In the wake of Brumadinho, the environment became a key political talking point, both in the corridors of Brasília and on social networks (FGV DAPP, 2019).[2] Leaked internal reports provided evidence that Vale knew of the weaknesses of the tailings dam and that it breached internal safety guidelines as early as October 2019; however, an appraisal by the German consultancy company Tüv Süd in September the same year found that the dam met legal requirements and that no action was required (BBC, 2019a, 2019b).

With Bolsonaro elected on a platform that included the loosening of environmental restrictions, the tragedy at Brumadinho occurred just three weeks after he took office, in what appeared to be a reversal. After previously speaking of the need for deregulation, the government began to discuss the need for monitoring and penalties for poor practices (Biller, Iglesias and Adghirni, 2019). However, any hope of an affirmation of environmental regulation under Bolsonaro quickly dissipated, particularly after Ricardo Salles argued in an interview three days after the collapse that the Brumadinho tragedy provided evidence that 'excessive bureaucracy' in environmental monitoring and inspection did not stop such tragedies from occurring (Sadi, 2019). At the time of writing, the assault on environmental regulation in Brazil continues. In May 2020, Salles was reported to have called on policymakers to use the Coronavirus pandemic as a public distraction from implementing further deregulation of environmental protections in Brazil (Spring, 2020).

As Bolsonaro celebrated his election to president, social movements prepared for a new period of resistance (Interview, 6 August 2019; Interview, 4 September 2019). Indigenous leaders appealed to the international community for assistance. One prominent figure, Sônia Guajajara, the leader of Articulação dos Povos Indígenas do Brasil (APIB) called on the European Union to impose trade sanctions to prevent environmental damage and violence towards indigenous communities (Nelsen, 2018). For some, Bolsonaro's worldview of the Amazon as a resource-rich area ripe for extraction harks back to that of the military junta, with the current government's policies likened to Operation Amazonia of the junta (Dias, 2019) The latter came at an extraordinary environmental and human cost, with widespread damage to the Amazon rainforest and the displacement and dislocation of local, particularly indigenous, communities (Bunker, 1988). Leaked audio reports lend credence to such fears, with documents showing military officers discussing development projects in the Legal Amazon Region (Dias, 2019). The Barao Rio Branco project – a resurrection of a project first-planned in the 1950s – includes the construction of a large hydroelectric dam on the Trombetas River, a bridge across the Amazon River, and an extension of the BR-163 highway to the Suriname border. This scheme, justified in the name of the national interest and the economic benefits it is expected to bring, will likely lead to new waves of deforestation and displacement and trauma for local communities in the Amazon region.

Conclusions

I have argued in this chapter that the 2016 decision to 'archive' the São Luiz do Tapajós Dam project was seen by anti-dam activists in Brazil and beyond as representative of a changing political context, within which such a decision suddenly became possible. For many of those interviewed, the uncovering of corruption by the Lava Jato investigation, the impeachment of Dilma Rousseff and the continuation of a crippling economic recession all set the foundations for Suely Araújo, the then-president of IBAMA, to not only criticise the project but remove it from the environmental licensing process entirely.

However, an understanding of the 2016 decision as one permitted by contextual factors also resulted in many of those interviewed claiming that the tides will turn again and the São Luiz do Tapajós project is likely to return in the future. This represents a continuation of the processes of 'scaling up' and repoliticisation that were discussed in previous chapters. While the political demise of Dilma Rousseff and the budgetary austerity of the Temer administration resulted in the project enjoying declining support, its removal from the licensing process was not celebrated for long. Instead, anti-dam activists asserted that many policies that they resist, of which this dam was a symbol, retained their significance in Brazilian politics. While IBAMA's decision was positive, it represented one victory in a far wider struggle. In light of this, many activists called for persistent vigilance and opposition to government policy.

This need for continued vigilance against encroachment and environmental damage is pertinent in light of the October 2018 election of Jair Bolsonaro as president. The Bolsonaro administration represents a new stage in the construction of hydroelectric dams in the Brazilian Amazon. It has pledged to streamline and downgrade the environmental licensing process to allow projects to be built quicker and easier. It has attacked environmental policies and regulations and the demarcation of indigenous territory as holding Brazil back from a brighter future. There are many in the Brazilian government and the wider bureaucracy who perceive the continued enforcement of environmental legislation as representing a barrier to the state's economic development. Political dismissal of the environmental licensing process has led to a lack of commitment to the process and the rights and norms that it protects, such as those of indigenous rights. Proposed legislation – at the time of writing – pledges to bring indigenous communities into the planning process of hydroelectric dams, offering payment and royalties in exchange for acquiescence (Gerlak et al., 2019). Elsewhere, the Bolsonaro administration has resumed a project to build a nuclear power plant near demarcated indigenous lands in Pernambuco (Assessoria de Comunicação do CPP, 2019). Interviewees argued that civil society organisations stand ready to oppose these changes and to support communities resisting hydroelectric dams into the future (Interview, 28 April 2017; Interview, 6 August 2019; Interview, 4 September 2019). This includes the São Luiz do Tapajós Dam project, with many activists now arguing that the shifting political terrain necessitates increased resistance and vigilance. As a respondent working at a Brazilian environmental organisation told me in August 2019:

> The government and those who support the view that preserving the environment and human rights goes against the country's economy ... We have agribusiness, large land grabbers, mining companies [all] wanting to end environmental protection and protection of indigenous peoples ... Everything indicates that this government will resume large hydroelectric plants in the Amazon – not only in the Tapajós [basin] ... We need the world to treat Bolsonaro for what he is: a global enemy of the environment, traditional peoples and [the] climate.
>
> (Interview, 4 September 2019)

The message of anti-dam activists is clear. The São Luiz do Tapajós project may be gone but the contest between local communities and external actors seeking to 'open up' the Amazon region – that is so dramatically symbolised in the planning and construction of hydropower in Brazil – continues.

Notes

1 In response to the fires, Germany cut its US$39.5 million contribution to the Amazon Fund, a mechanism to use international funding to slow deforestation in the Brazilian Amazon, due to Brasilia's lack of commitment to curbing the loss of the forest. Norway, previously the biggest donor contributor to the Amazon Fund, withdrew its donation in August 2019.
2 This was not the only such dam collapse in recent memory in Brazil. On 5 November 2015, a tailings dam, storing metal-rich, high-pollutant slurry from an iron mine operated by the mining company Samarco (co-owned by Vale and the Australian company BHP Billiton) collapsed in the Doce River, in the municipality of Mariana, Minas Gerais. The resulting tsunami of slurry fell upon the town of Bento Rodrigues, displacing 600 people and killing 19. This dam failure resulted in the release of between 55 and 62 million m^3 of tailings in Doce River – polluting the river from the point of the dam breach to the mouth of the river and sending a plume of pollutants into the ocean (Fernandes et al., 2016). It is understood that this pollution impacted the livelihoods of over 1 million people, reducing access to fisheries, clear water, agricultural sites, and hydroelectricity generation. It has in some way, affected people in 41 cities in the Doce basin, and caused up to US$20 billion of damage to ecosystems in the region (Fernandes et al., 2016).

Bibliography

Amazon Watch and International Rivers (2016). Brazilian government cancels megadam on the Amazon's Tapajós River. *Amazon Watch*, 4 August. Available at: https://amazonwatch.org/news/2016/0804-brazilian-government-cancels-mega-dam-on-the-amazons-tapajos-river (Accessed: 6 April 2020).

Amora, D (2016). Custo de energia pode mudar sem nova hidrelétrica, diz estatal. *Folha de S. Paulo*, 3 August. Available at: https://www1.folha.uol.com.br/mercado/2016/08/1798652-custo-de-energia-pode-mudar-sem-nova-hidreletrica-diz-estatal.shtml (Accessed: 6 April 2020).

Aranha, A, and Mota, J (2014). Exclusivo: Relatório da FUNAI determina que terra é dos Munduruku. *Agência Pública*, 11 December. Available at: https://apublica.org/2014/12/relatorio-funai-determina-que-terra-e-dos-munduruku/ (Accessed: 6 April 2020).

Assessoria de Comunicação do Conselho Pastoral dos Pescadores (2019). Mais de 100 organizações assinam carta contra a implantação de Usina Nuclear em Itacuruba (PE). *Conselho Pastoral dos Pescadores*, 6 June. Available at: http://www.cppnacional.org.br/noticia/mais-de-100-organiza%C3%A7%C3%B5es-assinam-carta-contra-implanta%C3%A7%C3%A3o-de-usina-nuclear-em-itacuruba-pe (Accessed: 6 April 2020).

Atkins, E (2017). Dammed and diversionary: the multi-dimensional framing of Brazil's Belo Monte dam. *Singapore Journal of Tropical Geography*, 38(3): 276–292.

BBC (2019a). Brumadinho dam collapse in Brazil: vale mine chief resigns. *BBC News*, 3 March. Available at: https://www.bbc.co.uk/news/business-47432134 (Accessed: 6 April 2020).

BBC (2019b). Vale 'knew collapsed dam was at risk,' says report. *BBC News*, 12 February. Available at: https://www.bbc.co.uk/news/business-47209265 (Accessed: 6 April 2020).

Benites, A (2016). Temer acena a ruralistas com apoio a mudança em demarcação de área indígena. *El País*, 13 July. Available at: https://brasil.elpais.com/brasil/2016/07/13/politica/1468363551_264805.html (Accessed: 6 April 2020).

Bilenky, T, and Fernandes, T (2018). Vamos preservar o ambiente sem ideologia", diz futuro ministro de Bolsonaro. *Folha de S. Paulo*, 9 December. Available at: https://www1.folha.uol.com.br/ambiente/2018/12/vamos-preservar-o-ambiente-sem-ideologia-diz-futuro-ministro-de-bolsonaro.shtml (Accessed: 6 April 2020).

Biller, D., Iglesias, S, and Adghirni, S (2019). Desastre da Vale em Brumadinho faz Bolsonaro reavaliar visão ambiental. *Exame*, 29 January. Available at: https://exame.abril.com.br/brasil/desastre-da-vale-em-brumadinho-faz-bolsonaro-reavaliar-visao-ambiental/ (Accessed: 6 April 2020).

Boas, BV (2016). Inflação atinge 10,67% em 2015 e estoura teto da meta do governo. *Folha de S. Paulo*, 8 January. Available at: https://www1.folha.uol.com.br/mercado/2016/01/1727284-inflacao-sobe-1067-em-2015-e-estoura-teto-da-meta-do-governo.shtml (Accessed: 6 April 2020).

Branford, S (2018). Brazil announces end to Amazon mega-dam building policy. *Mongabay*, 3 January. Available at: https://news.mongabay.com/2018/01/brazil-announces-end-to-amazon-mega-dam-building-policy/ (Accessed: 6 April 2020).

Bunker, SG (1988). *Underdeveloping the Amazon: Extraction, Unequal Exchange, and the Failure of the Modern State*. Chicago, IL: University of Chicago Press.

CIMI, Regional Sul (2017). Sem reconhecer indígenas como sujeitos de direitos, governo relembra Ditadura, denuncia. *Combate Racismo Ambiental*, 7 August. Available at: https://racismoambiental.net.br/2017/08/07/sem-reconhecer-indigenas-como-sujeitos-de-direitos-governo-relembra-ditadura-denuncia-cimi-regional-sul/ (Accessed: 6 April 2020).

Cruz, V (2019). Brumadinho serve de reflexão a quem defende acelerar licenças ambientais no governo Bolsonaro. *G1*, 28 January Available at: https://g1.globo.com/politica/blog/valdo-cruz/post/2019/01/28/brumadinho-serve-de-reflexao-a-quem-defende-acelerar-licencas-ambientais-no-governo-bolsonaro.ghtml (Accessed: 6 April 2020).

Cuadros, A (2017). Open talk of a military coup unsettles Brazil. *New Yorker*, 13 October. Available at: https://www.newyorker.com/news/news-desk/open-talk-of-a-military-coup-unsettles-brazil (Accessed: 6 April 2020).

Cury, A (2017). Desemprego fica em 12% no 4o trimestre de 2016 e atinge 12,3 milhões. *G1*, 31 January. Available at: https://g1.globo.com/economia/noticia/desemprego-fica-em-12-no-4-trimestre-de-2016.ghtml (Accessed: 6 April 2020).

Cury, A, and Caoli, C (2016). PIB do Brasil cai 3,8% em 2015 e tem pior resultado em 25 anos. *G1*, 3 March. Available at: http://g1.globo.com/economia/noticia/2016/03/pib-do-brasil-cai-38-em-2015.html (Accessed: 6 April 2020).

Dias, T (2019). Operation Amazon Redux. *Intercept*, 20 September. Available at: https://theintercept.com/2019/09/20/amazon-brazil-army-bolsanaro/ (Accessed: 6 April 2020).

Exame (2019). Bolsonaro diz que índios vivem "pré-históricos dentro de suas terras". *Exame*, 27 November. Available at: https://exame.abril.com.br/brasil/bolsonaro-diz-que-indios-vivem-pre-historicos-dentro-de-suas-terras/ (Accessed: 6 April 2020).

Fernandes, GW, Goulart, FF, Ranieri, BD, Coelho, MS, Dales, K, Boesche, N, Bustamente, M, Carvalho, FA, Carvalho, DC, Dirzo, R, Fernandes, S, Galetti Jr, PM, Garcia Millan, VE, Mielke, C, Ramirez, JL, Neves, A, Rogass, C, Ribeiro, SP and Soares-Filho, B (2016). Deep into the mud: ecological and socio-economic impacts of the dam breach in Mariana, Brazil. *Natureza e Conservacao*, 14(2): 35–45.

FGV DAPP (2019). Meio Ambiente é o principal tema associado ao governo após desastre em Brumadinho. *FGV DAPP*. Available at: http://dapp.fgv.br/meio-ambiente-e-o-principal-tema-associado-ao-governo-apos-desastre-em-brumadinho/ (Accessed: 6 April 2020).

Folha de S. Paulo (2017). Entenda o impacto da crise no governo na economia. *Folha de S. Paulo*, 18 May. Available at: https://www1.folha.uol.com.br/mercado/2017/05/1885077-entenda-o-impacto-da-crise-no-governo-na-economia.shtml (Accessed: 6 April 2020).

Folha de S. Paulo (2019). Bolsonaro nega ditadura e diz que regime viveu probleminhas. *Folha de S. Paulo*, 27 March. Available at: https://www1.folha.uol.com.br/poder/2019/03/nao-houve-ditadura-teve-uns-probleminhas-diz-bolsonaro-sobre-regime-militar-no-pais.shtml (Accessed: 6 April 2020).

Folha de S. Paulo (2020). Veja falas preconceituosas de Bolsonaro e o que diz a lei sobre injúria e racismo. *Folha de S. Paulo*, 26 January. Available at: https://www1.folha.uol.com.br/poder/2020/01/veja-falas-preconceituosas-de-bolsonaro-e-o-que-diz-a-lei-sobre-injuria-e-racismo.shtml (Accessed: 6 April 2020).

Folhapress (2018). Bolsonaro ataca 'indústrias' da reserva indígena e da expropriação de terras por trabalho escravo. *Bem Paraná*, 5 October. Available at: https://www.bemparana.com.br/noticia/bolsonaro-ataca-industrias-da-reserva-indigena-e-da-expropriacao-de-terras-por-trabalho-escravo#.XosX1IhKjIV (Accessed: 6 April 2020).

Freitas, R, and Almeida, F (2020). Um ano após tragédia da Vale, dor e luta por justiça unem famílias de 259 mortos e 11 desaparecidos. *G1*, 25 January. Available at: https://g1.globo.com/mg/minas-gerais/noticia/2020/01/25/um-ano-apos-tragedia-da-vale-dor-e-luta-por-justica-unem-familias-de-259-mortos-e-11-desaparecidos.ghtml (Accessed: 6 April 2020).

Fundação Nacional do Índio (2016). Funai aprova estudos das Terras Indígenas Sawré Muybu (PA), Ypoi/Triunfo (MS), Sambaqui (PR) e Jurubaxi-Téa (AM). *FUNAI*, 19 April. Available at: http://www.funai.gov.br/index.php/comunicacao/noticias/3712-funai-publica-estudos-das-terras-indigenas-sawre-muybu-pa-ypoi-triunfo-ms-sambaqui-pr-e-jurubaxi-tea-am (Accessed: 6 April 2020).

G1 Minas (2019). Barragem da Vale se rompe em Brumadinho, MG. *G1*, 25 January. Available at: https://g1.globo.com/mg/minas-gerais/noticia/2019/01/25/bombeiros

-e-defesa-civil-sao-mobilizados-para-chamada-de-rompimento-de-barragem-em-b rumadinho-na-grande-bh.ghtml (Accessed: 6 April 2020).
Gerlak, AK, Saguier, M, Mills-Novoa, M, Fearnside, P.M, and Albercht, TR (2019). Dams, Chinese investments, and EIAs: a race to the bottom in South America? *Ambio*, 49: 156–164.
Gonzales, J (2018). Brazilian elections and the environment: where top candidates stand. *Mongabay*, 17 September. Available at: https://news.mongabay.com/2018/09/brazil ian-elections-and-the-environment-where-top-candidates-stand/ (Accessed: 6 April 2020).
Greenpeace Brasil (2016). Hidrelétrica no Tapajós está cancelada. *Greenpeace Brasil*, 4 August. Available at: https://www.greenpeace.org/brasil/blog/hidreletrica-no-tapaj os-esta-cancelada/ (Accessed: 6 April 2020).
Ilg, J (n.d.). Bolsonaro é condenado por discurso racista, veja o que ele já disse contra os negros. *Esquerda Diario*. Available at: https://esquerdadiario.com.br/spip.php?page=g acetilla-articulo&id_article=18579 (Accessed: 6 April 2020).
Instituto Brasileiro do Meio Ambiente e dos Recursos Naturais Renováveis (2016). Ibama arquiva licenciamento da UHE São Luiz do Tapajós, no Pará. *IBAMA*, 5 August. Available at: http://www.ibama.gov.br/noticias/58-2016/162-ibama-arquiva-licenc iamento-da-uhesao-%0Aluiz-do-tapajos-no-para (Accessed: 19 March 2019).
Maisonnave, F (2019). Em 'dia do fogo,' sul do PA registra disparo no número de queimadas. *Folha de S. Paulo*, 14 August. Available at: https://www1.folha.uol.com.br/ ambiente/2019/08/em-dia-do-fogo-sul-do-pa-registra-disparo-no-numero-de-queimada s.shtml (Accessed: 6 April 2020).
Marques, A, and Rocha, L (2015). Bolsonaro diz que OAB só defende bandido e reserva indígena é um crime. *Campo Grande News*, 22 April. Available at: https://www.cam pograndenews.com.br/politica/bolsonaro-diz-que-oab-so-defende-bandido-e-reserva-indigena-e-um-crime (Accessed: 6 April 2020).
Martello, A (2015). BC sobe juro para 14,25% ao ano e indica manutenção no futuro. *G1*, 29 July. Available at: http://g1.globo.com/economia/noticia/2015/07/na-7-alta-seguida-juro-sobe-para-1425-ao-ano-maior-nivel-desde-2006.html (Accessed: 6 April 2020).
Mazui, G (2019). Presidente do Ibama se demite após ministro questionar contrato de aluguel de caminhonetes. *G1*, 7 January Available at: https://g1.globo.com/politica/ noticia/2019/01/07/presidente-do-ibama-pede-exoneracao-depois-de-ministro-questi onar-contrato-de-aluguel-de-carros.ghtml (Accessed: 6 April 2020).
Mendes, K (2019). Brazil's Congress reverses Bolsonaro, restores Funai's land demarcation powers. *Mongabay*, 5 June. Available at: https://news.mongabay.com/2019/06/brazil s-congress-reverses-bolsonaro-restores-funais-land-demarcation-powers/ (Accessed: 6 April 2020).
Mobilização Nacional Indígena (2017a). Festa indígena na Esplanada dos Ministérios. *Mobilização Nacional Indígena*, 27 April. Available at: https://mobilizacaonacion alindigena.wordpress.com/2017/04/27/festa-indigena-na-esplanada-dos-ministerios/ (Accessed: 6 April 2020).
Mobilização Nacional Indígena (2017b). O maior Acampamento Terra Livre da história! *Mobilização Nacional Indígena*, 28 April. Available at: https://mobilizacaonacion alindigena.wordpress.com/2017/04/28/o-maior-acampamento-terra-livre-da-historia/ (Accessed: 6 April 2020).
Mobilização Nacional Indígena (2017c). Protesto pacífico de povos indígenas é atacado pela polícia no Congresso. *Mobilização Nacional Indígena*, 25 April. Available at: https://

mobilizacaonacionalindigena.wordpress.com/2017/04/25/protesto-pacifico-de-pov os-indigenas-e-atacado-pela-policia-na-frente-do-congresso/ (Accessed: 6 April 2020).

Movimento dos Atingidos por Barragens (2017). Tapajós: Vencemos uma batalha, mas a guerra está só começando. *Movimento dos Atingidos por Barragens*, 18 January. Available at: https://www.mabnacional.org.br/noticia/tapaj-s-vencemos-uma-batalha-mas-gue rra-est-s-come-ando (Accessed: 6 April 2020).

Nelsen, A (2018). Indigenous leader urges EU to impose sanctions on Brazil. *The Guardian*, 18 December. Available at: https://www.theguardian.com/world/2018/dec/18/indi genous-leader-urges-eu-to-impose-sanctions-on-brazil (Accessed: 6 April 2020).

Nogueira, LA (2017). A Lava Jato está corroendo o PIB. E daí? *Istoé Dinheiro*, 2 June. Available at: https://www.istoedinheiro.com.br/lava-jato-esta-corroendo-o-pib-e-dai/ (Accessed: 6 April 2020).

Paiva, FM (2018). Diante de Bolsonaro, movimentos sociais preparam a resistência. *Instituto Humanitas Unisinos*, 7 November. Available at: http://www.ihu.unisinos.b r/188-noticias/noticias-2018/584451-diante-de-bolsonaro-movimentos-sociais-prepa ram-a-resistencia (Accessed: 6 April 2020).

Peron, I., Zaia, C, and Brigatto, G (2019). Presidente do Ibama pede demissão após críticas de Bolsonaro e Salles. *Valor Econômico*, 7 January. Available at: https://valor.globo. com/politica/noticia/2019/01/07/presidente-do-ibama-pede-demissao-apos-criticas-de-bolsonaro-e-salles.ghtml (Accessed: 6 April 2020).

Poirier, C (2016). Victory on Brazil's Tapajós River and the battle that lies ahead. *Amazon Watch*, 9 August. Available at: https://amazonwatch.org/news/2016/0809-victory-on-brazils-tapajos-river-and-the-battle-that-lies-ahead (Accessed: 6 April 2020).

Rocha, J (2019). Bolsonaro government reveals plan to develop the 'Unproductive Amazon'. *Mongabay*. 28 January. Available at: https://news.mongabay.com/2019/01/ bolsonaro-government-reveals-plan-to-develop-the-unproductive-amazon/ (Accessed: 6 April 2020).

Sadi, A (2019). Depois de Brumadinho, ministro do Meio Ambiente defende discussão da lei de licenciamento ambiental. *G1*, 28 January. Available at: https://g1.globo.com /politica/blog/andreia-sadi/post/2019/01/28/depois-de-brumadinho-ministro-do-mei o-ambiente-defende-discussao-da-lei-de-licenciamento-ambiental.ghtml (Accessed: 6 April 2020).

Sales, C, and Uhlig, A (2016). Ignorância ou má fé sobre as hidrelétricas em terra indígena. *Valor Econômico*, 14 September. Available at: https://valor.globo.com/opiniao/col una/ignorancia-ou-ma-fe-sobre-as-hidreletricas-em-terra-indigena.ghtml (Accessed: 6 April 2020).

Spring, J (2020). Brazil minister calls for environmental deregulation while public distracted by COVID. *Reuters*, 22 May. Available at: https://uk.reuters.com/article/us-b razil-politics-environment/brazil-minister-calls-for-environmental-deregulation-while -public-distracted-by-covid-idUKKBN22Y30Y (Accessed 23 July 2020).

Tuffani, M (2019). Já estava nos planos de Salles desde o ano passado 'reformatar o Conama.' *Direto da Ciência*, 27 March. Available at: http://www.diretodaciencia.com /2019/03/27/ja-estava-nos-planos-de-salles-desde-o-ano-passado-reformatar-o-cona ma/ (Accessed: 6 April 2020).

UOL (2020). Bolsonaro: 'O índio é cada vez mais um ser humano igual a nós.' *UOL*, 23 January. Available at: https://noticias.uol.com.br/politica/ultimas-noticias/2020/0 1/23/indio-ta-evoluindo-cada-vez-mais-e-ser-humano-igual-a-nos-diz-bolsonaro.htm   (Accessed: 6 April 2020).

8 Final remarks

The planning and construction of hydroelectric dams across the globe should be understood as taking the form of a long-term contest between a pro-dam coalition that locates hydropower on the government agenda and a resistance coalition that highlights the energy source's environmental and social impacts (Baviskar, 1995; Carvalho, 2006; Hochstetler, 2011; Bellette Lee, 2013). While pro-dam actors may assert the benefits of a particular scheme, those opposed to it highlight overlooked impacts and forgotten complexities. This text has followed the work of others in asserting the importance of the discourse present within this interplay between pro-dam and resistance coalitions, with the narratives put forward by these different groups engaging in a contest to inscribe a dam project with a particular meaning (Molle, 2008; Molle, Mollinga, and Wester, 2009; Warner, Hoogesteger, and Hidalgo, 2017). Following the work of Hajer (1993, 1995), I have defined the overarching body of these contests as taking the form of *storylines* that are put forward by actors to impose a prescribed meaning or significance on a policy, process or project.

Hydroelectricity in the 21st century is widely regarded by policymakers, engineers, and other actors as a crucial ingredient in any sustainable energy transition, due to it assumed provision of secure, cheap energy with limited social and environmental impacts. The asserted sustainability of contemporary hydropower projects is prevalent in the words the proponents of respective projects across the globe (Ahlers et al., 2015; Huber and Joshi, 2015). I understood this as representing an 'adaptive capacity' of pro-dam actors, absorbing emergent or alternative demands, grievances, or tropes into legitimising storylines to appeal to a 'moral legitimacy' that is prevalent at the time of their construction (Warner, Hoogesteger, and Hidalgo, 2017). Whilst historic dam projects were often legitimised via pro-dam storylines that linked respective schemes to wider contexts of nationalism or economic development, the hydroelectric projects of the 21st century have been justified as providing clean, green energy that contributes to contemporary sustainable development agendas.

The pro-dam storyline of sustainability is underpinned by international environmental policy instruments, with large dam projects able to secure funding through the Clean Development Mechanism (CDM) under the 1997 Kyoto Protocol. In light of Sustainable Development Goal 7, calling for *sustainable and modern energy for all*, governments across the globe continue to turn to hydroelectric dams as a source of energy. From the Ilisu Dam in Turkey that flooded one of the world's oldest continuous settlements in 2020 to the Myitsone Dam on the Irrawaddy River in Myanmar, the hydraulic mission continues across the globe. Despite the efforts of resistance actors in the cases studied, the pro-dam storyline of sustainability continues. The Clean Development Mechanism – as well as the World Bank, pension funds, and Chinese capital – all fund the construction of dam projects while asserting the projects' sustainability credentials (McDonald, Bosshard, and Brewer, 2009; Siciliano et al., 2019). Pro-dam actors continue to assert the role of hydropower in contemporary sustainable development agendas (Lane, 2015; Berga, 2016). Within this storyline of sustainability, numerous hydroelectric projects are provided with both financial support and a degree of legitimacy, with the projects cast as green technology within a climate-changing world.

Across the globe, rivers are being dammed and land inundated by hydroelectric plants, displacing populations and bringing traumatic impacts to many. Despite concerns regarding impacts and population displacement (World Commission on Dams, 2000) and cost overruns (Ansar et al., 2014), governments and funders across the globe invest time, money, and resources in the construction of hydroelectric projects as a source of clean, green energy. With new private and international funders becoming a central part of this new process of 21st-century dam construction, anti-dam movements will likely find it more difficult to hold the pro-dam coalition accountable and see their opportunities for resistance limited (Ahlers, Zwarteveen, and Bakker, 2017). At the time of writing, tensions are increasing around new dams across South America in response to the emergence of new funders, such as the Chinese state, and the politically-driven weakening of the environmental licensing process (Gerlak et al., 2019).

A central argument of this text is that the sustainability credentials of hydroelectric projects remain contestable – and contested. With the pro-dam storyline of sustainability predicated on the role of this infrastructure in GHG (particularly carbon dioxide) emissions, it holds a particularly narrow definition of a project's sustainability. It is within this context that the task of those opposing a hydropower project is to challlenge not only the dam itself but also its definition as a sustainable project. Across the globe, the social and environmental impacts of large hydroelectric dams continue, providing anti-dam movements with points of critique. In criticising and challenging hydroelectric dam projects, anti-dam movements simultaneously contest and reconfigure the pro-dam storyline of sustainability, broadening popular understanding of hydropower's social and environmental impacts.

To explore this storyline of sustainability and how it is contested and reconfigured, I have examined the planning and construction of the Belo Monte and São Luiz do Tapajós hydroelectric dams in the Legal Amazon Region of Brazil. Pro-dam actors in these cases have put forward a storyline of sustainability that argues that the hydroelectricity generated by the projects studied represents a form of 'clean' energy, with hydropower presented as having low emissions of greenhouse gases (GHGs). Pro-dam actors not only asserted the sustainability credentials of these projects in terms of climate change mitigation (via the reduction of GHG emissions that would be emitted from alternative fossil fuel sources) but also denied the extent of the impacts in the regions in which they were built. Within these storylines, the projects studied have been legitimised as key sites of the national transition away from fossil fuels and towards energy security. This text has explored the ways in which the civil society groups that are part of the resistance coalition in Brazil and beyond broaden and challenge such a definition to illuminate the unsustainability of the Belo Monte and São Luiz do Tapajós projects. In the previous chapters, I have explored how members of what I have labelled the 'resistance coalition' against the projects studied have not only opposed the projects but also challenged their promotion as *sustainable* energy. In particular, I have focused on the role and words of non-governmental organisations (NGOs), environmental organisations (EOs), and journalists in forwarding storylines of resistance that challenge dominant perceptions of the legitimacy of the Belo Monte and São Luiz do Tapajós projects and elevate the resistance against them to a wider audience.

Storylines of sustainability act to not only legitimise a dam project but also represent a process of depoliticisation, in which a project is rendered technical and apolitical, deflecting opposition criticism and excluding the demands and grievances of resistance actors, which are deemed to be illegitimate (Ferguson, 1994; Chhotray, 2007). Alternative definitions of sustainability or understandings of a hydroelectric dam's impacts are excluded from the storyline of sustainability, with the pro-dam storyline, instead, retaining a narrow focus on the role of this type of energy infrastructure in the reduction of greenhouse gases. However, the language of 'sustainability' is ambiguous (Leach, Scoones, and Stirling, 2010; Brown, 2016) resulting in the presence of diverse, often divergent understandings, including environmental justice, just transition, and socio-environmentalism. Perceptions of what is and what is not 'sustainable' at the local community level can differ from those definitions held by policymakers (Harris, 2009). Similarly, social movements in Brazil have a rich lineage in presenting the links between social and environmental components of sustainability. Following Cavanagh and Benjaminsen (2017), I understand these as the presence of 'alternative sustainabilities,' which challenge and complicate more dominant definitions of what sustainability and sustainable development look like. Whilst proponents of the Belo Monte and São Luiz do Tapajós projects have located the sustainability of the respective dams as above the political and as the provision of a technical solution to technical issues, resistance actors have put forward storylines that illuminate the political interests and motivations that drove the projects forward, regardless of the demands and grievances of those opposed to them, as well as the wide-ranging impacts that the projects would have – thus widening the terrain upon which this *sustainability* was set.

Across the previous chapters, I have argued that resistance actors have reconfigured – simultaneously challenging and modifying – the pro-dam storyline of sustainability not only by drawing attention to the social and environmental impacts of the Belo Monte and São Luiz do Tapajós projects but also by putting forward storylines that *repoliticise* the projects studied, render visible their respective impacts and scale up the local grievances and demands into wider storylines of opposition. In Chapter 4, I explored how anti-dam actors repoliticised the Belo Monte and São Luiz do Tapajós Dam projects by recontextualising their planning and construction within a terrain of political influence and will, impunity, and circumvention of legal norms. In doing so, these actors exposed the political nature of the projects discussed, characterising the Belo Monte project, in particular, as a site of political corruption and the storyline of sustainability as a mere instrument to conceal such deceit. In Chapter 5, I detailed the ways in which anti-dam actors critiqued and challenged the validity and accuracy of official Environmental Impact Assessments (EIAs) to *render visible* extensive impacts that remained undiscussed and unmitigated in the official definition of the projects' 'sustainability.' With the EIAs representing an overarching worldview that rendered the project technical and depoliticised the moment of contestation around them, anti-dam actors illumination these impacts allowed for not only the disputing of the accuracy of the storyline of sustainability but also the elevation of local communities impacted by the projects. Finally, in Chapter 6, I discussed how numerous anti-dam actors drew attention to the ways in which the planning and construction of hydroelectric projects in the Brazilian Amazon represent state-led encroachment on the territories and cultural lives of the region's indigenous communities. The projects, defined as representing a 'spearhead' that creates the ground for further encroachment in the area, were linked to the sudden dislocation of many communities in their region from their livelihoods and culture. In turn, this represents the *scaling up* of the anti-dam movement, with projects studied becoming two sites of a centuries-long process of exclusion of indigenous communities, encroachment on their territories and the loss of their cultures. In advancing these storylines, resistance actors contest the pro-dam storyline of sustainability, illustrating its limitations and exposing its weaknesses.

As discussed in previous chapters, I understand the resistance coalition opposing the Belo Monte and São Luiz do Tapajós Dams as a heterogeneous alliance of actors who, whilst working together against the projects studied, have different motivations, experiences and identities and make different demands. The analysis presented in previous chapters was primarily drawn from engagement with interviewees and respondents from and materials provided by national and international NGOs and EOs. In interviews, respondents often highlighted differences between the beliefs and strategies of their organisation and others, such as those related to the role of dialogue with the Brazilian government and the links between environmental politics and human rights (Interview, 3 October 2016; Interview, 7 November 2016a). This creates a complexity in analysis, with the variance of actors resulting in different and, at times, divergent storylines symbolising what, at times, can be a wider division in Brazilian environmentalism (Acselrad, 2008). Environmental and other non-governmental organisations adopt divergent definitions of sustainability (Scherrer, 2009), and this was evident in a number of interviews conducted within this research, in which respondents highlighted how others did not always subscribe to the same brand of environmentalism (Interview, 3 October 2016; Interview, 7 November 2016a). Socio-environmentalism represents a Brazilian brand of environmentalism that fuses social and ecological concerns to assert the need for sustainability policies to pay more attention to land rights, environmental justice, and community participation. This focus on social impacts and human rights was not always shared across the resistance coalition. When discussing the role of international civil society groups in opposition to Belo Monte and São Luiz do Tapajós projects, an interviewee based at a domestic human rights organisation commented:

> It is kind of tricky that some environmentalists do not consider themselves as human rights defenders.
> (Interview, 3 October 2016)

The interviewee is simultaneously arguing for the necessity of including the protection of human rights within a definition of 'sustainability' and highlighting how a number of other resistance actors do not commit to such an equivalence. This statement illuminates a disconnect between civil society groups, located within the resistance coalition, with some groups focused on storylines of the human rights of impacted communities and others put forward storylines linked to environmental impacts (Zhouri, 2004, 2010; Bolaños, 2011; Bratman, 2014). This is also evident in an interview conducted with a representative of the Brazilian arm of an international environmentalist organisation, with the interviewee explaining that the storyline that articulated the equivalence between the projects studied and a wider encroachment on indigenous territory by developmentalist or extractivist practices represented 'more a marketing strategy than really an issue' (Interview, 7 November 2016a). With the Brazilian pro-dam coalition previously absorbing certain issues, demands and grievances into pro-dam storylines as a 'wedge' to disrupt resistance groups (Bratman, 2014), this disconnect between domestic and international groups represents a potential weakness in the resistance coalition.

In focusing its attention and analysis on the storylines put forward by activists primarily working at national and international NGOs and EOs, this work has not engaged with the storylines put forward by other key constituencies involved in the moments of contestation surrounding the Belo Monte and São Luiz do Tapajós projects. However, research has previously demonstrated how the grievances and demands of these local communities can divergent from those of individuals who work at EO's and NGO's, which complicates their work together, both in resistance to projects and outside of it, and may lead to the invisibility of local communities and cultures (Zhouri, 2004; Chernela, 2005; Chernela and Zanotti, 2014). While national and international groups may adopt technocratic storylines that refer to a project's impacts, local actors put forward arguments based on emotions, identity and daily experiences (Zhouri, 2004; Bolaños, 2011; Tur et al., 2018). Hess and Fenrich (2017) conducted interviews with those in the region and found that the conflict surrounding the São Luiz do Tapajós project involved multiple sub-conflicts, linked to control over natural resources, economic and cultural difference and autonomy, and the perception and valorisation of the Tapajós River. These localised storylines not only confront pro-dam storylines but also interact with the storylines of other actors in the resistance coalition. Anti-dam activists at the national and international level are often university-educated, internationally mobile and economically prosperous and, as a result, distinct and detached from those individuals and communities facing the impacts of Belo Monte. They are well versed in the technical language and epistemology adopted within the environmental licensing process and are often experienced from action against other infrastructure projects elsewhere. The use of scientific and technical research and approaches to oppose a hydroelectric project – and its EIAs – represents the adoption of the same technical lens of analysis that is held by the pro-dam actors and excludes communities, grievances, and experience. This risks repeating the very 'epistemological violence' that is present within official EIAs, with civil society actors focused on environmental impacts adopting a technical, managerial perspective that functions to exclude other forms of environmental knowledge and experience of a scheme (Zhouri, 2018). This disconnect between constituent groups of the resistance coalition can result in the storylines put forward by national and international actors neglecting or overlooking the daily experience of those at the site of construction. The dominance of one mode of critique or frame of opposition can lead to the movement becoming detached from the demands, grievances, and identities of the local communities from which it stemmed (Rangan, 2000). This can be seen in how several anti-dam activists based in the UK presented indigenous communities impacted by the São Luiz do Tapajós project as passive and resisting the 'Modern World,' neglecting the complexity of the communities' relationships and networks (see Chapter 6). With the supremacy of a wider storyline often coming at the expense of initial local demands and grievances, it is important to interrogate this process further by engaging with local groups and understanding the perspectives of local actors regarding the role of national and international organisations, the 'scaling up' of local grievances and demands and the transformation of the Belo Monte and São Luiz do Tapajós Dam projects into sites of a wider struggle.

This plurality of demands, grievances, identities and types of expertise has historically been targeted by pro-dam actors in Brazil – who put forward a number of policies and storylines to drive a 'wedge' into the resistance coalition (Bratman, 2014). Pro-dam actors have also put forward storylines that dismiss the role of international actors in the resistance coalition as representing a form of eco-colonialism on the part of the Global North (Hochstetler and Keck, 2007; Zhouri, 2010; Bratman, 2014; Atkins, 2017). Within this storyline, international organisations are presented as undermining Brazilian sovereignty over the Amazon region and restricting the state's economic development. In 2002, the Federal Deputy for Pará, Asdrubal Bentes (PMDB-PA) argued that opposition networks 'wish to derail our development, who want to stifle the Amazon and not allow us to make the most of our hydroelectric potential, to use our riches in favour of Brazilians' (Bentes, 2002). Similarly, President Lula argued that:

> From time to time, along comes a gringo to take a shot at Brazil. We need to show the world that no one wants to care for our forest more than us; but it is ours and no gringo should poke his nose in where it is not wanted, because we shall care for our forest and we shall take care of our development.
> (da Silva, 2010)

This linking of international opposition to Belo Monte to a form of international conspiracy – and, with it, elements of Brazilian nationalism – ties the hydropower scheme to a particularly entrenched desire for sovereignty over the Amazon which has provided a strong mobilising device for Brazilian politicians past and present (Hochstetler and Keck, 2007; Zhouri, 2010). Within this storyline, Belo Monte becomes presented as a nationalist project, battling outsider influence. This putting forward of storylines by pro-dam actors to divide the opposition networks emphasises the plurality of the coalition, highlighting the differences between local, national and international actors. This weakens the resistance coalition due to the discrediting of one of the central successes of the 1989 movement against Kararaô – international support (Zhouri, 2010).[1] It is regretted that the analysis contained within this book has not explored this plurality within the resistance coalition. Yet, it provides a promising route for future research: How do these points of contention and difference originate, develop, and operate within the resistance coalition? Exploring this question will be particularly effective for research exploring the nuances of the 'scaling up' of local demands into a more global environmental storyline.

Whilst this text has explored a high-point of dam-building in Brazil, which seemingly came to a close in the 2016 removal of the São Luiz do Tapajós from the environmental licensing process, the anti-dam storylines discussed across this text serve to illuminate the need to further interrogate the sustainability credentials of hydropower, both in terms of social and environmental impacts and the wider political context in which they are built. By highlighting the potential for reconfiguration of pro-dam storylines, the analysis developed in this book broadens contemporary understandings of the politics of dams and the storylines that surround the construction of this type of infrastructure. While previous research has explored the emergence and consolidation of the pro-dam storyline of sustainability (Ahlers et al., 2015; Bratman, 2015; Warner, Hoogesteger, and Hidalgo, 2017), this book has illuminated the numerous ways in which resistance actors both contest and reconfigure this dominant narrative of legitimacy. The reconfiguration of the pro-dam storyline of sustainability highlights how dominant storylines are by no means assured and, rather than being hegemonic, remain open to contestation and reconfiguration by resistance actors. In exploring the processes of contestation and reconfiguration within the storylines put forward by pro- and resistance coalitions, the analysis developed throughout this book highlights the fact that it is necessary for contemporary research agendas to explore how the development of storylines surrounding dam projects in the 21st century is a two-way process, with resistance coalitions reconfiguring dominant pro-dam narratives by highlighting various impacts and characteristics that are neglected in the pro-dam storyline of sustainability. These moments of contestation provide an opportunity for future research to explore how the hegemony of the hydraulic mission is not set in stone and, instead, is subject to resistance and the emergence of alternative storylines.

The uncovering of the reconfiguration of the storyline of sustainability also presents an opportunity for future research to explore the moments of contestation surrounding contemporary dams as processes in which the term 'sustainability' is inscribed with new meaning, and the 'sustainability' of hydropower is contested. The divergences between pro-dam and resistance storylines represent the occurrence of alternative sustainabilities, in which the (un)sustainability of a particular project is subject to contestation by local communities and social movements (Harris, 2009; Cavanagh and Benjaminsen, 2017). Movements across the globe – from local communities to transnational non-governmental or environmental organisations – put forward a series of alternative sustainabilities (such as food sovereignty, ecological debt, post-extractivism and climate justice). These movements do not simply contest a project or policy. They put forward new storylines that highlight the contested meanings of the term sustainability and the component parts of contemporary energy transitions. From the supply chains of solar panels to the planning of on-shore wind farms, the construction of energy infrastructure has social and environmental impacts across both space and time. Movements and organisations opposing – or calling for the improvement of – these energy sources render visible overlooked impacts, repoliticise their construction and scale up the experience of local communities to represent wider questions related to environmental justice and a just transition. It is by illuminating the contested character of the concept of sustainability within the construction of contemporary hydropower projects that this book seeks to highlight a route forward for exploring the storylines advanced by other environmentalist movements.

Postscript

It is perhaps a twist of the pro-dam storyline of sustainability that hydroelectricity generation in the Brazilian Amazon is likely to be impacted by climate change. Climate change will increase air temperature and cause long-term shifts in patterns of rainfall, impacting both river runoff and the evaporation of water from reservoirs (Schaefli, 2015a; Spalding-Fecher et al., 2016). Climate change may, in some areas, increase the intensity of rainfall whilst, in others, leading to drought. Such factors will likely have an impact on water availability for energy generation in river basins across the globe. Research has predicted that climate change will lead to both an increased frequency and magnitude of droughts in the Amazon Basin (Fearnside, 2009; Broecker and Putnam, 2013; Marengo and Souza Jr., 2018). Due to their design allowing them to store vast quantities of water, reservoir-holding hydroelectric dams will be less susceptible to these impacts than run-of-the-river projects such as Belo Monte, which do not store water in a reservoir (de Souza Dias et al., 2018) A plant with no water storage is more subject to seasonal river flows, resulting in it having an intermittent nature as an energy source. If rain patterns change – or a drought occurs – the energy potential of the complex may drop dramatically. This was particularly evident in times of drought.

During the dry season of July to November 2019, the flow of the Xingu River reduced dramatically due to both the climate change-induced drought and decreased runoff associated with deforestation in the region (Higgins, 2020). While the project was initially to have a total capacity of 11,233 MW (Norte Energia, 2019), it has often failed to reach this potential (Higgins, 2020). During the dry season, Belo Monte barely produced 600 MW for the Brazilian grid per month, averaging only 568 MW in August, before dropping to 361 in September and 276 in October (Higgins, 2020). In October, Norte Energia declared a 'water emergency,' arguing that the water levels had dropped so far that they had exposed a vulnerable 14-km-long barrier of compacted earth that, when exposed to the movement of water, would be at risk of structural damage (Watts, 2019; Higgins, 2020). It was later reported that in the future, Belo Monte might be unable to generate energy for five months of the year due to low water levels brought by the dry season (Cruz, 2019). The failure of planners to take the regional variation of the Xingu's flow into account or to prepare mitigative measures was swiftly criticised by many, who also warned that this might impact the safety of the dam (Vargas, 2019). In a country still reeling from the Mariana and Brumadinho dam collapses of 2015 and 2019 respectively, many called on the government to increase monitoring of the dam and its stability (Watts, 2019). In November 2019, Norte Energia requested the permission of ANEEL to build two new plants alongside Belo Monte. These plants are likely to be thermoelectric, probably using fossil fuels (Borges, 2019; Higgins, 2020). After spending R$40 billion on the planning and construction of Belo Monte, the company that owned it was forced to return to using the fossil fuels that the dam was originally presented as symbolising a move away from within the pro-dam storyline of sustainability.

As I write this in the wake of the news of Belo Monte's failure, the problems faced by Norte Energia have a wider symbolism of the problematic character of the pro-dam storyline of sustainability. For many pro-dam actors, Belo Monte was symbolic of Brazil's commitment to clean, green and emission-free energy. However, with the turbines of Belo Monte failing to produce energy, Norte Energia has been forced to deploy the emissions-laden, unsustainable energy sources from which the pro-dam lobby had work so hard to distance the project from.

Note

1 Such a storyline of an 'international conspiracy' is evident in Brazil at the time of writing, in which President Jair Bolsonaro has without evidence, blamed the fires that gripped the Amazon region in 2019, on NGOs keen to secure international support for their activities and harm the Brazilian government.

Bibliography

Acselrad, H (2008). Grassroots reframing of environmental struggles in Brazil. In: Carruthers, DV (ed.) *Environmental Justice in Latin America: Problems, Promise, and Practice.* Cambridge, MA: MIT Press.

Ahlers, R, Budds, J, Joshi, D, Merme, V, and Zwarteveen, M (2015). Framing hydropower as green energy: assessing drivers, risks and tensions in the Eastern Himalayas. *Earth System Dynamics*, 6(1): 195–204.

Ahlers, R, Zwarteveen, M, and Bakker, K (2017). Large dam development: from Trojan Horse to Pandora's Box. In: B. Flyvbjerg (ed.) *The Oxford Handbook of Megaproject Management.* Oxford: Oxford University Press.

Aledo Tur, A, García-Andreu, H, Ortiz, G, and Domínguez-Gomez, JA (2018). Discourse analysis of the debate on hydroelectric dam building in Brazil. *Water Alternatives*, 11(1): 125–141.

Ansar, A, Flyvbjerg, B, Budzier, A, and Lunn, D (2014). Should we build more large dams? The actual costs of hydropower megaproject development. *Energy Policy*, 69: 43–56.

Atkins, E (2017). Dammed and diversionary: the multi-dimensional framing of Brazil's Belo Monte dam. *Singapore Journal of Tropical Geography*, 38(3): 276–292.

Atkins, E (2018). Dams, political framing and sustainability as an empty signifier: the case of Belo Monte. *Area*, 50(2): 232–239.

Baviskar, A (1995). *In the Belly of the River.* Oxford: Oxford University Press.

Bellette Lee, YC (2013). Global capital, national development and transnational environmental activism: conflict and the Three Gorges Dam. *Journal of Contemporary Asia*, 43(1): 102–126.

Bentes, A (2002). *Diário da Câmara dos Deputados ANO LVI N54 (08/05/2002).* Brasilia: Câmara dos Deputados.

Berga, L (2016). The role of hydropower in climate change mitigation and adaptation: a review. *Engineering*, 2(3): 313–318.

Bolaños, O (2011). Redefining identities, redefining landscapes: indigenous identity and land rights struggles in the Brazilian Amazon. *Journal of Cultural Geography*, 28(1): 45–72.

Borges, A (2019). Depois de pronta, Belo Monte quer erguer usina térmica para compensar baixa produção de energia. *Estadão*, 13 December. Available at: https://economia.estadao.com.br/noticias/geral,depois-de-100-pronta-belo-monte-quer-erguer-usina-termica-para-compensar-baixa-producao-de-energia,70003124128 (Accessed: 6 April 2020).

Bratman, E (2014). Contradictions of green development: human rights and environmental norms in light of Belo Monte Dam activism. *Journal of Latin American Studies*, 46: 261–289.

Bratman, E (2015). Passive revolution in the green economy: activism and the Belo Monte dam. *International Environmental Agreements: Politics, Law and Economics*, 15(1): 61–77.

Broecker, WS, and Putnam, AE (2013). Hydrologic impacts of past shifts of Earth's thermal equator offer insight into those to be produced by fossil fuel CO_2. *PNAS*, 110(42): 16710–16715.

Brown, T (2016). Sustainability as empty signifier: its rise, fall, and radical potential. *Antipode*, 48(1): 115–133.

Carvalho, G (2006). Environmental resistance and the politics of energy development. *Journal of Environment & Development*, 15(1): 245–268.

Cavanagh, CJ, and Benjaminsen, TA (2017). Political ecology, variegated green economies, and the foreclosure of alternative sustainabilities. *Journal of Political Ecology*, 24(1): 200–216.

Chernela, J (2005). The politics of mediation: local-global interactions in the Central Amazon of Brazil. *American Anthropologist*, 107(4): 620–631.

Chernela, J, and Zanotti, L (2014). Limits to knowledge: indigenous peoples, NGOs, and the moral economy in the Eastern Amazon of Brazil. *Conservation & Society*, 12(3): 306–317.

Chhotray, V (2007). The 'anti-politics machine' in India: depoliticisation through local institution building for participatory watershed development. *Journal of Development Studies*, 43(6): 1037–1056.

Cruz, I (2019). Por que Belo Monte não realiza seu potencial elétrico. *Nexo Jornal*, 17 December. Available at: https://www.nexojornal.com.br/expresso/2019/12/17/Por-q ue-Belo-Monte-n%C3%A3o-realiza-seu-potencial-el%C3%A9trico (Accessed: April 6, 2020).

da Silva, LIL (2010). Discurso do Presidente da República, Luiz Inácio Lula da Silva, no ato por Belo Monte e pelo desenvolvimento da região do Xingu – Altamira-PA. *Presidencia Da Republica, Biblioteca*, 22 June. Available at: http://www.biblioteca.pre sidencia.gov.br/presidencia/ex-presidentes/luiz-inacio-lula-da-silva/audios/2010-audi os-lula/22-06-2010-discurso-do-presidente-da-republica-luiz-inacio-lula-da-silva-no-a to-por-belo-monte-e-pelo-desenvolvimento-da-regiao-do-xingu-altamira-pa-08m in36s/view (Accessed: 30 March 2020).

de Souza Dias, V, da Luz, MP, Medero, GM, and Nascimento, DTF (2018). An overview of hydropower reservoirs in Brazil: current situation, future perspectives and impacts of climate change. *Water*, 10(5): 592.

Fearnside, PM (2009). Aquecimento Global na Amazônia: Impactos e mitigação. *Acta Amazonica*, 39(4): 1003–1011.

Ferguson, J (1994). *The Anti-politics Machine*. Minneapolis, MN: University of Minnesota Press.

G1 (2019). Fala de Bolsonaro sobre queimada na Amazônia é 'irresponsável' e 'leviana,' dizem ambientalistas. *G1*, 21 August. Available at: https://g1.globo.com/politica/notic ia/2019/08/21/fala-de-bolsonaro-sobre-queimada-na-amazonia-e-irresponsavel-e-lev iana-dizem-ambientalistas.ghtml (Accessed: 6 April 2020).

Gerlak, AK, Saguier, M, Mills-Novoa, M, Fearnside, PM, and Albercht, TR (2019). Dams, Chinese investments, and EIAs: a race to the bottom in South America? *Ambio*, 49: 156–164.

Hajer, M (1995). *The Politics of Environmental Discourse: Ecological Modernization and the Policy Process*. Oxford: Clarendon Press.

Hajer, MA (1993). Discourse coalitions and the institutionalization of practice: the case of acid rain in Britain. In: Fischer, F, and Forester, J (ed.) *The Argumentative Turn in Policy Analysis and Planning*. Durham, NC: Duke University Press

Harris, LM (2009). Contested sustainabilities: assessing narratives of environmental change in southeastern Turkey. *Local Environment*, 14(8): 699–720.

Hess, CEE, and Fenrich, E (2017). Socio-environmental conflicts on hydropower: the São Luiz do Tapajós project in Brazil. *Environmental Science and Policy*, 73: 20–28.

Higgins, T (2020). Belo Monte boondoggle: Brazil's biggest, costliest dam may be unviable. *Mongabay*, 17 January. Available at: https://news.mongabay.com/2020/01/belo-m onte-boondoggle-brazils-biggest-costliest-dam-may-be-unviable/ (Accessed: 6 April, 2020).

Hochstetler, K (2011). The politics of environmental licensing: energy projects of the past and future in Brazil. *Studies in Comparative International Development*, 46(4): 349–371.

Hochstetler, K, and Keck, ME (2007). *Greening Brazil: Environmental Activism in State and Society*. Durham, NC: Duke University Press.

Huber, A, and Joshi, D (2015). Hydropower, anti-politics, and the opening of new political spaces in the Eastern Himalayas. *World Development*, 76: 13–25.

Lane, T (2015). Sustainable development goals: how does hydropower fit in? *International Hydropower Association*, 1 October. Available at: https://www.hydropower.org/blog/sustainable-development-goals-how-does-hydropower-fit-in (Accessed: 30 March, 2020).

Leach, M, Scoones, I, and Stirling, A (2010). *Dynamic Sustainabilities: Technology, Environment, Social Justice*. London: Earthscan.

Marengo, JA, and Souza, C (2018). *Mudanças Climáticas: Impactos e Cenários para a Amazônia*. São Paulo: Greenpeace Brasil. Available at: https://www.conectas.org/wp/wp-content/uploads/2018/12/Relatorio_Mudancas_Climaticas-Amazonia.pdf (Accessed: 30 March 2020).

McDonald, K, Bosshard, P, and Brewer, N (2009). Exporting dams: China's hydropower industry goes global. *Journal of Environmental Management*, 90(3) Supplement 3: 294–302.

Molle, F (2008). Nirvana concepts, narratives and policy models: insight from the water sector. *Water Alternatives*, 1(1): 131–156.

Molle, F, Mollinga, P, and Wester, P (2009). Hydraulic bureaucracies and the hydraulic mission: flows of water, flows of power. *Water Alternatives*, 2(3): 328–349.

Moore, D, Dore, J, and Gyawali, D (2010). The World Commission on Dams + 10: revisiting the large dam controversy. *Water Alternatives*, 3(2): 3–13.

Norte Energia (2019). Belo Monte é inaugurada e está pronta para a plena operação, *Norte Energia*, 29 November. Available at: https://www.norteenergiasa.com.br/pt-br/imprensa/releases/belo-monte-e-inaugurada-e-esta-pronta-para-a-plena-operacao-100709 (Accessed: 6 April 2020).

Rangan, H (2000). *Of Myths and Movements*. London: Verso.

Schaefli, B (2015). Projecting hydropower production under future climates: a guide for decision-makers and modelers to interpret and design climate change impact assessments. *Wiley Interdisciplinary Reviews: Water*, 2(4): 271–289.

Scherrer, YM (2009). Environmental conservation NGOs and the concept of sustainable development. *Journal of Business Ethics*, 85(3): 555–571.

Siciliano, G, del Bene, D, Scheidel, A, Liu, J, and Urban, F (2019). Environmental justice and Chinese dam-building in the global South. *Current Opinion in Environmental Sustainability*, 37: 20–27.

Spalding-Fecher, R, Chapman, A, Yamba, F, Walimwipi, H, Kling, H, Tembo, B, Nyambe, I, and Cuamba, B (2016). The vulnerability of hydropower production in the Zambezi River Basin to the impacts of climate change and irrigation development. *Mitigation and Adaptation Strategies for Global Change*, 21(5): 721–742.

Vargas, A (2019). Incerteza em Belo Monte. *ISTOÉ Independente*, 22 November. Available at: https://istoe.com.br/incerteza-em-belo-monte/ (Accessed: 6 April, 2020).

Warner, JF, Hoogesteger, J, and Hidalgo, JP (2017). Old wine in new bottles: the adaptive capacity of the hydraulic mission in Ecuador. *Water Alternatives*, 10(2): 322–340.

Watts, J (2019). Poorly planned Amazon dam project 'poses serious threat to life.' *The Guardian*, 8 November. Available at: https://www.theguardian.com/environment/2019/nov/08/death-of-a-river-the-ruinous-design-flaw-in-a-vast-amazon-rainforest-dam (Accessed: 6 April, 2020).

World Commission on Dams (2000). *Dams and Development: A New Framework for Decision-Making*. London: World Commission on Dams.

Zhouri, A (2004). Global–local Amazon politics: conflicting paradigms in the rainforest campaign. *Theory, Culture & Society*, 21(2): 69–89.

Zhouri, A (2010). 'Adverse forces' in the Brazilian Amazon: developmentalism versus environmentalism and indigenous rights. *The Journal of Environment & Development*, 19(3): 252–273.

Zhouri, A (2018). Megaprojects, epistemological violence and environmental conflicts in Brazil. *Perfiles Economicos*, 5: 7–33.

Appendix

Interviews conducted:

Interview, 5 September 2017	Public Figure and Patron of Survival International*
Interview, 27 September 2016	National Journalist, Rio de Janeiro
Interview, 29 September 2016	Policy Advisor, Rio de Janeiro
Interview, 30 September 2016	International Journalist, Rio de Janeiro
Interview, 3 October 2016	Representatives, Justiça Global, Rio de Janeiro
Interview, 5 October 2017	Public Figure and Patron of Survival International*
Interview, 7 October 2017	National Researcher (Brazil)*
Interview, 18 October 2016	National Journalist, Folha de S. Paulo, Rio de Janeiro
Interview, 19 October 2016	Representative, Greenpeace Brasil, São Paulo
Interview 20 October 2016	Representative, Instituto Democracia e Sustentabilidade*
Interview, 27 October 2016a	Representative, The Nature Conservancy Brasil, São Paulo
Interview, 27 October 2016b	Representative, National human rights organisation, São Paulo
Interview, 28 October 2016	Representative, IPAM Amazonia, São Paulo
Interview, 2 November 2016	Representative, World Rainforest Movement*
Interview, 3 November 2016a	Representative, Department of Energy Planning, Ministério de Minas e Energia, Brasilia
Interview, 3 November 2016b	Representative, Instituto SocioAmbiental, Brasilia
Interview, 4 November 2016	Representatives, Instituto Brasileiro do Meio Ambiente e dos Recursos Naturais Renováveis, Brasilia
Interview, 7 November 2016a	Representative, WWF-Brasil, Brasilia
Interview, 7 November 2016b	Regional Prosecutor and Member of the Special Commission Affected by Dams, Ministério Público Federal, Brasilia

Interview, 8 November 2016	Researcher (Brazil)*
Interview, 9 November 2016	Researcher (Brazil)*
Interview, 10 November 2016a	Representative, Department for Environmental Licensing, FUNAI, Brasilia
Interview, 10 November 2016b	National Journalist, Reporter Brasil, Santarém
Interview, 18 November 2016	National Anti-Dam and Environmental Campaigner*
Interview, 1 December 2016a	International Researcher (Brazil), Manaus
Interview, 1 December 2016b	Representative, Interamerican Association for Environmental Defense (AIDA)*
Interview, 6 December 2016	Project Manager, Norte Energia, Rio de Janeiro
Interview, 9 December 2016	Representative, Society for Threatened Peoples (Gesellschaft für bedrohte Völker)*
Interview, 9 January 2017	Representative, Terra Direitos*
Interview, 1 February 2017	Federal Deputy, Partido Socialismo e Liberdade*
Interview, 28 April 2017	Representative, Amazon Watch*
Interview, 23 August 2017	National Anti-Dam Campaigner*
Interview, 16 September 2017	Representative, Xingu Vivo para Sempre*
Interview, 6 August 2019	Representative, Justiça Global*
Interview, 4 September 2019	Representative, Greenpeace Brasil*

* *interview conducted remotely and virtually.*

Summary timeline of the Belo Monte project

1975	Centrais Elétricas do Norte do Brasil S/A (Eletronorte) commissions studies to evaluate the hydroelectric potential of the Xingu River.
1979	Five potential dam sites on the Xingu river are identified, including Kararaô and Babaquara.
1980	Feasibility studies of Kararaô and Babaquara begin.
1987	Centrais Elétricas do Norte do Brasil S.A. (Eletrobrás) publishes its *Plano Decenal de Expansão de Energia, 1987–2010*. This document lists 297 dams to be built in Brazil, including Kararaô and Babaquara.
1988	Kayapó Caciques travel to Washington, DC to pressure the World Bank to suspend its funding for the project.
1989	19–24 February: The Altamira Gathering is held.
	11 October: Eletronorte submits final feasibility studies to the Departamento Nacional de Águas e Energia Elétrica (Department of Waters and Electric Energy, DNAEE) for review and approval. DNAEE rejects the project and it is removed from national energy plans.

1998	*Eletrobrás* publishes its *Plano Decenal de Expansão de Energia*, 1999–2008. The plan includes redeveloped versions of the Babaquara and Kararaô dams – now renamed Altamira and Belo Monte. The Altamira project will later be removed from this plan.
1999–2000	Ministério de Minas e Energia, Eletrobras, and Eletronorte all confirm interest in the redesigned Belo Monte project. Feasibility studies begin.
2001–2002	The Brazilian energy crisis, in which a prolonged period of drought leads to power shortages and rolling blackouts.
2001	25 August: Ademir Alfeu Federicci ('Dema'), prominent local opponent of Belo Monte, is found murdered.
2002	Eletrobras and Eletronorte submit feasibility studies to Agência Nacional de Energia Elétrica (ANEEL), with new Belo Monte plans including a run-of-the-river design and the construction of a total of three dams (Belo Monte, Pimental and Bela Vista).
2005	13 July: Legislative Decree No. 788 authorises the construction of Belo Monte.
2006	31 January: The environmental licensing process begins.
2007	The *Programa de Aceleração do Crescimento* is published, with Belo Monte considered a priority.
2008	Xingu Vivo para Sempre formed.
2010	1 February: The preliminary license for Belo Monte is provided by Instituto Brasileiro do Meio Ambiente e dos Recursos Naturais Renováveis (IBAMA), with the project's environmental impact assessment accepted. 18 February: O Banco Nacional de Desenvolvimento Econômico e Social (BNDES) announces that it will finance up to 80% of the investments needed to build Belo Monte.
2011	1 April: The Inter-American Court for Human Rights issues precautionary measures against Brazil, arguing that government violated its commitment to the International Labor Organization's Convention 169 by failing to consult with local indigenous communities. 30 April: President Dilma Rousseff withdraws Brazil's ambassador to the Organisation of American States and suspends annual payments to the organisation. 1 June: IBAMA issues a full installation license for the Belo Monte project. Construction begins.
2015	30 March: Belo Sun Mining Corporation announces feasibility study for its Volta Grande Gold Project.
2016	21 April: First turbine enters commercial operation at Belo Monte project.
2019	19 November: ANEEL authorises the last Belo Monte turbine to enter operations.

Summary timeline for the São Luiz do Tapajós project

2005   Eletronorte and Camargo Corrêa conduct preliminary studies of the hydroelectric potential of the Tapajós River.

2010   Brazil's Second *Programa de Aceleração do Crescimento* (PAC-2) is released, including six dams on the Tapajós and Jamanxim Rivers and five dams on the Teles Pires River (a tributary to the Tapajós).

2012   6 January: The Brazilian government publish Provisional Measure 558, which reduces the area of four conservation units in the Brazilian Amazon. This includes protected areas in the Tapajós basin.
17 February: IBAMA issues the terms of reference for the Environmental Impact Assessment for São Luiz do Tapajós project.

2013   Ten dams on the Tapajós, Teles Pires and Juruena rivers, including the São Luiz do Tapajós project, are included in the *Plano Decenal de Expansão de Energia, 2013–2022*.
'Operation Tapajós' begins, with biologists and support staff conducting impact assessments in the Tapajós basin. After a number of these technicians are expelled or captured by the Munduruku community, their presence in the region is supported by members of the Força Nacional de Segurança (National Security Force).

2014   Grupo de Estudos Tapajós submit the environmental impact assessment to IBAMA for review and approval.

2014   September: Leaders of the Munduruku community travel to meet with Maria Augusta Assirati, the president of Fundação Nacional do Índio (FUNAI), to pressure the agency to demarcate the Sawré Muybu indigenous territory.

2016   June: Assisted by Greenpeace, the Munduruku community begin the autonomous demarcation of the Sawré Muybu territory.
April: In response to a report, published by FUNAI, which confirmed the demarcation of the Sawré Muybu territory, IBAMA suspends the environmental licensing process of the São Luiz do Tapajós project.
August: IBAMA denies of the preliminary license for the São Luiz do Tapajós project, removing it from national energy plans.

Bibliography

Abbink, J (2012). Dam controversies: contested governance and developmental discourse on the Ethiopian Omo River dam. *Social Anthropology*, 20(2): 125–144.

Acselrad, H (2008). Grassroots reframing of environmental struggles in Brazil. In: Carruthers, DV (ed.) *Environmental Justice in Latin America: Problems, Promise, and Practice*. Cambridge, MA: MIT Press.

Adams, F (2013). 'Trataram a gente igual bicho', denúncia operário de Belo Monte. *Movimento dos Atingidos por Barragens*, 17 October. Available at: http://www.mabnacional.org.br/noticia/trataram-gente-igual-bicho-denuncia-oper-rio-belo-monte (Accessed: 8 January 2020).

Agência Nacional de Energia Elétrica (2009). *Atlas de Energia Elétrica do Brasil*. Brasilia: Agência Nacional de Energia Elétrica.

Aguilar-Støen, M, and Hirsch, C (2017). Bottom-up responses to environmental and social impact assessments: a case study from Guatemala. *Environmental Impact Assessment Review*, 62: 225–232.

Ahlers, R, Brandimarte, L, Kleemans, I, and Said, H.S (2014). Ambitious development on fragile foundations: criticalities of current large dam construction in Afghanistan. *Geoforum*, 54: 49–58.

Ahlers, R, Budds, J, Joshi, D, Merme, V, and Zwarteveen, M (2015). Framing hydropower as green energy: assessing drivers, risks and tensions in the Eastern Himalayas. *Earth System Dynamics*, 6(1): 195–204.

Ahlers, R, Zwarteveen, M, and Bakker, K (2017). Large dam development: from Trojan Horse to Pandora's box. In: B. Flyvbjerg (ed.) *The Oxford Handbook of Megaproject Management*. Oxford: Oxford University Press.

Akhter, M (2015a). Infrastructure nation: state space, hegemony, and hydraulic regionalism in Pakistan. *Antipode*, 47(4): 849–870.

Akhter, M (2015b). The hydropolitical Cold War: the Indus Waters Treaty and state formation in Pakistan. *Political Geography*, 46: 65–75.

Alarcon, DF, Millikan, B, and Torres, M (eds) (2016). *Ocekadi: Hidrelétricas, Conflitos Socioambientais e Resistência na Bacia do Tapajós*. Brasília: International Rivers. Available at: https://www.internationalrivers.org/sites/default/files/attached-files/tapajos_digital.pdf.

Alatout, S (2008). 'States' of scarcity: water, space, and identity politics in Israel, 1948–59. *Environment and Planning D: Society and Space*, 26(6): 959–982.

Aledo Tur, A, García-Andreu, H, Ortiz, G, and Domínguez-Gomez, JA (2018). Discourse analysis of the debate on hydroelectric dam building in Brazil. *Water Alternatives*, 11(1): 125–141.

Aleixos, J, and Conde, N (2016). *Quem São os Proprietários das Hidrelétricas da Amazônia?* Rio de Janeiro: Mais Democracia. Available at: http://www.corecon-rj.org.br/corecon/ckfinder/userfiles/files/pdf/Quem%20sao%20os%20proprietarios%20das%20hidroeletricas.pdf (Accessed: 23 July 2020).

Aleluia, JC (2005). *Diário da Câmara dos Deputados, ANO LX N° 110 (07/07/2005).* Brasilia: Câmara dos Deputados.

Aliança dos Rios da Amazônia,Movimento Xingu Vivo para Sempre, Aliança Tapajós Vivo, Movimento Teles Pires Vivo, Campanha Popular Viva o Rio Madeira Vivo, Coordenação das Organizações Indígenas da Amazônia Brasileira and Movimento dos Atingidos por Barragens (2011). Carta a Aliança em Defesa dos Rios Amazônicos o Presidente Dilma. *International Rivers*, 8th February 2011. Available at: https://www.internationalrivers.org/pt-br/resources/carta-a-aliança-em-defesa-dos-rios-amazônicos-o-presidente-dilma-3076 (Accessed: 8 January 2020).

Allouche, J (2005). *Water Nationalism: An Explanation of the Past and Present Conflicts in Central Asia, the Middle East and the Indian Subcontinent?* Thèse N ° 699, submitted to University of Geneva.

Altinbîlek, D (2002). The role of dams in development. *International Journal of Water Resources Development*, 18(1): 9–24.

Álvares, D (2019). Belo Monte, a violação de direitos humanos dos ribeirinhos e a ameaça ao Xingu. *The Huffington Post Brasil*, 4 September. Available at: https://www.huffpostbrasil.com/entry/belo-monte-altamira_br_5d6efef4e4b09bbc9ef644fd (Accessed: 8 January 2020).

Amaral, M, Aranha, A, Barros, CJ, Branford, S, Mota, J, Castro, A, and Rabello, T (2013). *Amazônia Pública.* São Paulo: Agência Pública.

Amazon Watch (2014). Issue brief: Brazil's Belo Monte dam: a major threat to the Amazon and its people. *Amazon Watch*, no date. Available at: https://amazonwatch.org/assets/files/belo-monte-dam-issue-brief.pdf (Accessed: 12 February 2020).

Amazon Watch (2016). Belo Monte a symbol of obscene destruction and corruption in Brazil. *Amazon Watch*, 17 March. Available at: https://amazonwatch.org/news/2016/0317-belo-monte-a-symbol-of-obscene-destruction-and-corruption-in-brazil (Accessed: 30 March 2020).

Amazon Watch (n.d.). Belo Monte facts: 10 myths the Brazilian government wants you to believe about Belo Monte. *Amazon Watch*, no date. Available at: https://amazonwatch.org/work/belo-monte-facts (Accessed: 12 February 2020).

Amazon Watch and International Rivers (2016). Brazilian government cancels megadam on the Amazon's Tapajós River. *Amazon Watch*, 4 August. Available at: https://amazonwatch.org/news/2016/0804-brazilian-government-cancels-mega-dam-on-the-amazons-tapajos-river (Accessed: 6 April 2020).

Amazon Watch and Xingu Vivo para Sempre (2011). Millions join Belo Monte protest in Brazil. *Amazon Watch*, 20 December. Available at: https://amazonwatch.org/news/2011/1220-millions-join-belo-monte-protest-in-brazil (Accessed: 30 March 2020).

Amazon Watch, Greenpeace, and International Rivers (2015). Brazilian indigenous movement received prominent UN environmental price at COP21 in Paris. *Amazon Watch*, 7 December. Available at: https://amazonwatch.org/news/2015/1207-brazilian-indigenous-movement-receives-prominent-un-environmental-prize-at-cop-21-in-paris (Accessed: 30 March 2020).

Amora, D (2016). Custo de energia pode mudar sem nova hidrelétrica, diz estatal. *Folha de S.Paulo*, 3 August. Available at: https://www1.folha.uol.com.br/mercado/2016/08/1798

652-custo-de-energia-pode-mudar-sem-nova-hidreletrica-diz-estatal.shtml (Accessed: 6 April 2020).

Amorim, PH (2011). ABIN identifica as ONGs estrangeiras que boicotam Belo Monte. *Conversa Afiada*, 5 July. Available at: https://www.conversaafiada.com.br/politica/20 11/07/05/abin-identifica-as-ongs-estrangeiras-que-boicotam-belo-monte (Accessed: 8 January 2020).

Anderson, M (2017). Displaced by Brazil's giant Belo Monte hydroelectric dam, 'river people' reoccupy reservoir. *Mongabay*, 13 March. Available at: https://news.mongaba y.com/2017/03/displaced-by-brazils-giant-belo-monte-hydroelectric-dam-river-peop le-reoccupy-reservoir/ (Accessed: 30 March 2020).

Angelo, C (2010). PT tenta apagar fama 'antiverde' de Dilma. *Folha de S.Paulo*, 10 October. Available at: https://www1.folha.uol.com.br/poder/812470-pt-tenta-apagar-fama-a ntiverde-de-dilma.shtml (Accessed: 8 January 2020).

Ansar, A, Flyvbjerg, B, Budzier, A, and Lunn, D (2014). Should we build more large dams? The actual costs of hydropower megaproject development. *Energy Policy*, 69: 43–56.

Aranha, A, and Mota, J (2014a). A batalha pela fronteira Munduruku. *Publica*, 11 December. Available at: http://apublica.org/2014/12/batalha-pela-fronteira-mund uruku/ (Accessed: 30 March 2020).

Aranha, A, and Mota, J (2014b). Exclusivo: Relatório da Funai determina que terra é dos Munduruku. *Agência Pública*, 11 December. Available at: https://apublica.org/2014/12/ relatorio-funai-determina-que-terra-e-dos-munduruku/ (Accessed: 6 April 2020).

Arias-Maldonado, M (2013). Rethinking sustainability in the Anthropocene. *Environmental Politics*, 22(3): 428–446.

Arnold, CF (2018). *The Third Bank of the River: Power and Survival in the Twenty-First Century*. London: Picador.

Aroeira, A (2019). Belo Monte forjou o massacre de altamira: novo presídio nunca entregue era obrigação da norte energia. *Intercept Brasil*, 7 August. Available at: https ://theintercept.com/2019/08/06/belo-monte-forjou-massacre-altamira/ (Accessed: 8 January 2020).

Arts, B (2004). The global-local nexus: NGOs and the articulation of scale. *Tijdschrift Voor Economische En Sociale Geografie*, 95(5): 498–510.

Assessoria de Comunicação do Conselho Pastoral dos Pescadores (2019). Mais de 100 organizações assinam carta contra a implantação de Usina Nuclear em Itacuruba (PE). *Conselho Pastoral dos Pescadores*, 6 June. Available at: http://www.cppnacional.or g.br/noticia/mais-de-100-organiza%C3%A7%C3%B5es-assinam-carta-contra-implan ta%C3%A7%C3%A3o-de-usina-nuclear-em-itacuruba-pe (Accessed: 6 April 2020).

Associação Internacional de Direito de Seguros (2018). Inter-American Commission urges Brazil to address damages to indigenous peoples caused by Belo Monte Dam. *AIDA*, 13 November. Available at: https://aida-americas.org/en/press/inter-american- commission-urges-brazil-address-damages-to-indigenous-peoples-caused-by-belo-mon te (Accessed: 16 July 2019).

Athayde, S, Matthews, M, Bohlman, S, Brasil, W, Doria, CRC, Dutka-Gianelli, J, Fearnside, PM, Loiselle, B, Marques, EE, Melis, TS, Millikan, B, Moretto, EM, Oliver-Smith, A, Rosette, A, Vacca, R, and Kaplan, D (2019). Mapping research on hydropower and sustainability in the Brazilian Amazon: advances, gaps in knowledge and future directions. *Current Opinion in Environmental Sustainability*, 37: 50–69.

Atkins, E (2017). Dammed and diversionary: the multi-dimensional framing of Brazil's Belo Monte dam. *Singapore Journal of Tropical Geography*, 38(3): 276–292.

Atkins, E (2018a). Building a dam, constructing a nation: the 'drowning' of Capel Celyn. *Journal of Historical Sociology*, 31(4): 455–468.

Atkins, E (2018b). Dams, political framing and sustainability as an empty signifier: the case of Belo Monte. *Area*, 50(2): 232–239.

Atkins, E (2019). Disputing the "national interest": the depoliticization and repoliticization of the Belo Monte Dam, Brazil. *Water*, 11(1): 103).

Baghel, R, and Nüsser, M (2010). Discussing large dams in Asia after the World Commission on Dams: is a political ecology approach the way forward? *Water Alternatives*, 3(2): 231–248.

Baiocchi, G (2004). The party and the multitude: Brazil s Workers Party (PT) and the challenges of building a just social order in a globalizing context. *Journal of World-Systems Research*, 10(1): 199–215.

Baird, IG, and Barney, K (2017). The political ecology of cross-sectoral cumulative impacts: modern landscapes, large hydropower dams and industrial tree plantations in Laos and Cambodia. *Journal of Peasant Studies*, 44(4): 884–910.

Bakker, K (1999a). The politics of hydropower: developing the Mekong. *Political Geography*, 18(2): 209–232.

Bakker, K (1999b). Deconstructing discourses of drought. *Transactions of the Institute of British Geographers*, 24(3): 367–372.

Bakker, K (2013). Neoliberal versus postneoliberal water: geographies of privatization and resistance. *Annals of the Association of American Geographers*, 103(2): 253–260.

Bakker, K, and Bridge, G (2006). Material worlds? Resource geographies and the "matter of nature." *Progress in Human Geography*, 30: 5–27.

Baletti, B (2016). Toward the worker state, or working for the state? Reorganization of political antagonisms in the Brazilian Amazon. *Latin American Perspectives*, 43(2): 22–47.

Barbon, J, and Maissonnave, F (2019). Maioria dos presos mortos no Pará era negra, tinha até 35 anos e cometeu crime violento. *Folha de S.Paulo*, 4 August. Available at: https://www1.folha.uol.com.br/cotidiano/2019/08/maioria-dos-presos-mortos-no-para-era-negra-tinha-ate-35-anos-e-cometeu-crime-violento.shtml (Accessed: 8 January 2020).

Barbosa, LC (2015). *Guardians of the Brazilian Amazon Rainforest: Environmental Organizations and Development*. London: Routledge Earthscan.

Barros, C, and Barcelos, L (2017). Conflitos, desmatamento e inundações marcam 6 anos das obras em Belo Monte. *UOL*, 7 November. Available at: https://noticias.uol.com.br/cotidiano/ultimas-noticias/2017/11/07/conflitos-inundacoes-e-desmatamento-marcam-6-anos-das-obras-em-belo-monte.htm (Accessed: 8 January 2020).

Barros, TA, and Ravena, N (2011). Representações sociais nas audiências públicas de Belo Monte: do palco ao recorte midiático. *Compolitica*, 13: 1–20.

Barrow, C (1988). The impact of hydroelectric development on the Amazonian environment: with particular reference to the Tucurui project. *Journal of Biogeography*, 15(1): 67–78.

Bautzer, T (2018). China's State Power considering bids for Brazilian hydro and thermal plants. *Reuters*, 19 September. Available at: https://www.reuters.com/article/brazil-power-china/chinas-state-power-considering-bids-for-brazilian-hydro-and-thermal-plants-idUSL2N1WY25M (Accessed: 30 March 2020).

Baviskar, A (1995). *In the Belly of the River*. Oxford: Oxford University Press.

Baviskar, A (2019). Nation's body, river's pulse: narratives of anti-dam politics in India. *Thesis Eleven*, 150(1): 26–41.

Bibliography

BBC (2019a). Brumadinho dam collapse in Brazil: vale mine chief resigns, *BBC News*, 3 March. Available at: https://www.bbc.co.uk/news/business-47432134 (Accessed: 6 April 2020).

BBC (2019b). Vale "knew collapsed dam was at risk", says report, *BBC News*, 12 February. Available at: https://www.bbc.co.uk/news/business-47209265 (Accessed: 6 April 2020).

Bellette Lee, YC (2013). Global capital, national development and transnational environmental activism: conflict and the Three Gorges Dam. *Journal of Contemporary Asia*, 43(1): 102–126.

Benford, RD, and Snow, DA (2002). Framing processes and social movements: an overview and assessment. *Annual Review of Sociology*, 26: 611–639.

Benites, A (2016). Temer acena a ruralistas com apoio a mudança em demarcação de área indígena. *El País*, 13 July. Available at: https://brasil.elpais.com/brasil/2016/07/13/politica/1468363551_264805.html (Accessed: 6 April 2020).

Bentes, A (2002). *Diário da Câmara dos Deputados ANO LVI N54 (08/05/2002)*. Brasilia: Câmara dos Deputados.

Berga, L (2016). The role of hydropower in climate change mitigation and adaptation: a review. *Engineering*, 2(3): 313–318.

Bezerra, RG, Prates, RC, EggertBoehs, CG, and Tripoli, ACK (2014). Discourse strategies to legitimize the Belo Monte project. *International Journal of Business and Social Science*, 5(12): 181–189.

Bilenky, T, and Fernandes, T (2018). Vamos preservar o ambiente sem ideologia", diz futuro ministro de Bolsonaro. *Folha de S. Paulo*, 9 December. Available at: https://ww w1.folha.uol.com.br/ambiente/2018/12/vamos-preservar-o-ambiente-sem-ideologia-di z-futuro-ministro-de-bolsonaro.shtml (Accessed: 6 April 2020).

Biller, D, Iglesias, S, and Adghirni, S (2019). Desastre da Vale em Brumadinho faz Bolsonaro reavaliar visão ambiental. *Exame*, 29 January. Available at: https://exame. abril.com.br/brasil/desastre-da-vale-em-brumadinho-faz-bolsonaro-reavaliar-visao-ambiental/ (Accessed: 6 April 2020).

Biswas, AK, and Tortajada, C (2001). Development and large dams: a global perspective. *International Journal of Water Resources Development*, 17(1): 9–21.

Blake, DJH, and Barney, K (2018). Structural injustice, slow violence? The political ecology of a "best practice" hydropower dam in Lao PDR. *Journal of Contemporary Asia*, 48(5): 808–834.

Blanc, J (2019). *Before the Flood: The Itaipu Dam and the Visibility of Rural Brazil*. Durham, NC: Duke University Press.

Blasberg, M, and Gluesing, J (2016). Brazil's Olympic-sized political headache. *Spiegel International*, 4 August. Available at: https://www.spiegel.de/international/world/a-visit -with-dilma-rousseff-on-eve-of-the-rio-olympics-in-brazil-a-1105811.html (Accessed: 8 January 2020).

Boas, BV (2016). Inflação atinge 10,67% em 2015 e estoura teto da meta do governo. *Folha de S.Paulo*, 8 January. Available at: https://www1.folha.uol.com.br/mercado/20 16/01/1727284-inflacao-sobe-1067-em-2015-e-estoura-teto-da-meta-do-governo. shtml (Accessed: 6 April 2020).

Boelens, R, Hoogesteger, J, Swyngedouw, E, Vos, J, and Wester, P (2016). Hydrosocial territories: a political ecology perspective. *Water International*, 41(1): 1–14.

Bolaños, O (2011). Redefining identities, redefining landscapes: indigenous identity and land rights struggles in the Brazilian Amazon. *Journal of Cultural Geography*, 28(1): 45–72.

Borges, A (2019). Depois de pronta, Belo Monte quer erguer usina térmica para compensar baixa produção de energia. *Estadão*, 13 December. Available at: https://economia.estadao.com.br/noticias/geral,depois-de-100-pronta-belo-monte-quer-erguer-usina-termica-para-compensar-baixa-producao-de-energia,70003124128 (Accessed: April 6, 2020).

Bornhausen, P (2010). *Diário da Câmara dos Deputados*, ANO LXV N° 51 (15/04/2010). Brasilia: Câmara dos Deputados.

BNDES (2012). BNDES approves R$ 22.5 billion in financing for Belo Monte. *BNDES*, 26 November. Available at: https://www.bndes.gov.br/SiteBNDES/bndes/bndes_en/Institucional/Press/Noticias/2012/20121126_belomonte.html (Accessed: 30 March 2020).

Bragança, D (2016). Dilma inaugura Belo Monte, maior obra do seu governo. *OECO*, 6 May. Available at: https://www.oeco.org.br/noticias/dilma-inaugura-belo-monte-maior-obra-do-seu-governo/ (Accessed: 8 January 2020).

Branford, S (2013). Prontos para resistir. In: Amaral, M (ed.) *Amazônia Pública*. São Paulo: Pública.

Branford, S (2018). Brazil announces end to Amazon mega-dam building policy, *Mongabay*, 3 January. Available at: https://news.mongabay.com/2018/01/brazil-announces-end-to-amazon-mega-dam-building-policy/ (Accessed: 6 April 2020).

Branford, S, and Rocha, J (2015). *Brazil under the Workers Party: From Euphoria to Despair*. Rugby: Practical Action Publishing.

Branford, S, and Torres, M (2017a). The end of a people: Amazon dam destroys sacred Munduruku "Heaven." *Mongabay*, 5 January. Available at: https://news.mongabay.com/2017/01/the-end-of-a-people-amazon-dam-destroys-sacred-munduruku-heaven/ (Accessed: 30 March 2020).

Branford, S, and Torres, M (2017b). Tapajós under attack 4: day of terror in Tapajós river basin. *Latin America Bureau*, 15 March. Available at: https://lab.org.uk/day-of-terror-in-tapajos-river-basin/ (Accessed: 30 March 2020).

Brasil, Ministério do Planejamento (2016). Dilma inaugura usina hidrelétrica de Belo Monte. Brasil. *Ministério do Planejamento*, 6 May. Available at: http://pac.gov.br/noticia/7be96908 (Accessed: 8 January 2020).

Brasil, Portal do Planalto (2011). Conversa com a Presidenta - Presidenta Dilma Rousseff conversa em sua coluna semanal sobre internet banda larga de baixo custo, política habitacional e Lei da Aprendizagem. *Portal Do Planalto*, 9 August. Available at: http://www.biblioteca.presidencia.gov.br/presidencia/ex-presidentes/dilma-rousseff/conversa-presidenta/conversa-com-a-presidenta-09-08-2011 (Accessed: 30 March 2020).

Bratman, E (2014). Contradictions of green development: human rights and environmental norms in light of Belo Monte Dam activism. *Journal of Latin American Studies*, 46: 261–289.

Bratman, E (2015). Passive revolution in the green economy: activism and the Belo Monte dam. *International Environmental Agreements: Politics, Law and Economics*, 15(1): 61–77.

Bratman, EZ (2020). *Governing the rainforest: sustainable development politics in the Brazilian Amazon*. Oxford: Oxford University Press.

Bringel, B (2016). 2013–2016: polarization and protests in Brazil. *Open Democracy*, 18 February. Available at: https://www.opendemocracy.net/en/democraciaabierta/2013-2016-polarization-and-protests-in-brazil/ (Accessed: 8 January 2020).

Broecker, WS, and Putnam, AE (2013). Hydrologic impacts of past shifts of Earth's thermal equator offer insight into those to be produced by fossil fuel CO2. *PNAS*, 110(42): 16710–16715.

Bromber, K, Féaux de la Croix, J, and Lange, K (2014). The temporal politics of big dams in Africa, the Middle East, and Asia: by way of an introduction. *Water History*, 6(4): 289–296.

Bronzatto, T, and Coutinho, F (2015). As suspeitas de tráfico de influência internacional sobre o ex-presidente Lula. *Epoca*, 30 April. Available at: https://epoca.globo.com/tempo/noticia/2015/04/suspeitas-de-trafico-de-influencia-internacional-sobre-o-ex-presidente-lula.html (Accessed: 8 January 2020).

Brown, T (2016). Sustainability as empty signifier: its rise, fall, and radical potential. *Antipode*, 48(1): 115–133.

Brum, E (2014). Belo Monte: a anatomia de um etnocídio. *El Pais*, 1 December. Available at: https://brasil.elpais.com/brasil/2014/12/01/opinion/1417437633_930086.html (Accessed: 30 March 2020).

Brum, E (2015a). Belo Monte, empreiteiras e espelhinhos. *El Pais*, 7 July. Available at: https://brasil.elpais.com/brasil/2015/07/06/opinion/1436195768_857181.html (Accessed: 30 March 2020).

Brum, E (2015b). O dia em que a casa foi expulsa de casa. *El Pais*, 14 September. Available at: https://brasil.elpais.com/brasil/2015/09/14/opinion/1442235958_647873.html (Accessed: 19 March 2019).

Brum, E (2015c). Vítimas de uma guerra amazônica. *El Pais*, 26 September. Available at: https://brasil.elpais.com/brasil/2015/09/22/politica/1442930391_549192.html (Accessed: 8 January 2020).

Brum, E (2016). Dilma compôs seu réquiem em Belo Monte. *El Pais*, 10 May. Available at: https://brasil.elpais.com/brasil/2016/05/09/opinion/1462804348_582272.html (Accessed: 25 April 2019).

Brum, E (2019). *The Collector of Leftover Souls*. Translated from Portuguese by Diane Grosklaus Whitty. London: Granta.

Buchs, A (2010). Water crisis and water scarcity as social constructions: the case of water use in Almería (Andalusia, Spain). *Options Méditerranéennes*, A(95): 207–211.

Budds, J (2004). Power, nature and neoliberalism: the political ecology of water in Chile. *Singapore Journal of Tropical Geography*, 25(3): 322–342.

Bunker, SG (1988). *Underdeveloping the Amazon: Extraction, Unequal Exchange, and the Failure of the Modern State*. Chicago, IL: University of Chicago Press.

Burrier, G (2014). *Ordem e Progresso: the Programa de Aceleração do Crescimento, Developmentalism, and Democracy in Brazil*. Thesis submitted to Department of Political Science, University of New Mexico.

Burrier, G (2016). The developmental state, civil society, and hydroelectric politics in Brazil. *Journal of Environment and Development*, 25(3): 332–358.

Calixto, B (2016). A corrupção nas obras de Belo Monte - segundo a delação de Delcídio. *Epoca*, 15 March. Available at: https://epoca.globo.com/colunas-e-blogs/blog-do-planeta/noticia/2016/03/corrupcao-nas-obras-de-belo-monte-segundo-delacao-de-delcidio.html (Accessed: 8 January 2020).

Calvi, MF (2019). *(Re)Organização Produtiva e Mudanças na Paisagem sob Influência da Hidrelétrica de Belo Monte*. Thesis submitted to Instituto de Filosofia e Ciências Humanas, Universidade Estadual de Campinas, Campinas.

Carvalho, C, and Dantas, D (2016). Palocci negociou propina de Belo Monte para PT e PMDB, diz delator. *O Globo*, 31 October. Available at: https://oglobo.globo.com/brasil/palocci-negociou-propina-de-belo-monte-para-pt-pmdb-diz-delator-20390567 (Accessed: 8 January 2020).

Carvalho, G (2006). Environmental resistance and the politics of energy development. *Journal of Environment & Development*, 15(1): 245–268.

Casanova, L, and Kassum, J (2013). *The Political Economy of an Emerging Global Power: In Search of the Brazil Dream*. Basingstoke: Palgrave Macmillan.

Castro-Diaz, L, Lopez, MC, and Moran, E (2018). Gender-differentiated impacts of the Belo Monte hydroelectric dam on downstream fishers in the Brazilian Amazon. *Human Ecology*, 46(3): 411–422.

Cavanagh, CJ, and Benjaminsen, TA (2017). Political ecology, variegated green economies, and the foreclosure of alternative sustainabilities. *Journal of Political Ecology*, 24(1): 200–216.

CDM Pipeline (2020). CDM pipeline. UNEP DTU Partnership. Available at: http://www.cdmpipeline.org/cdm-projects-type.htm#3 (Accessed: February 14, 2020).

Chapman, J (2007). India's Narmada dams controversy. *Journal of International Communication*, 13(1): 71–85.

Chayes, S (2017). A hidden cost of corruption: environmental devastation. *The Washington Post*, 16th June. Available at: https://www.washingtonpost.com/outlook/a-hidden-cost-of-corruption-environmental-devastation/2017/06/16/03f93c1e-52b8-11e7-b064-828ba60fbb98_story.html?utm_term=.e3995169b07a (Accessed: 8 January 2020).

Chernela, J (1988). Potential impacts of the proposed Altamira-Xingu hydroelectric complex in Brazil. *Cultural Survival Quarterly*, 12(2): 20–24.

Chernela, J (2005). The politics of mediation: local-global interactions in the Central Amazon of Brazil. *American Anthropologist*, 107(4): 620–631.

Chernela, J, and Zanotti, L (2014). Limits to knowledge: indigenous peoples, NGOs, and the moral economy in the Eastern Amazon of Brazil. *Conservation & Society*, 12(3): 306–317.

Chhotray, V (2007). The 'anti-politics machine' in India: depoliticisation through local institution building for participatory watershed development. *Journal of Development Studies*, 43(6): 1037–1056.

China Daily (2016). Chinese dam builders powering the Amazon nation. *Daily*, 9 May. Available at: https://www.chinadaily.com.cn/business/2016-05/09/content_25146582.htm (Accessed: 30 March 2020).

CIMI, Regional Sul (2017). Sem reconhecer indígenas como sujeitos de direitos, governo relembra Ditadura, denuncia. *Combate Racismo Ambiental*, 7 August. Available at: https://racismoambiental.net.br/2017/08/07/sem-reconhecer-indigenas-como-sujeitos-de-direitos-governo-relembra-ditadura-denuncia-cimi-regional-sul/ (Accessed: 6 April 2020).

CNEC Worley Parson Engenharia (2014). *Aproveitamento Hidrelétrico (AHE) São Luiz do Tapajós: Estudo de Impacto Ambiental, 1–25*. São Paulo: CNEC Worley Parsons Engenharia.

Comitê Brasileiro de Defensoras e Defensores de Direitos Humanos (CDDH) (2017). *Vidas em Luta Criminalização e Violência Contra Defensoras e Defensores de Direitos Humanos no Brasil*. Curitiba: CIDH. Available at: https://pdfs.semanticscholar.org/a26f/0c22df6d02d156c65af315e3dd3ee4055119.pdf.

Conklin, BA, and Graham, LR (1995). The shifting middle ground: Amazonian Indians and ecopolitics. *American Anthropologist*, 97(4): 695–710.

Corrêa dos Santos, M (2014). O conceito de "atingido" por barragens: Direitos humanos e cidadania. *Direito e Praxis*, 6(1): 113–140.

Costa, L (2017). UPDATE 1-State Grid, Eletrobras to deliver line for Brazil dam early - Reuters. *Reuters*, 16 October. Available at: https://www.reuters.com/article/brazil-utilities/update-1-state-grid-eletrobras-to-deliver-line-for-brazil-dam-early-idUSL2N1MR1H3 (Accessed: 30 March 2020).

Costa, L (2018). China's power investment group seeks new Brazil targets after $2 billion deal. *Reuters*, 16 May. Available at: https://www.reuters.com/article/us-spic-brazil/chinas-power-investment-group-seeks-new-brazil-targets-after-2-billion-deal-idUSKCN1IH08M (Accessed: 30 March 2020).

Criado, MA (2017). 500 presas amenazan con ahogar el Amazonas. *El País*, 14 June. Available at: https://elpais.com/elpais/2017/06/14/ciencia/1497430161_506854.html (Accessed: 19 March 2019).

Crow-Miller, B (2015). Discourses of deflection: the politics of framing China's south-north water transfer project. *Water Alternatives*, 8(2): 173–192.

Crow-Miller, B, Webber, M, and Molle, F (2017). The (re)turn to infrastructure for water management? *Water Alternatives*, 10(2): 195–207.

Crow-Miller, B, Webber, M, and Rogers, S (2017). The techno-politics of big infrastructure and the Chinese water machine. *Water Alternatives*, 10(2): 233–249.

Cruz, I (2019). Por que Belo Monte não realiza seu potencial elétrico. *Nexo Jornal*, 17 December. Available at: https://www.nexojornal.com.br/expresso/2019/12/17/Por-que-Belo-Monte-n%C3%A3o-realiza-seu-potencial-el%C3%A9trico (Accessed: April 6, 2020).

Cruz, V (2019). Brumadinho serve de reflexão a quem defende acelerar licenças ambientais no governo Bolsonaro. *G1*, 28 January Available at: https://g1.globo.com/politica/blog/valdo-cruz/post/2019/01/28/brumadinho-serve-de-reflexao-a-quem-defende-acelerar-licencas-ambientais-no-governo-bolsonaro.ghtml (Accessed: 6 April 2020).

Cuadros, A (2017). Open talk of a military coup unsettles Brazil. *New Yorker*, 13 October. Available at: https://www.newyorker.com/news/news-desk/open-talk-of-a-military-coup-unsettles-brazil (Accessed: 6 April 2020).

Cunningham, M (2007). Public policy and normative language: utility, community and nation in the debate over the construction of Tryweryn reservoir. *Parliamentary Affairs*, 60(4): 625–636.

Cury, A (2017). Desemprego fica em 12% no 4o trimestre de 2016 e atinge 12,3 milhões. *G1*, 31 January. Available at: https://g1.globo.com/economia/noticia/desemprego-fica-em-12-no-4-trimestre-de-2016.ghtml (Accessed: 6 April 2020).

Cury, A, and Caoli, C (2016). PIB do Brasil cai 3,8% em 2015 e tem pior resultado em 25 anos. *G1*, 3 March. Available at: http://g1.globo.com/economia/noticia/2016/03/pib-do-brasil-cai-38-em-2015.html (Accessed: 6 April 2020).

da Costa, A (2014). Sustainable dam development in Brazil: the roles of environmentalism, participation and planning. In: Scheumann, W, and Hensengerth, O (eds) *Evolution of Dam Policies: Evidence from the Big Hydropower States*. Berlin: Springer Berlin Heidelberg.

da Silva, LIL (2010). Discurso do Presidente da República, Luiz Inácio Lula da Silva, no ato por Belo Monte e pelo desenvolvimento da região do Xingu-Altamira- PA. *Presidencia Da Republica, Biblioteca*, 22 June. Available at: http://www.biblioteca.presidencia.gov.br/presidencia/ex-presidentes/luiz-inacio-lula-da-silva/audios/2010-audios-lula/22-06-2010-discurso-do-presidente-da-republica-luiz-inacio-lula-da-silva-no-ato-por-belo-monte-e-pelo-desenvolvimento-da-regiao-do-xingu-altamira-pa-08min36s/view (Accessed: 30 March 2020).

Datz, G (2013). Brazil's pension fund developmentalism. *Competition and Change*, 17(2): 111–128.

Davis, S (1977). *Victims of the Miracle: Development and the Indians of Brazil*. Cambridge: Cambridge University Press.

de Aguiar, D, Rodrigues, L, Nakagawa, L, Lila, L, Minami, T, Leal, V, and Brasil, G (2016). *The Battle for the River of Life*. São Paulo: Greenpeace Brasil. Available at: https://

www.greenpeace.de/sites/www.greenpeace.de/files/publications/greenpeace-report-the _battle_for_the_river_of_life-20160321.pdf (Accessed: 30 March 2020).

de Araújo, KR, Sawakuchi, HO. Bertassoli Jr, DJ, Sawakuchi, AO, da Silva, KD, Vieira, TB, Ward, ND, and Pereira, TS (2019). Carbon dioxide (CO_2) concentrations and emission in the newly constructed Belo Monte hydropower complex in the Xingu River, Amazonia. *Biogeosciences*, 16(18): 3527–3542.

de Moya Figueira Netto, CA, de Barros Franco, HC, and Souto Rezende, PFV (2007). AHE Belo Monte: Evolução Dos Estudos. *Paper pressented at XXVII Seminário Nacional De Grandes Barragens*, Belém, PA, 3–7 June. Available at: http://symbiont.ansp.org/ixingu/library/timeline_sources/Moya_et_al_2007.pdf (Accessed: 30 March 2020).

de Oliveira, GJ (n.d.). A suspensão de segurança e as cláusulas pétreas da constituição. Available at: https://ajufesc.org.br/wp-content/uploads/2017/02/Gelson-Jorge-de-Oliveira.pdf (Accessed: 30 March 2020).

de Souza Dias, V, da Luz, MP, Medero, GM, and Nascimento, DTF (2018). An overview of hydropower reservoirs in Brazil: current situation, future perspectives and impacts of climate change. *Water*, 10(5): 592.

de Toledo, JR, Burgarelli, R, and Bramatti, D (2014). Doações de campanha somam R$1bi, das quais metade vem de 19 empresas. *O Estado de S. Paulo*, 15 September. Available at: https://politica.estadao.com.br/noticias/geral,doacoes-de-campanha-somam-r-1-bi-das-quais-metade-vem-de-19-empresas-imp-,1560289 (Accessed: 8 January 2020).

Declaration of Temaca (2010). Endorsed at *Rivers for Life: the 3rd International Meeting of Dam Affected People and Their Allies, un Temacapulín*, Mexico, 1–7 October 2010. Available at: https://www.internationalrivers.org/resources/declaration-of-temaca-4290.

del Bene, D, Scheidel, A, and Temper, L (2018). More dams, more violence? A global analysis on resistances and repression around conflictive dams through co-produced knowledge. *Sustainability Science*, 13(3): 617–633.

della Porta, D, and Diani, M (1999). *Social Movements: An Introduction*. London: Blackwell.

della Porta, D, and Piazza, G (2007). Local contention, global framing: the protest campaigns against the TAV in Val di Susa and the bridge on the Messina Straits. *Environmental Politics*, 16(5): 864–882.

Delsontro, T, McGinnis, DF, Sobek, S, Ostrovsky, I, Wehrli, B (2010). Extreme methane emissions from a swiss hydropower Reservoir: contribution from bubbling sediments. *Environmental Science and Technology*, 44(7): 2419–2425.

Devlin, JF, and Yap, NT (2008). Contentious politics in environmental assessment: blocked projects and winning coalitions. *Impact Assessment and Project Appraisal*, 26(1): 17–27.

Dias, T (2019). Operation Amazon Redux. *Intercept*, 20 September. Available at: https://theintercept.com/2019/09/20/amazon-brazil-army-bolsanaro/ (Accessed: 6 April 2020).

Díaz-Caravantes, RE, and Wilder, M (2014). Water, cities and peri-urban communities: geographies of power in the context of drought in northwest Mexico. *Water Alternatives*, 7(3): 499–517.

Dinmore, EG (2014). "Mountain dream" or the "submergence of fine scenery"? Japanese contestations over the Kurobe Number Four Dam, 1920–1970. *Water History*, 6(4): 315–340.

Doval, GP, and Actis, E (2016). The political and economic instability of Dilma Rousseff's second government in Brazil: between impeachment and the pragmatic turn. *India Quarterly*, 72(2): 120–131.

Dye, B (2020). What holds back dam building? The role of Brazil in the stagnation of dams in Tanzania. Available at SSRN: https://doi.org/10.2139/ssrn.3538214 (Accessed: 23 July 2020).

EcoAlbania (2016). NO dams in Vjosa, "NO" to Poçem dam. *EcoAlbania*. http://www.ecoalbania.org/no-dams-in-vjosa-no-to-pocem-dam/ (Accessed: 23 July 2020).

Eden, S, Donaldson, A, and Walker, G (2006). Green groups and grey areas: scientific boundary-work, nongovernmental organisations, and environmental knowledge. *Environment and Planning. part A*, 38(6): 1061–1076.

Edwards, G (2013). Shifting constructions of scarcity and the neoliberalization of Australian water governance. *Environment and Planning. part A*, 45(8): 1873–1890.

Eletrobras (2009a). *Aproveitamento to Hidrelétrico Belo Monte: Estudo de Impacto Ambiental*. Rio de Janeiro, RJ, Brazil.

Eletrobras (2009b). *Relatório de Impacto Ambiental: Aproveitamento Hidrelétrico Belo Monte*. Brasilia. Available at: http://restrito.norteenergiasa.com.br/site/wp-content/uploads/2011/04/NE.Rima_.pdf (Accessed: 19 March 2019).

Eletrobras (2012). Assessoria de Comunicação da Eletrobras: Pela energia limpa. *Eletrobras*, 26 April. Available at: http://eletrobras.com/pt/Lists/noticias/ExibeNoticias.aspx?ID=590&ContentTypeId=0x0100C80727F9FEABA9499C54B2148B8BE07E (Accessed: 30 March 2020).

Empresa de Pesquisa Energética (2010). *Belo Monte Fatos e Dados*. Brasilia: Empresa de Pesquisa Energética. Available at: http://antigo.epe.gov.br//leiloes/Documents/Leilão Belo Monte/Belo Monte - Fatos e Dados - POR.pdf (Accessed: 30 March 2020).

Eren, A (2017). The political ecology of uncertainty: the production of truth by juridical practices in hydropower development. *Journal of Political Ecology*, 24: 386–405.

Estado de São Paulo (2015). O fim das obras dos 'barrageiros'. *Estado de São Paulo*, 27 June. Available at: https://economia.estadao.com.br/noticias/geral,-o-fim-das-obras-dos-barrageiros,1714868 (Accessed: 14 April 2020).

Estronioli, E (2016). Obras de belo monte aumentam casos de assédio e estupro. *Azmina*, 15 February. Available at: https://azmina.com.br/reportagens/obras-de-belo-monte-aumentam-casos-de-assedio-e-estupro/ (Accessed: 8 January 2020).

Everard, M (2013). *The hydropolitics of dams*. London: Zed Books.

Evers, HD, and Benedikter, S (2009). Hydraulic bureaucracy in a modern hydraulic society: strategic group formation in the Mekong delta, Vietnam. *Water Alternatives*, 2(3): 416–439.

Exame (2019a). Altamira é mais um capítulo da guerra de facções; relembre outros casos. *Exame*, 30 July. Available at: https://exame.abril.com.br/brasil/altamira-e-mais-um-capitulo-da-guerra-de-faccoes-relembre-outros-casos/ (Accessed: 8 January 2020).

Exame (2019b). Bolsonaro diz que índios vivem "pré-históricos dentro de suas terras". *Exame*, 27 November. Available at: https://exame.abril.com.br/brasil/bolsonaro-diz-que-indios-vivem-pre-historicos-dentro-de-suas-terras/ (Accessed: 6 April 2020).

Fachin, P, and Santos, JV (2015). A monstruosidade de Belo Monte e descalabro em Altamira que Dilma não teve coragem de ver. Entrevista especial com D. Erwin Kräutler. *IHU-Online*, 16 January. Available at: http://www.ihu.unisinos.br/entrevistas/539024-a-monstruosidade-de-belo-monte-dilma-nao-teve-coragem-de-ver-o-descalabro-provocado-pela-obra-entrevista-especial-com-d-erwin-kraeutler (Accessed: 30 March 2020).

FASE (2009). Belo Monte: Audiência discrimina e reprime população. *FASE*, 28 September. Available at: https://fase.org.br/pt/informe-se/noticias/belo-monte-audiencia-discrimina-e-reprime-populacao/ (Accessed: 8 January 2020).

Fearnside, PM (2009). Aquecimento global na Amazônia: Impactos e mitigação. *Acta Amazonica*, 39(4): 1003–1011.

Fearnside, PM (2015). Brazil's São Luiz do Tapajós dam: the art of cosmetic environmental impact assessments. *Water Alternatives*, 8(3): 373–396.

Fearnside, PM (2017). Planned disinformation: the example of the Belo Monte Dam as a source of greenhouse gases. In: Issberner, LR, and Lena, P (eds) *Brazil in the Anthropocene: Conflicts between Predatory Development and Environmental Policies*. New York: Routledge.

Fearnside, PM (2018). Belo Monte: Lições da Luta 11 – A farsa da audiência pública. *Amazonia Real*, 5 March. Available at: https://amazoniareal.com.br/belo-monte-licoes-da-luta-11-farsa-da-audiencia-publica/ (Accessed: 30 March 2020).

Fédération Internationale Pour Les Droits Humains (2014). *Vale e Belo Monte sob suspeita de espionagem: A justiça tem que investigar*. Fédération Internationale Pour Les Droits Humains, 17 February. Available at: https://www.fidh.org/pt/americas/brasil/14676-brasil-vale-e-belo-monte-sob-suspeita-de-espionagem-a-justica-tem-que (Accessed: 8 January 2020).

Ferguson, J (1994). *The Anti-politics Machine*. Minneapolis, MN: University of Minnesota Press.

Fernandes, GW, Goulart, FF, Ranieri, BD, Coelho, MS, Dales, K, Boesche, N, Bustamante, M, Carvalho, FA, Carvalho, DC, Dirzo, R, Fernandes, S, Galetti Jr, PM, Garcia Millan, VE, Mielke, C, Ramirez, JL, Neves, A, Rogass, C, Ribeiro, SP and Soares-Filho, B (2016). Deep into the mud: ecological and socio-economic impacts of the dam breach in Mariana, Brazil. *Natureza e Conservacao*, 14(2): 35–45.

Fernández, L, de la Sota, C, Andrade, JCS, Lumbreras, J, and Mazorra, J (2014). Social development benefits of hydroelectricity CDM projects in Brazil. *International Journal of Sustainable Development and World Ecology*, 21(3): 246–258.

Ferro, F (2010). *Diário da Câmara dos Deputados, ANO LXV No 51 (15/04/2010)*. Brasilia: Câmara dos Deputados.

Fisher, WH (1994). Megadevelopment, environmentalism, and resistance: the institutional context of Kayapó indigenous politics in Central Brazil. *Human Organization*, 53(3): 220–232.

FGV DAPP (2019). Meio Ambiente é o principal tema associado ao governo após desastre em Brumadinho. *FGV DAPP*. Available at: http://dapp.fgv.br/meio-ambiente-e-o-principal-tema-associado-ao-governo-apos-desastre-em-brumadinho/ (Accessed: 6 April 2020).

Fletcher, R (2010). When environmental issues collide: climate change and the shifting political ecology of hydroelectric power. *Peace and Conflict Review*, 5(1): 1–17.

Fleury, LC (2014). Belo Monte e o "interesse nacional": Entre ações civis públicas, suspensões de segurança e o estado de exceção. Presented at *29a Reunião Brasileira de Antropologia*. Natal, RN. Available at: http://www.29rba.abant.org.br/resources/anais/1/1402504521_ARQUIVO_2014_ABA_LorenaFleury_BeloMonteeoestadodeexcecao.pdf.

Fleury, LC, and Almeida, J (2013). A construção da Usina Hidrelétrica de Belo Monte: Conflito ambiental e o dilema do desenvolvimento. *Ambiente e Sociedade*, 16(4): 141–156.

Flick, U (2009). *An Introduction to Qualitative Research*. London: SAGE.

Folha de S.Paulo (2017). Entenda o impacto da crise no governo na economia. *Folha de S.Paulo*, 18 May. Available at: https://www1.folha.uol.com.br/mercado/2017/05/1885077-entenda-o-impacto-da-crise-no-governo-na-economia.shtml (Accessed: 6 April 2020).

Folha de S.Paulo (2019). Bolsonaro nega ditadura e diz que regime viveu probleminhas. *Folha de S.Paulo*, 27 March. Available at: https://www1.folha.uol.com.br/poder/2019/03/nao-houve-ditadura-teve-uns-probleminhas-diz-bolsonaro-sobre-regime-militar-no-pais.shtml (Accessed: 6 April 2020).

Folha de S.Paulo (2020). Veja falas preconceituosas de Bolsonaro e o que diz a lei sobre injúria e racismo. *Folha de S.Paulo*, 26 January. Available at: https://www1.folha.uol.com.br/poder/2020/01/veja-falas-preconceituosas-de-bolsonaro-e-o-que-diz-a-lei-sobre-injuria-e-racismo.shtml (Accessed: 6 April 2020).

Folhapress (2018). Bolsonaro ataca "indústrias" da reserva indígena e da expropriação de terras por trabalho escravo. *Bem Paraná*, 5 October. Available at: https://www.bemparana.com.br/noticia/bolsonaro-ataca-industrias-da-reserva-indigena-e-da-expropriacao-de-terras-por-trabalho-escravo#.XosX1IhKjIV (Accessed: 6 April 2020).

Freeman, S (2013). Voices of the Xingu: interview with Maini Militão. *Amazon Watch*, 28 March. Available at: https://amazonwatch.org/news/2013/0328-voices-of-the-xingu-interview-with-maini-militao (Accessed: 25 April 2019).

Freire, F (2015). Delator dirá que Camargo Corrêa pagou R$ 100 milhões em propina para PT e PMDB em Belo Monte. *O Globo*, 6 March. Available at: https://oglobo.globo.com/brasil/delator-dira-que-camargo-correa-pagou-100-milhoes-em-propina-para-pt-pmdb-em-belo-monte-15521906 (Accessed: 8 January 2020).

Freitas, R, and Almeida, F (2020). Um ano após tragédia da Vale, dor e luta por justiça unem famílias de 259 mortos e 11 desaparecidos. *G1*, 25 January. Available at: https://g1.globo.com/mg/minas-gerais/noticia/2020/01/25/um-ano-apos-tragedia-da-vale-dor-e-luta-por-justica-unem-familias-de-259-mortos-e-11-desaparecidos.ghtml (Accessed: 6 April 2020).

French, J, and Fortes, A (2012). Nurturing hope, deepening democracy, and combating inequalities in Brazil: Lula, the Workers' Party, and Dilma Rousseff's 2010 election as President. *Labor Studies in Working-Class History of the Americas*, 9(1): 7–28.

Fundação Nacional do Índio (2011). Nota sobre as medidas cautelares da Comissão Interamericana de Direitos Humanos (CIDH) da OEA. *Fundação Nacional Do Índio*, 5 April. Available at: http://www.funai.gov.br/index.php/comunicacao/noticias/1885-nota-sobre-as-medidas-cautelares-da-comissao-interamericana-de-direitos-humanos-cidh-da-oea (Accessed: 30 March 2020).

Fundação Nacional do Índio (2016). Funai aprova estudos das Terras Indígenas Sawré Muybu (PA), Ypoi/Triunfo (MS), Sambaqui (PR) e Jurubaxi-Téa (AM). *FUNAI*, 19 April. Available at: http://www.funai.gov.br/index.php/comunicacao/noticias/3712-funai-publica-estudos-das-terras-indigenas-sawre-muybu-pa-ypoi-triunfo-ms-sambaqui-pr-e-jurubaxi-tea-am (Accessed: 6 April 2020).

G1 (2019). Fala de Bolsonaro sobre queimada na Amazônia é "irresponsável" e "leviana", dizem ambientalistas. *G1*, 21 August. Available at: https://g1.globo.com/politica/noticia/2019/08/21/fala-de-bolsonaro-sobre-queimada-na-amazonia-e-irresponsavel-e-leviana-dizem-ambientalistas.ghtml (Accessed: April 6, 2020).

G1 Minas (2019). Barragem da Vale se rompe em Brumadinho, MG. *G1*, 25 January. Available at: https://g1.globo.com/mg/minas-gerais/noticia/2019/01/25/bombeiros-e-defesa-civil-sao-mobilizados-para-chamada-de-rompimento-de-barragem-em-brumadinho-na-grande-bh.ghtml (Accessed: 6 April 2020).

G1 PA (2014a). Dilma visita obras de Belo Monte e faz campanha no Pará. *G1*, 5 August. Available at: http://g1.globo.com/pa/para/eleicoes/2014/noticia/2014/08/dilma-rousseff-visita-obras-de-belo-monte-e-faz-campanha-no-para.html (Accessed: 8 January 2020).

G1 PA (2014b). Cheia do rio Xingu deixa mais famílias desabrigadas em Altamira. *G1*, 12 March. Available at: http://g1.globo.com/pa/para/noticia/2014/03/cheia-do-rio-xingu-deixa-mais-familias-desabrigadas-em-altamira.html (Accessed: 8 January 2020).

G1 PA (2016). Fim das obras de Belo Monte ressalta desemprego no sudoeste do Pará. *G1*, 28 June. Available at: http://g1.globo.com/pa/para/noticia/2016/06/fim-das-obras-de-belo-monte-revela-cenario-de-desemprego-na-regiao.html (Accessed: 8 January 2020).

G1 PA (2017). MPF faz audiência pública em para debater impacto de Belo Monte no PA. *G1*, 20 March. Available at: http://g1.globo.com/pa/para/noticia/2017/03/mpf-faz-audiencia-publica-em-para-debater-impacto-de-belo-monte-no-pa.html (Accessed: 9 January 2020).

Gandy, M (2014). *Fabric of Space: Water, Modernity, and the Urban Imagination.* Cambridge, MA: MIT Press.

Garavan, M (2007). Resisting the costs of "development": local environmental activism in Ireland. *Environmental Politics*, 16(5): 844–863.

Gauthier, C, Lin, Z, Peter, BG, and Moran, EF (2019). Hydroelectric infrastructure and potential groundwater contamination in the Brazilian Amazon: Altamira and the Belo Monte dam. *The Professional Geographer.* Routledge, 71(2): 292–300.

Gerlak, AK, Saguier, M, Mills-Novoa, M, Fearnside, PM, and Albercht, TR (2019). Dams, Chinese investments, and EIAs: a race to the bottom in South America? *Ambio*, 49: 156–164.

Giles, J (2006). Methane quashes green credentials of hydropower. *Nature*, 444(7119): 524–5.

Ginzburg, O (2006). *There you go!* London: Survival International.

Giraldo, CM (2017). Panama's Barro Blanco dam to begin operation, indigenous pleas refused. *Mongabay.* 24 March. Available at: https://news.mongabay.com/2017/03/panamas-barro-blanco-dam-to-begin-operation-indigenous-pleas-refused/ (Accessed: 30 March 2020).

Glass, V (2013). Adolescente é resgatada de prostíbulo em Belo Monte. *Reporter Brasil*, 14 February. Available at: https://reporterbrasil.org.br/2013/02/adolescente-e-resgatada-de-prostibulo-em-belo-monte/ (Accessed: 19 March 2019).

Goffman, E (1974). *Frame Analysis: An Essay on the Organization of Experience.* Cambridge, MA: Harvard University Press.

Goldman, M (2004). Imperial science, imperial nature: environmental knowledge for the World (Bank). In: Jasanoff, S, and Martello, ML (eds) *Earthly Politics: Local and Global in Environmental Governance.* Cambridge, MA: MIT Press.

Gómez Bruera, HF (2015). *Lula, the Workers' Party and the Governability Dilemma in Brazil.* Abingdon: Routledge.

Gonzales, J (2018). Brazilian elections and the environment: where top candidates stand. *Mongabay*, 17 September. Available at: https://news.mongabay.com/2018/09/brazilian-elections-and-the-environment-where-top-candidates-stand/ (Accessed: 6 April 2020).

Gosman, E (2015). Rechazo al rumbo económico de Dilma Rousseff. *Clarin Mundo*, 29 May. Available at: https://www.clarin.com/mundo/brasil-ajuste-dilma_rousseff-tercerizacion_0_H1geWsuFwml.html (Accessed: 8 January 2020).

Greenpeace Brasil (2016a). *Damming the Amazon: The Risky Business of Hydropower in the Amazon.* São Paulo: Greenpeace Brasil. Available at: https://www.greenpeace.org/usa/dam-amazon-hydropower/ (Accessed: 30 March 2020).

Greenpeace Brasil (2016b). Hidrelétrica no Tapajós está cancelada. *Greenpeace Brasil*, 4 August. Available at: https://www.greenpeace.org/brasil/blog/hidreletrica-no-tapajos-esta-cancelada/ (Accessed: 6 April 2020).

Greenwald, G, and Pougy, V (2019). Hidden plot: Brazil's top prosecutors who indicted Lula schemed in secret messages to prevent his party from winning 2018 election. *The Intercept*, 9 June. Available at: https://theintercept.com/2019/06/09/brazil-car-wash-prosecutors-workers-party-lula/ (Accessed: 22 July 2020).

Griffiths, H (2014). Water under the bridge? Nature, memory and hydropolitics. *Cultural Geographies*, 21(3): 449–474.

Grisotti, M (2016). The construction of health causal relations in the Belo Monte dam context. *Ambiente & Sociedade*, 19: 287–304.

Grupo de Estudos Tapajós (2014). *Avaliação Ambiental Integrada da Bacia do Tapajós: Sumário Executivo*. Available at: https://web.archive.org/web/20190217004707/http://www.http://grupodeestudostapajos.com.br/site/wp-content/uploads/2014/04/Sumario_AAI.pdf (Accessed: 30 March 2020).

Guidry, JA (2003). Not just another labor party: the Workers' Party and democracy in Brazil. *Labor Studies Journal*, 28(1): 83–108.

Hajer, M (1995). *The Politics of Environmental Discourse: Ecological Modernization and the Policy Process*. Oxford: Clarendon Press.

Hajer, MA (1993). Discourse coalitions and the institutionalization of practice: the case of acid rain in Britain. In: Fischer, F, and Forester, J (eds) *The Argumentative Turn in Policy Analysis and Planning*. Durham, NC: Duke University Press

Hanna, P (2016). *The Social Impacts of Large Projects on Indigenous Peoples: Procedures, Processes and Protests*. Thesis submitted to Department of Cultural Geography, University of Groningen.

Hanna, P, and Vanclay, F (2013). Human rights, Indigenous peoples and the concept of free, prior and informed consent. *Impact Assessment and Project Appraisal*, 31(2): 146–157.

Hanna, P, Vanclay, F, Langdon, EJ, and Arts, J (2016). The importance of cultural aspects in impact assessment and project development: reflections from a case study of a hydroelectric dam in Brazil. *Impact Assessment and Project Appraisal*, 34(4): 306–318.

Harris, LM (2009). Contested sustainabilities: assessing narratives of environmental change in southeastern Turkey. *Local Environment*, 14(8): 699–720.

Haynes, J (1999). Power, politics and environmental movements in the Third World. *Environmental Politics*, 8(1): 222–242.

Hecht, SB (2011). The new Amazon geographies: insurgent citizenship, "Amazon Nation" and the politics of environmentalisms. *Journal of Cultural Geography*, 28(1): 203–223.

Heckenberger, MJ, Kuikuro, A, Kuikuro, UT, Russell, JC, Schmidt, M, Fausto, C, and Franchetto, B (2003). Amazonia 1492: Pristine forest or cultural parkland? *Science*, 301(5640): 1710–1714.

Heckenberger, MJ, Russell, JC, Fausto, C, Toney, JR, Schmidt, MJ, Pereira, E, Franchetto, B, and Kuikuro, A (2008). Pre-Columbian urbanism, anthropogenic landscapes, and the future of the Amazon. *Science*, 321(5893): 1214–1217.

Heckenberger, MJ, Russell, JC, Toney, JR, and Schmidt, MJ (2007). The legacy of cultural landscapes in the Brazilian Amazon: implications for biodiversity. *Philosophical Transactions of the Royal Society of London series B Biological Sciences*, 362 (1478): 197–208.

Hemming, J (1978). *Red Gold: The Conquest of the Brazilian Indians*. Cambridge, MA: Harvard University Press.

Hensengerth, O (2015). Where is the power? Transnational networks, authority and the dispute over the Xayaburi Dam on the Lower Mekong Mainstream. *Water International*, 40(5–6): 911–928.

Hess, CEE, and Fenrich, E (2017). Socio-environmental conflicts on hydropower: the São Luiz do Tapajós project in Brazil. *Environmental Science and Policy*, 73: 20–28.

Higgins, T (2020). Belo Monte boondoggle: Brazil's biggest, costliest dam may be unviable. *Mongabay*, 17 January. Available at: https://news.mongabay.com/2020/01/belo-monte-boondoggle-brazils-biggest-costliest-dam-may-be-unviable/ (Accessed: April 6, 2020).

Hill, C, Phan, TNT, Storey, J, and Vongphosey, S (2017). Lessons learnt from gender impact assessments of hydropower projects in Laos and Vietnam. *Gender & Development*, 25(3): 455–470.

Hochstetler, K (2011). The politics of environmental licensing: energy projects of the past and future in Brazil. *Studies in Comparative International Development*, 46(4): 349–371.

Hochstetler, K, and Keck, ME (2007). *Greening Brazil: Environmental Activism in State and Society*. Durham, NC: Duke University Press.

Hochstetler, K, and Montero, AP (2013). The renewed developmental state: the national development bank and the Brazil model. *Journal of Development Studies*, 49(11): 1484–1499.

Hochstetler, K, and Viola, E (2012). Brazil and the politics of climate change: beyond the global commons. *Environmental Politics*, 21(5): 753–771.

Hommes, L, Boelens, R, and Maat, H (2016). Contested hydrosocial territories and disputed water governance: struggles and competing claims over the Ilisu Dam development in southeastern Turkey. *Geoforum*, 71: 9–20.

Huber, A, and Joshi, D (2015). Hydropower, anti-politics, and the opening of new political spaces in the Eastern Himalayas. *World Development*, 76: 13–25.

Hunter, W (2010). *The Transformation of the Workers' Party in Brazil, 1989–2009*. Cambridge: Cambridge University Press.

Hurwitz, Z (2011). IBAMA President resigns over Belo Monte licensing. *International Rivers*, 13 January. Available at: https://www.internationalrivers.org/blogs/258/ibama-president-resigns-over-belo-monte-licensing (Accessed: 8 January 2020).

Hurwitz, Z (2011). Mining giant joins Belo Monte dam. *International Rivers*, 2 May. Available at: https://www.internationalrivers.org/blogs/258/mining-giant-joins-belo-monte-dam (Accessed: 30 March 2020).

Ibor, CS, Mollá, MG, Reus, LA, and Genovés, JC (2011). Reaching the limits of water resources mobilization: irrigation development in the Segura river basin, Spain. *Water Alternatives*, 4(3): 259–278.

Ilg, J (n.d.). Bolsonaro é condenado por discurso racista, veja o que ele já disse contra os negros, *Esquerda Diario*. Available at: https://esquerdadiario.com.br/spip.php?page=g acetilla-articulo&id_article=18579 (Accessed: 6 April 2020).

Indigenous People's Cultural Support Trust (n.d.). Press release: Indians rally to fight dam proposal in the Amazon. *Indigenous People's Cultural Support Trust*. Available at: http://www.ipcst.org/Pdfs/AltamiraPR.pdf (Accessed: 2 April 2020).

Instituto Brasileiro de Geografia e Estatistica (IBGE) (n.d.). *Altamira População*. Instituto Brasileiro de Geografia e Estatistica. Available at: https://cidades.ibge.gov.br/brasil/pa/altamira/panorama (Accessed: 8 January 2020).

Instituto Brasileiro do Meio Ambiente e dos Recursos Naturais Renováveis (2016). Ibama arquiva licenciamento da UHE São Luiz do Tapajós, no Pará. *IBAMA*, 5 August. Available at: http://www.ibama.gov.br/noticias/58-2016/162-ibama-arquiva-licenc iamento-da-uhesao-%0Aluiz-do-tapajos-no-para (Accessed: 19 March 2019).

Instituto Humanitas Unisinos (2013a). Violência sexual em Altamira: uma realidade crescente. Entrevista especial com Assis Oliveira. *IHU-Online*, 1 April. Available at:

http://www.ihu.unisinos.br/entrevistas/518919-violencia-sexual-em-altamira-uma-r ealidade-crescente-entrevista-especial-com-assis-oliveira (Accessed: 8 January 2020).
Instituto Humanitas Unisinos (2013b). Boate Xingu: MPF/PA inicia investigação sobre exploração sexual em Belo Monte. *IHU-Online*, 19 February. Available at: http://www.ihu.unisinos.br/noticias/517747-boate-xingu-mpfpa-inicia-investigacao-sobre-exp loracao-sexual-em-belo-monte (Accessed: 8 January 2020).
Instituto Humanitas Unisinos (2016). Belo Monte e a proposição formal de participação. Entrevista especial com Maíra Borges Fainguelernt. *IHU-Online*, 26 June. Available at: http://www.ihu.unisinos.br/entrevistas/521268-belo-monte-e-a-proposicao-formal-d e-participacao-entrevista-especial-com-maira-borges (Accessed: 8 January 2020).
Instituto Socioambiental (2015a). *Dossiê Belo Monte: Não há condições para a Licença de Operação*. Brasilia. Available at: https://documentacao.socioambiental.org/noticias/a nexo_noticia/31046_20150701_170921.pdf.
Instituto Socioambiental (2015b). MPF denuncia ação etnocida e pede intervenção judicial em Belo Monte. *Instituto Socioambiental*, 11 December. Available at: https://www.socioambiental.org/pt-br/noticias-socioambientais/mpf-denuncia-acao-etnoc ida-e-pede-intervencao-judicial-em-belo-monte (Accessed: 30 March 2020).
Instituto Socioambiental (2018a). Em articulação inédita, ribeirinhos atingidos pela usina Belo Monte determinam os caminhos para retornarem ao seu território. *Instituto Socioambiental*, 17 December. Available at: https://medium.com/@socioambiental/ em-articulação-inédita-ribeirinhos-atingidos-pela-usina-belo-monte-determinam-os-caminhos-para-3743b8440973 (Accessed: 8 January 2020).
Instituto Socioambiental (2018b). Ribeirinhos atingidos por Belo Monte exigem retomar seu território. *Instituto Socioambiental*, 9 February. Available at https://www.socioamb iental.org/pt-br/noticias-socioambientais/ribeirinhos-atingidos-por-belo-monte-e xigem-retomar-seu-territorio (Accessed: 8 January 2020).
Inter-American Commission on Human Rights (2011). *Comuidades indigenas da Bacia do Rio Xingu, Pará (MC-382-10)*. Washington, DC: Inter-American Commission on Human Rights. Available at: http://www.xinguvivo.org.br/wp-content/uploads/201 0/10/Carta_otorgamiento_corregida_peticionario1.pdf.
International Energy Agency (2019a). *Renewables 2019*. Available at: https://www.iea .org/reports/renewables-2019/power#hydropower (Accessed: March 30, 2020).
International Energy Agency (2019b). *Sustainable Development Scenario – World Energy Model*. Available at: https://www.iea.org/reports/world-energy-model/sustainable-d evelopment-scenario (Accessed: March 30, 2020).
International Hydropower Association (2019). *2018 Hydropower Status Report*. London: International Hydropower Association.
International Rivers (2008). A knife in the water. *International Rivers*, 3 July. Available at: https://www.internationalrivers.org/blogs/232/a-knife-in-the-water (Accessed: 30 March 2020).
International Rivers (2009). Lula promises not to shove Belo Monte down our throats. *International Rivers*, 27 July. Available at: http://www.internationalrivers.org/blogs/232/ lula-promises-not-to-shove-belo-monte-down-our-throats (Accessed: 8 January 2020).
Irigaray, M (2014). Killing a people little by little: Belo Monte, human rights and the myth of clean energy. *Tipiti*, 12(2): 128–133.
Irigaray, M (2015). The Munduruku people: a living history of resistance. *Amazon Watch*, 30 April. Available at: https://amazonwatch.org/news/2015/0430-the-munduruku-pe ople-a-living-history-of-resistance (Accessed: 30 March 2020).

Isaacman, AF, and Isaacman, BS (2013). *Dams, Displacement and the Delusion of Development: Cahora Bassa and Its Legacies in Mozambique, 1965–2007*. Athens, OH: Ohio University Press.

Islar, M (2012). Privatised hydropower development in Turkey: a case of water grabbing? *Water Alternatives*, 5(2): 376–391.

Jensen-Cormier, S (2019). *Watered Down: How Do Big Hydropower Companies Adhere to Social and Environmental Policies and Best Practices?* Oakland, CA: International Rivers.

Jiang, X, Lua, D, Moran, E, Freitas Calvi, M, Vieira Dutra, L, and Li, G (2018). Examining impacts of the Belo Monte hydroelectric dam construction on land-cover changes using multitemporal Landsat imagery. *Applied Geography*, 97: 35–47.

Johnson, LB, Howell, JP, and Evered, KT (2015). "Where nothing was before": (re)producing population and place in Ghana's Volta River Project. *Journal of Cultural Geography*, 32(2): 195–213.

Jornal de Brasilia (2013). Índios e ribeirinhos voltam a ocupar Belo Monte. *Jornal de Brasilia*, 21 March. Available at: https://jornaldebrasilia.com.br/economia/indios-e-ribeirinhos-voltam-a-ocupar-belo-monte/ (Accessed: 8 January 2020).

Justiça Global, Justiça nos Trilhos, Sociedade Paraense de Direitos Humanos, Terra de Direitos, Instituto Socioambiental, Asociación Interamericana para la Defensa Del Ambiente, International Rivers (2014). *Situação do Direito ao Acesso à Justiça e a Suspensão de Decisões Judiciais (Ação de Suspensão de Segurança) no Brasil*. Washington, DC: International Rivers. Available at: https://www.internationalrivers.org/sites/default/files/attached-files/cidh_suspensao_seguranca_28mar2014.pdf.

Kaika, M (2003). Constructing scarcity and sensationalising water politics: 170 days that shook Athens. *Antipode*, 35(5): 919–954.

Keck, ME, and Sikkink, K (1998). *Activists beyond Borders: Advocacy Networks in International Politics*. Ithaca, NY: Cornell University Press.

Kenis, A, and Lievens, M (2014). Searching for "the political" in environmental politics. *Environmental Politics*, 23(4): 531–548.

Kenis, A, and Mathijs, E (2014). Climate change and post-politics: repoliticizing the present by imagining the future? *Geoforum*, 52: 148–156.

Khagram, S (2004). *Dams and Development: Transnational Struggles for Water and Power*. Ithaca, NY: Cornell University Press.

Kirchherr, J (2018). Strategies of successful anti-dam movements: evidence from Myanmar and Thailand. *Society and Natural Resources*, 31(2): 166–182.

Klein, PT (2015). Engaging the Brazilian state: the Belo Monte dam and the struggle for political voice. *Journal of Peasant Studies*, 42(6): 1137–1156.

Klingensmith, D (2007). *"One Valley and a Thousand": Dams, Nationalism and Development*. Oxford: Oxford University Press.

Kumar, A, Schei, T, Ahenkorah, A, Rodriguez, RC, Devernay, J-M, Freitas, M, Hall, D, Killingtveit, Å, and Liu, Z (2011). Hydropower. In: O. Edenhofer, R. Pichs-Madruga, Y. Sokona, K. Seyboth, P. Matschoss, S. Kadner, T. Zwickel, P. Eickemeier, G. Hansen, S. Schlömer, and C. von Stechow (eds) *IPCC Special Report on Renewable Energy Sources and Climate Change Mitigation*. Cambridge: Cambridge University Press.

Lakoff, G (2010). Why it matters how we frame the environment. *Environmental Communication*, 4(1): 70–81.

Lane, T (2015). Sustainable development goals: how does hydropower fit in? *International Hydropower Association*, 1 October. Available at: https://www.hydropower.org/blog/sustainable-development-goals-how-does-hydropower-fit-in (Accessed: March 30, 2020).

Latrubesse, EM, Arima, EY, Dunne, T, Park, E, Baker, VR, d'Horta, FM, Wight, C, Wittmann, F, Zuanon, J, Baker, PA, Ribas, CC, Norgaard, RB, Filizola, N, Ansar, A, Flyvbjerg, B, and Stevaux, JC (2017). Damming the rivers of the Amazon basin. *Nature*, 546(7658): 363–369.

le Mentec, K (2014). The Three Gorges Dam and the demiurges: the story of a failed contemporary myth elaboration in China. *Water History*, 6(4): 385–403.

Leach, M, Scoones, I, and Stirling, A (2010). *Dynamic Sustainabilities: Technology, Environment, Social Justice*. London: Earthscan.

Lees, AC, Peres, CA, Fearnside, PM, Schneider, M, and Zuanon, JAS (2016). Hydropower and the future of Amazonian biodiversity. *Biodiversity and Conservation*, 25(3): 451–466.

Leite, M, Amora, D, Kachani, M, de Almeida, L, and Machado, R (2013). A batalha de Belo Monte. *Folha de. S. Paulo*, 16 December. Available at: https://arte.folha.uol.com.br/especiais/2013/12/16/belo-monte/ (Accessed: 30 March 2020).

Lessa, ACR, Santos, MA, Maddock, JEL, and dos Santos Bezerra, C (2015). Emissions of greenhouse gases in terrestrial areas pre-existing to hydroelectric plant reservoirs in the Amazon: the case of Belo Monte hydroelectric plant. *Renewable and Sustainable Energy Reviews*, 51(C): 1728–1736.

Li, F (2015). *Unearthing Conflict: Corporate Mining, Activism and Expertise in Peru*. Durham, NC: Duke University Press.

Li, TM (2007). *The Will to Improve: Governmentality, Development and the Practice of Politics*. Durham, NC: Duke University Press.

Lima, LH, and Magrini, A (2010). The Brazilian Audit Tribunal's role in improving the federal environmental licensing process. *Environmental Impact Assessment Review*, 30(2): 108–115.

Linton, J, and Budds, J (2013). The hydrosocial cycle: defining and mobilizing a relational-dialectical approach to water. *Geoforum*, 57: 170–180.

Lopes, C (2011). *Diário da Câmara dos Deputados, ANO LXVI No 060 (13/04/2011)*. Brasilia: Câmara dos Deputados.

Lopes, RJ (2017). Novas hidreletricas na Amazonia poden prejudicar clima e ecossistemas. *Folha de S.Paulo*, 14 June. Available at: http://www1.folha.uol.com.br/ambiente/2017/06/1892979-novas-hidreletricas-na-amazonia-podem-prejudicar-clima-e-ecossistemas.shtml (Accessed: 8 January 2020).

Lopez-Gunn, E (2009). Agua para todos: a new regionalist hydraulic paradigm in Spain. *Water Alternatives*, 2(3): 370–394.

Lopez-Gunn, E, Zorrilla, P, Prieto, F, and Llamas, MR (2012). Lost in translation? Water efficiency in Spanish agriculture. *Agricultural Water Management*, 108: 83–95.

Loureiro, PM, and Saad-Filho, A (2018). The limits of pragmatism: the rise and fall of the Brazilian Workers' Party (2002–2016). *Latin American Perspectives*, 46(1): 66–84.

Loures, R (2018). The Karodaybi Government and its invincible warriors: the Munduruku Ipereğ Ayũ Movement versus large construction projects in the Amazon. *Vibrant: Virtual Brazilian Anthropology*, 15(2): 1–23.

Madeiro, C (2017). Após Belo Monte, Altamira (PA) supera taxa de homicídios de país mais violento do mundo. *IHU-Unisinos*, 6th March. Available at: http://www.ihu.unisinos.br/186-noticias/noticias-2017/565448-apos-belo-monte-altamira-pa-supera-taxa-de-homicidios-de-pais-mais-violento-do-mundo (Accessed: 19 March 2019).

Magalhães, SB, and Carneiro da Cunha, M (2017). *A Expulsão de Ribeirinhos em Belo Monte*. São Paulo. Sociedade Brasileira para o Progresso da Ciência: São Paulo. Available at: http://portal.sbpcnet.org.br/livro/belomonte.pdf.

Magalhães, SM, and Hernandez, FdM (eds) (2009). *Painel de Especialistas - Análise Crítica do Estudo de Impacto Ambiental do Aproveitamento Hidrelétrico de Belo Monte*. Belém, PA: Painel de Especialistas. Available at: https://www.socioambiental.org/banco_ima gens/pdfs/Belo_Monte_Painel_especialistas_EIA.pdf.
Maisonnave, F (2019). Em "dia do fogo", sul do PA registra disparo no número de queimadas. *Folha de S. Paulo*, 14 August. Available at: https://www1.folha.uol.com.br/ ambiente/2019/08/em-dia-do-fogo-sul-do-pa-registra-disparo-no-numero-de-queimada s.shtml (Accessed: 6 April 2020).
Manibeli Declaration (1994). Manibeli declaration calling for a moratorium on world bank funding of large dams. https://www.internationalrivers.org/resources/manibeli-declaration-4334 (Accessed: 30 March 2020).
Marcelino, AA, Santos, MA, Xavier, VL, Bezerra, CS, Silva, CRO, Amorim, MA, and Rodrigues, RP (2015). Emissões difusivas de metano e de dióxido de carbono oriundas de dois reservatórios hidrelétricos. *Brazilian Journal of Biology*, 75(2): 331–338.
Marin, REA, and da Costa Oliveira, A (2016). Violence and public health in the Altamira region: the construction of the Belo Monte hydroelectric plant. *Regions and Cohesion*, 6(1): 116–134.
Marino, A (2012). "The cost of dams": acts of writing as resistance in postcolonial India. *Citizenship Studies*, 16(5–6): 705–719.
Marques, A, and Rocha, L (2015). Bolsonaro diz que OAB só defende bandido e reserva indígena é um crime. *Campo Grande News*, 22 April. Available at: https://www.cam pograndenews.com.br/politica/bolsonaro-diz-que-oab-so-defende-bandido-e-reserva-indigena-e-um-crime (Accessed: 6 April 2020).
Marsiglia, I (2013). O futuro que passou. *O Estado de S. Paulo*, 22 June. Available at: https ://www.estadao.com.br/noticias/geral,o-futuro-que-passou,1045705 (Accessed: 10 July 2018).
Martello, A (2015). BC sobe juro para 14,25% ao ano e indica manutenção no futuro. *G1*, 29 July. Available at: http://g1.globo.com/economia/noticia/2015/07/na-7-alta-seguida-juro-sobe-para-1425-ao-ano-maior-nivel-desde-2006.html (Accessed: 6 April 2020).
Martinez-Alier, J, Temper, L, del Bene, D, and Scheidel, A (2016). Is there a global environmental justice movement? *The Journal of Peasant Studies*, 43(3): 731–755.
Matoso, F (2015). Governo Dilma tem aprovação de 9%, aponta pesquisa Ibope. *G1*, 1 July. Available at: https://web.archive.org/web/20170108192305/http://g1.http:// globo.com/politica/noticia/2015/07/governo-dilma-tem-aprovacao-de-9-aponta-pesqu isa-ibope.html (Accessed: 8 January 2020).
Matthews, N (2012). Water grabbing in the Mekong basin – an analysis of the winners and losers of Thailand's hydropower development in Lao PDR. *Water Alternatives*, 5(2): 392–411.
Mazui, G (2019). Presidente do Ibama se demite após ministro questionar contrato de aluguel de caminhonetes. *G1*, 7 January Available at: https://g1.globo.com/politica/ noticia/2019/01/07/presidente-do-ibama-pede-exoneracao-depois-de-ministro-questi onar-contrato-de-aluguel-de-carros.ghtml (Accessed: 6 April 2020).
McAllister, LK (2008). *Making Law Matter: Environmental Protection and Legal Institutions in Brazil*. Redwood City, CA: Stanford University Press.
McCartney, M (2009). Living with dams: managing the environmental impacts. *Water Policy*, 11(1): 121–139.
McCormick, S (2006). The Brazilian anti-dam movement: knowledge contestation as communicative action. *Organization and Environment*, 19(3): 321–346.

McCormick, S (2010). Damming the Amazon: local movements and transnational struggles over water. *Society and Natural Resources*, 24(1): 34–48.

McCully, P (1996). *Silenced Rivers: The Ecology and Politics of Large Dams*. London: Zed Books.

McDonald, K, Bosshard, P, and Brewer, N (2009). Exporting dams: China's hydropower industry goes global. *Journal of Environmental Management*, 90(3) Supplement 3: 294–302.

Members of the Pariri Indigenous Association and Ipereğ Ayũ Movement (2017). A government of death is plundering our ancient Munduruku lands. Help us stop it. *The Guardian*, 25 April. Available at: https://www.theguardian.com/global-developmen t/2017/apr/25/a-government-of-death-is-plundering-our-ancient-munduruku-lands-he lp-us-stop-it-brazil-amazon (Accessed: 30 March 2020).

Mendes, K (2019). Brazil's Congress reverses Bolsonaro, restores Funai's land demarcation powers. *Mongabay*, 5 June. Available at: https://news.mongabay.com/2019/06/brazil s-congress-reverses-bolsonaro-restores-funais-land-demarcation-powers/ (Accessed: 6 April 2020).

Menga, F (2015). Building a nation through a dam: the case of Rogun in Tajikistan. *Nationalities Papers*, 43(3): 479–494.

Menga, F (2017). Hydropolis: reinterpreting the polis in water politics. *Political Geography*, 60: 100–109.

Menga, F, and Swyngedouw, E (2018). *Water, Technology and the Nation-State*. Abingdon: Routledge.

Merme, V, Ahlers, R, and Gupta, J (2014). Private equity, public affair: hydropower financing in the Mekong Basin. *Global Environmental Change*, 24(1): 20–29.

Middleton, C, Grundy-Warr, C, and Yong, ML (2013). Neoliberalizing hydropower in the Mekong basin: the political economy of partial enclosure. *Social Science Journal*, 43(2): 299–334.

Miescher, SF (2014). "Nkrumah's Baby": the Akosombo Dam and the dream of development in Ghana, 1952–1966. *Water History*, 6(4): 341–366.

Millikan, B (2014). The Amazon: dirty dams, dirty politics and the myth of clean energy. *Tipití: Journal of the Society for the Anthropology of Lowland South America*, 12(2): 134–138.

Ministério de Minas e Energia and Empresa de Pesquisa Energética (2007). *Plano Nacional de Energia 2030*. Brasil: Ministério de Mines e Energia.

Ministério do Meio Ambiente (2012). Meio ambiente: Brasileiro está mais consciente. *Ministério do Meio Ambiente*, 6 June. Available at: https://www.mma.gov.br/informm a/item/8386-o-que-o-brasileiro-pensa-do-meio-ambiente-e-do-consumo-sustent% C3%A1vel (Accessed: March 30, 2020).

Ministério Público Federal (2019). MPF recomenda correção da licença de Belo Monte para preservar a vida na Volta Grande do Xingu (PA). *Ministério Público Federal*, 4 September. Available at: http://www.mpf.mp.br/pa/sala-de-imprensa/noticias-pa/mp f-recomenda-correcao-da-licenca-de-belo-monte-para-preservar-a-vida-na-volta-gra nde-do-xingu-pa (Accessed: 8 January 2020).

Ministério Público Federal, Procuradoria da República no Pará (2014). Indígenas denunciam agressões no canteiro de Belo Monte. *Ministério Público Federal*, 26 May. Available at: http://www.mpf.mp.br/pa/sala-de-imprensa/noticias-pa/indigenas-de nunciam-agressoes-no-canteiro-de-belo-monte (Accessed: 8 January 2020).

Ministério Público Federal, Procuradoria da República no Pará (2015). *Relatório de Inspeção Interinstitucional: Áreas ribeirinhas atingidas pelo processo de remoção compulsória da UHE Belo Monte*. MPF/PA: Altamira. Available at: http://pfdc.pgr.mpf.mp.br/tema

s-de-atuacao/populacao-atingida-pelas-barragens/relatorios/relatorio-inspecao-interin stitucional-belo-monte (Accessed: 8 January 2020).
Ministério Público Federal, Procuradoria da República no Pará (2016). Em Santarém (PA), mais de 500 pessoas debatem usinas, mas governo não manda representante. *MPF/PA*, 29 January. Available at: http://www.mpf.mp.br/pa/sala-de-imprensa/noti cias-pa/em-santarem-mais-de-500-pessoas-debatem-usinas-mas-governo-nao-mand a-representante (Accessed: 8 January 2020).
Ministério Público Federal, Procuradoria da República no Pará (2017). Ribeirinhos expulsos por Belo Monte apresentam lista de moradores que devem voltar ao Xingu. *MPF/PA*, 21 March. Available at: http://www.mpf.mp.br/pa/sala-de-imprensa/noti cias-pa/ribeirinhos-expulsos-por-belo-monte-apresentam-lista-de-moradores-que-de vem-voltar-ao-xingu (Accessed: 30 March 2020).
Mobilização Nacional Indígena (2017a). Festa indígena na Esplanada dos Ministérios. *Mobilização Nacional Indígena*, 27 April. Available at: https://mobilizacaonacion alindigena.wordpress.com/2017/04/27/festa-indigena-na-esplanada-dos-ministerios/ (Accessed: 6 April 2020).
Mobilização Nacional Indígena (2017b). O maior Acampamento Terra Livre da história! *Mobilização Nacional Indígena*, 28 April. Available at: https://mobilizacaonacion alindigena.wordpress.com/2017/04/28/o-maior-acampamento-terra-livre-da-historia/ (Accessed: 6 April 2020).
Mobilização Nacional Indígena (2017c). Protesto pacífico de povos indígenas é atacado pela polícia no Congresso. *Mobilização Nacional Indígena*, 25 April. Available at: https ://mobilizacaonacionalindigena.wordpress.com/2017/04/25/protesto-pacifico-de-pov os-indigenas-e-atacado-pela-policia-na-frente-do-congresso/ (Accessed: 6 April 2020).
Mohamud, M, and Verhoeven, H (2016). Re-engineering the state, awakening the nation: dams, Islamist modernity and nationalist politics in Sudan. *Water Alternatives*, 8(2): 182–202.
Mongabay (2011). Brazil's environment chief resigns over controversial Amazon dam. *Mongabay*, 14 January. Available at: https://news.mongabay.com/2011/01/brazils-env ironment-chief-resigns-over-controversial-amazon-dam/ (Accessed: 9 January 2020).
Monteiro, T (2016). Lula, Belo Monte e a Lava Jato II. *Telma Monteiro Blog*, 19 September. Available at: https://www.telmadmonteiro.com/2016/09/lula-belo-monte-e-lava-jat o-ii.html (Accessed: 8 January 2020).
Montero, AP (2014). *Brazil: Reversal of Fortune*. Cambridge: Polity Press.
Molle, F (2008). Nirvana concepts, narratives and policy models: insight from the water sector. *Water Alternatives*, 1(1): 131–156.
Molle, F, Mollinga, P, and Wester, P (2009). Hydraulic bureaucracies and the hydraulic mission: flows of water, flows of power. *Water Alternatives*, 2(3): 328–349.
Moore, D, Dore, J, and Gyawali, D (2010). The World Commission on Dams + 10: revisiting the large dam controversy. *Water Alternatives*, 3(2): 3–13.
Morais, H (2016). Militante social desaparecida foi assassinada a tiros em Rondônia. *G1*, 15 January. Available at: http://g1.globo.com/ro/rondonia/noticia/2016/01/militan te-social-desaparecida-foi-assassinada-tiros-em-rondonia.html (Accessed: 30 March 2020).
Mossallam, A (2014). We are the ones who made this dam 'High'!" A builders' history of the Aswan High Dam. *Water History*, 6(4): 297–314.
Movimento dos Atingidos por Barragens (2012). Índios e pescadores ocupam Belo Monte. *Movimento Dos Atingidos Por Barragens*, 9 October. Available at: http://www.mabn

acional.org.br/noticia/ndios-e-pescadores-ocupam-belo-monte (Accessed: 30 March 2020).

Movimento dos Atingidos por Barragens (2013). MAB denuncia exploração sexual em áreas de barragens. *Movimento dos Atingidos por Barragens*, 20 March. Available at: http://www.mabnacional.org.br/noticia/mab-denuncia-explora-sexual-em-reas-barragens (Accessed: 8 January 2020).

Movimento dos Atingidos por Barragens (2014a). Lula, Dilma e o Cavalo de pau. *Movimento dos Atingidos por Barragens*, 22 April. Available at: http://www.mabnacional.org.br/noticia/lula-dilma-e-cavalo-pau (Accessed: 8 January 2020).

Movimento dos Atingidos por Barragens (2014b). Ribeirinhos reafirmam não às barragens no Tapajós. *Movimento Dos Atinigos Por Barragens*, 7 May. Available at: http://www.mabnacional.org.br/noticia/ribeirinhos-reafirmam-n-s-barragens-no-tapaj-s (Accessed: 30 March 2020).

Movimento dos Atingidos por Barragens (2015). Indígenas bloqueiam acesso à canteiro de Belo Monte. *Movimento Dos Atingidos Por Barragens*, 11 January. Available at: http://www.mabnacional.org.br/noticia/ind-genas-bloqueiam-acesso-canteiro-belo-monte (Accessed: 30 March 2020).

Movimento dos Atingidos por Barragens (2016). Agricultores ocupam Incra para exigir reassentamento. *Movimento Dos Atingidos Por Barragens*, 22 April. Available at: http://mabnacional.org.br/noticia/agricultores-ocupam-incra-para-exigir-reassentamento (Accessed: 30 March 2020).

Movimento dos Atingidos por Barragens (2017a). Belo Monte faz de Altamira o município mais violento do Brasil. *Movimento dos Atingidos por Barragens*, 6 June. Available at: http://mabnacional.org.br/noticia/belo-monte-faz-altamira-munic-pio-mais-violento-do-brasil (Accessed: 19 March 2019).

Movimento dos Atingidos por Barragens (2017b). Por uma convivência sustentável com a Amazônia. *Movimento dos Atingidos por Barragens*, 2 August. Available at: http://www.mabnacional.org.br/noticia/por-uma-conviv-ncia-sustent-vel-com-amaz-nia (Accessed: 30 March 2020).

Movimento dos Atingidos por Barragens (2017c). Tapajós: Vencemos uma batalha, mas a guerra está só começando. *Movimento dos Atingidos por Barragens*, 18 January. Available at: https://www.mabnacional.org.br/noticia/tapaj-s-vencemos-uma-batalha-mas-guerra-est-s-come-ando (Accessed: 6 April 2020).

Movimento dos Atingidos por Barragens (2018). Inundação deixa atingidos por Belo Monte desabrigados. *Movimento dos Atingidos por Barragens*, 30 November. Available at: https://www.mabnacional.org.br/noticia/inunda-deixa-atingidos-por-belo-monte-desabrigados (Accessed: 8 January 2020).

Movimento dos Atingidos por Barragens (2019). Conquista: Norte Energia vai refazer vistoria no entorno da Lagoa em Altamira. *Movimento dos Atingidos por Barragens*, 19 March. Available at: https://www.mabnacional.org.br/noticia/conquista-norte-energia-vai-refazer-vistoria-no-entorno-da-lagoa-em-altamira (Accessed: 8 January 2020).

Movimento Xingu Vivo para Sempre (MXVPS) (2010). *Letter to Secretary of Development, Science and Technology of the State of Pará*. Translated by Survival International. Available at: http://assets.survivalinternational.org/documents/406/SEDEC_letter_English.pdf (Accessed: 23 July 2020).

MXVPS (2011). Com Belo Monte, violência sexual contra criança e adolescente cresce 138%. *Xingu Vivo para Sempre*, 11 October. Available at: http://www.xinguvivo.org.

br/2011/10/11/com-belo-monte-violencia-sexual-contra-crianca-e-adolescente-cresce-138/ (Accessed: 8 January 2020).
MXVPS (2014a). Xingu Vivo, No 50º aniversário do Golpe, ação pede condenação da Abin e de Belo Monte por espionagem. *Xingu Vivo para Sempre*, 1 April. Available at: http://www.xinguvivo.org.br/2014/04/01/no-50o-aniversario-do-golpe-acao-pede-condenacao-da-abin-e-de-belo-monte-por-espionagem/ (Accessed: 9 January 2020).
MXVPS (2014b). Leilão da usina de São Luiz do Tapajós: o governo mentiu para os Munduruku. *Xingu Vivo Para Sempre*, 14 September. Available at: https://xinguvivo.org.br/2014/09/14/leilao-da-usina-de-sao-luiz-do-tapajos-o-governo-mentiu-para-os-munduruku/ (Accessed: 30 March 2020).
MXVPS (2016). Fazem com você o que você fez conosco; mas nem assim, Dilma. *Xingu Vivo para Sempre*, 5 May. Available at: https://xinguvivo.org.br/2016/05/05/fazem-com-voce-o-que-voce-fez-conosco-mas-nem-assim-dilma/ (Accessed: 30 March 2020).
MXVPS (2019). Norte Energia descumpre acordos e provoca morte de ribeirinhos, denuncia Conselho. *Xingu Vivo para Sempre*, 21 May. Available at: http://www.xinguvivo.org.br/2019/05/21/norte-energia-descumpre-acordos-e-provoca-morte-de-ribeirinhos-denuncia-conselho/ (Accessed: 8 January 2020).
MXVPS (n.d.). *Belo 'Monstro' Não!* Altamira: MXVPS. Available at: http://assets.survivalinternational.org/documents/267/Xingu_Vivo_para_Sempre_panfle%0Ato.pdf.
Mouffe, C (1993). *The Return of the Political*. London: Verso.
Mouffe, C (2000). *The Democratic Paradox*. London: Verso.
Mouffe, C (2005). *On the Political*. London: Verso.
Mouffe, C (2013). *Agonistics: Thinking the World Politically*. London: Verso.
Murton, G, Lord, A, and Beazley, R (2016). A handshake across the Himalayas: Chinese investment, hydropower development, and state formation in Nepal. *Eurasian Geography and Economics*, 57(3): 403–432.
Nascimento, L (2015). Governo vai reduzir R$ 4,8 bilhões do Programa Minha Casa, Minha Vida. *Agencia Brasil*, 14 September. Available at: http://agenciabrasil.ebc.com.br/economia/noticia/2015-09/governo-vai-reduzir-r-48-bilhoes-do-programa-minha-casa-minha-vida (Accessed: 9 January 2020).
Nascimento, S (2015). Antônia Melo, liderança do Movimento Xingu Vivo para Sempre. *DR*, Issue 2. Available at: http://www.revistadr.com.br/posts/antonia-melo-lideranca-do-movimento-xingu-vivo-para-sempre (Accessed: 8 January 2020).
Nathan Green, W, and Baird, IG (2016). Capitalizing on compensation: hydropower resettlement and the commodification and decommodification of nature-society relations in Southern Laos. *Annals of the American Association of Geographers*, 106(4): 853–873.
Nelsen, A (2018). Indigenous leader urges EU to impose sanctions on Brazil. *The Guardian*, 18 December. Available at: https://www.theguardian.com/world/2018/dec/18/indigenous-leader-urges-eu-to-impose-sanctions-on-brazil (Accessed: 6 April 2020).
Nery, N (2011). Dilma retalia OEA por Belo Monte e suspende recursos. *Folha de S.Paulo*, 30 April. Available at: https://www1.folha.uol.com.br/fsp/mercado/me3004201117.htm (Accessed: 8 January 2020).
Neville, KJ, and Weinthal, E (2016). Scaling up site disputes: strategies to redefine 'local' in the fight against fracking. *Environmental Politics*, 25(4): 569–592.
Nilsson, C, Reidy, CA, Dynesius, M, and Revenga, C (2005). Fragmentation and flow regulation of the world's large river systems. *Science*, 308(5720): 405.
Nitta, R, and Naka, LN (2015). *Barragens do Rio Tapajós: Uma Avaliação Crítica do Estudo e Relatório de Impacto Ambiental (EIA/RIMA) do Aproveitamento Hidrelétrico São Luiz do*

Tapajós. São Paulo: Greenpeace Brasil. Available at: http://greenpeace.org.br/tapajos/docs/analise-eia-rima.pdf (Accessed: 30 March 2020).

Nixon, R (2011). *Slow Violence and the Environmentalism of the Poor*. Cambridge, MA: Harvard University Press.

Nogueira, LA (2017). A Lava Jato está corroendo o PIB. E daí? *Istoé Dinheiro*, 2 June. Available at: https://www.istoedinheiro.com.br/lava-jato-esta-corroendo-o-pib-e-dai/ (Accessed: 6 April 2020).

Norte Energia (2019). Belo Monte é inaugurada e está pronta para a plena operação. *Norte Energia*, 29 November. Available at: https://www.norteenergiasa.com.br/pt-br/imprensa/releases/belo-monte-e-inaugurada-e-esta-pronta-para-a-plena-operacao-100709 (Accessed: 6 April 2020).

Norte Energia (2020). Belo Monte. *Norte Energia*. https://www.norteenergiasa.com.br/pt-br/ (Accessed: 30 March 2020).

Nunes, J, and Peña, AM (2015). Marina Silva and the rise of sustainability in Brazil. *Environmental Politics*, 24(3): 506–511.

O'Faircheallaigh, C (2007). Environmental agreements, EIA follow-up and aboriginal participation in environmental management: the Canadian experience. *Environmental Impact Assessment Review*, 27(4): 319–342.

O'Faircheallaigh, C (2010). Public participation and environmental impact assessment: purposes, implications, and lessons for public policy making. *Environmental Impact Assessment Review*, 30(1): 19–27.

O Globo (2017). Odebrecht só fez Belo Monte e Itaquerão por pedido de Lula a Emílio. *O Globo*, 1 May. Available at: https://oglobo.globo.com/brasil/odebrecht-so-fez-belo-monte-itaquerao-por-pedido-de-lula-emilio-21279782 (Accessed: 8 January 2020).

Oliveira, M (2011). Posição da OEA sobre Belo Monte é 'absurda', diz subcomissão do Senado. *G1*, 5 April. Available at: http://g1.globo.com/politica/noticia/2011/04/posicao-da-oea-sobre-belo-monte-e-absurda-diz-subcomissao-do-senado.html (Accessed: 8 January 2020).

Ostrom, E (2008). The challenge of common-pool resources. *Environment: Science and Policy for Sustainable Development*, 50(4): 8–21.

Oswald, V, and Tavares, M (2012). País não se intimida com pressão contra Belo Monte, diz Lobão. *Jornal O Globo*, 2 January. Available at: https://oglobo.globo.com/economia/pais-nao-se-intimida-com-pressao-contra-belo-monte-diz-lobao-3555541 (Accessed: 30 March 2020).

Ottmann, G (2005). What is the PT? Brazil's Workers Party (PT) between formal representative and participatory democracy. *Journal of Iberian and Latin American Research*, 11(2): 93–102.

Ozen, H (2014). Overcoming environmental challenges by antagonizing environmental protesters: the Turkish Government discourse against anti-hydroelectric power plants movements. *Environmental Communication*, 8(4): 433–451.

Pace, CA (2018). *Ripple Effects of the Belo Monte Dam: A Syndemic Approach to Addressing Health Impacts for the Downstream Community of Gurupá*. Thesis submitted to Department of Anthropology, University of South Florida.

Paiva, FM (2018). Diante de Bolsonaro, movimentos sociais preparam a resistência. *Instituto Humanitas Unisinos*, 7 November. Available at: http://www.ihu.unisinos.br/188-noticias/noticias-2018/584451-diante-de-bolsonaro-movimentos-sociais-preparam-a-resistencia (Accessed: 6 April 2020).

Palit, C (2003). Monsoon risings. *New Left Review*, 21: 80–100.

Park, CC (2002). *Tropical Rainforests*. Abingdon: Routledge.

Parracho, L (2012). Com obras de Belo Monte, Altamira enfrenta insegurança e alta de preços. *Terra*, 27 March. Available at: https://istoe.com.br/196393_COM+OBRAS+DE+BELO+MONTE+ALTAMIRA+ENFRENTA+INSEGURANCA+E+ALTA+DE+PRECOS/ (Accessed: 8 January 2020).

Partido dos Trabalhadores (PT) (2014). Norte Energia desmente Marina e investe R$ 1,2 bi em projetos de compensação. *Partido dos Trabalhadores*, 16 September. Available at: https://pt.org.br/norte-energia-desmente-marina-e-investe-r-12-bi-em-projetos-de-compensacao/ (Accessed: 14 March 2020).

Pedruzzi, P (2012). Centenas de desempregados dormem nas ruas de Altamira à espera de vagas em Belo Monte. *Agencia Brasil*, 18 April. Available at: http://memoria.ebc.com.br/agenciabrasil/noticia/2012-04-18/centenas-de-desempregados-dormem-nas-ruas-de-altamira-espera-de-vagas-em-belo-monte (Accessed: 8 January 2020).

Peluso, NL (1995). Whose forests are these? Territories in Kalimantan, counter-mapping forest Indonesia. *Antipode*, 274: 383–406.

Pepermans, Y, and Maeseele, P (2014). Democratic debate and mediated discourses on climate change: from consensus to de/politicization. *Environmental Communication*, 8(2): 216–232.

Peron, I, Zaia, C, and Brigatto, G (2019). Presidente do Ibama pede demissão após críticas de Bolsonaro e Salles. *Valor Econômico*, 7 January. Available at: https://valor.globo.com/politica/noticia/2019/01/07/presidente-do-ibama-pede-demissao-apos-criticas-de-bolsonaro-e-salles.ghtml (Accessed: 6 April 2020).

Pinho, VA, and Oliveira Costa, A (2012). *Rodas de Direito: Diálogo, Empoderamento e Prevenção Não Enfrentamento da Humano Sexual Contra Crianças e Adolescentes*. Altamira, PA: Universidade Federal do Pará. Available at: http://pair.ledes.net/gestor/titan.php?target=openFile&fileId=1000.

Pinto, K (2016). Em dia de visita de Dilma, grupo fecha único acesso a Belo Monte. *Folha de S.Paulo*, 5 May. Available at: https://www1.folha.uol.com.br/paywall/login.shtml?https://www1.http://folha.uol.com.br/poder/2016/05/1768004-em-dia-de-visita-de-dilma-grupo-fecha-unico-acesso-a-belo-monte-no-para.shtml (Accessed: 8 January 2020).

Poirier, C (2010). Letter to President Luiz Inácio Lula da Silva. *Comité Pour Les Droits Humains En Amérique Latine*, 12 March. Available at: https://www.cdhal.org/open-letter-against-belo-monte-hydroelectric-dam-project-xingu-river-brazil/ (Accessed: 8 January 2020).

Poirier, C (2016). Victory on Brazil's Tapajós River and the battle that lies ahead. *Amazon Watch*, 9 August. Available at: https://amazonwatch.org/news/2016/0809-victory-on-brazils-tapajos-river-and-the-battle-that-lies-ahead (Accessed: 6 April 2020).

Poirier, C (2017). Toxic mega-mine looms over Belo Monte's affected communities. *Amazon Watch*, 4 April. Available at: https://amazonwatch.org/news/2017/0404-toxic-mega-mine-looms-over-belo-montes-affected-communities (Accessed: 30 March 2020).

Pontes, N (2016). Índios travam "guerra moderna" contra hidrelétricas no Tapajós. *Deutsche Welle*, 12 July. Available at: https://www.dw.com/pt-br/%C3%ADndios-travam-guerra-moderna-contra-hidrel%C3%A9tricas-no-tapaj%C3%B3s/a-19394652 (Accessed: 30 March 2020).

Pontes Jr, F (2011). Speaking at À margem do Xingu: Vozes não consideradas, 2011. *Rede Brasil Atual*, 15 September. Available at: https://www.redebrasilatual.com.br/ambiente/2011/09/projeto-da-ditadura-militar-belo-monte-significa-o-mesmo-retrocesso-de-30-anos-atras/ (Accessed: 8 January 2020).

Power, ME., Dietrich, WE, and Finlay, JC (1996). Dams and downstream aquatic biodiversity: potential food web consequences of hydrologic and geomorphic change. *Environmental Management*, 20(6): 887–895.

Puzone, V, and Miguel, LS (eds) (2019). *The Brazilian Left in the 21st Century: Conflict and Conciliation in Peripheral Capitalism*. London: Palgrave Macmillan.

Raco, M (2014). The post-politics of sustainability planning: privatisation and the demise of democratic government. In: Wilson, J, and Swyngedouw, E (eds) *The Post-political and Its Discontents: Spaces of Depoliticisation, Spectres of Radical Politics*. Cambridge: Cambridge University Press.

Radkau, J (2008). *Nature and Power: A Global History of the Environment*. Cambridge: Cambridge University Press.

Ramos, AR (1998). *Indigenism: Ethnic Politics in Brazil*. Madison, WI: University of Wisconsin Press.

Randell, H (2016). The short-term impacts of development-induced displacement on wealth and subjective well-being in the Brazilian Amazon. *World Development*, 87: 385–400.

Rangan, H (2000). *Of Myths and Movements*. London: Verso.

Redclift, M (2005). Sustainable development (1987–2005): an oxymoron comes of age. *Sustainable Development*, 13(4): 212–227.

Resk, SS (2017). Povo Munduruku defende patrimônio espiritual indígena. *Instituto Centro de Vida*, 30 August. Available at: https://www.icv.org.br/2017/08/povo-munduruku-defende-patrimonio-espiritual-indigena/ (Accessed: 30 March 2020).

Reuters (2009). China says Three Gorges Dam cost $37 billion. *Reuters*, 14 September. Available at: https://www.reuters.com/article/idUSPEK84588 (Accessed: March 30, 2020).

Reuters (2015). Brazil's Vale concludes sale of 49 pct stake in Belo Monte dam. *Reuters*, 1 April. Available at: https://www.reuters.com/article/vale-cemig-belo-monte-idUSE6N0T70B120150401 (Accessed: 30 March 2020).

Reuters (2016). Rousseff benefited from Belo Monte dam graft: report. *Reuters*, 12 March. Available at: https://www.reuters.com/article/us-brazil-corruption-belomonte/brazils-rousseff-benefited-from-belo-monte-dam-graft-report-idUSKCN0WE04U (Accessed: 8 January 2020).

Revkin, Andrew (1990). *The Burning Season: The Murder of Chico Mendes and the Fight for the Amazon Rainforest*. New York: Collins.

Ribeiro, AP, and Zimmermann, P (2007). Com PAC, governo espera investimento de R$ 504 bi até 2010. *Folha de S.Paulo*, 22 January. Available at: https://www1.folha.uol.com.br/folha/dinheiro/ult91u113888.shtml (Accessed: 30 March 2020).

Ribeiro, PF (2014). An amphibian party? Organisational change and adaptation in the Brazilian Workers' Party, 1980–2012. *Journal of Latin American Studies*, 46(1): 87–119.

Riethof, M (2017). The international human rights discourse as a strategic focus in socio-environmental conflicts: the case of hydro-electric dams in Brazil. *International Journal of Human Rights*, 21(4): 482–499.

Ritter, CD, McCrate. Nilsson, RH, Fearnside, PM, Palme, U, and Antonelli, A (2017). Environmental impact assessment in Brazilian Amazonia: challenges and prospects to assess biodiversity. *Biological Conservation*, 206: 161–168.

Rocha, B, and Millikan, B (2013). Brazil: Operation Tapajós suspended. *International Rivers*, 18 April. Available at: https://www.internationalrivers.org/resources/brazil-operation-tapaj%C3%B3s-suspended-7932 (Accessed: 30 March 2020).

Rocha, J (2019). Bolsonaro government reveals plan to develop the 'Unproductive Amazon'. *Mongabay*. 28 January. Available at: https://news.mongabay.com/2019/01/

bolsonaro-government-reveals-plan-to-develop-the-unproductive-amazon/ (Accessed: 6 April 2020).
Roosevelt, AC, Lima da Costa, M, Lopes Machado, C, Michab, M, Mercier, N, Valladas, H, Feathers, J, Barnett, W, Imazio da Silveira, M, Henderson, A, Sliva, J, Chernoff, B, Reese, DS, Holman, JA, Toth, N, and Schick, K (1996). Paleoindian cave dwellers in the Amazon: the peopling of the Americas. *Science*, 272(5260): 373–384.
Rootes, C (1999). Environmental movements: from the local to the global. *Environmental Politics*, 8(1): 1–12.
Rosa, G (2015). A política munduruku. *Reporter Brasil*, 21 December. Available at: https:// reporterbrasil.org.br/2015/12/a-politica-munduruku/ (Accessed: 30 March 2020).
Rothman, FD (2001). A comparative study of dam-resistance campaigns and environmental policy in Brazil. *Journal of Environment and Development*, 10(4): 317–344.
Rothman, FD, and Oliver, P (1999). From local to global: the anti-dam movement in Southern Brazil, 1979–1992. *Mobilization: An International Quarterly*, 4(1): 41–57.
Routledge, P (2003). Voices of the dammed: discursive resistance amidst erasure in the Narmada Valley, India. *Political Geography*, 22(3): 243–270.
Saad-Filho, A (2013). Mass protests under "left neoliberalism": Brazil, June-July 2013. *Critical Sociology*, 39(5): 657–669.
Sadi, A (2019). Depois de Brumadinho, ministro do Meio Ambiente defende discussão da lei de licenciamento ambiental. *G1*, 28 January. Available at: https://g1.globo.com /politica/blog/andreia-sadi/post/2019/01/28/depois-de-brumadinho-ministro-do-mei o-ambiente-defende-discussao-da-lei-de-licenciamento-ambiental.ghtml (Accessed: 6 April 2020).
Sakamoto, L (2016). Belo Monte: Antes de denúncias de corrupção, um crime contra a humanidade. *Blog do Sakamoto*, 12 March. Available at: https://blogdosakamoto.bl ogosfera.uol.com.br/2016/03/12/belo-monte-antes-de-denuncias-de-corrupcao-um-cri me-contra-a-humanidade/ (Accessed: 8 January 2020).
Sales, C, and Uhlig, A (2016). Ignorância ou má fé sobre as hidrelétricas em terra indígena. *Valor Econômico*, 14 September. Available at: https://valor.globo.com/opiniao/col una/ignorancia-ou-ma-fe-sobre-as-hidreletricas-em-terra-indigena.ghtml (Accessed: 6 April 2020).
Salisbury, C (2017). International action a must to stop irreversible harm of Amazon dams, say experts. *Mongabay*, 19 June. Available at: https://news.mongabay.com/2017/06/i nternational-action-a-must-to-stop-irreversible-harm-of-amazon-dams/ (Accessed: 8 January 2020).
Salm, R (2009). Belo Monte: a farsa das audiências públicas. *EcoDebate*, 8 October. Available at: https://www.ecodebate.com.br/2009/10/08/belo-monte-a-farsa-das-au diencias-publicas-artigo-de-rodolfo-salm/ (Accessed: 8 January 2020).
Samuels, D (2004). From socialism to social democracy party organization and the transformation of the workers' party in Brazil. *Comparative Political Studies*, 37(9): 999–1024.
Santos, JV (2015). Belo Monte: Atualização do processo de destruição dos povos indígenas. *Instituto Humanitas Unisinos*, 30 November. Available at: http://www.ihuonline.unis inos.br/artigo/6284-thais-santi (Accessed: 30 March 2020).
Santos, LQ, and Gomes, EG (2015). *Suspensão de Segurança: Neodesenvolvimentismo e violações de direitos humanos no Brasil*. Curitiba: Terra de Direitos. Available at: https:// terradedireitos.org.br/uploads/arquivos/suspensao-e-seguranca-min.pdf.
Saunders, C (2013). *Environmental Networks and Social Movement Theory*. London: Bloomsbury.

Savarese, M (2010). Lula visita local de obras da usina de Belo Monte e se irrita com manifestantes. *UOL Notícias*, 22 June. Available at: https://noticias.uol.com.br/politica/ultimas-noticias/2010/06/22/lula-vai-local-de-obras-de-belo-monte-e-se-irrita-com-manifestantes.htm (Accessed: 30 March 2020).

Schaefli, B (2015). Projecting hydropower production under future climates: a guide for decision-makers and modelers to interpret and design climate change impact assessments. *Wiley Interdisciplinary Reviews: Water*, 2(4): 271–289.

Scheidel, A, Temper, L, Demaria, F, and Martínez-Alier, J (2018). Ecological distribution conflicts as forces for sustainability: an overview and conceptual framework. *Sustainability Science*, 13(3): 585–598.

Scherrer, YM (2009). Environmental conservation NGOs and the concept of sustainable development. *Journal of Business Ethics*, 85(3): 555–571.

Schmitt, G (2019). Em quase cinco anos, Lava-Jato de Curitiba condenou 155 pessoas. *O Globo*, 7 March. Available at: https://oglobo.globo.com/brasil/em-quase-cinco-anos-lava-jato-de-curitiba-condenou-155-pessoas-23506151 (Accessed: 8 January 2020).

Schneider, H (2013). World Bank turns to hydropower to square development with climate change. *The Washington Post*, 8 May. Available at: https://www.washingtonpost.com/business/economy/world-bank-turns-to-hydropower-to-square-development-with-climate-change/2013/05/08/b9d60332-b1bd-11e2-9a98-4be1688d7d84_story.html (Accessed: March 30, 2020).

Schulz, C, and Adams, WM (2019). Debating dams: the World Commission on Dams 20 years on. *Wiley Interdisciplinary Reviews: Water*, 6(5): e1396.

Scudder, T (2005). *The Future of Large Dams: Dealing with Social, Environmental, Institutional and Political Costs*. London: Routledge.

Secreto, MV (2007). A ocupação dos "espaços vazios" no governo Vargas: do "Discurso do rio Amazonas" à saga dos soldados da borracha. *Estudos Históricos*, 2(40): 115–135.

Senado Federal (2011). Pronunciamento de Francisco Dornelles em 25/04/2011. *Senado Federal*, 25 April. Available at: https://www25.senado.leg.br/web/atividade/pronunciamentos/-/p/texto/387756 (Accessed: 30 March 2020).

Senado Federal (2019). Subcomissão de Belo Monte quer resolver disputa por terra com ribeirinhos no Pará. *Senado Federal*, 23 October. Available at: https://www12.senado.leg.br/noticias/materias/2019/10/23/subcomissao-de-belo-monte-quer-resolver-disputa-por-terra-com-ribeirinhos-no-para (Accessed: 8 January 2020).

Scoones, I (2007). Sustainability. *Development in Practice*, 17(4/5): 589–596.

Scoones, I (2016). The politics of sustainability and development. *Annual Review of Environment and Resources*, 41(1): 293–319.

Scott, JC (1999). *Seeing Like a State: How Certain Schemes to Improve the Human Condition Have Failed*. New Haven, CT: Yale University Press.

Siciliano, G, del Bene, D, Scheidel, A, Liu, J, and Urban, F (2019). Environmental justice and Chinese dam-building in the global South. *Current Opinion in Environmental Sustainability*, 37: 20–27.

Sikor, T, and Norgaard, R (1999). Principles for sustainability: protection, investment, cooperation and innovation. In Kohn, J, Gowdy, JM, Hinterberger, D, and Van der Straaten, J (eds) *Sustainability in Question: The Search for a Conceptual Framework*. Cheltenham: Edward Elgar.

Silva, GC, and Lucas, FCA (2019). Ribeirinhos e a hidrelétrica belo monte: a desterritorialização e influências no cultivo de plantas alimentícias. *Ambiente & Sociedade*, 22: e02961.

Singer, A (2010). A segunda alma do partido dos trabalhadores. *Novos estudos CEBRAP*, 88: 89–111.
Sneddon, C, and Fox, C (2008). Struggles over dams as struggles for justice: the World Commission on Dams (WCD) and anti-dam campaigns in Thailand and Mozambique. *Society and Natural Resources*, 21(7): 625–640.
Soito, JLDS, and Freitas, MAV (2011). Amazon and the expansion of hydropower in Brazil: vulnerability, impacts and possibilities for adaptation to global climate change. *Renewable and Sustainable Energy Reviews*, 15(6): 3165–3177.
Southgate, T (2016). *Belo Monte: After the Flood*. Oakland, CA: International Rivers & Amazon Watch.
Spalding-Fecher, R, Chapman, A, Yamba, F, Walimwipi, H, Kling, H, Tembo, B, Nyambe, I, and Cuamba, B (2016). The vulnerability of hydropower production in the Zambezi River Basin to the impacts of climate change and irrigation development. *Mitigation and Adaptation Strategies for Global Change*, 21(5): 721–742.
Spiegel, SJ (2017). EIAs, power and political ecology: situating resource struggles and the techno-politics of small-scale mining. *Geoforum*, 87: 95–107.
Sposati, R (2013). Abin espionou indígenas e ONGs no governo Dilma. *Folha de S. Paulo*, 29th May. Available at: http://www1.folha.uol.com.br/poder/2017/05/1882257-abin-espionou-indigenas-e-ongs-no-governo-dilma.shtml (Accessed: 8 January 2020).
Spring, J (2020). Brazil minister calls for environmental deregulation while public distracted by COVID. *Reuters*, 22 May. Available at: https://uk.reuters.com/article/us-brazil-politics-environment/brazil-minister-calls-for-environmental-deregulation-while-public-distracted-by-covid-idUKKBN22Y30Y (Accessed 23 July 2020).
Sullivan, Z (2016). Brazil's dispossessed: Belo Monte dam ruinous for indigenous cultures. *Mongabay*, 8 December. Available at: https://news.mongabay.com/2016/12/brazils-dispossessed-belo-monte-dam-ruinous-for-indigenous-cultures/ (Accessed: 30 March 2020).
Sullivan, Z (2017). Unexamined synergies: dam building and mining go together in the Amazon. *Mongabay*, 22 June. Available at : https://news.mongabay.com/2017/06/unexamined-synergies-dam-building-and-mining-go-together-in-the-amazon/ (Accessed: 30 March 2020).
Survival International (2016). "Stop Brazil's genocide": Brazil blocks dangerous dam. *Survival International*, 5 August. Available at: https://www.survivalinternational.org/news/11378 (Accessed: 30 March 2020).
Switkes, G (2008). The Madeira hydroelectric and hidrovia project – Cornerstone of IIRSA. *International Rivers*, 25 June. Available at: https://www.internationalrivers.org/resources/introduction-and-article-the-madeira-hydroelectric-and-hidrovia-project-%E2%80%93-cornerstone-of (Accessed: 30 March 2020).
Swyngedouw, E (1999). Modernity and hybridity: nature, regeneracionismo, and the production of the Spanish waterscape, 1891–1930. *Annals of the Association of American Geographers*, 89(3): 37–41.
Swyngedouw, E (2009). The political economy and political ecology of the hydro-social cycle. *Journal of Contemporary Water Research and Education*, 142(1): 56–60.
Swyngedouw, E (2010). Impossible sustainability and the post-political condition. In: Cerreta, M, Concilio, G, and Monno, V (eds) *Making Strategies in Spatial Planning*. Dordrecht: Springer Netherlands.
Swyngedouw, E (2011). Depoliticized environments: the end of nature, climate change and the post-political condition. *Royal Institute of Philosophy Supplements*, 69: 253–274.

Swyngedouw, E (2015a). The non-political politics of climate change. *ACME: An International Journal for Critical Geographies*, 12(1): 1–8.

Swyngedouw, E (2015b). *Liquid Power: Contested Hydro-modernities in Twentieth-Century Spain*. Cambridge, MA: MIT Press.

Talento, A (2014). Operarios de Belo Monte pagam sexo com vale alimentacao. *Folha de S.Paulo*, 14 June. Available at: https://www1.folha.uol.com.br/cotidiano/2014/06/14 69550-operarios-de-belo-monte-pagam-sexo-com-vale-alimentacao.shtml (Accessed: 8 January 2020).

Tarrow, SG (ed.) (2011). *Power in Movement: Social Movements and Contentious Politics*. Cambridge: Cambridge University Press.

Teixeira, M, and Costa, L (2015). UPDATE 1-China's State Grid to build Brazil's longest power line. *Reuters*, 17 July. Available at: https://www.reuters.com/article/brazil-p ower-auction/update-1-chinas-state-grid-to-build-brazils-longest-power-line-idUS L2N0ZX0P420150717 (Accessed: 30 March 2020).

Temper, L, Walter, M, Rodriguez, I, Kothari, A, and Turhan, E (2018). A perspective on radical transformations to sustainability: resistances, movements and alternatives. *Sustainability Science*, 13(3): 747–764.

The Guardian (2016). Brazil must recognise Munduruku lands. *The Guardian*, 10 August. Available at: https://www.theguardian.com/environment/2016/aug/10/brazil-must-r ecognise-munduruku-lands (Accessed: 30 March 2020).

Thorkildsen, K (2018). 'Land yes, dam no!' Justice-seeking strategies by the anti-dam movement in the Ribeira Valley, Brazil. *The Journal of Peasant Studies*, 45(2): 347–367.

Tilly, C, and Tarrow, SG (2007). *Contentious Politics*. Oxford: Oxford University Press.

Tischler, J (2014). Cementing uneven development: the Central African Federation and the Kariba Dam scheme. *Journal of Southern African Studies*, 40(5): 1047–1064.

Tolmasquim, MT (2007). *Presentation at Public Audience, Organised by Comissões de Minas e Energia e de Meio Ambiente*. Rio de Janeiro: Câmara dos Deputados, 12 April. Available at: http://www2.camara.leg.br/atividade-legislativa/comissoes/comissoes-pe rmanentes/cme/audiencias-publicas/anos-anteriores/2007/12-04-2007-leiloes-de-ene rgia-a-5-2007-e-a-3-2007-e-mercado-de-energia-eletrica-para-o-proximo-decenio/EP E-Mauricio Tolmasquim.pdf (Accessed: 30 March 2020).

Tribunal de Contas da União (2015). Acórdão TCU 1569/2015. *Tribunal de Contas da União*, 24 June, Available at: https://pesquisa.apps.tcu.gov.br/#/documento/acordao-co mpleto/*/KEY%253AACORDAO-COMPLETO-1456217/DTRELEVANCIA% 2520desc/0/sinonimos%253Dfalse (Accessed: 30 March 2020).

Tribunal Regional Federal da Primeira Região (2010). *Suspensão de liminar ou antecipação de tutela 0022487-47.2010.4.01.0000/PA*. Belém: PAL Tribunal Regional Federal. Available at: https://aasp.jusbrasil.com.br/noticias/2160403/trf-1-suspensas-as-limi nares-que-impediam-a-realizacao-do-leilao-de-usina?ref=amp (Accessed: 16 April 2020).

Tuffani, M (2019). Já estava nos planos de Salles desde o ano passado 'reformatar o Conama'. *Direto da Ciência*, 27 March. Available at: http://www.diretodaciencia.com /2019/03/27/ja-estava-nos-planos-de-salles-desde-o-ano-passado-reformatar-o-cona ma/ (Accessed: 6 April 2020).

Turner, T (1993). The role of indigenous peoples in the environmental crisis: the example of the Kayapo of the Brazilian amazon. *Perspectives in Biology and Medicine*, 36(3): 526–545.

United Nations Framework Convention on Climate Change (2018). How hydropower can help climate action. *United Nations Framework Convention on Climate Change*,

21 November. Available at: https://unfccc.int/news/how-hydropower-can-help-climate-action (Accessed: March 30, 2020).
United Nations Symposium on Hydropower and Sustainable Development (2004). *Beijing Declaration on Hydropower and Sustainable Development*. Beijing: United Nations.
UOL (2020). Bolsonaro: "O índio é cada vez mais um ser humano igual a nós". *UOL*, 23 January. Available at: https://noticias.uol.com.br/politica/ultimas-noticias/2020/01/23/indio-ta-evoluindo-cada-vez-mais-e-ser-humano-igual-a-nos-diz-bolsonaro.htm   (Accessed: 6 April 2020).
Urquijo, J, de Stefano, L, and La Calle, A (2015). Drought and exceptional laws in Spain: the official water discourse. *International Environmental Agreements: Politics, Law and Economics*, 15: 273–292.
van Oel, PR, Krol, MS, and Hoekstra, AY (2009). A river basin as a common-pool resource: a case study for the Jaguaribe basin in the semi-arid Northeast of Brazil. *International Journal of River Basin Management*, 7(4): 345–353.
van Wijk, J, and Fischhendler, I (2017). The construction of urgency discourse around mega-projects: the Israeli case. *Policy Sciences*, 50(3): 469–494.
Vandergeest, P, and Peluso, NL (1995). Territorialization and state power in Thailand. *Theory and Society*, 24(3): 385–426.
Vargas, A (2019). Incerteza em Belo Monte. *ISTOÉ Independente*, 22 November. Available at: https://istoe.com.br/incerteza-em-belo-monte/ (Accessed: April 6, 2020).
Various (2010). Final declaration from the Terra Livre Encampment: "In defense of the Xingu: against Belo Monte!" *Amazon Watch*, 12 August. Available at: https://amazonwatch.org/news/2010/0812-final-declaration-from-the-terra-livre-encampment (Accessed: 30 March 2020).
Verdum, R (2012). *As Obras de Infraestrutura do PAC e os Povos Indígenas na Amazônia Brasileira*. São Paulo: Instituto de Estudos Socio-Economicos. Available at: https://www.amazonia.org.br/wp-content/uploads/2012/10/Obras-de-Infraestrutura-do-PAC-e-Povos-Indigenas.pdf (Accessed: 30 March 2020).
Vieira, M (2016). Belo Monte. 'Um monumento à insanidade'. Entrevista com D. Erwin Kräutler. *IHU-Online*, 5 April. Available at: http://www.ihu.unisinos.br/185-noticias/noticias-2016/553178-belo-monte-um-monumento-a-insanidade-entrevista-com-d-erwin-kraeutler (Accessed: 30 March 2020).
Vieira, MA, and Dalgaard, KG (2013). The energy-security–climate-change nexus in Brazil. *Environmental Politics*, 22(4): 610–626.
Vieira, R (2012). O transformismo petista: considerações acerca das transformações históricas do Partido dos Trabalhadores no Brasil. *Red de Revistas Científicas de América Latina, el Caribe, España y Portugal*, 17: 1–58. Available at: https://www.redalyc.org/articulo.oa?id=85524080003 (Accessed: 30 March 2020).
Vieira, M (2016). Fim de festa em Belo Monte. *Projecto Colabora*, 29 March. Available at: https://projetocolabora.com.br/florestas/fim-de-festa-em-belo-monte/ (Accessed 22 July 2020).
Villas-Bôas, A, Rojas Garzón, B, Reis, C, Amorim, L, and Leite, L (2015). *Dossiê Belo Monte: Não há condições para a Licença de Operação*. Brasilia: Instituto Socioambiental.
von Sperling, E (2012). Hydropower in Brazil: overview of positive and negative environmental aspects. *Energy Procedia*, 18: 110–118.
Warner, J (2010). Hydro-hegemonic politics: a crossroads on the Euphrates-Tigris. In: Wegerich, K, and Warner, J (eds) *The Politics of Water: A Survey*. London: Routledge.

Warner, JF (2004). Plugging the GAP Working with Buzan: the Ilisu Dam as a security issue. SOAS Water Issues Study Group, School of Oriental and African Studies/King's College London, Occasional Paper No 67, 1–24.

Warner, JF, Hoogesteger, J, and Hidalgo, JP (2017). Old wine in new bottles: the adaptive capacity of the hydraulic mission in Ecuador. *Water Alternatives*, 10(2): 322–340.

Watts, J (2017). Operation Car Wash: is this the biggest corruption scandal in history? *The Guardian*, 1 June. Available at: https://www.theguardian.com/world/2017/jun/01/brazil-operation-car-wash-is-this-the-biggest-corruption-scandal-in-history (Accessed: 8 January 2020).

Watts, J (2019). Poorly planned Amazon dam project "poses serious threat to life". *The Guardian*, 8 November. Available at: https://www.theguardian.com/environment/2019/nov/08/death-of-a-river-the-ruinous-design-flaw-in-a-vast-amazon-rainforest-dam (Accessed: April 6, 2020).

Wester, P, Rap, E, and Vargas-Velázquez, S (2009). The hydraulic mission and the Mexican hydrocracy: regulating and reforming the flows of water and power. *Water Alternatives*, 2(3): 395–415.

Whitefield, M (2017). Brazil engulfed in a corruption scandal with plots as convoluted as a telenovela. *Miami Herald*, 5 September. Available at: https://www.miamiherald.com/news/nation-world/world/americas/article171222962.html (Accessed: 8 January 2020).

Whitehead, M, Jones, R, and Jones, M (2007). *The Nature of the State: Excavating the Political Ecologies of the Modern State*. Cambridge: Cambridge University Press.

Wilson, J, and Swyngedouw, E (eds) (2014). *The Post-political and Its Discontents: Spaces of Depoliticisation, Spectres of Radical Politics*. Cambridge: Cambridge University Press.

Wittfogel, K (1957). *Oriental Despotism: A Comparative Study of Total Power*. London: Random House.

Wolford, Wendy (2010). *This Land is Ours Now: Social Mobilization and the Meanings of Land in Brazil*. Durham, NC: Duke University Press.

World Bank (2009). *Directions in Hydropower*. Washington, DC: World Bank.

World Commission on Dams (2000). *Dams and Development: A New Framework for Decision-Making*. London: World Commission on Dams.

World Commission on Environment and Development (1987). *Our Common Future*. Oxford: WCED.

Worster, D (1985). *Rivers of Empire: Water, Aridity, and the Growth of the American West*. Oxford: Oxford University Press.

Yang, SL, Milliman, D, Xu, KH, Deng, B, Zhang, XY, and Luo, XX (2014). Downstream sedimentary and geomorphic impacts of the Three Gorges Dam on the Yangtze River. *Earth-Science Reviews*, 138: 469–486.

Yasuda, Y (2015). *Rules, Norms and NGO Advocacy Strategies: Hydropower Development on the Mekong River*. London: Routledge Earthscan.

Zanotti, L (2015). Water and life: hydroelectric development and indigenous pathways to justice in the Brazilian Amazon. *Politics, Groups, and Identities*, 3(4): 666–672.

Zanotti, L (2016). *Radical Territories in the Brazilian Amazon*. Tucson, AZ: University of Arizona Press.

Zhouri, A (2004). Global–local Amazon politics: conflicting paradigms in the rainforest campaign. *Theory, Culture & Society*, 21(2): 69–89.

Zhouri, A (2010). "Adverse forces" in the Brazilian Amazon: developmentalism versus environmentalism and indigenous rights. *The Journal of Environment & Development*, 19(3): 252–273.

Zhouri, A (2015). From "participation" to "negotiation": suppressing dissent in environmental conflict resolution in Brazil. In: Bryant, RL (ed.) *The International Handbook of Political Ecology*. Cheltenham: Edward Elgar.

Zhouri, A (2018). Megaprojects, epistemological violence and environmental conflicts in Brazil. *Perfiles Economicos*, 5: 7–33.

Zhouri, A, and Laschefski, K (2010). Desenvolvimento e conflitos ambientais: um novo campo de investigação. In: Zhouri, A, and Laschefski, K (eds) *Desenvolvimento e Conflitos Ambientais*. Belo Horizonte: Editora UFMG.

Index

Page numbers in **bold** denote tables

actors: anti-dam 12–13, 15–17, 24, 31–37, 46, 56, 58, 60–63, 74, 76, 78, 81, 83, 86, 99, 110–111, 121, 126–128, 132–133, 135, 137–139, 146, 148–158, 170; civil society 8, 16–17, 57–58, 124, 172; commercial 47, 83, 85; government 48, 137, 154; hybrid 8; international 35, 123, 125, 172–173; key 14, 16, 52–54, 155; local 52, 56, 155, 171–173; national 35, 51, 125, 172–173; numerous 30, 45, 47–48, 52, 170; opposition 16–17, 35, 60, 150; political 16, 83, 85–86, 131; powerful 25, 31; private 7–8, 25; pro-dam 3–4, 9–11, 13, 15, 24, 26–32, 34–35, 46–47, 53, 58–63, 72, 74, 77–78, 81, 86, 96, 106, 111, 121, 127, 129, 131, 134–135, 137, 139, 147–148, 151–152, 167–169, 172–173, 175; resistance 10–11, 13, 16–17, 56, 125, 129–130, 134, 146–148, 150, 154–155, 157, 168–171, 173
Agência Brasileira de Inteligência *see* Brazilian Intelligence Agency
Agência Nacional de Energia Elétrica *see* National Electric Energy Agency
Aleluia, JC 50
Altamira Dam 45
Altamira Gathering 56–58, 63, 94, 121, 149
Amazon: Brazilian 15–17, 24, 53, 55, 57–58, 63, 74, 76, 78, 85–86, 120–121, 125, 133–134, 138, 146, 148, 154–155, 158–159, 161, 162n1, 170, 174; Watch 52, 54–55, 80, 83–86, 102–103, 122, 125, 129, 155–157
Andrade Gutierrez 51, 81–83, 96
Araújo, S 146, 149, 153, 159, 161
Arias-Maldonado, M 10

Articulação dos Povos Indígenas do Brasil (APIB) 160
Asmal, K 1
Assirati, MA 137
Avancini, D 82
Azevedo, AB 76

Banco Nacional de Desenvolvimento e Social *see* National Bank for Economic and Social Development
Barra Grande Dam 3, 47
Beijing Declaration on Hydropower and Sustainable Development 6
Belo Monte Dam 2–4, 13–17, 17n3, 24, 37, 44–56, **46**, 58–63, 64n2, 64n4, 64n5, 71–86, 87n3, 94–97, 99–112, 121–135, 138–139, 147, 149–155, 157, 168–173, 175
Benjaminsen, TA 12, 36, 62, 169, 174
Berga, L 5–6, 168
biodiversity 2, 9, 57, 62, 100, 108, 122
Blanc, J 47
Bolsonaro, J 17, 87n5, 87n6, 120, 146, 158–162, 175n1
Brazilian Democratic Movement Party (PMDB) 81–82, 153, 172
Brazilian Institute of the Environment and Renewable Natural Resources (IBAMA) 14, 46, 56, 76, 79, 96, 98, 109, 146–154, 157, 159, 161
Brazilian Intelligence Agency (ABIN) 80
Brazilian Supreme Court 78
Brum, E 72, 77, 94–95, 129–131
Brumadinho 159–160, 175

Cabal, MJ 12
Caceres, B 12

Index

Camargo Corrêa 48, 51, 81–82, 97
Cameron, J 55
Capobianco, JP 76
carbon dioxide (CO2) 4–5, 168
Cardoso, FH 78, 87n1
Casaes, R 77
Casanova, L 3, 48, 50
Cavanagh, CJ 12, 36, 62, 169, 174
Centrais Elétricas do Norte do Brasil SA (Eletronorte) 45, 48, 51, 57
Certified Emission Reduction (CERS) 5
Chico Mendes Institute for Biodiversity Conservation (ICMBIO) 76
China 2, 7–8, 23, 46, 50, 153, 168
Class A Command (CCA) 104
Clean Development Mechanism (CDM) 5, 17n2, 36, 50, 167–168
climate change 4–7, 10, 12, 15, 28, 30, 34, 62, 111, 159, 169, 174–175
Collective Urban Resettlement (RUC) 107
Colombia 32, 44
Comando Classe A *see* Class A Command
Comando Vermelho *see* Red Command
Companhia Hidro-Elétrica do São Francisco (CHESF) 48, 50
Conference of Parties (COP) (UNFCCC) 5, 125
Conselho Indigenista Missionário *see* Missionary Indigenous Council
Conselho Ribeirinho (Ribeirinho Council) 109–111
Construction Consortium [of] Belo Monte (CCBM) 51, 98, 104
Coordenação das Organizações Indígenas da Amazônia Brasileira *see* Coordination of Indigenous Organisations of the Brazilian Amazon
Coordination of Indigenous Organisations of the Brazilian Amazon (COIAB) 53, 56
Corrêa dos Santos, M 53
Costa Rica 30
Costa, J 26
Costa, PR 81
Costa, R 98
Cunha, E 85

da Silva, JP 94–95
da Silva, LI 2, 4, 48–50, 59–62, 72–77, 80–81, 83–84, 87n2, 87n5, 131, 152–154, 157, 173
da Silva Benjamin, LT 76

Datz, G 50
de Souza Magalhães, N (Nicinha) 47, 87n3
Del Bene, D 11–12, 32, 36
della Porta, D 55
Diani, M 55
Dornelles, F 50, 59, 61
'Drop of Water' 55

economic development 4, 6, 9–10, 24, 26–30, 34–36, 47, 59–60, 71, 74–75, 102–103, 126, 132, 140n6, 154, 161, 167, 172
ecosystem 2, 36, 105, 108, 162n2
Électricité de France SA (EDF) 8, 48, 51
employment 4, 28, 78, 101–103, 112n2, 153
Empresa de Pesquisa Energética *see* Energy Research Company
energy: renewable 4–6, 9, 30, 59, 61; security 4, 6–7, 28, 49, 71, 74, 78, 139, 147, 154, 169
Energy Research Company (EPE) 45, 49, 59, 147
Engineer Souza Dias Dam *see* Jupiá Dam
environmental impact assessments (EIAs) 16, 77, 95–103, 105–111, 121, 127, 133, 137–139, 149, 170, 172
environmental organisation (EO) 7, 14–15, 45, 54, 64n6, 64n7, 79–80, 100, 111, 123–124, 129, 148–149, 151, 155, 157, 162, 169–171, 174

Federal Public Ministry (MPF) 14, 55–56, 77–79, 87n5, 94, 96, 100, 106–107, 122, 128, 131, 149, 154
Federicci, AA (Dema) 52, 87n3
Fenrich, E 171
Ferguson, J 30–31, 169
Fiennes, R (Sir) 55
Filho, JS 152–153
flooding 6, 9, 45–46, **46**, 57, 61, 75, 94, 106–107, 121–122, 127–128, 147, 159, 168
fossil fuel 5–6, 61, 169, 175
free, prior and informed consent (FPIC) 76, 125–126, 140n4
Freitas, V 84
Friends of the Earth 80
Fundação Nacional do Índi *see* National Indian Foundation

Goto d'Agua *see* 'Drop of Water'
Green Party (PV) 63, 76

greenhouse gases (GHG) 5–7, 10–13, 30, 36, 61–62, 99, 111, 168–169
Greenpeace Brasil 54, 102, 122, 125, 134, 137–138, 148, 150, 152, 155
Growth Acceleration Programme (PAC) 3, 49–51, 74, 132, 135
Growth Acceleration Programme (PAC-2) 3, 49–51, 74, 132, 135
Growth Acceleration Programme *see Programa de Aceleração do Crescimento*
Guajajara, S 160

Hajer, MA 9–10, 28, 167
Hess, CEE 171
Hochstetler, K 3, 14, 47–50, 54, 58, 62–63, 64n7, 73, 76, 96, 110, 167, 172–173
Hommes, L 25
Huber, A 4, 11, 13, 29–32, 167
Hurwitz, Z 76, 82, 133
hydroelectric: dams 1–2, 5, 7–9, 11–12, 14, 17, 23, 25–27, 30, 44–46, 49–51, 56–57, 61, 72, 74–76, 78–80, 83–84, 87, 110–112, 120–121, 133, 147–148, 152, 154, 160–161, 167–169, 174; generation 2, 61, 152, 162n2, 168, 174; plants 49–50, 61, 71, 125, 140n5, 162, 168; potential 44–45, 173; projects 1–2, 9, 11–12, 24–26, 30–31, 35, 47, 49, 53, 59–60, 63, 74–75, 78, 81, 98–99, 107–108, 110–111, 122, 125–126, 136–138, 147, 150, 167–168, 170, 172; schemes 8, 32, 86
Hydropower Sustainability Assessment Protocol (HSAP) 8
hydropower: dams 103; expansion 7, 25, 137, 146, 154; projects 4–7, 9, 12, 14–16, 24, 26–28, 30, 32, 35–37, 44, 48–49, 55, 58–60, 63, 74, 100–101, 103, 108, 121, 123, 137, 139, 152, 167–168, 174; schemes 31, 173

IEA 5
Ilisu Dam 28, 168
India 7, 27, 29, 32, 35–37
indigenous communities 16–17, 34, 36, 47, 52–53, 55, 57, 64n8, 71, 76–77, 85, 95, 100, 109, 120–132, 134–135, 138–139, 140n2, 140n4, 146–148, 154–158, 160–161, 170, 172
Iniciativa de Integração da Infraestrutura Regional da América do Sul *see* Initiative for the Integration of the Regional Infrastructure of South America
Initiative for the Integration of the Regional Infrastructure of South America (IIRSA) 49, 74, 132, 135
Instituto Brasileiro do Meio Ambiente e dos Recursos Naturais Renováveis *see* Brazilian Institute of the Environment and Renewable natural Resources
Instituto Socioambiental *see* Socio-Environmental Institute
Inter-American Commission on Human Rights (IACHR) 53, 76–77
International Conference on Renewable Energies (Bonn) 6
International Hydropower Association 5–6, 44
International Rivers 7, 54, 57, 80, 82, 100, 103, 155
Irigaray, M 129–130, 135–136
Ishii, N 82
Itaipu Dam 1, 3, 47, 60–61, 64n3, 101

Jennings, E 100
Jirau Dam 3, 47, 49–50, 64n1, 101
Jornadas de Junho (June Days) 83–84, 151
Joshi, D 4, 11, 13, 29–32, 167
Jupiá Dam 3, 5
Juruna community 64n5, 122, 130, 140n1
Juruna, S 130
justice: climate 12, 32, 174; environmental 12, 32, 62, 169, 171, 174; social 62–63, 82

Kararaô project 45, 52, 56–58, 63, 87n3, 94, 106, 121, 123, 140n3, 149, 173
Kassum, J 3, 48, 50
Keck, ME 14, 47, 54, 58, 62, 64n7, 73, 172–173
Kräutler, E 54, 79
Kyte, R 7

Landless Workers' Movement (MST) 73
Lane, T 6, 168
Lava Jato investigation 81–85, 87n5, 151–153, 155, 161
Legal Amazon Region 2–4, 17, 44, 120, 132, 135, 154, 160, 168
legitimacy 3–4, 9–11, 13, 23, 27–28, 31, 58–60, 71–72, 78, 147–148, 153, 167–169, 173
Licença Prévia 96, 105, 147
liquid natural gas (LNG) 33

Lobão, E 60, 62, 82
Lopes, C 59, 61–62
Lopes, JAM 57, 94
Lumley, J 55

Maggi, B 156
Magnus, H 81
Manibeli Declaration 34–35
Margarido, B 76
McCartney, P (Sir) 55
Melo, A 75, 79, 94–95
Mendes, C 62, 140n3
military junta 47, 64n1, 79–80, 120, 158, 160
Minc, C 76
Ministério da Pesca e Aquicultura *see* Ministry of Fisheries and Aquaculture
Ministério de Minas e Energia *see* Ministry of Mines and Energy
Ministério do Meio Ambiente *see* Ministry of the Environment
Ministério Público Federal *see* Federal Public Ministry, Public Prosecutor's Office
Ministry of Fisheries and Aquaculture (MPA) 56
Ministry of Mines and Energy (MME) 14, 56, 60, 75, 82, 106, 127, 146–148
Ministry of the Environment (MMA) 4, 60, 62, 159
Missionary Indigenous Council (CIMI) 53–54, 157
Mohamud, M 25
Moraes, CA 106
Moraes, R 98
Moro, S 82, 87n5, 87n6
morphology 2, 9, 25, 62
Mouffe, C 11
Movement for the Development of Transamazon and Xingu (MDTX) 52, 59
Movement of Dam-Affected People (MAB) 14–15, 53, 55, 71, 80, 85, 99, 103–104, 106, 112n3, 122, 133, 140n6, 150, 157
Movimento dos Atingidos por Barragens *see* Movement of Dam-Affected People
Movimento dos Trabalhadores Sem Terra *see* Landless Workers' Movement
Movimento pelo Desenvolvimento da Transamazônica e Xingu *see* Movement for the Development of Transamazon and Xingu

Movimento Tapajós Vivo *see* Tapajós Alive Movement
Movimento Xingu Vivo para Sempre (Xingu Vivo) (MXVPS) *see* Xingu Alive Forever Movement
Munduruku, A 135
Munduruku: community 2, 16, 53–54, 64n5, 79, 122, 124–126, 135–139, 147, 155, 183; ideology 136; opposition 122–123, 135, 155; resistance 137; territory 123, 137–138, 143

Narmada Bachao Andolan (NBA) 35
Nasser, GA 27
National Bank for Economic and Social Development (BNDES) 48, 50, 58, 87n5
National Electric Energy Agency (ANEEL) 44, 55, 175
National Environmental Council (CONAMA) 159
National Indian Foundation (FUNAI) 14, 55–56, 72, 79, 96–98, 122, 125, 129, 131, 137–139, 146–147, 149, 159
nationalism 9–10, 26–27, 29–30, 33–34, 36, 167, 173
Nehru, J 27
Nepal 7, 30, 32
Neto, JV 82
Neville, KJ 29, 33–34
Nkrumah, K 27
non-governmental organisations (NGOs) 14, 47, 54, 64n6, 80, 83, 87n4, 111, 123–124, 129, 155, 169–171, 175n1
Norte Energia 14, 46, **46**, 48, 52, 56, 77, 94, 96, 98–99, 102–111, 121, 128–132, 139, 175

O Conselho Nacional do Meio Ambiente *see* National Environmental Council
Odebrecht 51, 81–83, 87n4, 87n5, 97
Organization of American States (OAS) 51, 76–77

Paiakan, P 58
Palocci, A 82
Paris Climate Change Agreement 5, 95
Partido da Social Democracia Brasileira (PSDB) 84
Partido do Movimento Democrático Brasileiro *see* Brazilian Democratic Movement Party
Partido dos Trabalhadores *see* Workers' Party

222 Index

Partido Progressista *see* Progressive Party
Partido Verde *see* Green Party
Petróleo Brasileiro SA (Petrobras) 48, 51, 81
Pires, SC 76
Plano Emergencial (Emergency Plan) 128–131, 139
Plano Nacional de Expansão Energética 45
Poirier, C 81, 126, 133, 155, 157
Programa de Aceleração do Crescimento, 2007 see Growth Acceleration Programme PAC
Programa de Aceleração do Crescimento, 2010 see Growth Acceleration Programme PAC-2
Progressive Party (PP) 61, 81
Public Prosecutor's Office (MPF) 14, 55–56, 77–79, 94, 96, 100, 106–107, 122, 128, 131, 149, 154

Queiroz Galvão 51, 81, 83

Raoni, C (Chief) 94
Reassentamento Urbano Coletivo *see* Collective Urban Resettlement
Red Command (CV) 104
Reis, C 129
Ribeiro, F 76
Roddick, A 56
Rousseff, D 2, 17, 48, 50, 55, 59, 71–77, 80–85, 127, 131, 136, 151–157, 161
run-of-the-river (ROR) 45, 106, 127, 175

Salles, Ricardo 159–160
Salles, Rodrigo 159
Santi, T 130
Santo Antônio Dam 3, 47, 49–50, 64n1, 101
São Luiz do Tapajós Dam 2–4, 13–18, 24, 37, 44–48, **46**, 50–52, 54–55, 58–60, 63–64, 64n5, 72, 74, 78, 80–83, 85–86, 87n4, 95, 97, 100–101, 110, 112, 121–123, 125–127, 131–139, 146–157, 159, 161–162, 168–173
Sarney, J 153
scaling up 13, 33–34, 53, 57–58, 63, 111, 131–132, 135, 147, 161, 170, 172–173
Schwarzenegger, A 55, 94
Scott, JC 26
security suspension 77–79, 85
Sikkink, K 14, 54, 58
Silva, M 62, 75–76, 153

Socio-Environmental Institute (ISA) 53, 78, 80, 94, 103, 105, 107, 109, 111, 129, 131, 151
solar power 4, 6, 44, 148, 174
South-North Water Transfer Project (SNWTP) 23
Souza, MdG 127
Spain 1, 26, 29
Sposati, R 80
stakeholders 1, 8, 24–25
Sting (musician) 56, 94
storyline: anti-dam 12, 23–24, 33–35, 37, 81, 83, 148, 155, 173; of legitimacy 4, 13, 59, 147; of sustainability 4, 10–17, 18n3, 24, 30–32, 36–37, 45, 59–63, 72, 86, 96, 100–101, 105–106, 110–111, 121, 128, 131, 139, 147, 151, 154, 167–170, 173–175; pro-dam 4, 10, 12–15, 18, 23–24, 28, 30, 32–37, 45, 47, 59–60, 62–63, 72, 86, 96, 101, 110–111, 121, 128, 131, 147, 151, 154, 167–175
Suspensões de Segurança *see* security suspension
Sustainable Development Goals (SDG) 5–6, 13, 167

Tapajós Alive Movement (MTV) 52
Teixeira, I 76
Teles Pires Dam 3, 46, 53, 78, 133, 135, 137, 155
Temaca Declaration 36
Temer, M 17, 84–85, 146, 153–154, 156–158, 161
Three Gorges Dam 2, 8, 50
Tuíra (Kayapó warrior) 57, 94
Turkey 1, 25, 28–29, 168

United Nations Framework Convention on Climate Change (UNFCCC) 5, 125

Vanucchi, P 77
Verhoeven, H 25

Warner, JF 3–4, 9, 13, 24, 27–31, 167, 173
water supply 4, 28
Weaver, S 55
Weinthal, E 29, 33–34
Whitehead, M 23, 37n2
wind power 4, 6, 44, 75, 148, 174
Wittfogel, K 23
Workers' Party (PT) 2, 48–50, 61, 63, 71–78, 80–86, 87n1, 105, 120–121, 128, 131–132, 134–135, 152, 155

World Bank 1, 6–8, 13, 34–35, 58, 140n3, 168
World Commission on Dams (WCD) 1–2, 8, 31, 34–35, 62, 140n4, 168
World Conservation Union 1
World Rainforest Movement 111
WWF 80; Brasil 14, 54, 105, 148

Xingu Alive Forever Movement (MXVS) 52, 55, 75, 79–80, 82, 87n4, 95, 99, 102, 109, 126

Zenawi, M 29
Zhouri, A 49, 62, 97, 108, 110, 112n1, 138, 171–173